**MOLOKA'I AND
LĀNA'I**
Pages 94–105

0 kilometers 50
0 miles 25

MAUI
Pages 106–129

MOLOKA'I

LĀNA'I

• Kahului

MAUI

KAHO'OLAWE

HAWAI'I ISLAND
Pages 130–155

• Kailua-Kona

Hilo •

HAWAI'I
ISLAND

EYEWITNESS TRAVEL
HAWAII

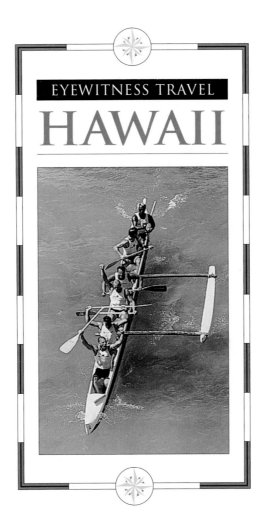

The rugged, sharply incised Nā Pali Coast on Kaua'i's North Shore

SURVIVAL GUIDE

Dancer at the Polynesian Cultural Center at Lāʻie, Oʻahu

Yellow 'ilima, a Hawaiian hibiscus relative and O'ahu's official flower

Historic cape made with the feathers of thousands of birds

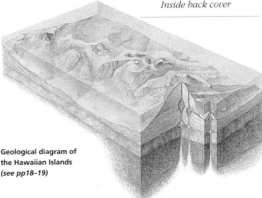

Geological diagram of the Hawaiian Islands
(see pp18–19)

HOW TO USE THIS GUIDE

This guide helps you to get the most from your visit to Hawai'i. It provides both detailed practical information and expert recommendations. *Introducing Hawai'i* maps the island chain and sets it in its historical and cultural context. The five island chapters, plus *Honolulu and Waikīkī*, describe important sights, using maps, photographs, and illustrations. Tips for hotels, restaurants, shops, entertainment, and sports are found in *Travelers' Needs*. The final section, *Survival Guide*, contains practical advice on everything from personal security to using public transportation.

HONOLULU AND WAIKĪKĪ

This chapter is divided into three areas: Downtown Honolulu, Waikīkī, and Greater Honolulu. Each area has its own section that opens with a list of the sights described. All sights are numbered and plotted on the chapter's *Area Map*. Information on each sight is easy to locate as it follows the numerical order on the map.

Sights at a Glance lists the chapter's sights by category: Cathedrals and Churches, Museums and Galleries, Historic Streets and Buildings, Parks and Gardens, Cemeteries and Memorials.

Each area has colour-coded thumb tabs.

A locator map shows where you are in relation to other areas on the island of O'ahu.

1 Area Map
For easy reference, the sights in each area are numbered and plotted on a map. The sights are also shown on the Honolulu and Waikīkī Street Finder *(see pp76–9).*

2 Street-by-Street Map
This gives a bird's-eye view of the key areas in each chapter.

A suggested route for a walk is shown in red.

3 Detailed information
The sights in the three main areas are described individually. Addresses, telephone numbers, opening hours, admission charges, tours, photography, and wheelchair access are also provided, as well as public transportation links.

1 Introduction
The landscape, history, and character of each island is outlined here, showing how the area has developed over the centuries and what it has to offer to the visitor today.

HAWAI'I AREA BY AREA
Apart from an initial section on Honolulu and Waikīkī, the state has been divided into five island groups, each of which has a separate chapter. The most interesting towns and places to visit are numbered on a *Regional Map* at the beginning of each chapter.

2 Regional Map
This shows the main road network and gives an illustrated overview of the whole island group. All interesting places to visit are numbered and there are also useful tips on getting around the region.

Each area of Hawaii can be quickly identified by its colour coding, shown on the inside front cover.

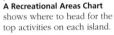

A Recreational Areas Chart shows where to head for the top activities on each island.

3 Detailed information
All the important towns and other places to visit are described individually. They are listed in order, following the numbering on the Regional Map. Within each town or city, there is detailed information on important buildings and other sights.

A Visitors' Checklist provides the practical information you will need to plan your visit.

4 Hawai'i's top sights
These are given two or more full pages. Museums and galleries have color-coded floor plans to help locate the most interesting exhibits; national parks have maps showing facilities and trails.

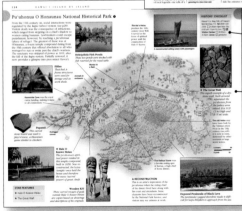

INTRODUCING HAWAI'I

DISCOVERING HAWAI'I

The only island state in the United States, each one of the major six Hawaiian islands has its own distinctive character. From the spectacular sun-drenched beaches and world-renowned surf enjoyed on O'ahu to Maui's rugged coastlines,

Native hibiscus flower

Hawai'i Island's active volcano, peaceful Moloka'i and Lāna'i, and Kaua'i's awe-inspiring lush beauty, this is a land of breathtaking extremes. The following pages are designed to help visitors pinpoint the highlights of each unique and fascinating island.

High-rise buildings bordering the famous beachfront at Waikīkī

HONOLULU AND WAIKĪKĪ

- World-class beaches
- Historic Capitol District
- Vibrant Chinatown
- Pearl Harbor

Honolulu is the state capital as well as Hawai'i's largest city. This sprawling urban metropolis includes **Waikīkī** *(see pp62–3)*, the center of the tourist industry, with thousands of high-rise hotels, restaurants, boutique stores, and nightclubs. The world famous golden sand and clear blue ocean in Waikīkī lure millions of visitors each year. Be sure to visit the statue on **Kūhiō Beach** *(see p65)* of Duke Kahanamoku, the father of modern surfing. Honolulu's Capitol District is a treasure of architecture, history, and culture. Highlights include the **State Capitol** *(see p55)*, **Kawaiha'o Church** *(see p54)*, and, most glorious of all, **'Iolani Palace** *(see p55)*. The state's most important

art collection is housed at the **Honolulu Academy of Arts** *(see p71)*, and the nearby **Bishop Museum** *(see pp68–9)* offers a fascinating insight into Hawaiian culture. **Chinatown** *(see pp58–9)* is well worth exploring for the food markets, ethnic restaurants, *lei* sellers, antique shops, and art galleries. The relics and memorials of the infamous World War II site **Pearl Harbor** *(see p73)* draw 1.5 million visitors each year and should not be missed.

O'AHU

- Snorkeling at Hanauma Bay
- Polynesian Cultural Center
- Legendary surf on the North Shore

Visitors who remain in Waikīkī miss much of O'ahu's scenic and cultural beauty as well as its history.
Snorkeling in shallow water with Hawai'i's myriad variety of reef fish is the major attraction at popular

Hanauma Bay *(see p65)*. The **Polynesian Cultural Center** *(see p92)* is Hawai'i's top visitor attraction. **Hale'iwa** *(see pp92–3)* is the quaint town at the core of the surfing community. There are surf shops galore, boutiques, and a surfing museum. The town is also home to **Matsumoto's** *(see p199)* – Hawai'i's most famous shave ice spot. The North Shore is the site of some of the most spectacular surf in the world and each winter many world-class surf meets are held here. North Shore beaches are for extremely experienced and skilled surfers only.

Powerful breaks on O'ahu's North Shore attract world-class surfers

MOLOKA'I AND LĀNA'I

- Enchanting Hālawa Valley
- Remote Kalaupapa
- The lunar landscape of Lāna'i's Garden of the Gods

The idyllic islands of Moloka'i and Lāna'i provide a serene and remote retreat. **Kaunakakai** *(see p98)*, Moloka'i's main town, is a

◁ Early 19th-century lithograph, by Ludwig Choris, depicting the port of Honolulu

charming location for a stroll. The untouched east side of the island is where visitors can experience Hawai'i's striking natural beauty. Sheltered **Hālawa Valley** *(see p99)* and **Kalaupapa National Historical Park** *(see pp100–101)* boast spectacular and haunting landscapes.

Once known as The Pineapple Isle, **Lāna'i** *(see pp104–5)* offers visitors a host of wonders. The **Garden of the Gods** *(see p105)* is a lunar-like landscape filled with rocks of every shape and size, formed by wind erosion over many millennia.

Glowing red boulders at Garden of the Gods, Lāna'i

MAUI

• **The thriving town of Lahaina**
• **Hiking in 'Īao Valley**
• **Haleakalā National Park**
• **The rugged Hāna Coast**

The second largest island in the chain, Maui is the destination of choice for more than two million visitors each year. **Lahaina** *(see pp110–13)*, once the capital of the Hawaiian Islands, is packed with shops, galleries, restaurants, and tourists.

The Central Valley town of **Wailuku** *(see p118)* merits a visit. See Maui's largest collection of Hawaiian artifacts at Bailey House Museum and continue on to picturesque Kepaniwai Gardens. Nearby **'Īao Valley** *(see p119)* has excellent

Sun-drenched 'Anaeho'omalu Bay, Hawai'i Island

hiking trails. To escape the crowds, **Upcountry Maui** *(see pp122–3)* offers incredible vistas, rolling pastureland, artistic **Makawao** *(see p123)*, and Maui's only winery, **Tedeschi Winery** *(see p121)*. Head to the magnificent and diverse slopes of **Haleakalā National Park** *(see pp128–9)* for a spectacular sunrise. The scenery along **The Road to Hāna** *(see pp124–5)* is stunning, with the ocean crashing against the cliff faces of the rugged coast.

HAWAI'I ISLAND

• **Lava flows at Hawai'i Volcanoes National Park**
• **Stunning beaches**
• **World-famous Kona coffee**

Experience the extraordinary thrill of seeing a continuously erupting volcano in **Hawai'i Volcanoes National Park** *(see p152–5)*. Extensive hiking trails give visitors a close-up view of the lava flows. Sun worshippers should head to Makalawena, a stunning beach on the Kona Coast near **Kekaha Kai State Park** *(see p134)*, **Hāpuna Bay** *(see p140)* on the Kohala Coast, or to the popular coconut-fringed white sand beach of 'Anaeho'omalu Bay, **Waikoloa Coast** *(see p137)*. Visit **Waimea** *(see p134)* to glimpse the tradition of *paniolo* (cowboy) culture. Kona district farms, famous for **Kona Coffee** *(see p135)* also merit exploration.

Nearby **Pu'uhonua O Hōnaunau National Historical Park** *(see pp138–9)* is one of the most sacred places in the Hawaiian island chain.

KAUA'I

• **The lush North Shore**
• **Magnificent Nā Pali Coast**
• **Dramatic Waimea**

Kaua'i's lush and tropical landscape is breathtaking. Visit the amazing North Shore, the nature preserve near **Kīlauea Point** *(see p164)*, atmospheric **Princeville** *(see p165)* and **Hanalei** *(see p166)*, and the Nā Pali Coast with **Kalalau Trail** *(see pp168–9)* winding through **Kalalau Valley** *(see p169)*. **Waimea Canyon and Kōke'e State Park** *(see pp170–71)* offers spectacular views.

Soaring cliffs lining Kaua'i's verdant Nā Pali coast

Putting Hawai'i on the Map

Hawai'i is an isolated archipelago in the middle of the Pacific Ocean and is one of the United States. It consists of eight main islands covering 6,425 sq miles (16,650 sq km). Most visitors arrive in Honolulu, the state capital, and travel to the other islands by inter-island flights or cruises.

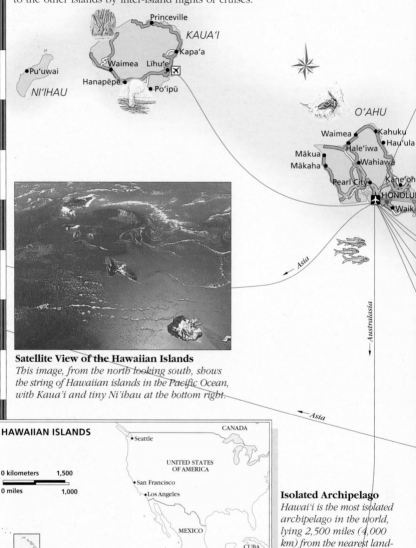

Princeville

KAUA'I

Kapa'a

Waimea   Līhu'e

Pu'uwai

Hanapēpē

Po'ipū

NI'IHAU

O'AHU

Waimea   Kahuku
                Hau'ula
Mākua   Hale'iwa
Mākaha   Wahiawā

Pearl City   Kāne'ohe

HONOLULU

Waikīkī

Asia

Australasia

Asia

Satellite View of the Hawaiian Islands
This image, from the north looking south, shows the string of Hawaiian islands in the Pacific Ocean, with Kaua'i and tiny Ni'ihau at the bottom right.

HAWAIIAN ISLANDS

CANADA

Seattle

UNITED STATES
OF AMERICA

| 0 kilometers | 1,500 |
| 0 miles | 1,000 |

San Francisco

Los Angeles

MEXICO

CUBA

BELIZE
GUATEMALA HONDURAS
NICARAGUA
COSTA RICA
PANAMA
COLOMBIA
ECUADOR

Isolated Archipelago
Hawai'i is the most isolated archipelago in the world, lying 2,500 miles (4,000 km) from the nearest landmass – the west coast of North America. In 1959 it became the 50th state to join the United States. It has a population of over 1 million, with nearly 75 percent living on O'ahu.

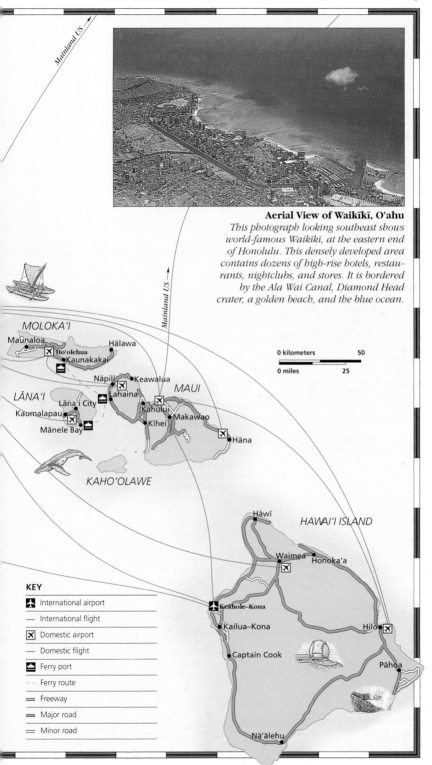

Aerial View of Waikīkī, O'ahu
This photograph looking southeast shows world-famous Waikīkī, at the eastern end of Honolulu. This densely developed area contains dozens of high-rise hotels, restaurants, nightclubs, and stores. It is bordered by the Ala Wai Canal, Diamond Head crater, a golden beach, and the blue ocean.

Mainland US

Mainland US

MOLOKA'I
Maûnaloa
Ho'olehua
Hālawa
Kaunakakai

Nāpili
Keawalua
LĀNA'I
Lāna'i City
Lahaina
MAUI
Kaumalapau
Kahului
Mānele Bay
Kīhei
Makawao
Hāna

KAHO'OLAWE

0 kilometers   50
0 miles   25

Hāwī
HAWAI'I ISLAND
Waimea
Honoka'a
Keāhole–Kona
Kailua–Kona
Hilo
Captain Cook
Pāhoa
Nā'ālehu

KEY

International airport	
—	International flight
International flight	
Domestic airport	
—	Domestic flight
Domestic flight	
Ferry port	
- -	Ferry route
Ferry route	
══	Freeway
Freeway	
Major road	
Minor road	

A PORTRAIT OF HAWAI'I

*H*awai'i is, quite simply, America's paradise. Its long stretches of white sand, crystal blue waters, swaying palms, and lush tropical rainforests dotted with pristine waterfalls attract millions of visitors each year. Hawai'i represents an ever-growing population encompassing a myriad of ethnic groups, development and tourism, agricultural diversity, and it is the homeland of a rich cultural heritage.

The most isolated land masses and the longest island chain on earth, the Hawaiian Islands were all formed by volcanic eruptions deep beneath the sea and are, technically, the summits of submerged volcanoes. Of the archipelago's numerous islands and atolls, the six main islands are O'ahu, Moloka'i, Lāna'i, Maui, Hawai'i Island, and Kaua'i. The state's unique topography is most vividly apparent on Hawai'i Island where the world's most active volcano, Kīlauea, has been erupting constantly since 1983. As Kīlauea's lava empties into the sea, the island continues to grow and change shape. The isolation of the Hawaiian islands and their diverse habitats have resulted in spectacular native flora and fauna. These impressive and fragile ecosystems are home to more endangered species than anywhere else in the world. Climates vary considerably, with 12 of the earth's 13 climactic zones represented. Windward coasts to the north and west receive more rainfall and are characterized by jagged cliffs, lush valleys, and dense foliage. The sunnier leeward sides to the south and west are drier and make ideal locations for popular tourist resorts.

Modern hula dancer

A pristine stretch of beach on Maui's north shore, bordered by the West Maui mountains

◁ Kīlauea volcano spewing molten lava, Hawai'i Island

Tourists flock to the clear blue waters of O'ahu's North Shore

TOURISM AND ECONOMICS

Tourism is, by far, the islands' biggest industry and it continues to grow annually. More than seven million people from around the globe visit the Hawaiian islands each year. Resort hotels, restaurants, retail outlets, and operators that organize sports activities dominate the industry. Military installations, including Pearl Harbor, are the second leading source of outside income. The agricultural industry remains an

One of Hawai'i's many surf schools

important facet of Hawai'i's economy. Major agricultural products include coffee, macadamia nuts, tropical flowers, cane sugar, pineapples, bananas, and papayas. In addition to these larger agricultural ventures, small farmers are making a resurgence and are today driving a diversified agriculture movement thanks, in large measure, to their partnerships with island chefs. A myriad variety of vegetables, herbs, beef cattle, and locally grown and produced foodstuffs now appear on restaurant menus throughout the islands.

Hawai'i's strategic location in the Pacific Rim also fuels the state's modern economy. Hi-tech companies and financial institutions establish themselves here, the closest place in the United States to the markets of Asia.

PEOPLE AND SOCIETY

To call Hawai'i an ethnic melting pot is an understatement. Immigration to these islands started more than six

Pineapple plantation, West Maui

centuries ago, with the arrival of the first Polynesian settlers, and continued during the plantation era with waves of Chinese, Portuguese, Japanese, Filipino, Korean, German, and Puerto Rican laborers. Today, more ethnic and cultural groups are represented in Hawaiʻi than in any other state. Each group has brought traditions that have been tightly woven into the fabric of modern Hawaiian life.

The tradition of removing one's shoes before entering a home, the annual O-Bon and Floating Lantern Festival which honors ancestors, the proliferation of sushi restaurants, and the extreme reverence for elders are all Japanese customs that today know few ethnic boundaries. The roots of the cattle industry, ranches, rodeos, ʻukulele music, and sweet bread lie in the influx of Portuguese immigrants in the 19th century.

Crafting of a boat using traditional methods

CULTURE AND THE ARTS

Hawaiʻi's cultural renaissance began in the late 1970s and continues to grow strongly and steadily to this day. There are many organizations and workshops dedicated to the preservation and perpetuation of the Hawaiian culture. Most important is the revival of the Hawaiian language in recent years. A

Traditional Hawaiian drummer

lively contemporary music scene also flourishes throughout the islands which blends mainstream reggae, rock 'n' roll, and jazz with more traditional sounds, including Hawaiian slack key guitar. It is still possible to see traditional *hula* performances, and the arts of Polynesian navigation and *lua,* a Hawaiian martial art, are also thriving. Hawaiian crafts – such as the making of hula implements, feather *lei* (garlands), and weaving – are also experiencing a welcome revival. And, of course, the ancient sports of surfing and canoe paddling are more popular than ever.

Artists from all over the world have been inspired by the people and beauty of Hawaiʻi, and Western and Asian visual and performing arts are very well represented. Honolulu boasts two world-class art institutions – the Honolulu Academy of Arts and The Contemporary Museum – and all of the islands are home to a number of galleries and artists' studios.

Floating lanterns at the annual O-Bon festival, Honolulu

Formation of the Hawaiian Islands

The Hawaiian Islands are the tips of a large chain of volcanoes stretching almost 3,100 miles (5,000 km) from Hawai'i Island to the Aleutian Trench in the north Pacific. Most are now underwater stumps, fringed by coral reefs, but many were once great shield (dome-shaped) volcanoes. The oldest, northernmost volcano is slowly disappearing into the Aleutian Trench. The youngest volcano – Kīlauea – today spews out basaltic lava, creating new land on Hawai'i Island. This cycle of destruction and creation, driven by the conveyor-belt movement of the Pacific plate over a stationary hot spot of magma, has been occurring for 70 million years.

Moloka'i's sea cliffs (see pp100–1) *constitute the back wall of giant landslide scars formed when half of the Wailau shield volcano slumped into the sea. Marine erosion keeps the cliffs steep by undercutting the bases.*

The areas of undulating ocean floor are deposits of giant landslides. Little is known about them because they sit in deep water, and their precise age of formation is unknown.

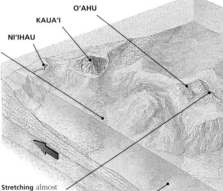

O'AHU

KAUA'I

NI'IHAU

Kaua'i's *amazing Waimea Canyon (see pp170–71) is carved into the Wai'ale'ale shield volcano. The layers of lava flows that created the volcano are visible. Large canyons of this nature are typical of Hawaiian volcanoes in their late erosional stage.*

Stretching almost halfway along O'ahu, the spectacular Nu'uanu Pali (cliffs) formed when a large section of the Ko'olau shield volcano slumped into the sea.

Ocean floor

The Pacific plate moves northwesterly at a rate of 2–3.5 in (5–9 cm) a year.

CONVEYOR BELT

As it moves, the Pacific plate – the huge slab of earth's crust underlying the Pacific Ocean – rides over a stationary hot spot (mantle plume) that feeds heat and basaltic magma toward the surface. Mauna Loa, Kīlauea, and the "new" underwater volcano Lō'ihi, are presently over the hot spot. As the plate moves to the northwest, volcanoes are gradually pulled off the hot spot while new volcanoes grow in their place.

O'ahu's Hanauma Bay (see p88) *is a late-stage volcanic crater, one of several forming a line of cones, craters, and vents caused by an eruption at least 10,000 years ago. The ash cones are the result of explosive interaction of rising magma with sea water. Either the bay's present shape is due to breaching of the crater wall or, more likely, the wall was never complete.*

Maui's Haleakalā (see pp128–9), *in its erosional, middle to late stage, is Hawai'i's only active shield volcano outside Hawai'i Island. Its last lava eruption was in 1790. Young cones and lava flows occur in and around the misnamed crater – actually an erosional depression formed where two large valleys coalesced.*

VOLCANO LIFE CYCLE

Shield volcanoes form while over a hot spot. As they move off it, volcanic activity decreases and erosion begins. Late stage volcanoes occur from a magma source deeper than the hot spot. Eventually volcanoes disappear under the ocean surface.

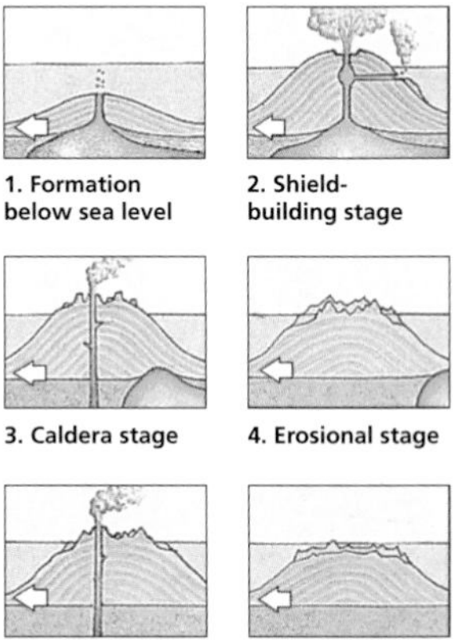

1. Formation below sea level   **2. Shield-building stage**

3. Caldera stage   **4. Erosional stage**

5. Post-erosional late stage volcano   **6. Atoll stage**

MOLOKA'I   KAHO'OLAWE

LĀNA'I   MAUI

HAWAI'I ISLAND

Mauna Kea

Rift zone

Kīlauea, a growing volcano perhaps calved off Mauna Loa some 200,000 years ago, has been erupting since 1983 and shows no sign of stopping *(see pp152–3)*. During this period lava has extended the coastline and formed about 2 sq miles (5 sq km) of new land.

Volcanic material

Lō'ihi, Hawai'i's newest shield volcano, lurks nearly 1 mile (1.5 km) below the ocean surface and is not expected to emerge for 100,000 to 200,000 years. It has all the features of a Hawaiian shield volcano, but none of its eruptions has broken the surface.

Main conduit   Vent   Lithosphere   **Underplating**
Hot spot

Magma reservoir

Mauna Loa *(see p147)* makes up over one-half the volume of Hawai'i Island.

Hawai'i Island's Mauna Kea *(shown here) and Mauna Loa, a pair of giant shield volcanoes, are hard to distinguish at their base beneath the sea. Mauna Kea (see p146) is older, in its post-shield stage with many smaller cones, giving it a rough appearance. Bulkier Mauna Loa's mass is so heavy that it has depressed the ocean floor. Together they make up the earth's largest single volcanic structure.*

Flora of the Hawaiian Islands

Prior to human settlement, the location of the Hawaiian islands in the middle of the Pacific Ocean was a natural barrier to the colonization of plants from other parts of the world. In prehistoric times, fewer than 300 immigrant flowering plant species – seeds borne by wind, carried by birds, or drifting on the ocean – colonized the islands. Extreme isolation produced a limited flora in comparison with continental floras; for example, Hawai'i has only three native orchids out of a worldwide family of 20,000 species. Some species evolved into new forms able to exploit a wide variety of habitats. Thorns and other defensive adaptations have largely been lost in Hawaiian plants as they conferred no advantage in a flora isolated from natural predators. As a result, native flora is unique, with 89 percent of its flowering species found only in Hawai'i.

Koa *is one of the most important forest trees in the Hawaiian islands. The largest specimens can attain heights of over 115 ft (35 m), and their huge trunks were used by Hawaiians to make voyaging canoes.*

Grasses are found in virtually all vegetation zones, occasionally as the dominant species. In dry, lowland areas *pili* grasslands provided thatching material for early Hawaiians *(see p69).* About 150 native and naturalized species of this important and large family occur in Hawai'i.

'Ōhi'a lehua, *probably the most common tree in the Hawaiian flora, occurs from near sea level to elevations of 7,200 ft (2,200 m). It is also one of the most variable, with mature forms ranging from a few inches in bog habitats to 80 ft (24 m) or more in forest habitats. Epiphytes and a tree fern understory also characterize wet 'ōhi'a lehua forests.*

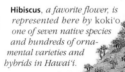

Iliau, a relative of the silversword

Hibiscus, *a favorite flower, is represented here by koki'o, one of seven native species and hundreds of ornamental varieties and hybrids in Hawai'i.*

Palm trees imported from Polynesia

Bougainvillea imported from Brazil

Pōhuehue, a typical beachfront plant

Naupaka *is a dune-binding shrub with distinctive "half" flowers. Ocean currents have dispersed its buoyant fruits throughout the Pacific Basin. Scientists believe that two separate colonizations account for eight endemic species growing in a variety of upland habitats.*

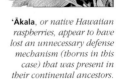

'Ākala, *or native Hawaiian raspberries, appear to have lost an unnecessary defense mechanism (thorns in this case) that was present in their continental ancestors.*

The silversword, *or 'āhinahina* (see p129), *occurs on Maui and Hawai'i Island in alpine desert habitats to elevations of over 12,000 ft (3,650 m). This species, together with the bog greensword and 25 other shrubs, trees, and a liana, actually evolved in the Hawaiian islands from one single ancestral immigrant.*

VEGETATION ZONES

Alpine vegetation, *a sparse array of shrubs dominated by silverswords and kūpaoa, occurs at 9,850–11,150 ft (3,000–3,400 m). A harsh, dry zone, it may freeze at night.*

Subalpine communities *occur in a relatively cool, dry zone from about 5,575–9,850 ft (1,700–3,000 m). Vegetation varies from grassland or shrubland to stunted trees.*

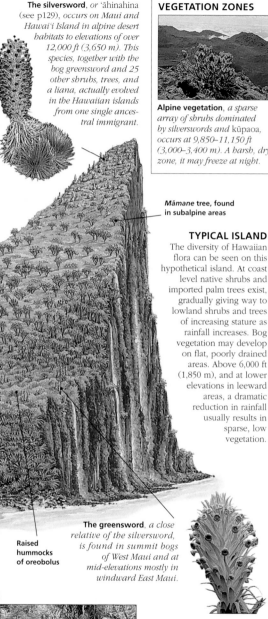

Māmane tree, found in subalpine areas

TYPICAL ISLAND

The diversity of Hawaiian flora can be seen on this hypothetical island. At coast level native shrubs and imported palm trees exist, gradually giving way to lowland shrubs and trees of increasing stature as rainfall increases. Bog vegetation may develop on flat, poorly drained areas. Above 6,000 ft (1,850 m), and at lower elevations in leeward areas, a dramatic reduction in rainfall usually results in sparse, low vegetation.

Montane dry areas *are characteristic of leeward slopes at an elevation of 1,650–8,850 ft (500–2,700 m). Vegetation varies from dry grasslands to dry forests with a canopy 10–65 ft (3–20 m) high.*

Montane wetlands, *in areas of high rainfall at elevations of 3,950–7,200 ft (1,200–2,200 m), include wet herblands, sedgelands, shrublands, bogs, and forests with canopies up to 130 ft (40 m) high.*

Raised hummocks of oreobolus

The greensword, *a close relative of the silversword, is found in summit bogs of West Maui and at mid-elevations mostly in windward East Maui.*

Lowland and coastal communities *include a diverse array of dry, medium, and wet herb, grass, shrub, and forest vegetation occurring below 5,000 ft (1,500 m) elevation.*

Tropical plants *from around the world thrive in Hawai'i. This lush planting on O'ahu includes giant aroids and bananas. Alien plants pose a real threat to native species by displacing them and preventing their regeneration.*

Marine Life of Hawai'i

Parrot fish

Hawai'i's remote location in the middle of the Pacific Ocean supports a rich population of marine life and a relatively undisturbed coral reef habitat. This dynamic reef ecosystem is home to more than 7,000 marine species, of which approximately one third are unique to the Hawaiian Islands. It is also home to many endangered species which are protected under the 1973 Endangered Species Act, including Hawaiian monk seals and green sea turtles. In 2006, the Northwestern Hawaiian Islands National Monument was created in order to protect 140,000 sq miles (360,000 sq km) of this precious marine habitat, including ten islands and atolls, making this the largest area dedicated to marine conservation in the world.

Humuhumunukunukuāoua'a (reef triggerfish) *is the designated state fish of Hawai'i. Its name means "triggerfish with a snout like a pig". With sharp teeth and powerful jaws, it feeds off molluscs and crustaceans.*

Cauliflower coral has heavy, leaf-like branches.

Corals are living animals that eat, grow, and reproduce.

Urchins inhabit crevices in the coral reef.

Antler coral, *common in Hawai'i, is usually found in depths of 35 ft (11 m) to 150 ft (46 m). Its branches resemble moose antlers.*

The seven eleven crab *has seven prominent spots on the top of its shell and four more along the bottom for a total of eleven. It is most commonly seen at night.*

The pencil-slate sea urchin *is bright red and has large, blunt, pencil-thick spines.*

The green sea turtle *measures more than 3 ft (1 m) across and weighs up to 220 lbs (100 kg). Once a food source for islanders, it is now a protected species.*

SHARKS OF THE COASTLINE

There are about 40 species of sharks found in Hawaiian waters, ranging in size from the deep-water pygmy shark, about 0.7 ft (0.2 m) long, to the whale shark, up to 50 ft (15 m) long. The most frequently encountered near Hawaiian reefs are the whitetip reef, hammerhead, and, occasionally, tiger sharks. Sharks are essential in maintaining the balance of the ecosystem.

Whitetip reef shark

Hammerhead shark

Whale shark

CORAL REEFS

Hawai'i's coral reefs are home to thousands of fish and other sea animals and plants that come in every size, shape, and color imaginable. The reefs house the majority of coral found in U.S. waters. They grow only 0.25 inches (0.6 cm) each year.

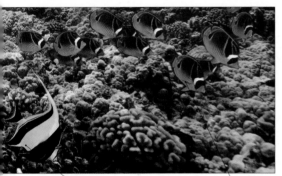

Moorish Idols are brightly-colored and move gracefully through the water feeding off the coral.

Butterfly fish live in depths of less than 20 ft (6 m). There are 25 species in Hawaiian waters.

The octopus *is a master of camouflage. It escapes detection by changing its color to match its environment.*

The Hawaiian stilt *is a rare and threatened species. This slender wading bird with long pink "stilt" legs is endemic to the Hawaiian island chain. It can grow up to 1.3 ft (0.4 m) tall.*

Spinner dolphins *are the most common dolphin species in Hawai'i. They can be observed daily off the coast of O'ahu.*

Hawaiian monk seals, *so named because their folds of skin resemble a monk's hood, are the most endangered marine mammal in the U.S. Adults can grow to 600 lbs (272 kg).*

Voices of Hawai'i

Ancient Hawai'i produced a wealth of oral literature and myth, which was passed down from generation to generation. A 12-letter alphabet, the smallest in the world, was developed by the missionaries in the early 19th century. Notable literary visitors wrote accounts of the islands and completed other works during their stays. Today, a new generation of Hawaiians is creating modern native literature, while maintaining a profound respect for the myths and chants that perpetuate the old ways of Hawai'i.

David Malo

The demigod Maui fishing the Hawaiian islands out of the sea

ORAL TRADITION

The oral traditions of pre-contact Hawai'i played a vital role in island life. The literature, committed to memory, was often chanted to the accompaniment of music and dance. There were *oli* (chants), *mo'olelo* (stories and narratives), *mele* (songs), and *'ōlelo no'eau* (proverbs). The *kāhuna* (priests) composed and simply recited poetry to preserve history, genealogies, and the knowledge of traditional crafts. *Haku mele* (composers) often composed verses for special occasions, such as the birth of an *ali'i* (royal) child; such songs were considered sacred.

19th-century image of Kū

The *haku mele* took advantage of the fact that many words sound alike, building on repetitions and word play. The similarity of words was not considered accidental; if a sea creature's name matched that of a geographical feature, these phenomena were considered *kino*, manifestations of the same spiritual force.

The most famous creation chant, the *Kumulipo*, tells of life and the islands growing up gradually, on their own initiative. The progenitors of

humans were the male *Wākea* (the Heavens) and the female *Papa* (the Earth). Hawaiians venerated four main gods: Kāne (light, life, water), Lono (productivity of the land), Kū (war, courage), and Kanaloa (sea). Each had numerous manifestations, all with names, and their deeds were visible in everyday nature.

Stories tell of Pele, the fiery-tempered volcano goddess who migrated from *Kahiki* (Tahiti, or simply the distant homeland) seeking a dry place for her eternal fires. Tracing the geological evolution of the islands, she resided first on Kaua'i and then O'ahu before settling for a time in Maui's Haleakalā Crater. She now lives in Hawai'i Island's Kīlauea Caldera *(see pp152–3)*. Myths are told of Pele's entire clan, especially her jealous relationship with her beautiful youngest sister, Hi'iaka, the first dancer of the *hula*. Pele's opponent in many stories is the shape-shifting pig-man Kamapua'a, a carnal, violent manifestation of Lono. Representing the productivity of the mountains and fields, his unending quest is to tame and fertilize the destructive goddess of lava. A cinder cone near Hāna on Maui is called Ka Iwi o Pele, or Pele's bones *(see p125)*, because the two titans met there for a cataclysmic battle.

Other stories tell of Maui, the Prometheus of Hawaiian mythology, who brought fire to the human race, lifted the roof of the heavens, slowed the speed of the sun, and fished the islands out of the sea with a magic hook.

EARLY RECORDS

The first written words about Hawai'i are found in the logbooks and journals of the early visitors. Thomas Manby, on an expedition in 1791, wrote candidly of the seamen's amorous relations with Hawaiian women and gave a humorous portrait of Kamehameha I's first sight of a cow – startled, the great warrior knocked over half his retinue fleeing for his life.

The first missionaries kept more restrained records. The Reverend Hiram Bingham, leader of the first mission in

An 1834 edition of *Ka Lama Hawaii* (The Hawaiian Luminary)

1820, set the pattern with his *Missionaries versus Man-of-Warsmen*. Within 14 years of their arrival the missionaries had created a Hawaiian alphabet, translated the Bible, established a printing press, and put out the first Hawaiian language newspaper, *Ka Lama Hawaii*.

Native oral tradition was suppressed but never lost during this time. Traditional songs *(mele)* passed through the filter of hymns *(hīmeni)* and the introduction of the guitar and *'ukulele* to emerge as "Hawaiian music." King Kalākaua (1874–91) started a renaissance of Hawaiian culture by calling for a revival of the *mele*, chants, and *hula*. In the same era, scholarly converts such as Samuel M. Kamakau and David Malo wrote invaluable records of life in precontact Hawai'i.

Jack and Charmian London on Waikīkī Beach in 1915

Following in Melville's footsteps, the 31-year-old Mark Twain explored the islands in 1866 as a correspondent for the *Sacramento Union*. While touring, he wrote a series of *Letters from the Sandwich Islands* and later put several chapters about Hawai'i in his book *Roughing It*. Though he never visited again, he wrote that "no other land could so lovingly and so beseechingly haunt me, sleeping and waking, through half a lifetime, as that one has done."

In 1889, the Scottish writer Robert Louis Stevenson dined with King David Kalākaua. Suffering from tuberculosis, the author of *Treasure Island* traveled the South Seas from 1888 until his death in 1894. In Hawai'i he befriended the royal family, studied the language, and visited Kalaupapa leprosy colony *(see pp100–1)*. Stevenson worked at fever pitch during his five-month visit, finishing *The Master of Ballantrae*, conceiving his novel *The Wrecker*, roughing out a collection of sketches about Hawai'i called *The Eight Islands*, and writing numerous poems and letters. Two of his best stories, "The Bottle Imp" and "The Isle of Voices," were also penned here.

Jack London arrived in Honolulu aboard his yacht *Snark* in 1907. The islands became his second home and

Portrait of Robert Louis Stevenson by Girolamo Piero Nerli (1892)

LITERARY VISITORS

In the opening chapter of Herman Melville's *Moby Dick*, Ishmael says, "I love to sail forbidden seas and land on barbarous coasts." This urge to explore exotic realms was an echo of that felt by Ishmael's creator and many other writers, and in the 1800s the lure of the South Seas was particularly strong. In 1843, Melville himself spent four months in Hawai'i, working in a Honolulu bowling alley and beachcombing in Lahaina.

where he wrote some of his famous works, such as *The Call of the Wild* and *White Fang*. He was the first literary figure to call himself a *kama'āina* (child of the land). His volumes of island-set stories, *On The Makaloa Mat* and *The House of Pride*, angered the authorities by depicting racial snobbery and the cruelty of official responses to leprosy.

HAWAI'I CALLS

Twentieth-century tourism produced a new mythology, casting the islands as a "paradise" filled with relaxed, *'ukulele*-strumming natives. A surge of interest in 1916 stimulated songs such as "Oh, How She Could Yacki Hacki Wicki Wacki Woo (That's Love In Honolu)." A second wave in the 1930s prompted a string of Hollywood Waikīkī fantasies, including the 1936 film *Honolulu*, which turned *hula* into a form of tap dance.

Today, the Hawai'i Visitors and Convention Bureau continues to romanticize Hawai'i. However, island-born writers such as Oswald A. Bushnell and Milton Murayama are creating a wealth of native literature. With support from local intellectuals, many now write in pidgin, the hybrid language that evolved on the plantations so that different ethnic groups could communicate. The stories of Lois-Ann Yamanaka, for example, have received international acclaim.

Wild Meat and the Bully Burgers, a novel by Lois-Ann Yamanaka

Hula and Hawaiian Music

Traditional 'ulī'ulī rattle

Hula began, it is believed, as a form of religious ritual to honor the ancient gods and chiefs while providing entertainment for the ruling classes. The traditional *hula kāhiko* was accompanied only by the human voice through chants *(oli)* or song *(mele)*, and by percussion instruments. In the early 19th century the missionaries tried to abolish *hula* but succeeded only in driving it underground. King Kalākaua, the Merrie Monarch, encouraged the revival of *hula* in the late 19th century, giving rise to the modern *hula 'auwana*. This style was influenced by Western music and clothing – women wore, and still do, long-sleeved, floor-length dresses *(holokū)*. The 1930s ushered in the "Sweet Leilani" era when dancers in cellophane skirts and flower *lei* greeted the ocean liners bringing tourists to Honolulu. Today *hula* enjoys great respect.

This 19th-century engraving *is a European interpretation of a native woman with traditional tattoos dancing* hula noho *(sitting hula) in a* kapa *skirt.*

The earliest hula *was, some say, the domain of men, although there is no documented evidence. However, there has been a great resurgence of male hula in recent years.*

Knee-length *ti*-**leaf skirts** are worn in *hula kāhiko*. The flat leaves rustle with the dancers' movements.

Dog-tooth leg ornaments, *or* kūpe'e niho 'īlio, *were traditionally worn exclusively by male dancers. Only four teeth from each dog were used, and it took nearly 3,000 dogs to make some ornaments.*

The 'ulī'ulī is a small gourd containing seeds and fitted with a handle. It is often decorated with feathers.

The ipu heke *is a percussion instrument made of two gourds. It is the most common accompaniment for* hula kāhiko. *The* kumu *(teacher) here is wearing a dried* ti*-leaf cape, which originally would have functioned as a raincoat.*

The standing pahu drum *is traditionally made from a section of coconut tree covered with shark skin, played with the hands. Pahu are often used in conjunction with the smaller* pūniu – *a drum made of coconut, lashed to the chanter's right thigh and played with a thong of braided fiber.*

WHERE TO ENJOY HULA AND MUSIC

Merrie Monarch Festival (p37)
Polynesian Cultural Center (p92)
Moloka'i Ka Hula Piko (p34)
Prince Lot Hula Festival (p35)
Nā Mele O Maui (p36)

Pū'ili are made of bamboo; one end is a handle and the other is split into a narrow "fringe" that makes a rattling sound.

This group of kūpuna (*respected elders*) *dressed in* mu'umu'u *are singing and playing instruments that typically accompany* hula 'auwana – 'ukulele, guitar, and standing bass. The ipu heke *and* 'ulī'ulī *lying in the foreground are used for* hula kāhiko.

The 'ukulele *is one of many instruments brought to Hawai'i by immigrants, in this case the Portuguese. It is integral to contemporary Hawaiian music.*

Flower lei are not authentic to *hula kāhiko*; dancers traditionally wear fern anklets and bracelets.

Maui's Keali'i Reichel *is a well-known chanter,* hula *dancer, singer, composer, and teacher dedicated to the preservation of the culture.*

HULA KĀHIKO

This old form of *hula* is shown here with contemporary twists. The *ti*-leaf skirts, *pū'ili*, and *'ulī'ulī* are traditional, while the plumeria flower *lei* and colorful fabric tops are modern. Visitors can see this combined style of old and new elements on all the Hawaiian islands.

THE REVIVAL OF HULA AND HAWAIIAN MUSIC

Today *hula kāhiko* is pursued by hundreds of students performing the same chants and using the same instruments as their ancestors, and *hula 'auwana* is more popular than in King Kalākaua's time. *Hula*'s connection to Hawaiian music is inextricable. The "music" accompanying traditional dancers took the form of musical poetry – chants and song. When Western musical influence became widespread, *hula* embraced it in the *'auwana* style. In the early 19th century missionaries brought sober hymns to Hawai'i, and increased sea traffic brought musicians from Europe and Asia with their varied secular music. The era from 1900 to the Hawaiian Renaissance of the 1970s saw an explosion of *hapa haole* – Hawaiian music influenced by ragtime, Tin Pan Alley, and even orchestrations from films and television shows. The instruments brought by immigrants – *'ukulele*, Hawaiian guitar, standing bass, piano – were stirred into the musical pot. The ongoing Hawaiian Renaissance has brought an enthusiastic revival of early Hawaiian music.

Child dancing hula kāhiko

Traditional Hawaiian Crafts

What we consider crafts today – woven baskets, feather *lei* (garlands), *poi* (taro paste) pounders, wooden bowls – were integral to the lives of ancient Hawaiians. They were made with care from readily available sources, such as coconut fronds, feathers of the *mamo* bird, local stone, and native *koa* wood. Many crafts are still made in the old, precontact ways. Even the ancient, almost lost art of beating and printing *kapa* (bark cloth) is undergoing a revival. Traditional implements are often favored over the modern, but certain tools have been updated. For instance, metal needles for stringing *lei* have replaced those made from coconut palm frond midribs. Not all crafts are indigenous. The missionaries introduced quilting, an art that is still passed from generation to generation *(see p68)*. Both the ancient and modern crafts are time-consuming pursuits requiring patience and skill – not unusual attributes among Hawaiians.

Netting *was the most efficient method of fishing in old Hawai'i. The best nets were made with a netting needle and mesh gauge, using cord from the* olonā *shrub.*

These two wooden bowls, *connected by a human figure crowned with feathers, were probably used by an ali'i (chief) for Poi (taro paste) or 'awa (a ceremonial drink).*

THE STARBUCK CAPE

This superb 19th-century 'ahu'ula (cape) with a unique geometric pattern was made with the feathers of thousands of birds, which were released after giving up just a few feathers each. It was probably given to Captain Starbuck by Kamehameha II, who with his wife sailed to London on the captain's ship in 1824.

Feathers were arranged by size, tied together at the quills, and attached to the net with *olonā* thread.

Decorating *kapa* **cloth**

KAPA CLOTH

Common garments *('a'ahu)* in ancient Hawai'i were made of *kapa* (bark cloth). The *wauke* (paper mulberry tree) produced the best cloth, which was pounded with wooden *kapa* beaters. Using dyes from native plants in every imaginable hue, bamboo implements were used to stamp patterns on the cloth. Today *kapa* is still made for certain ceremonies and is highly regarded for its variety of textures and beautiful, intricate designs.

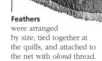

This late 18th-century pe'ahi *(fan) is made out of coconut leaves, human hair, cordage, and dyes. Fans with this distinctive shape were probably used exclusively by the* ali'i *(chiefs).*

Gourds with tubular necks were used in ancient Hawai'i to hold drinking water. It is believed that dyes created with infusions of bruised leaves, bark, or black mud were used to make the dark patterns on gourd bowls and water containers. Gourds of different shapes and sizes were also used as percussion instruments (see pp26–7).

HAWAIIAN LEI

Lei are wreaths or garlands, made of flowers, leaves, shells, ivory, or feathers, which are worn around the neck. They range from simple strings of blossoms to complex woven garlands of native leaves and plants. *Lei* have always been important symbols of affection in Hawai'i and are bestowed frequently with a kiss. They are worn by everyone with pride on Lei Day *(see p34)*.

Two-ply cord made from the bark of the *olonā* shrub was used in the net foundation and the fasteners.

The irregular black shapes are made from the feathers of the *'ō'ō* bird. Black feathers were rarely used.

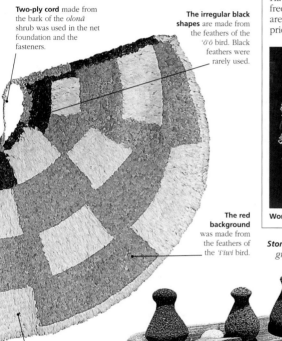

The red background was made from the feathers of the *'i'iwi* bird.

Woman with colorful flower *lei*

The '*ō'ō* bird also provided the bright yellow feathers.

Stone poi pounders were used to grind taro (see p125), a vital food source, into poi (a thick paste eaten with the fingers). It was heavy work, done by men who sat at a wooden pounding board, which was moistened with water, and mashed the cooked taro.

TRADITIONAL BRAIDING

In ancient Hawai'i, braiding or weaving was an important method of creating everyday objects, such as floor coverings, sleeping mats, pillows, baskets, and fans. *Lauhala* – the large leaves *(lau)* of the pandanus tree *(hala)* – were one of the most common materials. Sedge grass, including the coveted fine sedge *makaloa*, and certain palms were also used. The most extraordinary sleeping mats were made of *makaloa* on the island of Ni'ihau. In preparing the leaves for braiding, the weaver had to be careful because their edges and spines were sharp. Today, coconut palm fronds are commonly woven into hats and baskets. Generally speaking, the tighter the weave, the more valuable the item.

Coconut frond hat

Stiff, sharp leaves used as braiding material

Surfing in Hawai'i

Sign for Hale'iwa, O'ahu's surf town

Past and present, surfing has occupied an honored place in Hawaiian culture. Though its exact origins are unclear, *he'e nalu* (wave sliding) has been practiced here for centuries. The sport was dominated by the *ali'i* (chiefs), who had their own surf breaks that commoners were not permitted to enjoy; Kamehameha the Great himself was an avid wave rider. In the 19th century the sport went into decline after the missionaries discouraged it. A revival started in the early 20th century when Waikīkī became an international playground. Today the islands remain the ultimate place to surf.

Hawaiian surfers *ride the waves in this 19th-century engraving. In ancient times, entire villages flocked to the beach when the surf was up.*

The face of the wave, just before it breaks, is where the energy is most concentrated.

Duke Kahanamoku, *shown here with fellow surfers in front of the Moana Hotel c.1915, was the father of modern surfing (see p65). The Duke was a gifted surfer and the epitome of the carefree Waikīkī Beach life in the early 20th century.*

The surfer keeps knees bent and arms out for balance and to control speed and movement.

Most modern surfboards *are made of lightweight fiberglass and range in length from 6–12 ft (2–4 m). They usually have three fins attached to the underside of their tails, though longer boards may only have one.*

Long boards may be wide for riding gently sloped waves, like those of Waikīkī, or narrow for riding steep, very large waves, like those of Waimea Bay.

Fins add stability and maneuverability. They come in different shapes and sizes. In big waves, the fin would be backward and in small waves, it would be forward.

BANZAI PIPELINE

This spectacular wave on O'ahu's North Shore shows an expert surfer engulfed in a tube of water. He must maintain an exact position inside the "barrel" or risk being thrown over the "falls."

Short boards, the most maneuverable boards, are used for steep small- to medium-size waves. They are more difficult to stand on than long boards.

Boogie boards are small foam boards coated with fiberglass used to surf steep waves, often in shallow water. Riders lie flat on the boards and kick with fins to gain enough speed to catch the waves.

O'ahu's North Shore *sees towering waves from October to April, when storms sweep across the North Pacific producing powerful swell lines. Waimea Bay (above) has always been known for the largest waves that can be surfed.*

In the 1960s *daredevil surfers like American Mike Doyle, seen here with Duke Kahanamoku, came to Hawai'i in search of challenging surf. They found it on Oahu's North Shore, which soon became the surfing capital of the world.*

The wave breaks just behind the surfer, creating a cascade of spray and foam.

Special techniques *in surfing can involve the use of foot straps for aerial tricks, exotic board shapes, and towing by jet skis to surf giant waves.*

TRIPLE CROWN OF SURFING

Every year for three weeks in late November to mid-December O'ahu's North Shore is transformed into a surf carnival. During this time the Triple Crown of Surfing, the world's most prestigious series of surfing contests, takes place at Banzai Pipeline and Sunset Beach near Waimea, and at Ali'i Beach Park in Hale'iwa *(see p92)*. Giant waves and spectacular rides create a level of excitement and performance found almost nowhere else in surfing. The contests attract surfers from around the globe for competitions that often decide the world championship. The highlight is the PipeMasters at the Banzai Pipeline – the most coveted title in surfing. Live commentary makes the events accessible even to spectators watching surfing for the first time. Food is not generally available at the beach parks so spectators take a picnic.

Winners of O'ahu's famous Triple Crown, which is contested on waves bigger than 20 ft (6 m)

Scuba Diving and Snorkeling

Diving and snorkeling in Hawai'i is an experience like no other. The warm, crystalline waters teem with an incredible array of fish, coral, and other marine life. Visibility often exceeds 100 ft (33 m). Below the ocean's surface, the spectacular scenery includes reefs, lava formations, caves, and sandy plains. Beginners quickly get the hang of snorkeling. You can rent or buy a mask, snorkel, and fins on every island; if you go on a snorkeling boat excursion, instruction and gear are provided. Scuba diving usually takes place on the calmer, leeward sides of the islands. Instruction and gear are provided by dive shops and charter boats. Most offer introductory dives and internationally recognized certification courses. A wet suit is always recommended for scuba diving.

Snorkeling *is a popular pastime on each of the islands and there are many sites to choose from. It offers the chance to see schools of tropical fish and colorful marine life at close range.*

Kaua'i (see pp156–73) *has some of the best protected reef lagoons. Po'ipū Beach Park offers a sheltered, shallow cove ideal for novice snorkelers. Kaua'i is known for its rugged and pristine diving. Popular sites include General Store, a reef 65–80 ft (20–24 m) deep with a 19th-century sunken steamship.*

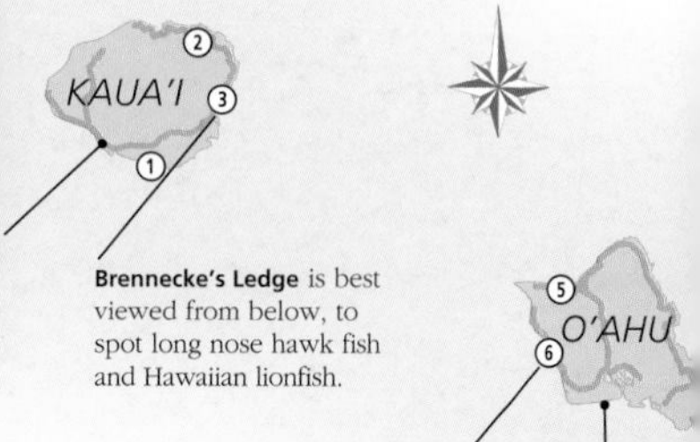

Brennecke's Ledge is best viewed from below, to spot long nose hawk fish and Hawaiian lionfish.

Mahi Shipwreck is a former minesweeper where lemon butterflyfish and other tropical species practically pose for photographs.

0 kilometres 50

0 miles 50

DIVE SITE RATINGS

There is a good variety of dive sites around the Hawaiian island chain. Divers should find out the level of experience required at any dive site before braving the waters.

	SNORKELING	NOVICE DIVING	ADVANCED DIVING	EXPERT DIVING
PO'IPŪ BEACH PARK (1)	●	■		
GENERAL STORE (2)			●	
BRENNECKE'S LEDGE (3)			●	
HANAUMA BAY (4)	●	■	●	■
HALE'IWA BEACH PARK (5)	●	■	●	
MAHI SHIPWRECK (6)			●	
MURPHY'S BEACH (7)	●	■		
FISH BOWL (8)			●	■
HULOPO'E BEACH (9)	●	■		
CATHEDRALS (10)			●	
MOLOKINI (11)	●	■	●	■
CARTHAGINIAN (12)			●	
RICHARDSON'S BEACH PARK (13)	●	■		

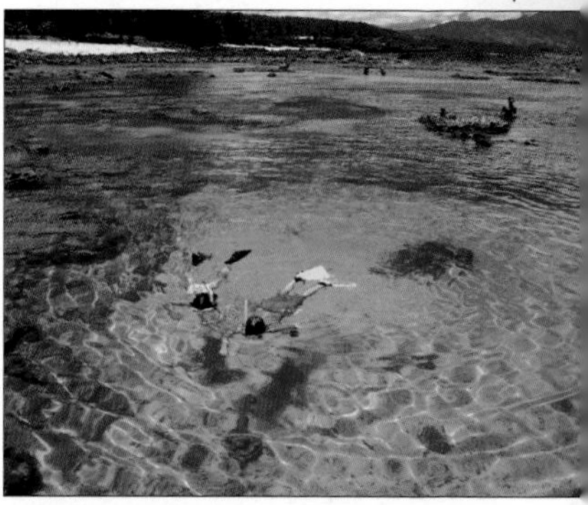

O'ahu (see pp84–93) *has dive sites that range from lava formations to shipwrecks. Hanauma Bay, the most popular snorkeling destination, is a natural "fish bowl". Originally the cone of a volcano, depths range from 15 ft (5 m) to 70 ft (21 m). Hale'iwa Beach Park is also good.*

GETTING TO THE DIVE SITES

Organized diving excursions include equipment and transportation by boat or motor van. If you are certified and wish to dive on your own, you can get directions and maps at any dive shop when you pick up your equipment.
Getting there: *Each island has at least one major airport, and regular ferry services run between Maui and the islands of Lāna'i and Moloka'i. See pages 12–13 for the location of airports, ferry ports, and major roads.*

Moloka'i (see pp94–103) *boasts the longest barrier reef in Hawai'i. The best snorkeling spots are between mile markers 18 and 20, heading east from Kaunakakai along Kamehameha V Highway, such as Murphy's Beach. Sites like Fish Bowl offer superb scuba diving, but are seldom visited due to weather and sea conditions.*

Hulopo'e Beach on Lāna'i (see pp104–5) *is renowned for its snorkeling; it is edged by tide pools full of tiny fish and anemones. The most popular scuba site is Cathedrals, named for the size of its lava tubes and the stained-glass effect created by the sun's rays coming through holes in the lava ceiling.*

Most dive sites in Maui (see pp106–29) *are located off the west coast, including Molokini. Maui's newest scuba diving attraction is the Carthaginian, a replica of a double-masted brigantine, which was sunk in 2005 off Lahaina to create an artificial reef.*

ꓳLOKA'I ⑧
⑦

LĀNA'I ⑫
⑨ ⑩
⑪ MAUI

Molokini *(see p121)* is perfect for snorkelers and learner divers. Charter boats drop anchor here so both can view the abundant trumpetfish, octopus, and other marine life.

HAWAI'I ⑬

On Hawai'i Island (see pp130–55), *Richardson's Beach Park, east of Hilo, is a good place for beginner snorkelers. The more adventurous can swim around the lava rock outcroppings to a reef with fish and sea turtles.*

HAWAI'I THROUGH THE YEAR

Contrary to popular belief, Hawai'i does have distinct seasons but only two: summer and winter. To residents, the distinctions are clear. It is summer if the mango tree in the garden is weighed down with fruit, or the intoxicating aroma of white ginger wafts in the air. Sudden rains or storms mean the onset of winter, as do the big waves that surfers eagerly await. Residents

Statue decorated for King Kamehameha Day

in the cooler upcountry areas of Kaua'i, Maui, and Hawai'i Island spend Christmas Eve gathered around the fireplace. A fair generalization for visitors is that May to October is hot and dry; November through April is slightly cooler and wetter. Happily for visitors, though, there are very few days during the year when Hawai'i's fine beaches do not beckon.

SUMMER

By May the winter rains have ceased and summer bursts into life all over the Hawaiian islands with blooming flowers and myriad festivals. **Lei Day** takes advantage of the abundance of beautifully scented flowers, with everyone young and old donning a flowered garland. Hawai'i's oldest state holiday, **King Kamehameha Day**, dates back to 1872; there are many celebrations on all the islands to honor the great chief who united Hawai'i *(see p41)*. All summer long there are cultural, music, and food festivals, as well as great sports competitions, from big rodeos to outrigger canoe races and the grueling **Ironman Triathlon**. The summer draws to a close with the grandest of all annual parties, the **Aloha Week Festivals**.

MAY

Lei Day *(May 1)*, all islands. Everyone is adorned with at least one of these traditional Hawaiian garlands; *lei*-making contests are held on the islands of O'ahu and Kaua'i.
Moloka'i Ka Hula Piko *(3rd Sat)*, Pāpōhaku Beach County Park *(see p103)*, Moloka'i. This celebration of the birth of *hula* features music, dancing, food, and traditional crafts.
International Festival of Canoes *(mid-May)*, Lahaina, Maui. Carvers create canoes from logs and launch them to sea.
Memorial Day *(last Mon)*, all islands. This national holiday commemorates soldiers who lost their lives in battle.

JUNE

Dolphin Days Summer Festival is a weekend of food, golf, and fun held at the Hilton Waikoloa Village Resort *(see p189)* on Hawai'i Island.
King Kamehameha Day *(Jun 11 and surrounding days)*, all islands. This state holiday is celebrated with parades, *hula* and chant performances, crafts festivals, and much more. The biggest celebration is held at the Neal Blaisdell Center in Honolulu *(see p219)*.
Hawaiian Slack Key Guitar Festival *(June to Jul)*, Maui, O'ahu, and Hawai'i. This uniquely Hawaiian guitar tuning is used in performances by the state's best guitarists.
O-Bon Festivals *(late Jun to end Aug)*, all islands. At every Buddhist temple in Hawai'i, Japanese Bon dancers honor their ancestors. There are spectacular floating lantern ceremonies in Lahaina, Maui, *(Jul)* and at Honolulu's Ala Wai Canal *(Aug)*.

Dancers at the traditional Buddhist O-Bon Festival in Honolulu

JULY

Pu'uhonua O Hōnaunau Cultural Festival *(weekend closest to Jul 1)*, Pu'uhonua O Hōnaunau National Historical Park *(see pp138–9)*, Hawai'i Island. A royal court and demonstrations of traditional Hawaiian crafts.
Makawao Rodeo *(weekend closest to Jul 4)*, Makawao *(see p123)*, Maui. Hawai'i's biggest rodeo, where *paniolo*, Hawaiian cowboys *(see p143)*, demonstrate their skill.

Crowd-pleasing bull-riding at the annual Makawao Rodeo

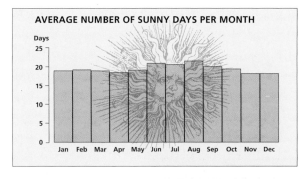

AVERAGE NUMBER OF SUNNY DAYS PER MONTH

Days: 25, 20, 15, 10, 5, 0

Jan Feb Mar Apr May Jun Jul Aug Sep Oct Nov Dec

Sunshine Chart
Hawai'i has few days without at least some sunshine, with leeward (southwest) coasts being, on the whole, sunnier than windward (northeast) ones. Blue skies and warm days are thus a fairly consistent feature, except at higher altitudes, which are often misty. The chart gives the number of days per month with little or no cloud cover, averaged across the islands.

Parker Ranch Rodeo *(weekend closest to Jul 4)*, Waimea *(see p137)*, Hawai'i Island. Set in the ranching heartland.
Prince Lot Hula Festival *(3rd Sat)*, Moanalua Gardens, O'ahu. Local *hālau hula* *(hula* schools) honor Prince Lot (Kamehameha V) with both the ancient and modern styles.
Kōloa Plantation Days *(late Jul)*, Kōloa, Kaua'i. A parade and other celebrations which commemorate one of the first sugar plantations to be established in Hawai'i.

AUGUST

Hawaiian International Billfish Tournament *(late Jul to early Aug, or 1st half of Aug)*, Kailua-Kona *(see p134)*, Hawai'i Island. The world's leading international marlin fishing tournament. Fishermen and avid fans are drawn to this renowned event from all over the world.

SEPTEMBER

Aloha Week *(mid-Sep to late Oct)*, all islands. Dozens of music and dance events, craft fairs and demonstrations, floral parades, delicious food, and even a royal ball make up this grandest of Hawai'i's annual celebrations. The festival begins on O'ahu and continues on each of the other main islands, lasting a week on each island.
Kaua'i Mokihana Festival *(Sep or Oct)*, Lihu'e *(see pp160–61)* and island-wide, Kaua'i. This weeklong celebration showcases contemporary Hawaiian music and *hula*, with concerts and competitions.

Traditional costumes and flower-decked float at an Aloha Week parade

Nā Wahine O Ke Kai *(late Sep)*, Hale O Lono, Moloka'i. The most important women's outrigger canoe race of the year; finishes on O'ahu.

OCTOBER

Princess Ka'iulani Keiki Hula Festival *(date varies)*, Princess Ka'iluani Hotel, O'ahu. More than 200 children, aged between 5 and 12, from local hula schools perform here.
Ironman Triathlon *(Sat closest to full moon)*, Kailua-Kona *(see p134)*, Hawai'i Island. The ultimate physical challenge for the 1,250 participants, this race combines a 2.4- mile (3.8-km) swim with a 112-mile (180-km) bike ride before finishing with a grueling 26-mile (42-km) marathon.
Coconut Festival *(early Oct)*, Kapa'a Beach Park *(see p163)*, Kaua'i. The

cultural, social, and historical importance of the versatile fruit is celebrated with coconut food items, crafts, games, contests, and entertainment.
Nā Moloka'i Hoe *(mid-Oct)*, Hale O Lono, Moloka'i. More than 50 men's teams from around the world compete in this outrigger canoe race to O'ahu. It has become the most important annual event in the sport in the world.
Halloween Mardi Gras of the Pacific *(Oct 31)*, Lahaina *(see pp110–13)*, Maui. The streets are closed to all traffic for this rollicking Halloween party.

Start of the Ironman Triathlon in Kailua-Kona

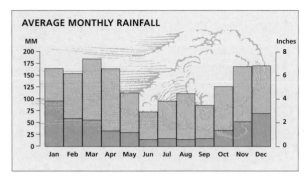

AVERAGE MONTHLY RAINFALL

MM | Inches

| | Jan | Feb | Mar | Apr | May | Jun | Jul | Aug | Sep | Oct | Nov | Dec |

Rainfall Chart
This two-tiered chart gives average figures for all of Hawai'i. The dark blue indicates rainfall on the sheltered, leeward coasts, while the light blue indicates the higher rainfall on the exposed windward coasts. The winter months, from November through April, receive the most rainfall, while the summer months, May to October, receive the least.

WINTER

In ancient Hawai'i, winter was the time of Lono, the god of agriculture and peace (*see p24*). Lono made himself known with extreme weather that could change from minute to minute. Traditionally, wars were concluded by the onset of winter, and it was time for the people and the land to rest from the year's labors.

November, December, and January are the most unpredictable months, but Hawaiian winters are generally mild, and there are many sports and cultural events. The remarkable **Triple Crown of Surfing** displays feats of great skill and courage, while major Pro-Am golf tournaments are held statewide. Winter ends with the famous **Merrie Monarch Festival** of *hula*.

NOVEMBER

Kona Coffee Cultural Festival, Kona district (*see p135*), Hawai'i Island. With parades, arts and crafts, gourmet tasting, and a coffee-picking contest, the Kona district pays homage to the bean that made it famous.

Float at the Kona Coffee Cultural Festival

Hawai'i International Film Festival (*early to mid-Nov*), all islands. Dozens of screenings, workshops, and symposia starting on O'ahu, and then running concurrently on the other islands. Except for some films on O'ahu, screenings are free.
Triple Crown of Surfing (*late Nov to mid-Dec*), North Shore (*see p92*), O'ahu. The world's most prestigious surfing competition, which spans three weeks (*see p31*), waves and weather permitting.
Thanksgiving Day (*4th Thu*), all islands. National holiday celebrated with family feasts.
Mission Houses Museum Annual Christmas Fair (*last weekend in Nov*), O'ahu. An open-air market features artists and craftspeople showing and selling Christmas-related handicrafts.

DECEMBER

Honolulu City Lights and Festival of Trees (*early Dec to early Jan*), Honolulu. A must-see display of lights and one-of-a-kind trees, all created by employees of different county and city departments.
Nā Mele O Maui (*1st weekend*), Kā'anapali (*see p114*), Maui. Cultural celebration of music featuring a student song contest to help preserve the knowledge and love of Hawaiian traditions.
Honolulu Marathon (*2nd Sun*), Honolulu. One of the most popular and scenic marathons in the US, it stretches 26 miles (42 km) from the Aloha Tower to Kapi'olani Park, drawing 15,000 runners.
Christmas (*Dec 25*), all islands. National holiday.
Sheraton Hawai'i Bowl (*Dec 25*), Aloha Stadium, O'ahu. Annual event contended by college football teams.

Lion dancer at the Narcissus Festival in Honolulu's Chinatown

JANUARY

Narcissus Festival (*Jan-Mar, lasting 12 weeks*), all islands. This celebration of the Chinese New Year features lion dances, fireworks, a coronation ball, and traditional food. Honolulu's Chinatown (*see pp58–9*) hosts the best parties.
Ka Moloka'i Makahiki (*late Jan*), Kaunakakai (*see p98*), Moloka'i. Week-long cultural festival beginning with a fishing contest in outrigger canoes. There are traditional Hawaiian games, sports, *hula*, and music.
Hula Bowl (*late Jan to early Feb*), Aloha Stadium, O'ahu. College football with all-stars from around the US.

AVERAGE MONTHLY TEMPERATURE

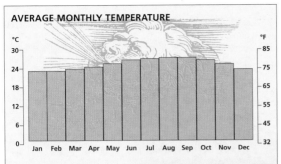

°C		°F
30		85
24		75
18		65
12		55
6		45
0	Jan Feb Mar Apr May Jun Jul Aug Sep Oct Nov Dec	32

Temperature Chart
Hawai'i has consistently warm temperatures year round, with little variation between summer and winter. The coastal areas are warmest, particularly the leeward coasts, which are more sheltered from wind and rain. The upcountry and mountainous areas can be much cooler, with a marked difference in the mornings and evenings.

Sony Open in Hawai'i
(mid-Jan), Wai'alae Golf and Country Club, O'ahu. Major tournament on the PGA tour.

FEBRUARY

Cherry Blossom Festival
(late Jan or early Feb to Mar or early Apr), all over O'ahu. Japanese festival with tea ceremonies, cooking and flower arranging demonstrations, *mochi*-pounding, and traditional Taiko drumming.
Panaewa Stampede Bud Light Pro-Am Rodeo *(mid-Feb)*, Equestrian Center next to zoo outside Hilo *(see p148)*, Hawai'i. Professional and amateur cowboys and cowgirls compete for prizes.
NFL Pro Bowl *(early Feb)*, Aloha Stadium, O'ahu. NFL stars play a post-season game. Reserve tickets early.

The annual NFL Pro Bowl game at O'ahu's Aloha Stadium

MARCH

World Championship of Women's Bodyboarding
(mid-Mar–mid-Apr), Banzai Pipeline, north shore O'ahu. Pro women bodyboarders compete for prize money.

Hula dancers with their flower *leis* at the Merrie Monarch Festival

Ocean Arts Fest *(mid-Feb to early Mar)*, Banyan Tree Lahaina *(see pp110–13)*, Maui. Celebration of marine life and the humpback whales that spend winters in Maui's coastal waters *(see p115)*.
Prince Kūhiō Day *(Mar 26)*, all islands. Holiday in celebration of Hawai'i's first delegate to the US Congress and a well-liked "people's prince." There are ceremonies at the Federal Building in Honolulu.
Windward Orchid Society Annual Spring Show *(late Mar)*, O'ahu. Beautiful orchids on display in every imaginable hue. Demonstrations on plant care and plant sale.

APRIL

Easter Sunrise Service *(Easter Sun)*, National Memorial Cemetery of the Pacific *(see p71)*, Honolulu. An inspiring ceremony held at "Punchbowl" crater with views of the city.
Merrie Monarch Festival *(week starting Easter Sun)*, Hilo *(see pp148–9)*, Hawai'i Island. This week-long Hilo festival honoring King David

Kalākaua culminates with the "Olympics" of *hula*. Plan well in advance for this extremely popular event, as tickets sell out almost immediately.

PUBLIC HOLIDAYS

New Year's Day (Jan 1)
Martin Luther King Day (3rd Mon in Jan)
Presidents' Day (3rd Mon in Feb)
Prince Kūhiō Day (Mar 26)
Memorial Day (last Mon in May)
King Kamehameha Day (Jun 11)
Independence Day (Jul 4)
Admission Day (3rd Fri in Aug)
Labor Day (1st Mon in Sep)
Columbus Day (2nd Mon in Oct)
Election Day (1st Tue in Nov)
Veterans' Day (Nov 11)
Thanksgiving Day (4th Thu in Nov)
Christmas Day (Dec 25)

THE HISTORY OF HAWAI'I

*S*panning less than 2,000 years, Hawaiian history is one of the briefest in the world, with much of it shrouded in legend. And yet it equals the world's best for bloodshed, irony, and heroism. *Hawai'i has had to adapt to waves of invasion and immigration, and now supports one of the world's most ethnically diverse cultures.*

The islands were formed by volcanic eruptions in the Pacific Ocean, more than 2,500 miles (4,000 km) from the nearest landmass. Life on the isolated Hawaiian archipelago evolved from wind-borne spores and seeds, corky fruits that drifted in the sea, and the occasional hardy bird blown off course by a storm. Sea creatures had difficulty reaching the islands, as the North Pacific currents push life-rich plankton away from Hawai'i. As a result, the unspoiled island ecosystem consisted of thousands of unique species that evolved by adapting to the new environment.

Ancient petroglyph from Hawai'i Island

The Polynesians, whose culture was established in the island clusters of Samoa and Tonga between 2,000 and 1,500 BC, possessed a remarkable seafaring technology. They traveled in twin-hulled voyaging canoes that carried up to 100 passengers plus planting stocks of crops (taro, coconut, sweet potato, banana) and pairs of domesticated animals (pigs, dogs, and chickens). These explorers colonized the Society Islands (Tahiti) and the Marquesas Islands in the first century AD. Around AD 300 the Marquesans dared the 3,000-mile (5,000-km) ocean crossing to discover the Hawaiian islands. Archaeologists have based this date on excavations of habitation sites at Waimānalo (O'ahu), Hālawa Valley (Moloka'i), and Ka Lae (Hawai'i Island). Hawaiian ancestral chants, which were rigorously preserved in oral tradition, carried family lines back further, to the first century.

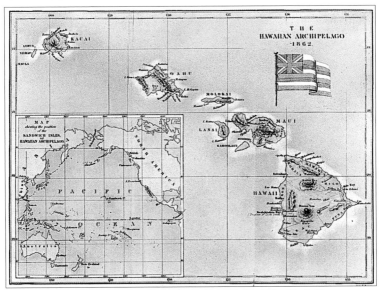

Map from 1862 showing the Hawaiian archipelago and its location in the middle of the Pacific

◁ Early Hawaiians gathered around a thatched *hale* (house)

KĀNAKA MAOLI ("REAL PEOPLE")

The early Hawaiians established an advanced, spiritual culture. Dedicated farmers and stone-builders, they were the first to alter a landscape that had evolved in isolation for millions of years.

Hawaiian men dancing in front of a crowd

They divided the land into *ahupua'a*, pie-shaped wedges running from the mountaintop to the sea, providing each district with access to the full range of island resources. They also built monumental *heiau* (temples) and some of the largest irrigation systems in Polynesia.

Life centered on the *'ohana* (extended family) of 250 to 300 people, in which everyone from *keiki* (child) to *kupuna* (grandparent) was vital to the whole. Cultural values included *aloha 'āina* (love of land), *laulima* (cooperation), and *pa'ahana* (hard work).

INVASION OF THE ALI'I

During the 12th and 13th centuries, new waves of Polynesian settlers came from the Society Islands (Tahiti). According to oral tradition, the invasions were cruel and bloody. Casting themselves as reformers of a weakened Polynesian race, they established a rigid class system with themselves as

Traditional *ali'i* attire, as worn in the 13th century

ali'i (chiefs) who regulated the lives of the *maka'āinana* (commoners) through the harshly enforced *kapu* system. Derived from the Tahitian term "taboo," *kapu* designated any activity that was forbidden because it interfered with the apportionment of *mana* (supernatural power). Women, for example, were forbidden to eat with men. Commoners could not touch the clothes or shadows of the nobility, or lift their heads higher than the chiefs'. Punishment for infractions was quick and fatal, and the *ali'i* rededicated temples as *luakini heiau*, for human sacrifice.

The chief figure in this reform was the Tahitian priest Pā'ao, who probably made several journeys between the two archipelagos. He established a line of *kuhina nui* (high priests) and brought a chief named Pili, probably from Samoa, to consolidate political power. For unknown reasons, these voyages ceased after the 13th century.

CONTACT

Although British sea captain and explorer James Cook is credited with the "discovery" of Hawai'i in 1778, convincing evidence suggests that Spanish ships preceded him by more than 200 years. In the mid-16th century, Spanish galleons made annual voyages across the Pacific between their colonies in Mexico and recently established bases in the Philippines. In 1542 a fleet commanded by Ruy Lopes de Villalobos and led by Portuguese navigator Joao Gaetano stumbled onto islands they named the Isla de Mesa group. Navigators were ordered not to mention

TIMELINE

AD 300 Marquesans discover and settle Hawaiian islands	*Hawaiian stone idol*		**1250** Arrival of Tahitian priest Pā'ao, who rededicates *heiau* (temples) for human sacrifice	*Early hale (house)*
AD 300	600	900	1200	1500
Early voyaging canoe (c.300)		**AD 1100–1300** Tahitians invade Hawai'i	**1542** Spanish expedition, led by Joao Gaetano, finds Hawai'i and suppresses the information	

the islands in their logs for fear that knowledge of them would fall into British hands. In 1742, the British burst into the Pacific with their man-of-war *Centurion*, commanded by Lord Anson, and captured a Spanish galleon in its annual crossing. They seized its treasure and a chart showing the Isla de Mesa group; Cook must have had a copy of that chart.

Confrontation at Kealakekua Bay, Hawai'i Island, in 1779

The timing of Cook's arrival at Hawai'i Island's Kealakekua Bay constitutes one of history's oddest ironies. His ships the *Resolution* and *Discovery* appeared at the height of the annual *makahiki* festival honoring the Hawaiian god of agriculture, Lono. The British ships bore a startling resemblance to Hawaiian prophecies that said that one day Lono would return on a floating island. Much to Cook's surprise, the Hawaiians greeted him with reverence beyond anything he had experienced in the Pacific.

All went well until his departure in February 1779, when a storm snapped a mast, forcing Cook back to Kealakekua Bay. By now the Hawaiians surmised that the *haole* (Westerners) were less than divine, and a series of squabbles, including the killing of a chief, escalated into violent confrontation over a stolen boat. Cook was knifed to death in the fray.

Other explorers followed, including Frenchman La Pérouse in 1786, the first Westerner on Maui. Four years later, American Simon Metcalf ordered the slaughter of dozens of Maui natives in the Olowalu Massacre. In 1792 British captain George Vancouver introduced cattle, goats, and sheep to Hawai'i. Within a generation of "discovery," domestic animals had begun to denude the forests, and imported diseases were killing large numbers of Hawaiians.

KAMEHAMEHA THE GREAT

An ambitious chief from Kohala (Hawai'i Island), Kamehameha could claim a direct kinship to the powerful chief Pili, who lived 500 years earlier. A skilled warrior and shrewd opportunist, he managed to quell centuries of internecine warfare by systematically conquering each of the islands. In 1790 he demoralized the Hawai'i Island chiefs by constructing Pu'ukoholā Heiau *(see p140)* and sacrificing his key rival on its altar. In 1795 he stormed Maui, terrifying the enemy with cannon plundered from an American ship. O'ahu fell the same year after bloody fighting along the Nu'uanu *pali* (cliffs). Twice he tried to invade Kaua'i, but storms turned back his fleet. Kamehameha then invited chief Kaumuali'i to visit him on O'ahu.

Kamehameha the Great, ruler from 1795 to 1819

1758 Kamehameha I born	**1779** Cook killed at Kealakekua Bay		**1795** Kamehameha conquers Maui, Moloka'i, Lāna'i, and O'ahu	
	1778 British captain James Cook first sights Ni'ihau and Kaua'i		**1790** Hundreds killed in Olowalu Massacre	
1750	**1760**	**1770**	**1780**	**1790**
Captain Cook (1728–79)		**1786** La Pérouse explores Hawaiian islands		
		1791 Kamehameha begins conquest of islands		

Through threats and rewards, he forced the chief to cede Kaua'i, and Hawai'i became a united kingdom in 1809.

When the old conqueror died in 1819, he left a leadership void that his son Kamehameha II was unable to fill. The

Mid-19th-century painting of an enormous whale effortlessly destroying a whaling boat

drunken youth was coerced that same year to abandon the strict *kapu* system. The crucial moment came when he shared a meal with women – his mother Keōpūolani and his father's favorite wife, Ka'ahumanu. This act of *'ai noa* (free eating) was taken as a symbolic deed that invalidated all traditional rules. Thus the kingdom was reduced to a class of leaders with no precise set of laws.

MISSIONARY YEARS
The American Board of Foreign Missions provided relief just six months later. On April 19, 1820, the brig *Thaddeus* landed in Kailua Bay *(see p135)* carrying 23 Congregationalists, the first of 12 such groups to come to Hawai'i over the next three decades. In 1823 the second group established a church in Lahaina, Maui, which was by now the whaling capital. The missionaries had running battles with rowdy whalers. They also baptized

Missionary preaching to Hawaiians on Kaua'i, 1840

Keōpūolani, the dying queen mother, who commanded her people to embrace Christianity.

Kamehameha II had bankrupted the kingdom by now, despite stripping the native forests to sell Hawaiian sandalwood to China. To distract himself from his problems, he and his wife sailed to England where they arrived unannounced and unrecognized. Instead of meeting King George IV as they had hoped, they both contracted measles and died of the disease in July 1824. This misfortune left Kamehameha III, the king's 11-year-old brother, to rule. Power, however, was wielded by the formidable regent, Queen Ka'ahumanu. By the time of her death eight years later, Ka'ahumanu had engineered the peaceful conversion of the entire kingdom to Christianity.

THE RISE OF AMERICAN BUSINESS
Generally speaking, the missionary children showed a greater appetite for commerce than for religion. They and other Western entrepreneurs began to experiment with agribusiness ventures, particularly plantation-style production of sugar. In 1832 Kamehameha III leased land in Kōloa, Kaua'i for this purpose.

The king's unenviable job was to push ancient Hawai'i into the Western-dominated world. Guided by his *haole* (Western) advisors, he developed a constitution in 1840. Then, needing an infusion of revenues for the monarchy and maintaining that the *maka'āinana* (commoners) deserved to own land, he announced the Great *Mahele* (land division) in 1848. This released millions

TIMELINE

1800	1810	1820	1830	1840

1809 Kaua'i joins united Hawaiian Kingdom

Kamehameha III (1814–54)

1820 First missionary party arrives in Kailua-Kona

1840 Kamehameha III proclaims Hawai'i's first constitution

1825 Kamehameha III becomes king, with Ka'ahumanu as regent

A blubber pot used in the whaling trade

1819 Kamehameha I dies; Kamehameha II discards *kapu* system. Whaling commences

1825 Sugar and coffee plantations begun on O'ahu

1842 US recognizes independence of Hawaiian Kingdom

Sugar plantation workers gathered around a steam plow in the mid-19th century

of acres for sale to private owners. Ironically, the *maka'āinana* possessed a weak understanding of "owning" land, and most of the deeds went to Western planters. For the next 100 years, sugar ruled the Hawaiian economy.

Large plantations required a labor force willing to endure long hours, poor pay, and cruel treatment, and native Hawaiians, demoralized by social change and crippling foreign plagues, largely declined. Instead, the planters began importing contract laborers, first from China in 1852. Later recruitments drew from the Portuguese islands of Madeira and the Azores, Japan, Puerto Rico, Korea, and the Philippines. As workers finished their contracts, a great number assimilated into island life. Many Chinese married into Hawaiian families. The Portuguese came, with their families, intent on settling. Other workers, particularly Japanese men, saw little incentive for returning to their former lives of hardship; they opted to

Queen Kapi'olani and Princess Lili'uokalani, wife and sister of Kalākaua, visiting the White House in 1887

pioneer lands leased in the Hawaiian wilderness, eventually writing home for brides and family members to join them. By 1900, over half the population of Hawai'i was of Japanese origin.

THE ENDANGERED MONARCHY

After Kamehameha III's death in 1854, a succession of short-lived rulers did what they could for the rapidly dwindling native population. Kamehameha IV and his wife Queen Emma established Queen's Medical Center to help stave off the effects of contagious disease on Hawaiians. Kamehameha V issued a new constitution in 1864 that strengthened the power of the monarchy, and introduced laws to protect the rights of foreign laborers. Lunalilo ruled only a year. By 1873 high tariffs on sugar were causing the planters to talk openly of annexation to the US. In 1874 David Kalākaua took the throne. Called the "Merrie Monarch," he initiated a cultural renaissance by promoting a revival of the *hula* and ancient chants, spending lavishly to build 'Iolani Palace *(see p55)*, and planning a Polynesian empire with Hawai'i as its capital. The tide of history, however, had turned against him. Pressure applied by armed *haole* planters forced the king to secure a reciprocity treaty with the US. It eliminated tariffs on Hawaiian sugar, creating an economic dependency on agribusiness and US imports. In 1887 a league of planters forced Kalākaua to sign the Bayonet Constitution, which restricted the power of the monarchy.

1848 Kamehameha III proclaims Great *Mahele*. Imported diseases kill 10,000 Hawaiians *Father Damien (1840–89)*		1866 Leprosy patients taken to Moloka'i's Kalaupapa Peninsula	1876 H.P. Baldwin completes Hāmākua Ditch, bringing wide-scale sugar production to Maui. Reciprocity Treaty with US	
1850	**1860**	**1870**	**1880**	**1890**
1863 Kamehameha IV dies 1845 Seat of government moves from Lahaina to Honolulu	1864 Kamehameha V issues constitution strengthening the monarchy	1874 Kalākaua ascends the throne 1873 Lunalilo reigns for a year		1887 Royal power curtailed by Bayonet Constitution

The king's sister Lili‘uokalani took the throne in 1891 and attempted to broaden constitutional powers, but was deposed in 1893 by the all-white "Committee of Safety" backed by illegally requisitioned American troops. Queen Lili‘uokalani turned to the United States government for justice. President Grover Cleveland examined the facts and demanded that the queen be restored. However, the Provisional Government, led by missionary son Sanford P. Dole, refused.

Hula **dancers accompanied by musicians at Waikīkī, with Diamond Head in the background (c.1920)**

THE STOLEN KINGDOM

The Provisional Government established itself as the Republic of Hawai‘i in 1894, but its clear intention was to be absorbed into the United States. Cleveland refused to annex the pirated kingdom, but his successor McKinley did so gladly in 1898. In 1900, Hawai‘i became a US territory. The territorial government was largely an oligarchy of white Republicans who controlled every aspect of island life from their positions as directors of Hawai‘i's five main agribusiness companies. Attempts to unionize plantation labor in the 1930s were firmly squelched. Ironically, it took the threat of Japanese invasion to force democracy on the nearly feudal institutions of territorial Hawai‘i.

On December 7, 1941, Japanese bombers crippled US military installations on O‘ahu, sinking or severely damaging 18 battleships at rest in Pearl Harbor, destroying or disabling nearly 200 aircraft, and killing more than 2,000 officers and men. Within 24 hours, Hawai‘i's government was replaced by a military one that stayed in power throughout World War II. Five years of direct federal involvement forced territorial leaders to adopt more democratic methods. After the war, a strike – violent, but ultimately effective – shut down the plantations for 79 days. At the same time, Hawai‘i's underclass began wielding the power of the ballot, and soon the children of the plantation camps were being swept into positions of political power. In 1959 the US Congress offered to make Hawai‘i the 50th state of the union, and a majority of citizens voted to accept, led by a strong endorsement from the Japanese population.

Celebration of the US annexation of Hawai‘i in 1898

TIMELINE

1890	1900	1910	1920	1930	1940	1950
1893 Monarchy is overthrown		**1922** Dole creates world's largest pineapple plantation on Lāna‘i	**1936** *Hawai‘i Clipper* flies from San Francisco to Honolulu, initiating commercial air traffic to Hawai‘i	**1949** Strikes cripple Hawai‘i, shifting political power away from "Big Five" companies		
	1894 Hawai‘i is declared a republic	**1917** Lili‘uokalani dies				
	1898 Hawai‘i annexed by US	**1927** Royal Hawaiian Hotel is built, catering to cruise liner trade	**1941** Japan attacks Pearl Harbor; many Japanese-Americans sent to mainland internment camps	**1954** Labor-backed Democrats swamp Republicans in Territorial elections		
	1895 Citizens attempt an armed insurrection	*US Territory seal*				

Japanese bombing of US naval base at Pearl Harbor in 1941, bringing the United States into World War II

The invention of air travel has changed Hawai'i perhaps more than any other imported technology, not only because it turned O'ahu into the center of US military defense in the Pacific but also because it opened the door for mass tourism. Commercial flights had begun in the 1930s with Pan Am's *Hawai'i Clipper*, but it was the introduction of jet travel in 1959 that brought the world to the islands. Suddenly, Hawai'i, especially Waikīkī, was an affordable four-and-a-half hour flight from the US mainland. Hotel development and population growth hit O'ahu first; by 1959 more than half the people in the state lived in Honolulu. Soon the large agribusiness landholders on all islands began diversifying. During the 1960s, the development of West Maui's Kā'anapali as a resort community signaled a new era for island economy. Whereas the plantations were once the driving economic force, many of the great sugar and pineapple fields now lay fallow, and Hawai'i's fortunes began to rise and fall with the moods of tourism and the price of real estate.

Anniversary of the monarchy's overthrow (1993)

At the same time, some 140,000 resident Hawaiians have started taking political action to reclaim autonomy in their ancient homeland. During the 1970s, Hawaiians began demanding the release of Kaho'olawe from the grip of the US military, which had been using the island for target practice for 50 years. A renewed interest in Hawaiian culture, language, and crafts culminated in 1976 with the building of the *Hōkūle'a* – the first authentic voyaging canoe to be built in over 500 years *(see p57)*. In 1993 the US government apologized for any complicity in the wrongful overthrow of the monarchy, and the "nation of Hawai'i" began a movement to reestablish its own sovereignty.

Today the Hawaiian islands support a population of over 1 million, with Hawaiians accounting for 12.5 percent, and each year over 6 million tourists visit. The island chain accommodates one of the most ethnically diverse and tolerant populations in the world, where over 15 entrenched cultures jostle for position with an embattled heritage. No matter where you go in the islands, however, Polynesian roots grow very close to the surface.

The crowded golden sand of Waikīkī Beach, Hawai'i's most popular visitor destination

		"Statehood" newspapers	1983 Kīlauea begins present eruption	1992 Closure of Hāmākua Sugar, Hawai'i Island's last plantation. Hurricane Iniki devastates Kaua'i	2006 The US Government announces the Northwestern Hawaiian islands as a national monument; it is the largest marine sanctuary in the world
59 wai'i comes h US state		1982 Hurricane Iwa devastates Kaua'i			
60	**1970**	**1980**	**1990**	**2000**	**2010**	**2020**
	1977 Activists George Helm and Kimo Mitchell die while trespassing on Kaho'olawe	1986 John Waihe'e becomes first Hawaiian governor	1996 Citizens vote to convene on the issue of sovereignty		2002 Linda Lingle, the former mayor of Maui County, is elected as the first woman governor of Hawai'i	2009 Father Damien canonized

HONOLULU AND WAIKĪKĪ

Honolulu and Waikīkī at a Glance

Hawai'i's capital city has two focal points, the historic and business district of Downtown Honolulu and the world-famous resort of Waikīkī. The downtown area first gained prominence as a trading port in the early 19th century. Waikīkī, by contrast, was still a swamp when its first luxury hotel went up in 1901. With Honolulu's best beach, however, the resort's success was guaranteed.

Chinatown (see pp58–9) *is a lively district. The streets are lined with exotic emporia, religious shrines, and lei stands.*

'Iolani Palace (see p55) *was built in 1882 and served as home for Hawai'i's last two monarchs, King Kalākaua and Queen Lili'uokalani.*

0 meters   500
0 yards   500

Mission Houses Museum (see p54) *preserves three mission buildings from the early 1800s.*

DOWNTOWN HONOLULU
(see pp50–59)

The Aloha Tower (see p56), *built in 1926 to a height of 184 ft (56 m), was at the time Honolulu's tallest building. A street-level marketplace contains shops and restaurants.*

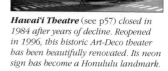

Hawai'i Theatre (see p57) *closed in 1984 after years of decline. Reopened in 1996, this historic Art-Deco theater has been beautifully renovated. Its neon sign has become a Honolulu landmark.*

◁ Joggers in 'Āinamoana State Recreation Area with Ala Wai Yacht Harbor behind it

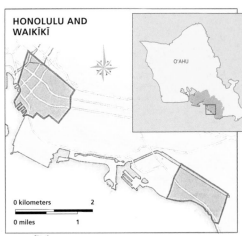

HONOLULU AND WAIKĪKĪ

O'AHU

0 kilometers   2

0 miles   1

The Royal Hawaiian Hotel (see p62), *or "Pink Palace," affords tranquil respite from Waikīkī's incessant bustle. This landmark hotel, opened in 1927, has played host to Roosevelts and Rockefellers.*

International Market Place *(see p64), a huge open-air plaza, offers an amazing array of handicrafts and souvenir items.*

King's Village *(see p65) is a Victorian-theme shopping mall.*

WAIKĪKĪ *(see pp48–53)*

Kūhiō Beach *(see p65) features a statue of Duke Kahanamoku, the "Father of Surfing."*

The Waikīkī Beach Front *(see pp62–3) is lined by high-rise hotels, restaurants, and nightclubs, with the distinctive Diamond Head crater at the far end. Every day of the year this 2-mile (3-km) stretch of golden sand attracts sun-seekers by the thousands.*

The Moana Surfrider Hotel *(see p64) dates from the early 20th century. The seaside Banyan Court bar is the perfect spot for sipping cocktails while watching glorious sunsets over the ocean.*

DOWNTOWN HONOLULU

Once a fishing village called Kou, Honolulu was described in the 1820s as "a mass of brown thatched huts looking like haystacks." In the course of that century, however, it became a vital port of call for fur traders and whaling vessels visiting Oʻahu, and in 1866 the novelist Mark Twain commented that every step in the city revealed a new contrast. This is no less true today. In a relatively small and compact area,

Seal on the gates of the State Capitol

downtown Honolulu manages to squeeze together towering skyscrapers, Japanese shrines, New England-style missionary houses, a cathedral, a royal palace, former opium dens, strip joints, and fish markets.

This bustling capital has a strong ethnic mix, and the downtown streets mirror the diversity. Hawaiian businessmen in three-piece suits, children in school uniforms, and Samoans in bright sarongs mingle in harmony.

SIGHTS AT A GLANCE

Historic Streets and Buildings
Aloha Tower Marketplace ❽
Chinatown pp58–9 ⓫
Fort Street Mall ❼
Hawaiʻi Theatre ❾
ʻIolani Palace ❹
State Capitol ❺

Museums and Galleries
Hawaiʻi State Art Museum ❿
Mission Houses Museum ❸

Cathedrals and Churches
Kawaiahaʻo Church ❷
St. Andrew's Cathedral ❻

Monuments
King Kamehameha Statue ❶

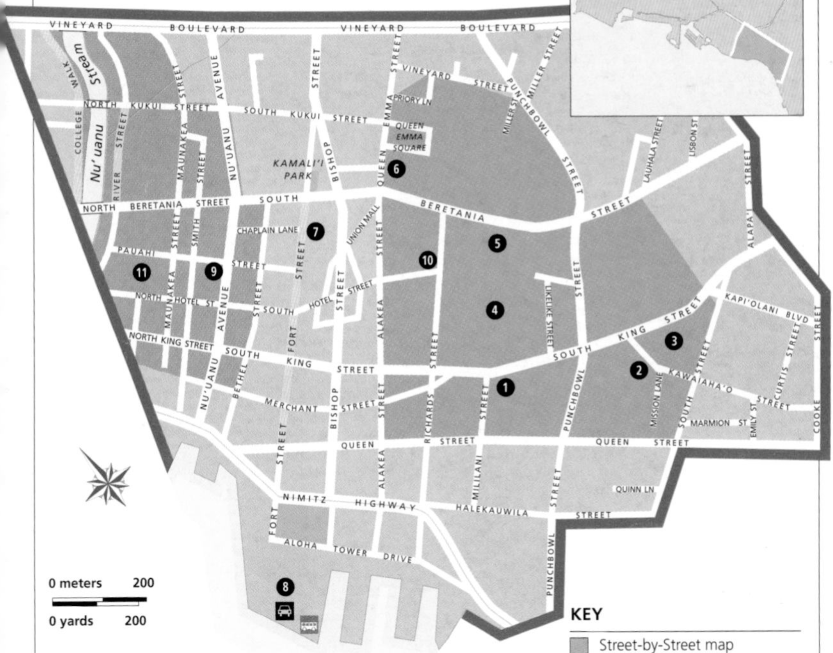

KEY

	Street-by-Street map *See pp52–3*
	Street-by-Street map *See pp58–9*
	Main bus terminal
	Taxi stand
---	Pedestrian street

GETTING THERE

Downtown Honolulu is 3 miles (5 km) *ʻEwa* (to the west) of Waikīkī. From Waikīkī, take *TheBus* 2, 13, 19, 20, or 47 westbound, or the Aloha Tower Trolley or Waikīkī Trolley. For more details, see inside back cover.

◁ **The King Kamehameha Statue, draped with dozens of *lei* in celebration of Kamehameha Day (June 11)**

Street-by-Street: Capitol District

'Iolani Palace crest

The architectural contrasts in this compact area mirror Hawai'i's cultural medley and trace its fascinating history. A short walk takes you from clapboard missionary homes to a sophisticated, Victorian-style palace where Hawaiian kings hosted lavish parties and the last queen of the islands was imprisoned. This majestic survivor of the island monarchy soon gives way, though, to a nearby symbol of 20th-century democracy – one of the few domeless state capitol buildings in the United States.

The 'Iolani Barracks were built in 1871 to house royal soldiers.

Chinatown (see pp58–9)

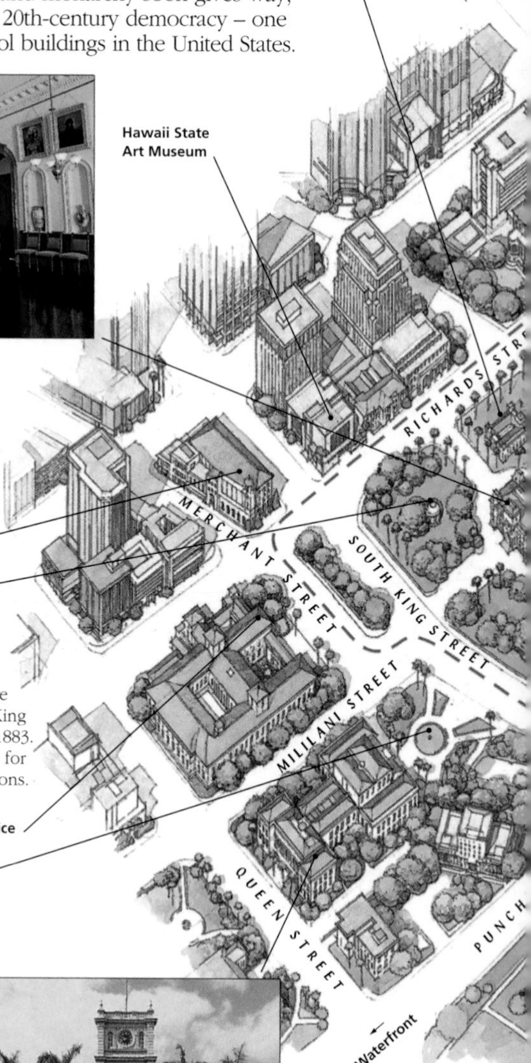

Hawaii State Art Museum

★ 'Iolani Palace
The only royal residence in the United States, 'Iolani ("Royal Hawk") Palace was completed in 1882. The interior has an elegant koa-wood staircase ❹

Hawaiian Electric Company building

The Royal Bandstand, set in the shaded grounds of 'Iolani Palace, was built for the coronation of King Kalākaua in 1883. It is still used for official functions.

Post Office

King Kamehameha Statue
The king's bronze statue stands proudly in front of Ali'iōlani Hale ❶

RICHARDS STR

MERCHANT STREET

SOUTH KING STREET

MILILANI STREET

QUEEN STREET

PUNCH

Waterfront

STAR SIGHTS

- ★ 'Iolani Palace
- ★ Kawaiaha'o Church
- ★ Mission Houses Museum

Ali'iōlani Hale ("House of the Heavenly King") was designed as a palace and built in 1874. It now houses the Supreme Court and the Judiciary History Center.

St. Andrew's Cathedral
Built in 1867, this cathedral features a large window of vivid stained glass 6

Washington Place, a Georgian-style frame house built in 1846, is now a museum for Hawai'i's last queen, Lili'okulani.

DOWNTOWN
HONOLULU

LOCATOR MAP
See Street Finder, map 1

MILLER STREET
SOUTH BERETANIA STREET
PUNCHBOWL STREET
SOUTH KING STREET
KAWAIAHA'O STREET

Eternal Flame War Memorial

State Capitol
The design of this unique building represents the formation of Hawai'i's volcanic islands 5

LILI'UOKALANI

The Statue of Queen Lili'uokalani commemorates Hawai'i's last monarch, who took the throne in 1891 but was deposed by the "Committee of Safety" just two years later *(see p44)*.

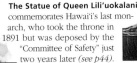

★ Kawaiaha'o Church
Prior to the completion of this New England-style church in 1842, missionaries used to preach from thatched huts on the same site. Sunday services are conducted here in both English and Hawaiian 2

Kawaiaha'o Cemetery

0 meters 100

0 yards 100

KEY

– – – Suggested route

★ Mission Houses Museum
This excellent museum is housed in three buildings, including a printing house, erected by missionaries between 1821 and 1841 3

Bronze statue of the king, his hand extended in a gesture of welcome

King Kamehameha Statue **❶**

Corner of King St & Mililani St.
Map 1 B3. 🚌 *2, 13.*

Kamehameha the Great, who ruled the islands from 1795 to 1819, is Hawai'i's most revered monarch. This Hawai'i Island chief turned the islands from chiefdoms riddled by internecine warfare into a respected monarchy. As a young warrior, Kamehameha met illustrious foreigners, including Captain Cook in 1778. He soon grasped the importance of Western technology and incorporated ships and cannons into his conquest of the war-ring chiefs. After consolidating the kingdom, Kamehameha I turned his attention to looking after his people.

With its gold-leaf feathered helmet and cloak, the bronze statue in front of Ali'iōlani Hale is one of the most famous sights in Hawai'i. The original statue was lost in a storm, and this replica was unveiled by King Kalākaua in 1883. The original was recovered by divers the same year and erected in Kapa'au *(see p141)*.

Kawaiaha'o Church **❷**

957 Punchbowl St. **Map** 1 B3. *Tel (808) 522-1333.* 🚌 *2, 13.* ⏰ *8:30am–4pm daily.* ⚫ *public hols.* ♿ 🎥 *by appt.*

This imposing edifice is a monument to Hawai'i's missionary days. With the collapse of the old Hawaiian religion around 1820 – shortly after Kamehameha I's death – the missionaries soon gained influential converts, including the formidable Ka'ahumanu, the king's favorite wife. In earlier thatched churches on the site, the Reverend Hiram Bingham preached to as many as 2,000 penitent Hawaiians, who would attend in what one missionary wife described in 1829 as "an appalling state of undress." With their first exposure to Western clothing, some wore just a shirt and others only a top hat. By the time the present church was built in 1842, the women wore decorous *mu'umu'u* (long dresses), and most worshipers sported shoes, a habit encouraged by the planting of thorn-shedding *kiawe* trees.

The church's New England-style architecture is softened by the coral-block construction. The upper gallery has 21 portraits of the Hawaiian monarchs and their families, most of whom were baptized, married, and crowned here.

Outside are two cemeteries for missionaries and their early converts, and a mausoleum where King Lunalilo is buried. Apart from Kamehameha I, whose bones were hidden so that no one could steal his *mana* (spiritual power), most of the other royalty lie in the Royal Mausoleum *(see p70)*.

Mission Houses Museum **❸**

553 South King St. **Map** 1 C3. *Tel (808) 531-0481.* 🚌 *2, 13.* ⏰ *10am–4pm Tue–Sat.* ⚫ *public hols.* 🎥 ♿ *first floor only.* 🎥 **www**.missionhouses.org

This bucolic enclave of the past contains the oldest timber frame house in Hawai'i, a testament to the persuasive powers of the New England missionaries. In 1821, one year after their arrival, Kamehameha II allowed Reverend Bingham to build a Christian house and to establish Hawai'i's first printing press. A more elegant house followed, part of which contains a replica press. The interiors have been lovingly preserved. Especially interesting are the clothes worn by the missionaries, including long underwear.

King Lunalilo's Gothic-style mausoleum

The missionaries were so good at converting the rowdy whalers and Sandwich Island heathens that in 1825 a Russian visitor described Honolulu as follows: "streets deserted, games prohibited [and] singing, dancing [and] riding horseback on Sundays all punishable offenses."

Elegant coral-block house at the Mission Houses Museum

South façade of 'Iolani Palace, with steps up to the main entrance

'Iolani Palace ❹

King St & Richards St. **Map** 1 B3.
Tel (808) 522-0832. 🚌 2, 13.
⏰ 9am–2:15pm Tue–Sat. 🚫 Jan 1,
Jul 4, Thanksgiving, Dec 25. 🎟 🎭
♿ 📷 recommended (except at
gallery). **www**.iolanipalace.org

King David Kalākaua was
inspired by English
Victorian architecture when he
commissioned this royal residence on the site of an earlier
palace. Drawing heavily on
sugarcane profits, Hawai'i's
"Merrie Monarch" tried to
recreate the pomp and circum-
stance of the English court in
the palace's luxurious interiors.

The only royal palace in the
US, 'Iolani ("Royal Hawk")
Palace served that function for
just 11 years. Kalākaua took up
residence in 1882, followed by
his sister, Lili'uokalani, who
reigned for only two years
before the monarchy was
overthrown in 1893 (see p44).

The palace became the seat
of government, and in 1895,
Lili'uokalani was imprisoned
here for nine months. The first
governor used Kalākaua's bedroom as his office, and the
legislature met in the chambers
downstairs. After the government moved to the Capitol
building, the palace became a
set for Jack Lord's office in
the television series *Hawaii
Five-0*. Fans will recognize the
arched floor-to-ceiling windows. Children under five are
not admitted to the palace.

The grounds make a pleasant
place for a stroll. The barracks
of Kalākaua's royal guard,
which date from 1871, serve as
a gift shop and visitor center.

The grass near Kalākaua's
coronation bandstand makes
an ideal picnic spot, and every
Friday at noon – except in
August – the Royal Hawaiian
Band gives a free concert.

State Capitol ❺

Beretania St & Richards St. **Map** 1 B2.
Tel (808) 586-0178. 🚌 2, 13.
⏰ 7:45am–4:30pm Mon–Fri. 🚫 public
hols. ♿ 📷 by appointment.
Washington Place 📷 Mon–Fri;
reservations required: (808) 586-0248.

Crossing beneath the canopy
of banyans from 'Iolani Palace
to the back of Hawai'i's State
Capitol is a trip from old to
new, from Victorian monarchy
to contemporary crossroads
of the Pacific.

America's youngest state
boasts the most imaginative
statehouse, its architecture
symbolizing Hawai'i's majestic
environment. The building rises
from a reflecting pool just as
the islands rise from the blue
Pacific. Fluted columns,

suggesting lofty palms, circle
the veranda, and two volcano-
shaped chambers contain the
houses of the legislature. At the
rear, by the Capitol veranda,
stands a statue of Queen
Lili'uokalani, holding the music
to "Aloha 'Oe," a famous ballad
she composed. The words
mean "may you be loved or
greeted." The statue is often
decked with flower *lei*. In front
of the building is a modern
statue of Father Damien
(see p101) by Marisol Escobar.

Across Beretania Street
("British" street in Hawaiian),
is the **Eternal Flame**, a memorial to World War II soldiers.
Farther down the street is
Washington Place, formerly
the governor's mansion and
Hawai'i's oldest continuously
occupied dwelling. This
Georgian-style frame house
was built by John Dominis,
Queen Lili'uokalani's father-
in-law, in 1846. After release
from imprisonment in the
palace, the queen lived out
her days in this house and it is
now a museum in her honor.

The Eternal Flame, a war memorial across from the State Capitol

St. Andrew statue at the cathedral

St. Andrew's Cathedral **6**

229 Queen Emma Square.
Map 1 B2. **Tel** (808) 524-2822.
🚌 2, 13. ⏰ 6:30am–6pm daily.
www.saintandrewscathedral.net

The oldest Episcopal edifice in Hawai'i, St. Andrew's was built as an Anglican cathedral in 1867. (It turned Episcopalian in 1898, when Hawai'i became an American territory.) Alexander Liholiho (Kamehameha IV), Hawai'i's most Anglophile king, brought Anglicanism to Honolulu following a trip to England during which he was enchanted by English church rituals. His wife Queen Emma, the granddaughter of Englishman John Young, an advisor of Kamehameha the Great, was baptized by the first Anglican clergymen to arrive in the islands.

After the death of the king in 1863, Emma traveled to England to raise funds and to find an architect for the cathedral. Her husband's brother and successor, Kamehameha V, laid the cornerstone four years later. Much of the stone was imported from England, although the arched walkways are more suggestive of Gothic churches in France.

The cathedral was not consecrated until 1958, when the final phase of construction,

Detail of stained glass at St. Andrew's

including a huge stained-glass mural, was completed. Outside, a statue of St. Andrew appears to preach to fish rising from a surrounding pool. The carved message reads "Preach the Gospel to every creature."

Fort Street Mall **7**

Fort St. **Map** 1 A3. 🚌 2, 13.

This street was named after the former Kekuanohu fort. Kamehameha I decided to build a harbor fort after he fought off a Russian bid to colonize the islands in 1816. John Young, the king's advisor, supervised the work, and the whitewashed walls stood until 1857. According to early documents, the stronghold also functioned as a prison. By the 1860s the adjacent street was a thriving business center, with a dressmaker, milliner, hardware store, and lumberyard. Some small shops remain today, but the four-block street has been turned into a pedestrian mall. At the *mauka* end (toward the mountains) is **Our Lady of Peace**, an austere Catholic cathedral built of coral in 1843. Father Damien (*see p101*), the "Martyr of Moloka'i," was ordained here in 1864. Opposite is the contemporary **Hawai'i Pacific University** building. Eating places nearby reflect the university's international student body – Vietnamese, Korean,

Chinese, French gourmet, and even a Filipino-Polish restaurant. Midway down the mall, the benches are often occupied by retired Filipino grandpas who spend their time people watching, strumming *'ukulele*, and chatting away in Tagalog. The mall affords interesting views both *mauka* and *makai* (toward the sea).

View down Fort Street Mall, lined with diverse eating establishments

Aloha Tower Marketplace **8**

Pier 9, Honolulu Harbor. **Map** 1 A3.
Tel (808) 528-5700. 🚌 19, 20, 47.
⏰ 9am–9pm Mon–Sat, 9am–6pm
Sun. 🚢 **Navatek I** Pier 6. **Tel** (808)
548-6262. 📷 ♿ main deck only.
www.alohatower.com

Originally known as the "Gateway to Fort Street," the Aloha Tower was constructed in 1926, in the days when tourists arrived by steamship. Locals flocked to the tower

View of Aloha Tower Marketplace and the Honolulu Harbor

and terminals to sell *lei* to the arriving passengers, dance the *hula*, dive for coins, and partake vicariously of the excitement of travel only few could afford. Departing passengers threw multicolored streamers from the decks while the Royal Hawaiian Band played the famous and much loved ballad, "Aloha 'Oe" *(see p55)*.

Standing ten stories high, with four clocks facing the four points of the compass, what was once Honolulu's tallest building is now dwarfed by gleaming skyscrapers. An elevator carries visitors to an observation deck, which delivers a 360° view of Honolulu Harbor and the mountains.

Today the tower is the hub of a tasteful complex that houses upscale stores, and restaurants offering sheltered outdoor seating, perfect for sunsetwatching. Local musicians play throughout the complex. Cruise liners still pull up at the pier, as do working ships from all over the world. Some naval vessels welcome visitors free of charge during designated hours. Sightseeing vessels run harbor tours, and **Navatek I** offers whale-watching cruises from January to April.

Clock face at the top of the Aloha Tower

Hawai'i Theatre ❾

1130 Bethel St. **Map** 1 A2. *Tel (808) 528-0506.* 🚌 *2, 13.* ⬜ *9am–5pm Tue–Sat (box office).* ◐ *most public hols.* ♿ www.hawaiitheatre.org

Opened in 1922 to present vaudeville, musicals, plays, and silent movies, the Hawai'i Theatre was dubbed "The Pride of the Pacific". Hawaiian architects Walter Emory and Marshall Webb created a Neoclassical exterior with a variety of decorative elements – Byzantine, Corinthian, and Moorish – and a lavish interior with plush carpets, ornate columns, marble statuary, and a gilded dome. When talking pictures took off in the 1930s, the Hawai'i became an upscale movie theater, but eventually it went into decline, finally closing down in 1984. A local campaigning group raised funds to save the building and restore it to its former glory. It reopened in 1996 as a multi-purpose venue offering films, concerts, and stage performances. Exterior renovations were completed in 2005. In recognition of its historic importance, the theater is listed on the US National Register of Historic Places.

Model of a sailing canoe in Hawai'i State Art Museum

Hawai'i State Art Museum ❿

2nd floor, No.1 Capitol Building, 250 South Hotel St. **Map** 1 A2. *Tel (808) 586-0900.* ⬜ *10am–4pm Tue–Sat.* ◐ *public hols.* 📷 🎁 ♿ www.hawaii.gov/sfca

This museum, housed in a handsome Spanish-Mission-style building, is dedicated to Hawaiian art, including bark cloth items, embroidery, quilts, and pottery. Many items blend Western forms and traditional folk art. The museum is also home to Art in Public Places, which brings together over 5,000 works of art by more than 1,400 Hawaiian artists.

THE HŌKŪLE'A

Hawai'i's first modern reconstruction of an ancient sailing canoe, the *Hōkūle'a* sailed to Tahiti and back in 1976 without radar or compass. This feat proved that the first Hawaiians arrived in these islands thanks to their mastery of celestial navigation, rather than by chance, and helped to spark off a full-blown renaissance of Hawaiian culture.

Ancient navigators were carefully chosen as infants for a lifelong training to read the stars, ocean currents, and flights of birds. Because this knowledge had been lost to modern Hawaiians, the *Hōkūle'a* relied on a Micronesian, Mau Pialug, to steer that first voyage. Over the years he has passed on his wisdom to a young Hawaiian, Nainoa Thompson, who, with Hawai'i's Polynesian Voyaging Society, is training new generations in the ancient arts of canoe building and navigation. Since 1976 the society has sponsored further voyages of rediscovery.

The *Hōkūle'a* ("Star of Joy") at sea with billowing sails

Street-by-Street: Chinatown

Hawai'i's first Chinese arrived on merchant ships in 1789, followed in 1852 by large numbers who came to work on O'ahu's sugar plantations. On completion of their contracts, many gravitated to downtown Honolulu to build restaurants, herb shops, and clubhouses. Chinatown also developed a flourishing opium trade. A fire in 1886 destroyed the area, and in 1900 another was started by health officials to wipe out bubonic plague. By this time Chinese immigration was a divisive political issue, and some believe the fire was intended to ruin the area. However, Chinatown rose from the ashes and today is a thriving community.

★ **Izumo Taisha Shrine**
The oldest Japanese Shinto shrine in Hawai'i, this was built in 1923 without nails. Facing the Nu'uanu Stream is a traditional gate.

Footbridge

Nu'uanu Stream

Dr. Sun Yat-sen (1866–1925), the Chinese statesman who became the first president of the Republic of China, is honored with this statue next to the Nu'uanu Stream. On the other side of the stream is a statue of Jose Rizal (1861–96), a Filipino hero.

Maunakea Market Place

The Wo Fat building, with its pagoda-style roof, was once a landmark Chinese restaurant. Mr. Wo Fat, a baker, opened the original establishment in the 1880s. The present pink building dates from 1936.

At O'ahu Market you can haggle for fresh fish, exotic fruits and vegetables, and delicacies such as pigs' heads.

COLLEGE WALK
RIVER
NORTH
RIVER STREET
PAUAHI STREET
NORTH HOTEL STREET
MAUNAKEA STREET
KEKAULIKE STREET
NORTH KING STREET
SMITH STREET
Waterfront

STAR SIGHTS

★ Izumo Taisha Shrine

★ Open-Air Markets

★ Hawai'i Theatre

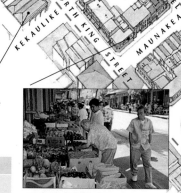

★ **Open-Air Markets**
Chinatown's abundant open-air markets sell everything from duck and salmon heads to fresh ginger.

0 meters   100
0 yards   100

For hotels and restaurants in this region see pp178–81 and pp196–9

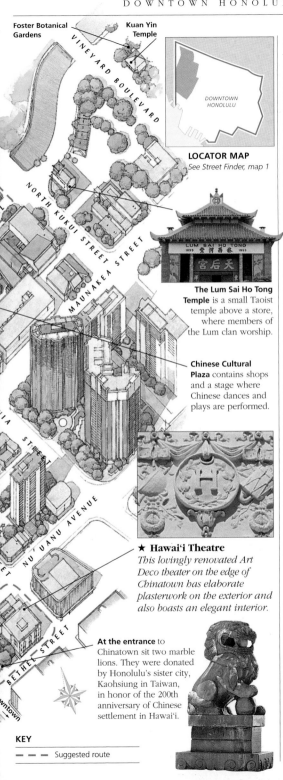

Foster Botanical Gardens

Kuan Yin Temple

VINEYARD BOULEVARD

NORTH KUKUI STREET

MAUNAKEA STREET

NU'UANU AVENUE

BETHEL STREET

DOWNTOWN HONOLULU

LOCATOR MAP
See Street Finder, map 1

The Lum Sai Ho Tong Temple is a small Taoist temple above a store, where members of the Lum clan worship.

Chinese Cultural Plaza contains shops and a stage where Chinese dances and plays are performed.

★ **Hawai'i Theatre**
This lovingly renovated Art Deco theater on the edge of Chinatown has elaborate plasterwork on the exterior and also boasts an elegant interior.

At the entrance to Chinatown sit two marble lions. They were donated by Honolulu's sister city, Kaohsiung in Taiwan, in honor of the 200th anniversary of Chinese settlement in Hawai'i.

KEY

– – – Suggested route

Chinatown ⓫

Map 1 A2. 🚌 *2, 13.* ℹ️ *HVCB, Waikīkī, (808) 924-0266.* 🎎 *Chinese New Year (early Jan–Mar).* **Foster Botanical Gardens** *50 N Vineyard Blvd.* **Map** 1 A1. **Tel** *(808) 522-7066.* 🚌 *4.* 🕐 *9am–4pm daily.* ⬤ *Jan 1, Dec 25.* 🏛️ ♿ 🎬

This exotic neighborhood is full of colorful flower *lei* (garlands worn around the neck) stands, open markets with hanging ducks and tropical fish, herbal medicine shops displaying dried snakes and rats, trendy art galleries, and acupuncture and tattooing emporia. There are also less salubrious saloons with topless dancing, especially on Pauahi and North Hotel streets, downtown Honolulu's red light district – the legacy of World War II soldiers on leave.

The twin lions on Bethel and North Hotel streets, the gateway to Chinatown from the adjacent business district, are symbols of a major rejuvenation project. Many buildings, such as the Hawai'i Theatre, have been beautifully restored.

Visitors to Chinatown may be lucky enough to witness a Chinese wedding with full percussion orchestra and a prancing lion dance. At the Maunakea Market Place, you can sample food from all over Asia, and the noodle shops along River Street are much favored by local residents.

At the edge of Chinatown, the **Foster Botanical Gardens** are an oasis of tranquillity in the heart of a fast-paced city. They contain some protected trees and a prehistoric plant exhibit. The gift shop sells plants that can be sent home.

Chinese herbalist in a North King Street shop weighing his goods

WAIKĪKĪ

Waikīkī was a nondescript place of taro patches and fish ponds when Kamehameha I, the chief who united the Hawaiian islands, landed here to launch an invasion in 1795 *(see p41)*. After conquering the chiefs of O'ahu, he built a bungalow facing the ocean, not far from the present Royal Hawaiian Hotel. Now Waikīkī has one of the world's famous beaches, a sliver of people-packed sand against the backdrop of Diamond Head crater.

Waikīkī Trolley sightseeing bus

Waikīkī's "golden mile" of glass and concrete skyscrapers is a hectic hodge-podge of Western, Asian, and Pacific cultures bustling with some 65,000 tourists a day. The streets are packed with T-shirt vendors, sunburned honeymooners, Japanese matrons with Christian Dior bags, and barefoot boys carrying surfboards on their bikes. Local people strum *'ukulele* at beachfront bars, music throbs from nightclubs, and a band of performers roams the streets.

The turquoise water is dotted with swimmers and multicolored inflatables. Beyond them, outrigger canoes cut swaths through the ranks of surfers, and farther out, red and yellow sailboats bob on the horizon.

SIGHTS AT A GLANCE

Historic Hotels
Moana Surfrider ❸
Royal Hawaiian Hotel ❶

Shopping Areas
International Market Place ❷
King's Village ❹

Beaches
Kūhiō Beach ❺

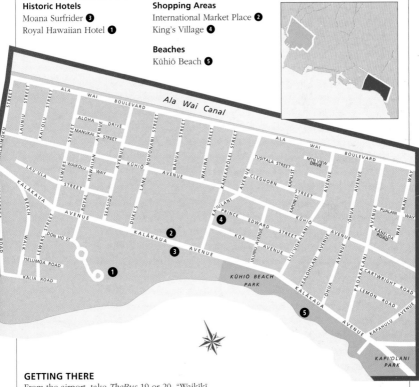

GETTING THERE

From the airport, take *TheBus* 19 or 20, "Waikīkī Beach & Hotels" (hand luggage only), or one of the many shuttle buses or taxis. From downtown Honolulu, catch *TheBus* 2, 13, 19, or 20, "Waikīkī Beach & Hotels," or the Aloha Tower or Waikīkī Trolleys. Buses 4, 8, 22, and 58 also serve Waikīkī. For more details, see inside back cover.

0 meters	250
0 yards	250

◁ **Vacationers relaxing on the terrace of Waikīkī's "Pink Palace" – the Royal Hawaiian Hotel**

Beachfront façade of the Royal Hawaiian Hotel, known to countless tourists as the "Pink Palace"

Royal Hawaiian Hotel ❶

2259 Kalākaua Ave. **Map** 4 D5.
Tel (808) 923-7311. 📧 many buses.
www.royal-hawaiian.com

An oasis in the high-rise surroundings of Waikīkī, the Royal Hawaiian Hotel occupies 10 acres of land in a former coconut grove where Kamehameha V built a summer cottage in the 1870s. Some of the hotel's palms are thought to survive from that period. Paths meander across emerald green lawns under cathedral-size banyan trees to arrive at this Spanish-Moorish-style gem, known affectionately as the "Pink Palace." Almost every-thing here is coral pink, from the rooftop cupolas to the telephones, and carpets.

When it opened in 1927, the Royal Hawaiian Hotel was hailed by the *Honolulu Star-Bulletin* as "the finest resort hostelry in America." It soon became famous for its rollicking parties and was

Waikīkī Beach Front

This world-famous sandy beach actually encompasses several individually named, smaller beaches stretching 2.5 miles (4 km) from the Hilton Hawaiian Village *(see p181)* to Diamond Head. The whole beach is open to the public.

Thousands of tourists *flock to Waikīkī Beach daily to sunbathe on the golden sand, swim in the sheltered water, and surf the gentle waves.*

The coral-pink Royal Hawaiian Hotel *is a pocket of luxury at the west end of the beach* (see p180).

The Sheraton Waikīkī Hotel's Hanohano Room, on the 30th floor, offers stupendous views, especially at sunset *(see p180).*

Outrigger Waikīkī *(see p179).*

The International Market Place is a pop-ular center for vacation souvenirs *(see p64).*

Moana Surfrider, a Westin Resort and Spa *(see p180).*

Royal Hawaiian Shopping Center

Hawai'i Visitors and Convention Bureau

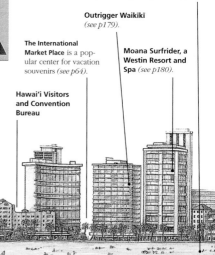

patronized by the wealthy and fashionable. Some guests even brought along their own servants and Rolls Royces.

The Depression of the 1930s slowed business down, and during World War II the hotel was leased to the US Navy as a center for rest and recreation for sailors in the Pacific Fleet. After refurbishment, the hotel was reopened in 1947. It was closed again in 2008 for a $110 million restoration that includes a new lobby, new pools, renovated guest rooms, and the addition of spa suites.

The aura of Hollywood glitz still lingers. On the beach, the "beautiful people" can be seen tanning and attracting all sorts of local commerce.

Behind the hotel, covering three city blocks, is the **Royal Hawaiian Shopping Center**. This modern arcade contains dozens of upscale shops, boutiques, and fast-food places.

EARLY TOURISM IN WAIKĪKĪ

Prior to the development of tourism, Waikīkī was a swampy marshland, consisting mainly of taro patches (see p125) and rice paddies. The land was reclaimed in the early part of the 20th century; large areas were filled in and the Ala Wai Canal was dug to drain the area by diverting streams from the hills above Waikīkī to the sea. Tourism began gradually around 1901 with the building of the Moana Hotel (now the Sheraton Moana Surfrider), which included a wooden pier that extended 300 ft (90 m) into the sea. Tourism accelerated in the 1920s with the opening of the Royal Hawaiian Hotel, which was host to movie stars and millionaires.

A view toward the gracious Moana Hotel in April 1920

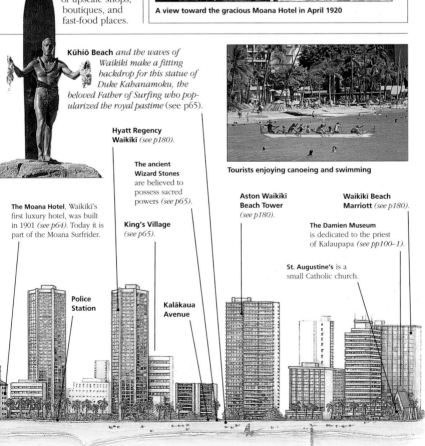

Kūhiō Beach and the waves of Waikīkī make a fitting backdrop for this statue of Duke Kahanamoku, the beloved Father of Surfing who popularized the royal pastime (see p65).

Hyatt Regency Waikīkī (see p180).

The ancient **Wizard Stones** are believed to possess sacred powers (see p65).

Tourists enjoying canoeing and swimming

The Moana Hotel, Waikīkī's first luxury hotel, was built in 1901 (see p64). Today it is part of the Moana Surfrider.

King's Village (see p65).

Aston Waikīkī Beach Tower (see p180).

Waikīkī Beach Marriott (see p180).

The Damien Museum is dedicated to the priest of Kalaupapa (see pp100–1).

St. Augustine's is a small Catholic church.

Police Station

Kalākaua Avenue

The façade of the Moana Surfrider Hotel, the "First Lady of Waikīkī," restored to its original splendor in 1989

International Market Place ❷

2330 Kalākaua Ave. **Map** 4 E5.
Tel (808) 971-2080. many buses.
10:30am–10pm daily.

Situated across the street from the Royal Hawaiian Shopping Center *(see p63),* the open-air International Market Place occupies a city block between Kalākaua and Kūhiō Avenues. This theme-park shopping plaza is a labyrinth of food stalls (on the Kūhiō Avenue side) and souvenir-crammed carts. Choose from shell sculptures, funky cigarette lighters, and racks of identical chains and watches, or pick up an "island" candle or silk flower *lei* – often manufactured in Korea, unfortunately.

Typically vivid Hawaiian shirt on sale at International Market Place

Elsewhere in the market, visitors can watch local sculptors at work, ship home a painted coconut, have their fingernails painted with tropical scenes, or even consult the on-site palm reader. They can have their pictures taken in grass skirts, with green and red parrots, in front of a waterfall, or next to a fiberglass wave.

Just like the wave, this shopping plaza is plastic Polynesia at its worst, but it is a good, central place to shop for T-shirts and colorful island wear. Bargaining is *de rigueur,* and it is always wise to

Souvenir plate at International Market Place

check the prices of similar merchandise around the market. When the going gets too hot, you can rest in the shade of the huge banyan tree in the middle. If you get lost, follow the yellow stripe on the floor to get back to the street.

Moana Surfrider Hotel ❸

2365 Kalākaua Ave. **Map** 4 E5.
Tel (808) 922-3111.
many buses. daily.
www.moana-surfrider.com

The colonial-style Moana, Waikīkī's oldest hotel, opened in 1901 to cater to an international steamship crowd. It became famous for gala events attended by movie stars. In 1920, the Prince of Wales stayed at the hotel and was given outrigger canoe and surfing lessons from local hero Duke Kahanamoku.

An award-winning restoration project, begun in 1986, returned the hotel to something approaching its original look. Restorers used original drawings and templates that were found in the hotel basement. Memorabilia now on display throughout the hotel include a 1905 guest register, photos of famous visitors, and monogrammed woolen swimsuits that were issued to guests in the 1930s. There are free daily tours.

Although nowadays the Moana is part of the Starwood Group's Westin Resort and Spa chain *(see p179),* the hotel's quiet luxury still seems a world away from brash and bustling Kalākaua Avenue, just outside the grand entrance. On a front porch bedecked with rocking chairs, visitors are greeted with *lei* by South Seas beauties dressed in Victorian attire. The nostalgic lobby is decorated with period furniture and huge vases of anthuriums, while over on the ocean side, guests are served high-tea on the airy veranda.

For hotels and restaurants in this region see pp178–81 and pp196–9

King's Village ❹

131 Ka'iulani Ave. **Map** 4 E4.
Tel (808) 237-6344. 🚌 many buses.
⬤ 9am–10pm daily. ♿

King's Village is a cobble-stone shopping mall that recreates the period of David Kalākaua, ruler of the islands from 1874–91. Kalākaua was the last Hawaiian king and is known as the Merrie Monarch, thanks to his revival of the *hula*, which had been banned by the missionaries as a "lewd and lascivious dance." As the first Hawaiian monarch to travel the world, Kalākaua was particularly impressed with the British Empire and modeled 'Iolani Palace *(see p55)* and his guards' uniforms on what he saw in Victorian London.

King's Village itself consists of mock 19th-century shops selling souvenirs, clothing, jewelry, and fabrics. There are various food stalls and themed restaurants. Local street artists gather here at night to provide impromptu entertainment.

Every day at 6:15pm the center puts on a changing-of-the-guard ceremony, set against the backdrop of a Victorian-style Burger King! This is followed three nights a week by a *hula* show that demonstrates both ancient and modern styles *(see pp26–7)*.

Changing of the guard at King's Village

Lifeguard keeping watch over water activities at Kūhiō Beach

The area where King's Village and the Princess Ka'iulani and Hyatt hotels now stand was once a royal estate called 'Āinahau, famous for its lush gardens and flocks of peacocks. Here, in a grass hut, Robert Louis Stevenson told tales of England and Scotland to Ka'iulani, a half-Scottish, half-Hawaiian princess who was next in line to the Hawaiian throne. Later, distressed by the US annexation of Hawai'i *(see p44)*, Stevenson left the islands, heading farther into the Pacific, to Samoa. Princess Ka'iulani died in 1899 at the age of 23, some say from a broken heart caused by the loss of her beloved land.

Kūhiō Beach ❺

Map 4 F5. 🚌 many buses.

Wide Kūhiō Beach stretches eastward from Duke Kahanamoku's statue in central Waikīkī. Near the statue are four sacred boulders, known as the **Wizard Stones**, that represent healers who came from Tahiti before the 16th century. The healers are said to have passed their powers to the stones before returning home. The beach is a calm haven amid Waikīkī's swirling crowds. It is often rich in local color – grandmas in *mu'umu'u* (long, loose dresses) string *lei* garlands and weave coconut fronds, locals play back-gammon, and *hula* schools entertain in the evenings.

DUKE KAHANAMOKU

Duke Kahanamoku (1890–1968) first swam into fame at the 1912 Olympics, when he broke the world record for the 100-yard freestyle. It was as the father of modern surfing, though, that "the Duke" really made his name. He popularized the Hawaiian pastime, called *he'e nalu* (wave sliding), by giving demonstrations in the US, Europe, and Australia, and has been credited with putting Hawai'i on the map almost single-handedly. Back home, the popular hero was sheriff of Honolulu and unofficial goodwill ambassador. When he danced the *hula* with Queen Elizabeth, the photos were captioned "royalty dancing with royalty." At his funeral in 1968, 10,000 people turned out to see his ashes scattered in the seas off Waikīkī. His statue on Kūhiō Beach, always draped with *lei* from devoted fans, stands with its back to the sea. Some say it should be turned around so that the Duke can face his beloved ocean.

Sports hero Duke Kahanamoku receiving an award from Mayor Hylan of New York in 1920

GREATER HONOLULU

The landscape around Honolulu and Waikīkī is dominated by the peaks of the Ko'olau Range. Here, wild boar roam freely and hiking trails lead to waterfalls splashing into mountain pools. Set in these wooded hills, the Lyon Arboretum offers the chance to marvel at Hawai'i's botanical heritage, while nearby, the Queen Emma Summer Palace provides respite from the city heat, just as it did for the Queen herself back in the 1850s.

Closer to the city, the extinct craters of Diamond Head and Punchbowl stand guard. Kapi'olani Park, which sprawls beneath Diamond Head's

Rhinoceros at Honolulu Zoo

famous profile, is home to the Honolulu Zoo and Waikīkī Aquarium. The National Memorial Cemetery of the Pacific, in Punchbowl Crater, contains the graves of thousands of US war dead, and the horror of war is also remembered to the west, at Pearl Harbor. Here, on the site of the infamous 1941 attack, visitors tour the memorials and pay their respects to those who died.

Many of Honolulu's museums and galleries are situated on the outskirts of the city. Most significant among them is Bishop Museum, which houses the world's finest collection of Hawaiian and Polynesian artifacts.

SIGHTS AT A GLANCE

Museums and Galleries
Bishop Museum pp68–9 **1**
Honolulu Academy of Arts **6**
The Contemporary
  Museum **7**

Historic Buildings
Queen Emma
  Summer Palace **4**

Parks and Gardens
Kapi'olani Park **9**
Lyon Arboretum **8**

Cemeteries and Memorials
National Memorial Cemetery
  of the Pacific **5**
O'ahu Cemetery **2**
Pearl Harbor **10**
Royal Mausoleum **3**

0 kilometers   5
0 miles   3

KEY

▦	Main sightseeing areas
▢	Urban area
▦	Military/restricted area
✈	Airport
═	Freeway
═	Major road
═	Minor road

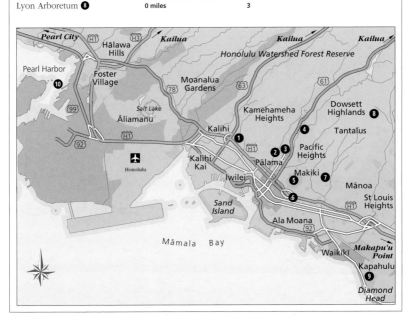

Bishop Museum ❶

Considered the world's finest museum of Polynesian culture, Bishop Museum was created as an American businessman's farewell to his beloved wife. When Princess Bernice Pauahi, the last royal descendant of Kamehameha the Great *(see p41)*, died in 1884, she left all her family heirlooms to her husband,

Princess Bernice Pauahi Bishop

Charles Bishop. Her cousin, Queen Emma, died shortly afterward and bequeathed her own Hawaiian artifacts to Bishop. He immediately set about building a home for the priceless collection, and Bishop Museum opened in 1902. Designated the "State Museum of Natural and Cultural History," it has over a million Pacific artifacts, plus millions of specimens of regional fauna and flora.

Third floor

STAR EXHIBITS

★ *Pili*-grass *Hale*

★ Tamate Costume

KEY

▢	Hawaiian Hall
▢	Polynesian Hall
▢	Picture Gallery
▢	J.M. Long Gallery
▢	Kāhili Room
▨	Nonexhibition space

★ Tamate Costume
Worn in dances involving a mock chase of women, this Melanesian shredded-fiber costume is a very rare artifact, as most are burned after the dance.

Entered from outside only, this vine-covered pavilion leads to a shell collection.

TRADITIONAL HAWAIIAN QUILTS

The Hawaiians' style of quilting reflects both their own tradition with *kapa* (bark cloth) and the quilting methods of missionaries. The designs, which are said to have been

inspired by the shadows cast by breadfruit leaves on a piece of cloth, often honor the Hawaiian monarchy or depict the natural beauty of the islands. The habit of stitching Hawaiian flags into quilts began in 1843, when a British admiral ordered all flags to be destroyed.

The Bishop Museum has a fine collection of old and contemporary quilts.

Traditional Hawaiian quilt

***Kāhili* Room**
Feather standards, or Kāhili, which accompanied high chiefs, are exhibited here in this room. They were made from feathers of forest and sea birds.

★ *Pili-grass Hale*
The timbers of this full-sized hale *(traditional house), thatched with* pili *grass, were brought from Kaua'i in 1902. It sits on a platform to discourage dampness, has woven floor mats and a low doorway.*

VISITORS' CHECKLIST

1525 Bernice Street. **Tel** (808) 847-3511. 🚌 2. ☐ 9am–5pm Wed–Sun. ⏰ Dec 25. 🎟 ⛪ 📷 📹 📶 *Daily craft, music & dance events.* **Hawaiian Hall** ☐ 9am–5pm **Planetarium** ☐ 11:30am, 1:30 & 3:30pm daily. **www**.bishopmuseum.org

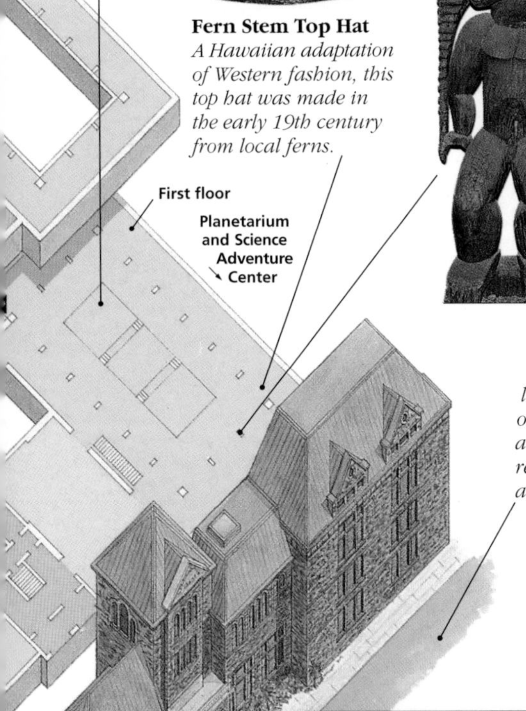

Kū, the War God
This large sacred image of the war god Kū, carved from 'ōhi'a wood, dates from the early 19th century. It probably came from a heiau *(temple) on Hawai'i Island.*

Fern Stem Top Hat
A Hawaiian adaptation of Western fashion, this top hat was made in the early 19th century from local ferns.

Second floor

First floor

Planetarium and Science Adventure Center

Moai
This Moai looms large on the lawn at the museum. It is a life-size replica of an Easter Island Rapanui, *and was a gift from Japan.*

MUSEUM GUIDE
The Hawaiian Hall has three floors: the first covers pre-contact Hawaiian culture, including a replica heiau; *the second illustrates the importance of nature to Hawaiians in daily life and culture; and the third deals with the complexity of modern Hawaiian life. Artifacts from the whole Pacific region can be seen in the Polynesian Hall, while the Kāhili Room displays the treasures of Hawai'i's monarchy. Other parts of the complex include a Science Adventure Center, planetarium, a library, and the Castle Building, which usually houses contemporary traveling exhibitions.*

Castle Building

Main entrance

Three tiers of galleries overlooking the heart of the impressive Hawaiian Hall

Tombstones at Oʻahu Cemetery, established in 1844

Oʻahu Cemetery ②

2162 Nuʻuanu Avenue. **Tel** (808)
538-1538. 🚌 4. ◯ 7am–6pm
daily. 📷 only 5 or 6 times a year.

Oʻahu Cemetery (1844) was
one of the first cemeteries
established in Hawaiʻi. It
was created to bury foreigners who did not belong to
Kawaiahaʻo Church (see p54),
including members of prominent 19th-century missionary
and merchant families. The
cemetery is still in use, and
many notable people of Asian,
European, and Hawaiian descent are buried here. Among
them are A.J. Cartwright, the
"father of baseball"; Martha
Root, spokesperson for the
Baha'i faith; and several of
Hawaiʻi's governors. Veterans
of the Civil War who settled
in Hawaiʻi are laid to rest
here, as are casualties of the
bombing of Pearl Harbor on
December 7, 1941 (see p44).

Royal Mausoleum ③

2261 Nuʻuanu Avenue. **Tel** (808)
587-0300. 🚌 4. ◯ 8am–4:30pm
Mon–Fri. ● public hols, except
Mar 26 & Jun 11.

A few hundred yards from
Oʻahu Cemetery is the
Gothic-influenced Royal
Mausoleum, enclosed by a
wrought-iron fence with gold
crowns on each post. The final
resting place of the kings and
queens of Hawaiʻi, and their
families, their bodies lie in
tombs placed about the lawns.

Only two royal names are
missing from this sanctuary:
Kamehameha the Great (1758–
1819), who was buried in the
traditional way – in secret, his
whereabouts unknown to this
day – and Lunalilo (1835–74),
who is buried in the grounds
of Kawaiahaʻo Church (see
p54) in downtown Honolulu.

Other people buried at the
Royal Mausoleum include John
Young, the English advisor to
Kamehameha the Great, and
Charles Bishop, the founder
of the Bishop Museum (see
pp68–9). The original mausoleum building (1865) is now
a chapel. The interior is made
entirely of rich, dark koa-wood.

Queen Emma
Summer Palace ④

2913 Pali Highway (Hwy 61).
Tel (808) 595-3167. 🚌 4, 55,
56, 57. ◯ 9am–4pm daily.
● public hols. 📷 🚫 🎫
www.daughtersofhawaii.org

Built in the 1840s, this airy
retreat in the Nuʻuanu
Valley was used as a summer
home by Queen Emma and
her husband, Kamehameha IV.
More modest than its name
implies, it is a unique
combination of Greek Revival
architecture and local touches,
such as the long lānai (porch).
Emma's uncle, John Young II,
left the palace to her in 1850.

Set in extensive gardens, it is
still a cool oasis surrounded
by huge trees, some planted by
the royal family over 100
years ago. The mango trees
planted at their wedding in
1856 are now 100-ft (30-m)
tall and still bear fruit. The
tamarind tree was planted by
the couple's only son, Prince
Albert, who died soon
afterward, at the age of four.

The building houses many
of the royal couple's personal
belongings, including valuable
period pieces, jewelry,
household items, and artifacts
from their Hawaiian heritage.
Among the beautiful koa-wood
furniture is the couple's large
bed and their son's cradle,
famous for its wave design.

The gift shop is run by the
Daughters of Hawaiʻi, a
group of women descended
from missionary families,
who rescued the house from
demolition in 1913, restored it
and then reopened it two years
later. They also give daily tours
to groups of ten or more.

The elegant façade of Queen Emma Summer Palace

The Honolulu Memorial at the National Memorial Cemetery of the Pacific

National Memorial Cemetery of the Pacific ❺

2177 Pūowaina Drive. **Map** 1 C1.
Tel (808) 532-3720. 🚌 15, then short
walk. ⬜ 8am–5:30pm daily. ▨

Looming above downtown
Honolulu is Punchbowl, an
extinct volcanic crater. Within
it lies a 116-acre US military
cemetery, dedicated in 1949.
By 1991 the plot was filled to
capacity with over 33,000
graves, nearly half of them for
World War II dead, including
victims of the Pearl Harbor
attack in 1941 *(see p44)*.
There are also casualties from
the Korean War (1950–3) and
the Vietnam War (1964–75).

Dominating the grounds
is the **Honolulu Memorial**
(dedicated in 1966), which
consists of a chapel, marble
slabs bearing the names of
over 28,000 soldiers missing in
action, and a staircase topped
by **Columbia**, a huge memorial statue. South of here a
short walk leads to a great
viewpoint over the city.

Honolulu Academy of Arts ❻

900 S Beretania St. **Map** 2 D2. **Tel**
(808) 532-8700. 🚌 2, 13. ⬜ 10am–
4:30pm Tue–Sat; 1–5pm Sun. ⬤
Mon, public hols. ▨ 🚻 Ward Ave
Gate. ▨ Shangri La Wed–Sat by reservation. **www**.honoluluacademy.org

Founded in 1927 by Mrs.
Charles Montague Cooke,
the light, airy Academy has
30 galleries displaying a

permanent collection of Asian,
European, American, and
Pacific works. It has an
outstanding array of Asian art,
including Chinese jades and
bronzes, Korean ceramics, and
the James Michener Collection
of Japanese prints.

European art includes
Italian Renaissance paintings as
well as works by Dürer, Van
Gogh, Monet, Rembrandt, and
Picasso. American works on
display include work by Mary
Cassatt and Winslow Homer.
The Pacific Collection has
items from Micronesia, Papua
New Guinea, and Hawai'i as
well as works by contem-
porary Hawaiian artists.

Shangri La is one of Hawaii's
most architecturally significant
homes, containing a collection of Islamic art. Tours start
at the Academy with a short
video presentation and groups
are taken by bus to the house.
Tours last 2.5 hours and cover
the public rooms of the main
house and part of the grounds.

The Contemporary Museum ❼

2411 Makiki Heights Drive.
Tel (808) 526-0232. 🚌 15.
⬜ 10am–4pm Tue–Sat; noon–4pm
Sun. ⬤ Mon, public hols.
▨ 🚻 ▨ 🖥 **www**.tcmhi.org

Honolulu's only museum
dedicated to modern art, TCM
started life in the downtown
News Building. It moved to the
present site in 1988, when the
Honolulu Advertiser donated
this luxurious estate as a
permanent home. The house,
a mixture of Asian and Western
architectural elements, was
built in 1925 for Mrs. C.M.
Cooke, the founder of the
Honolulu Academy of Arts,
and has great views of the city.

TCM has a permanent collection of sculptures, ceramics,
paintings, prints, photos, and
videos by national and international artists, spanning the
years from 1940 to the present.
There are also numerous temporary exhibitions. The **Cades
Pavilion** displays *L'Enfant et
les Sortilèges* (1983), David
Hockney's walk-through instal-
lation based on his set for
Ravel's opera, staged by New
York's Metropolitan Opera.

The estate that surrounds
the museum has innovative
sculpture, huge trees, sloping
lawns, orchids, bromeliads,
and a path that encourages
meditation as it winds among
grottoes designed by a local
minister turned gardener.

The Contemporary Museum
Café, set in a secluded corner,
has delicious food *(see p197)*.

Part of Hockney's *L'Enfant et les Sortilèges* at The Contemporary Museum

Lyon Arboretum ⑧

3860 Mānoa Rd. *Tel (808) 988-0456.* ▭ 5. ◐ 9am–4pm daily. ● *public hols. Donation* ▣ 🔲
www.hawaii.edu/lyonarboretum

Only a short drive from busy Waikīkī, this serene, wooded retreat is an ideal tonic for the weary sightseer. Short, verdant trails wind through the trees and reveal botanical delights at every turn.

Founded in 1918 in an effort to reforest land made barren by cattle grazing, the Lyon Arboretum is now home to over 5,000 plant species, both native and introduced. It is nationally recognized as a center for the conservation of Hawaiian plants, and its 194 acres support over 80 endangered and rare species. These include the state flower, *ma'o hau hele* (a yellow hibiscus), and the tree gardenia, *nānū*, whose scientific name, *Gardenia brighamii*, honors W.T. Brigham, the first director of the Bishop Museum *(see pp68–9)*. The arboretum now features around 600 varieties of palm, more than any other botanical garden in the world.

A substantial part of the arboretum is open to the public; the rest is set aside for research. The on-site hybridization program has resulted in more than 160 new cultivars, including hybrids of hibiscus and rhododendron.

There are three quiet memorial gardens and an aromatic spice and herb patch near the main building. A little farther away, the Beatrice H. Krauss Ethnobotanical Garden displays plants that have been used by native Hawaiians as medicine, food, and building materials.

View of Kapi'olani Park from Diamond Head

Kapi'olani Park ⑨

Map 4 F5. ▭ *4, 8, 19, 20, 47.* ◐ *daily.* 🔲 **Zoo** 151 Kapahulu Ave. *Tel (808) 971-7171.* ◐ 9am–4:30pm daily. ● *Dec 25.* ▣ 🔲
www.honoluluzoo.org **Aquarium** 2777 Kalākaua Ave. *Tel (808) 923-9741.* ◐ 9am–5pm daily. ● *Dec 25.* ▣ 🔲 www.waquarium.hawaii.org

This 300-acre expanse of green offers a 2-mile (3-km) jogging path, tennis courts, barbecues, and special areas

---

HONOLULU'S MAKIKI-TANTALUS TRAILS

Forming a loop around lush Makiki Valley 3 miles (5 km) north of Waikīkī, Round Top Drive and Tantalus Drive offer fine views of the city. The trails that lace between the roads delve deep into the rain forest and teem with bird life and exotic flora. Weekday mornings are quietest, but weekend hikes run by the Sierra Club or Nature Conservancy *(see p235)* are informative and tackle the more challenging areas. On any hike, be well prepared: dress for comfort, wear sturdy shoes, bring a flashlight and plenty of water and food, and stick to the main trails. Most importantly, never hike alone. The Hawai'i Nature Center, off Makiki Heights Drive, provides maps and good advice.

View from Pu'u 'Ōhi'a Trail

'Aihualama Trail

Mānoa Falls

Mānoa Cliff Trail

Pu'u 'Ōhi'a Trail

Mānoa Falls Trail

Tantalus ▲ 2,013ft 614m

Lyon ℗ Arboretum

Tantalus Drive

Kaneale Trail

Makiki Valley Trail

Moleka Trail

Mānoa Cliff Trail

• Paradise Park

Hawai'i Nature Center ℗

Maunalaha Trail

Round Top Drive

DOWNTOWN HONOLULU

℗ Pu'u 'Ualaka'a State Wayside

Round Top 1,048ft 319m

Mānoa Road

KEY

═══ Road

■ ■ Hiking trail

❋ Vista

℗ Parking

| 0 meters | 750 |
| 0 yards | 750 |

---

for softball, archery, and kite-flying. It is also the site of crafts fairs and many celebrations.

The north end of the park is devoted to **Honolulu Zoo** whose highlight is an extensive African savanna section. On Sunday mornings, local artists display their works on the zoo fence facing Monsarrat Avenue.

The **Waikīkī Aquarium**, on the southwest side, features the usual sea life as well as a special exhibit on the endangered Hawaiian monk seal and a hands-on tide pool. The aquarium also organizes reef walks, some specially for children.

The park acts as a gateway to **Diamond Head**. To see the extinct volcano, either take the scenic circle drive to Diamond Head lighthouse, whose lawn is a favorite spot for tourist weddings and sunset watching, or you can hike to the summit from a parking lot in the crater. Entrance to the crater is marked by a sign on Diamond Head Road, the continuation of Monsarrat Avenue. The trail is quite steep, but the sweeping view is worth the hour-long ascent. Part of the hike involves climbing a staircase in a tunnel; take a flashlight if you are claustrophobic.

The white-marble USS *Arizona* Memorial in Pearl Harbor

A huge Galapagos tortoise at Honolulu Zoo

Pearl Harbor ⑩

7 miles (11 km) NW of downtown Honolulu. 20, 42. **USS *Arizona*** 1 Arizona Memorial Drive. *Tel (808) 422-0561.* 7:30am–5pm daily. Jan 1, Thanksgiving, Dec 25. **www**.nps.gov/usar **USS *Bowfin*** 11 Arizona Memorial Drive. *Tel (808) 423-1341.* 8am–5pm daily. Jan 1, Thanksgiving, Dec 25. museum only. **www**.bowfin.org **USS *Missouri*** and **Battleship Missouri Memorial** 11 Arizona Memorial Drive. *Tel (808) 423-2263.* 9am–5pm daily. Jan 1, Thanksgiving, Dec 25. **www**.ussmissouri.com

When Honolulu was made capital of Hawai'i in 1845, a major reason was its proximity to one of the world's best

natural harbors – Pearl Harbor. In the time of Kamehameha the Great, the inlet supported oysters that were farmed for their pearls. Later, the port was crucial for whalers, trade with China, and both the sugar and pineapple industries. Leased to the US in 1887 as part of a trade treaty, it was first used militarily in the Spanish-American War of 1898. Today it houses modern warships, military museums, and memorials. Most significant among these is the **USS *Arizona* Memorial**, perched above the sunken ship of that name. The ship went down with hundreds of its crew during the Japanese attack on December 7, 1941 that brought the US into World War II. For many people the visit to this site is a pilgrimage, so appropriate dress is requested.

On busy days tickets may all be allocated by 1pm, and there is often a wait of up to 2 hours for the boat to the offshore memorial. It is best to get your ticket first and then browse in the museum, which features details of the attack and histories of the ships, planes, and personnel involved, both US and Japanese. It offers a balanced and personal view of the participants. Near the ticket desk is a panel describing the volunteers for the day. They are usually Pearl Harbor survivors and are available to answer questions and share their stories. Ceremonies are held here on important days. Another place to visit during

a day at Pearl Harbor is the nearby award-winning **USS *Bowfin* Submarine Museum and Park**, a tribute to the role of the submarine in war and peacetime security. The museum covers the history of submarines, beginning with the first attempt to build one in 1776. Visitors can view the inner workings of a Poseidon missile, and they can also inspect control panels from retired submarines and see how the crew whiled away their time in cramped quarters.

The USS *Bowfin* submarine is moored nearby and is open for public viewing. The park itself contains a memorial to the crews of the 52 US submarines lost in World War II.

The most recent addition to the harbor was the **USS *Missouri***, which opened to the public in 1999 as the **Battleship *Missouri* Memorial**. On September 2, 1945, General MacArthur, aboard this ship, accepted the Japanese surrender that ended World War II. Check the website for additional information: (www.ussmissouri.com).

The crew's tightly packed bunks inside the USS *Bowfin* submarine

STREET FINDER

The map references given for sights, shops, and entertainment places in Honolulu and Waikīkī refer to the four pages of maps in this section. The key map below shows the area of the city that is covered, with the two major sightseeing districts color-coded red. All the principal sights mentioned in the text are marked as well as useful information such as transit stations, parking lots, tourist offices, and post offices; a full list is given in the key. Map references are also given in the Travelers' Needs section for the hotels *(see pp178–81)* and restaurants *(see pp196–9)* in Honolulu and Waikīkī.

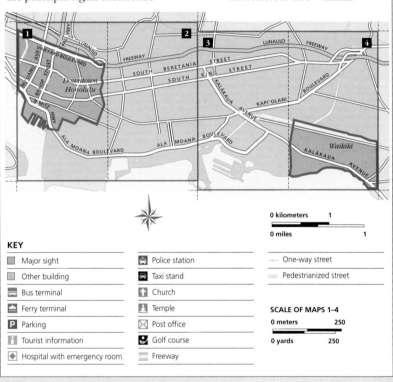

KEY

Major sight	Police station	One-way street
Other building	Taxi stand	Pedestrianized street
Bus terminal	Church	
Ferry terminal	Temple	**SCALE OF MAPS 1–4**
Parking	Post office	0 meters 250
Tourist information	Golf course	0 yards 250
Hospital with emergency room	Freeway	

A
'A'ala Street 1 A1
'Ahana Street 3 A2
'Āhui Street 1 C5
'Ākala Lane 2 F2
Akoko Street 2 F2
Ala Moana Boulevard 1 B4 & 3 A4
Ala Wai Boulevard 3 B4
Alakea Street 1 A3
Alapa'i Street 1 C3
Alder Street 2 F3
Alexander Street 3 B1
Algaroba Street 3 B2
Aloha Drive 4 D4
Aloha Tower Drive 1 A3
'Alohi Way 2 E3
'Āmana Street 3 A3
Artesian Street 3 B1

Artesian Way 3 B1
Atkinson Drive 3 A4
Auahi Street 1 B4
Avon Way 2 D1

B
Barron Lane 1 B1
Beach Walk 4 D4
Bethel Street 1 A3
Beverly Court 2 E2
Bingham Street 3 B1
Birch Street 2 F3
Bishop Street 1 A3
Bowers Lane 1 B2

C
Captain Cook Avenue 1 C2
Cartwright Road 4 F5
Cary Circle 2 D3

Cedar Street 2 F3
Channel Street 1 A5
Chapin Street 2 D3
Chaplain Lane 1 A2
Church Lane 4 E2
Citron Street 3 B2
Clark Street 3 A1
Clayton Street 2 D3
Cleghorn Street 4 E4
College Walk 1 A1
Cooke Street 1 C5
Coolidge Street 4 D2
Coral Street 1 B5
Coyne Street 3 B1
Cummins Street 2 D4
Curtis Street 1 C3

D
Date Street 3 C2

Davenport Place 2 E1
Davenport Street 2 E1
Dewey Court 3 C5
Dole Street 3 A1
Don Ho Street 4 D5
Dreier Street 1 C3
Dudley Street 3 C4
Dudoit Lane 3 C4

E
'Ekela Avenue 4 F3
Elm Street 2 E3
Elsie Lane 3 A2
Emerson Street 2 D1
Emma Lane 1 B2
'Ena Road 3 B4
Enos Lane 3 A1
Ernest Street 2 E2
Evelyn Lane 3 B1

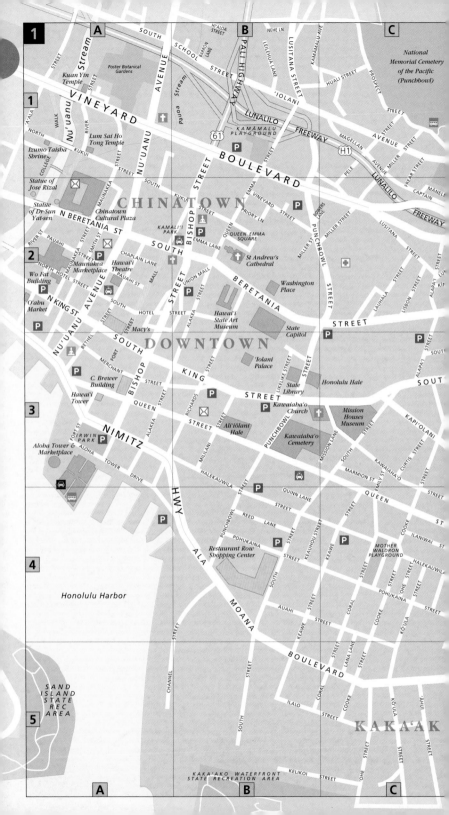

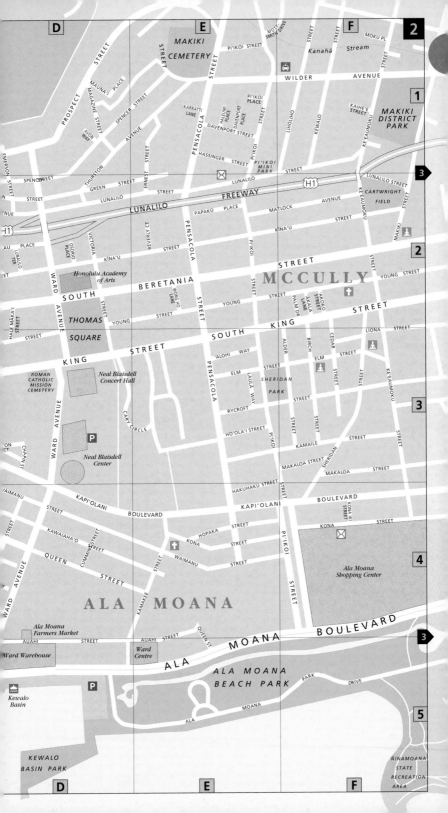

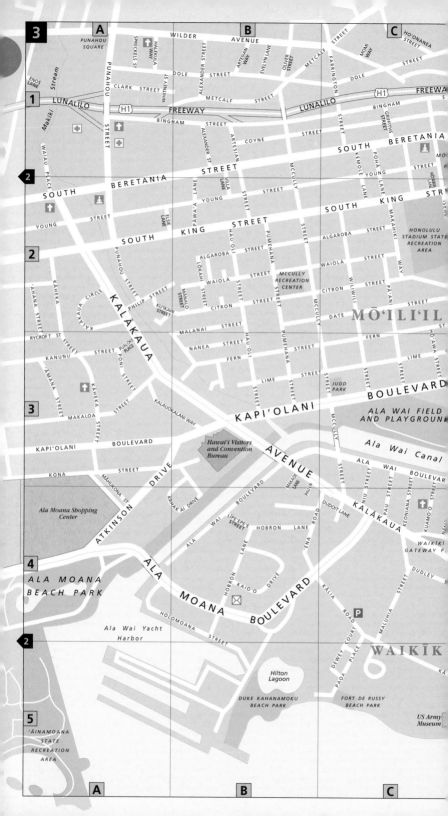

HAWAI'I ISLAND BY ISLAND

The Hawaiian Islands at a Glance

The Hawaiian Islands offer an outstanding array of natural beauty spots and places of cultural interest. The landscape is incredibly diverse, from beach-fringed coastal shores to lush, grassy uplands and alpine summits. Visitors may experience volcanic eruptions, see world-class surfing, explore the fascinating cultural heritage of Polynesia, or simply relax in the sea and sun.

Princeville (see p165), *a resort community on Kaua'i's lush North Shore, is a favorite with golfers for its excellent courses.*

KAUA'I
(see pp156–73)

NI'IHAU

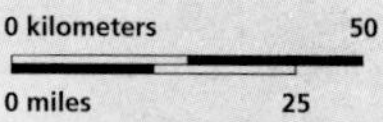

0 kilometers   50

0 miles   25

Kaua'i's Nā Pali Coast (see pp168–9) *features stunning, sharply incised cliffs, slender beaches, and deep blue seas. Enthusiastic hikers can see the scenery up close by following the rugged Kalalau Trail.*

O'AHU
(see pp84–93)

Honolulu and Waikiki

Waimea Bay on O'ahu's North Shore (see p31) *is home to some of the world's biggest waves. Expert surfers flock here from around the world to demonstrate their skill and courage in front of appreciative onlookers.*

The Polynesian Cultural Center (see p92) *in Lā'ie on O'ahu's windward shore displays Polynesian heritage. Through dances and craft demonstrations, visitors witness the traditional cultures of Tonga, Hawai'i, Samoa, Tahiti, Fiji, the Marquesas, and New Zealand.*

◁ Makapu'u Beach on southeast O'ahu, backed by the peaks of the Ko'olau Range

Kalaupapa National Historical Park (see pp100–1) *commemorates the more than 8,000 victims of leprosy who suffered and died on this remote Moloka'i peninsula, and the saintly work of Father Damien who tended the sick. He was buried in the garden of St. Philomena.*

Wailea Beach *is one of a string of beautiful sheltered beaches on South Maui's leeward coast (see p127). Visitors flock here to relax on the golden sands and in the calm coastal waters, and to take advantage of the ideal swimming, snorkeling, and diving conditions.*

MOLOKA'I
AND
LĀNA'I
(see pp94–105)

MAUI
(see pp106–29)

KAHO'OLAWE

Maui's sheltered coastal waters are home to wintering whales.

Mauna Kea, snow-capped for part of the year, is Hawai'i's tallest mountain.

Hawai'i Volcanoes National Park (see pp152–3), *with its active East Rift Zone, is the site of both spectacular fire cones and lava flows. Billowing steam plumes, such as this one at Lae'apuki at sunrise, form when fiery lava enters the ocean.*

HAWAI'I ISLAND
(see pp130–55)

Pu'uhonua o Hōnaunau National Historical Park (see pp138–9), *an ancient place of refuge, provides a unique glimpse into traditional Hawaiian culture and its laws.*

O'AHU

The third largest island in the archipelago with an area of 600 sq miles (1,550 sq km), O'ahu was born of two volcanoes that formed the Wai'anae Mountains to the west and the Ko'olau Range to the northeast. Three-quarters of Hawai'i's million residents live here, mostly in the greater Honolulu area or nestled in the deep valleys that cut between the mountains. This island also receives the largest number of visitors.

O'ahu was conquered in 1795 by Kamehameha the Great, whose forces chased rival chiefs Kai'ana and Kalanikūpule and their men back into Nu'uanu Valley, forcing them off a precipice at the top. Kai'ana was killed outright, and though Kalanikūpule escaped, he was later captured and sacrificed by the great king. The battle was an important victory in Kamehameha's campaign to unify the islands (see pp41–2).

In the 1800s, farmers began growing pineapples in the highlands, and by the middle of the century sugar-cane plantations had become big business. Workers came from China, Japan, Portugal, and elsewhere – the origin of Hawai'i's ethnic diversity. But increasingly, as both the sugar and pineapple industries have declined, much of central O'ahu has been given over to malls and nondescript housing complexes, crammed together on expensive acreage. Some residents now link tourism with overdevelopment and the resultant threat to ancestral lands. Many local people live in relative poverty.

Beautiful scenery, however, is never far away. From Wahiawā the road rolls through undulating fields of pineapple down to the bohemian North Shore surfing town of Hale'iwa. From here to Makapu'u Point on O'ahu's southeast corner, the narrow highway skirts a chain of green velvet, mist-draped mountains. Islets dot the turquoise sea as you pass seaside villages and one deserted beach after another. Along the way are fruit stands, sparkling waterfalls, and Buddhist temples. In the west, the old town of Waipahu is a living museum of plantation history, and the arid Wai'anae Coast offers perfect sunsets and a chance to see an unspoiled slice of Hawaiian life.

Traditional dancing at the Polynesian Cultural Center in Lā'ie, a popular tourist attraction

◁ Fearless surfers riding the record-breaking waves of Waimea Bay, on O'ahu's legendary North Shore

Exploring O'ahu

Hawai'i's most visited island, O'ahu has much to offer besides the clamor of humanity in Honolulu, Waikīkī, and the central 'Ewa plain. The rest of the island is amazingly rural, with large areas of sugarcane fields and rain forest where wild boar still roam. It is easy to escape into O'ahu's spectacular scenery as jungle-clad roads and trails transport you from the high-rises of Honolulu. The Wai'anae Mountains and the Ko'olau Range form the backbones of the island, while tropical beaches line the shimmering coast. The snorkelers' paradise of Hanauma Bay and the world-class surf breaks on the North Shore draw the crowds, but the Wai'anae Coast is peaceful. Cultural attractions range from the popular Polynesian Cultural Center to the tranquil Byodo-In Temple.

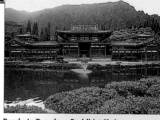

Byodo-In Temple, a Buddhist Shrine

Kawela
Sunset Beach
Waiale'e
'Ehukai Beach Park
Waimea
Pūpūkea
WAIMEA VALLEY 6
Waimea Falls
83
Kawailoa
Ali'i Beach Park
7 HALE'IWA
KA'ENA POINT 11
Mokulē'ia Beach
Mokulē'ia
Waialua
KAMEHAMEHA HWY
FARRINGTON HWY
803
99
FARRINGTON HWY
Yokohama Bay
Makua Valley
Wai'anae Mountains
DOLE PLANTATION 8
930
Mākaha
Schofield Barracks
Wahiawā
Kāne'āki Heiau
Mākaha Beach
Mākaha
Mililani Mauka
750
WAI'ANAE COAST 10
Wai'anae
KUNIA ROAD
Mililani Town
Maili'ili
99
Poka'i Bay
Ma'ili
Honolulu Forest Reserve
Waipahu
Nānākuli
9
93
HAWAI'I PLANTATION VILLAGE
H1
Makakilo
Kapolei
'Ewa
Hawaiian Waters Adventure Park
760
'Ewa Beach

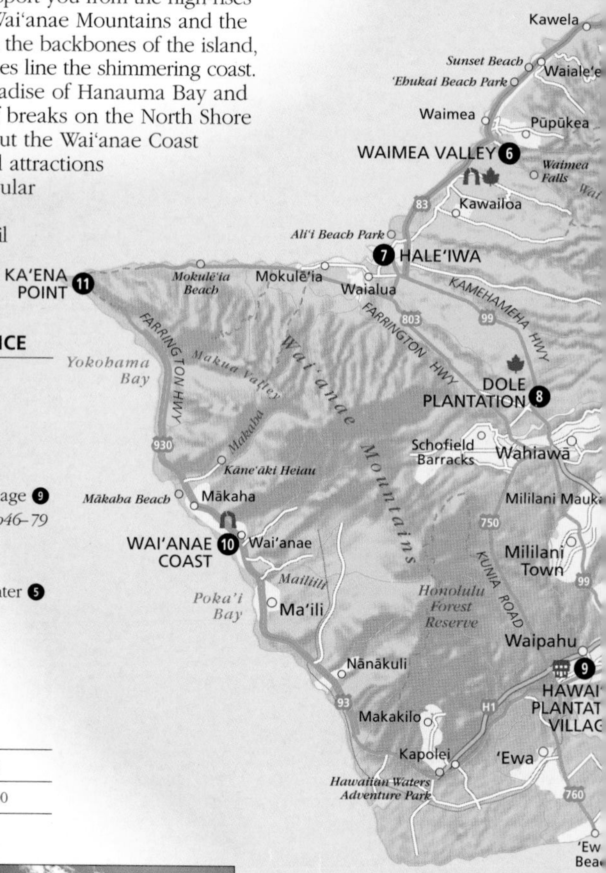

SIGHTS AT A GLANCE

Byodo-In Temple 3
Dole Plantation 8
Hale'iwa 7
Hanauma Bay 1
Hau'ula Trails 4
Hawai'i's Plantation Village 9
HONOLULU & WAIKĪKĪ pp46–79
Ka'ena Point 11
Makapu'u Point 2
Polynesian Cultural Center 5
Wai'anae Coast 10
Waimea Valley 6

SEE ALSO

- ***Where to Stay*** pp182–3
- ***Where to Eat*** pp199–200

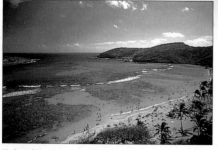

Sheltered Hanauma Bay, a favorite with snorkelers

KEY

- Freeway
- Major road
- Minor road
- Track
- Scenic route
- Summit

For additional map symbols *see back flap*

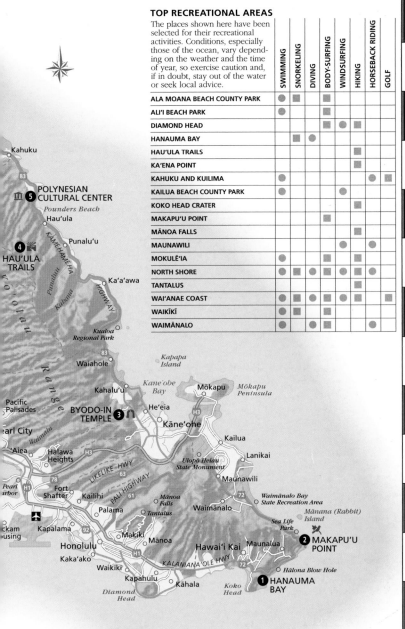

TOP RECREATIONAL AREAS

The places shown here have been selected for their recreational activities. Conditions, especially those of the ocean, vary depending on the weather and the time of year, so exercise caution and, if in doubt, stay out of the water or seek local advice.

	SWIMMING	SNORKELING	DIVING	BODY-SURFING	WINDSURFING	HIKING	HORSEBACK RIDING	GOLF
ALA MOANA BEACH COUNTY PARK	●	■		■				
ALI'I BEACH PARK	●			■				
DIAMOND HEAD				■	●	■		
HANAUMA BAY		■	●					
HAU'ULA TRAILS						■		
KA'ENA POINT						■		
KAHUKU AND KUILIMA	●						●	■
KAILUA BEACH COUNTY PARK	●				●			
KOKO HEAD CRATER						■		
MAKAPU'U POINT				■				
MĀNOA FALLS						■		
MAUNAWILI						●	●	
MOKULĒ'IA	●			■		■		
NORTH SHORE	●	■	●	■	●	■	●	
TANTALUS						■		
WAI'ANAE COAST	●	■	●	■	●	■		■
WAIKĪKĪ	●	■		■				
WAIMĀNALO	●		●	■			●	

GETTING AROUND

O'ahu is served by Honolulu International Airport. There is a good road network, and the best way to get around is by rented car. Three freeways radiate out from Honolulu: H1 takes you to the Wai'anae Coast, H2 veers north toward Hale'iwa, and H3 crosses to the windward (northeast) coast. *TheBus* company runs two routes (52, 55) that link Honolulu with central O'ahu, the windward coast, and the North Shore *(see inside back cover)*.

0 kilometers 5

0 miles 5

Trained dolphins performing graceful maneuvers at Sea Life Park

Hanauma Bay ❶

Honolulu Co. Kalanianaʻole Highway (Hwy 72), 10 miles (16 km) E of Waikīkī. **Tel** (808) 396-4229. 🚌 🅿 6am–6pm Wed–Mon. 🎫 🚫 🔲 🎁

Snorkeling in this sheltered bay is like swimming in a gigantic aquarium with more than 400 species of fish, some of which exist only here. A sandy-bottomed hole in the reef is perfect for first-time snorkelers. Fish-feeding, once a popular tourist activity, is no longer allowed since this is a conservation district. A Marine Education Center presents an orientation video and offers restrooms, a snack bar; and a tram service to the beach. To avoid the crowds, visit early in the morning.

Makapuʻu Point ❷

Honolulu Co. Kalanianaʻole Highway (Hwy 72), 14 miles (23 km) E of Waikīkī. 🚌 Sea Life Park.

It is worth stopping at the lookout below the Makapuʻu lighthouse for humbling views of sky and sea, with rock islets artistically arranged. You can watch the action on nearby **Makapuʻu Beach**, a pocket cove that boasts the island's best body-surfing waves. Local kids make the wave-hopping look easy, but it requires precise timing to avoid being dragged onto the rocks.

Hiking trails lead upward into black mountains, but you do not need to climb beyond the first 100 ft (30 m) or so for

spectacular photos. Hikers can continue to the hang-glider launch site at 1,250 ft (380 m) and watch the intrepid fliers.

Facing Makapuʻu Beach, the educational **Sea Life Park** features a huge Hawaiian reef tank and regular performances by penguins, sea lions, and dolphins. The park has spectacular views of Oʻahu's breathtaking coastline. Buses link up with Waikīkī.

🐬 Sea Life Park
41-202 Kalanianaʻole Hwy (Hwy 72). **Tel** (808) 259-7933. 🅿 9:30am–5pm daily. 🎫 🚫 🎁 **www**.sealifeparkhawaii.com

Byodo-In Temple ❸

Honolulu Co. 47-200 Kahekili Highway (Hwy 83), Kāneʻohe. **Tel** (808) 239-8811. 🚌 on Kahekili Hwy (Hwy 83), then 10-min walk. 🅿 9am–5pm Mon–Sat; 10am–4pm Sun. ⬤ Dec 25. 🎫 🚫

This replica of a 900-year-old Japanese temple cannot be seen from the highway. The only marker is a Hawaiʻi Visitors and Convention Bureau sign for a historic sight. Once you turn into the Valley of Temples – a nondenominational cemetery – the road winds into the valley to reach this hidden treasure, its walls red against fluted, green cliffs. After crossing the curved vermilion footbridge, you can ring a three-ton bell to assure long life and to receive the blessings of the Buddha.

Remove your shoes before entering the shrine, where a 9-ft (3-m) gold and lacquer Buddha presides.

Visiting the temple just before sunset provides a tranquil experience. You will not be able to see the Buddha (the temple closes at 4pm), but the profound silence will be punctuated only by the singing of birds. The sun setting behind the cliffs gives off pink and mauve hues, and, if you are lucky, you may have the scene all to yourself.

Hauʻula Trails ❹

Honolulu Co. Kamehameha Hwy (Hwy 83), 20 miles (30 km) NW of Kāneʻohe, approximately 2 miles (3 km) past Punaluʻu. **Tel** (808) 973-9782. 🅿 weekends and holidays. **www**.hawaiitrails.org

The three trails that make up the Hauʻula Trails area – Hauʻula Loop Trail, Maʻakua Ridge Trail, and Maʻakua Gulch Trail – provide everything that hikers love best about Hawaiʻi's finest trails. They are wide with excellent footing and offer spectacular mountain, valley, and ocean views. You should allow approximately two hours for a round-trip of any of the trails, all of which begin beyond the end of Maʻakua Road, off Hauʻula Homestead Road which is just beyond the tiny town of Hauʻula.

The beautifully crafted Buddha, centerpiece of the Japanese Byodo-In Temple

Beaches of Southeast O‘ahu

From Makapu‘u Point at the southern tip to the commuter suburbia of Kāne‘ohe, O‘ahu's southeast coast features a range of delightful beaches, with free access to the public. Waimānalo Beach offers lazy swimming in calm seas, Lanikai Beach is exclusive and quiet, and the tree-lined community of Kailua has extensive beach facilities. To discourage break-ins in the area, do not leave items of value in your car.

Kāne‘ohe Bay, *protected by a barrier reef, features two prominent islands: Mokoli‘i (Chinaman's Hat) and Moku o Lo‘e (Coconut Island). Kāne‘ohe itself is a bedroom town for the local military base.*

0 kilometers   4

0 miles   2

He‘eia State Park
He‘eia
836
Kahekili Hwy
Kāne‘ohe Bay
MŌKAPU PENINSULA
KĀNE‘OHE
H3
83
630
HONOLULU
63
H3
83
61
HONOLULU
Kailua Bay
KAILUA
Kailua Beach
61
Lanikai
Lanikai Beach
Kalaniana‘ole Hwy
Bellows Field Beach Park
72
Waimānalo Bay State Recreation Area
Waimanalo Bay
Kaupō Beach County Park
Sea Life Park
Makapu‘u Beach
Makapu‘u Point
HONOLULU
72

Lanikai Beach *is one of the most beautiful beaches on O‘ahu. The white sands stretch for a little over a mile (1.5 km) and are overlooked by the beachfront mansions of affluent Lanikai.*

At Kailua Beach, a 30-acre park with full facilities, you can rent a kayak or a sailboard for windsurfing, snorkel to a deserted island, or just sit back and enjoy the scenery. The reef-protected waters are popular with local families.

KEY

▬▬	Freeway
▬▬	Major road
▬▬	Minor road
⛳	Golf course
❀	Vista

Waimānalo Beach, *the longest on O‘ahu at 3 miles (5 km), has safe seas and gently sloping sand.*

Couple riding bikes at Kualoa Ranch, East O‘ahu ▷

Polynesian Cultural Center ❺

Honolulu Co. 55-370 Kamehameha Highway (Hwy 83), Lā'ie. *Tel (808) 293-3333.* 🅿 🕐 *noon–9pm Mon–Sat.* 🌙 *Thanksgiving, Dec 25.* 🖼 ♿ www.polynesia.com

The village of Lā'ie was founded by Mormon missionaries in 1864 after a failed attempt to settle on the island of Lāna'i. Lā'ie now contains a Mormon temple, a branch of Brigham Young University, and a 42-acre educational theme park known as the Polynesian Cultural Center.

At the Center, students from all over the Pacific demonstrate crafts and dancing in seven Polynesian "villages": Tongan, Hawaiian, Samoan, Tahitian, Fijian, Maori, and Marquesan. The instruction, whether it be Tongan drumming or Samoan fire-making, is delivered in almost continuous minishows, and audience participation is encouraged. The afternoon show, **Rainbows of Paradise**, presents legends from all the islands with singing, dancing, and martial arts performed on double-hulled canoes.

The Center is worth the hefty admission fee. However, some critics question the authenticity of the exhibits and shows – not all the "islanders" in the villages are the real thing. Despite this, the PCC remains Hawai'i's most popular paid attraction, with 900,000 visitors a year. Regular shuttle buses connect with Waikīkī.

Waimea Valley ❻

Honolulu Co. 59-864 Kamehameha Highway (Hwy 83), Waimea. *Tel (808) 638-7766.* 🚌 *52, 55.* 🕐 *9am–5pm daily.* 🌙 *Jan 1, Thanksgiving, Dec 25.* 🖼 ♿ www.waimeavalley.net

One of a few intact examples of an *ahupua'a* – a Hawaiian land division from mountain to sea – Waimea Valley is a beautiful, unspoilt environment, a sacred place for native Hawaiians, and an important educational resource. After periods as an attraction, with glitzy *hula* shows and cliff divers, and as a facility run by the Audubon Society, it is now operated by the Office of Hawaiian Affairs.

The 1,875-acre (759-hectare) area includes a waterfall, a 5,000-plant botanical collection, a refuge for endangered wildlife, and archaeological sites, including a 15th-century *heiau* (temple) dedicated to Lono, god of peace, agriculture, and music.

Walking tours and cultural activities such as *lei* making, *hula* lessons, and storytelling are included in the cost of admission. Bring binoculars, as the park has great opportunities for bird-watching. After your visit, enjoy a swim or a snorkel at **Waimea Beach Park** across the street.

Matsumoto's shave ice

Environs: Set above Waimea Bay at an elevation of 300 ft (90 m), **Pu'u O Mahuka Heiau State Monument** offers fine views. Here the ruins of three sacred rock terraces make up the largest *heiau* (temple) on

O'ahu. Ironically called "hill of escape" in Hawaiian, this was once a site of human sacrifice.

⛩ **Pu'u O Mahuka Heiau State Monument**
Off Pūpūkea Road, half a mile (800 m) E of Kamehameha Hwy (Hwy 83), just N of Waimea.

Hale'iwa Beach Park on the North Shore, a sheltered spot for a swim

Hale'iwa ❼

Honolulu Co. 🏠 *2,500.* 🚌 ℹ️ *HVCB, Waikīkī, (808) 924-0266.* 🎎 *O-Bon Buddhist Festival (Jul or Aug).*

Once a plantation town and more recently a hippie hangout, Hale'iwa is now the hub for the North Shore surfing community. Graced by local color from these subcultures, the town has a single main street with art galleries, boutiques, general stores, restaurants, and coffee shops. Tin-roofed **Matsumoto's** is the best place to try a Hawaiian specialty known as shave ice (thinly shaved ice flavored with exotic syrups and toppings, such as adzuki beans).

Flanking a picturesque boat harbor are well-appointed public beaches. **Ali'i Beach Park** is famous for big waves and surfing contests *(see p31)*, but the adjacent **Hale'iwa Beach Park**, protected by a breakwater, is one of the few North Shore spots where it is usually safe to swim in winter.

The town's biggest event, the O-Bon Festival, is held every summer at a seaside Buddhist temple. It involves folk dancing and the release of thousands of floating lanterns into the sea, a truly enchanting sight.

Dancers performing aboard a canoe at the Polynesian Cultural Center

Environs: Driving west from Hale'iwa, you pass a former sugar plantation at Waialua and arrive at **Mokulē'ia**, where polo fields border on empty, white-sand beaches. Here you can spend a pleasant afternoon watching parachutists from nearby Dillingham Airfield float down across the surf like clouds of colorful butterflies.

Dole Plantation ❽

Honolulu Co. 64-1550 Kamehameha Highway (Hwy 99), 2 miles (3 km) N of Wahiawā. *Tel* (808) 621-8408. 🚌 Wahiawā. ⏰ 9am–5:30pm daily. 🚫 Dec 25. ♿ www.dole-plantation.com

The Dole Cannery, built by James Dole in 1903 next to his Wahiawā pineapple plantation, was at that time the world's largest fruit cannery. In 1907 operations moved to Honolulu, eventually closing in 1991 due to increasing competition from Asia. The original Dole Cannery in Wahiawā now functions as a distribution warehouse.

Dole's famous company logo

Across from the warehouse is Dole Plantation, a gift shop selling a range of pineapple products and a demonstration garden showing the different stages of the fruit's growth.

The Plantation is also home to the **Pineapple Garden Maze** which is the largest maze in the world, with 1.7 miles of paths and covering more than two acres.

🌿 **Pineapple Garden Maze**
⏰ 9am–5pm daily. 📷

Hawai'i's Plantation Village ❾

Honolulu Co. 94-695 Waipahu Street, Waipahu. *Tel* (808) 677-0110. 🚌 Waipahu. ⏰ 10am–2pm Mon–Sat. 🚫 public hols. 📷 ♿ 📷 www.hawaiiplantationvillage.org

This $3 million restored village portrays over 100 years of sugar plantation culture. It

Interior of the Chinese Cookhouse at Hawai'i's Plantation Village

shows how plantation owners segregated workers along strict ethnic lines and how, in spite of this, a common pidgin language developed *(see p25)*.

The village contains some recreated buildings from the major ethnic groups that worked the plantations, from the Korean, Puerto Rican, and Japanese homes to a Japanese bathhouse and a Shinto shrine. Personal objects placed in the houses give the impression that the occupants have just left.

Wai'anae Coast ❿

Honolulu Co. 🚌 Nānākuli, Wai'anae and Mākaha Beach. 🛈 HVCB, Waikīkī, (808) 924-0266.

With no souvenir stands and very few restaurants, O'ahu's sunny leeward coast is home to a population of native Hawaiians and other Pacific islanders. One of the coast's prettiest beaches is **Pōka'ī Bay**, where a breakwater shelters an aquamarine lagoon with sand as soft as cloth under your feet.

Farther northwest is **Mākaha Beach**, famous for its 30-ft (9-m) waves. In Mākaha Valley is **Kāne'ākī Heiau**, with thatched houses and *ki'i* (carved idols). It was used as a war temple by Kamehameha I. Mākaha means "ferocious," and the valley was once notorious for bandits. The area still has a reputation for car break-ins; camping is not advised.

🛖 **Kāne'ākī Heiau**
Off Mākaha Valley Rd. *Tel* (808) 695-8174. ⏰ Tue–Sun.

Ka'ena Point ⓫

Honolulu Co. Beyond end of Farrington Highway (Hwy 930), 7 miles (11 km) N of Mākaha.

O'ahu's western extremity, Ka'ena Point has a stark, mountainous coastline and spectacular sunsets. A hot but relatively easy 2-mile (3-km) trail leads to the point.

Legend tells that the rock off the point is a chunk of Kaua'i that the demigod Maui pulled off when he was trying to unite the two islands. On clear days Kaua'i can be spotted to the north. You may also see rare monk seals, green turtles, and humpback whales *(see p115)*. The world's highest waves slam against the rocks here. So far no one has been suicidal enough to surf them. The point can also be reached from the road's end in Mokulē'ia. The two roads do not connect.

Ka'ena Point, reached by the exposed trail in the foreground

MOLOKA'I AND LĀNA'I

The small island of Moloka'i tends to be overlooked by vaca-tioners scurrying between O'ahu and Maui. Far less developed for tourism than its neighbors, Moloka'i is the place to get away from it all, and most visitors are enchanted by its gentle pace. Across the Kalohi Channel to the south lies the smaller island of Lāna'i. This former pineapple plantation is now an exclusive tourist destination.

Moloka'i is formed from two extinct volcanoes that were once, along with Lāna'i and Kaho'olawe, attached to Maui. Its higher eastern peak, at some 5,000 ft (1,500 m), is topped by dense rain forest. The north shore is lined by the world's highest, steepest sea cliffs and indented by vast green valleys. The sheltered southern slopes traditionally held the bulk of the inhabitants, who planted crops along the coastline and raised fish in artificial enclosures just offshore. The western volcano, Mauna Loa, has been eroded to a smooth, rounded monolith, which receives so little rain that it is technically desert. Until recently this end of Moloka'i was barely populated, but since the 1970s, thanks to guaranteed sun and beaches like vast Pāpōhaku, it has been the site of what little development Moloka'i has seen. Despite repeatedly falling to invading armies from O'ahu, Maui, and Hawai'i Island, Moloka'i acquired a reputation for great spiritual power. Partly thanks to that sense of mystery and isolation, the Kalaupapa Peninsula was set aside in the 1860s as a leprosarium. The work of the Belgian priest Father Damien (canonized in 2009) in tending its exiled patients became famous, and pilgrims now flock to the peninsula from all around the world.

Lying in the rainshadow of Moloka'i and Maui, Lāna'i is now largely owned by the Castle & Cooke Corporation, and its luxury resorts have begun to shift the island's economy from agriculture to tourism. Visitors will find an open, sun-baked terrain, spectacular sea cliffs, unpopulated beaches, and the haunting remains of ancient native Hawaiian settlements.

Moloka'i's isolated Kalaupapa Peninsula, backed by the world's highest sea cliffs

◁ Native *kauna'oa* vine growing along Polihua Beach on Lāna'i's northern shore

Exploring Moloka'i and Lāna'i

Most of Moloka'i's accommodations are in the resort of Kaluako'i at the island's sunnier west end. Kaluako'i offers wonderful beaches. Kaunakakai, on the south coast, has a few charming hotels and most of the island's restaurants. No visitor should miss a drive along the flower-decked south coast to Hālawa Valley or a trip to Kalaupapa National Historical Park, backed by the north shore's huge sea cliffs. Lāna'i, Moloka'i's smaller and drier neighbor to the south, has luxury hotels, deserted beaches, and ancient ruins. Most residents live in the island's one small town, Lāna'i City.

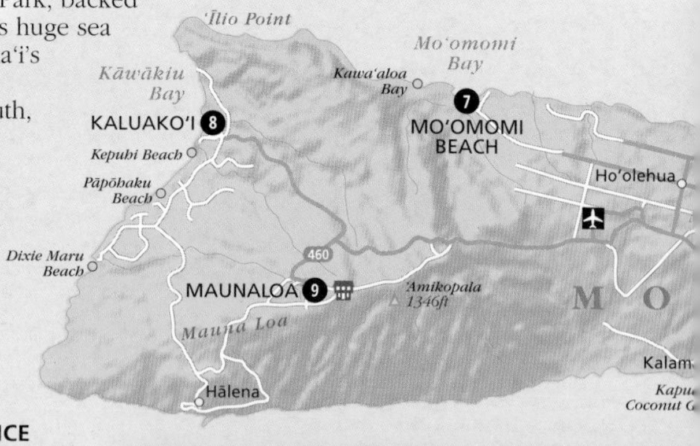

SIGHTS AT A GLANCE

Hālawa Valley **3**
Kalaupapa National Historical Park pp100–101 **4**
Kaluako'i **8**
Kamakou Rain Forest **5**
Kaunakakai **1**
Kualapu'u **6**
Lāna'i pp104–5 **10**
Maunaloa **9**
Mo'omomi Beach **7**

Tours

A Tour of East Moloka'i **2**

The golden sands of Polihua Beach on Lāna'i's remote north coast

TOP RECREATIONAL AREAS

The places shown here have been selected for their recreational activities. Conditions, especially those of the ocean, vary depending on the weather and the time of year, so exercise caution and, if in doubt, stay out of the water or seek local advice.

	SWIMMING	SNORKELING	DIVING	BODY-SURFING	WINDSURFING	HIKING	HORSEBACK RIDING	GOLF
DIXIE MARU BEACH	●	■						
HĀLAWA VALLEY	●			■				
HULOPO'E/MĀNELE BAY (LĀNA'I)	●	■	●					■
KALAUPAPA NAT'L HISTORICAL PARK						■	●	
KAMAKOU RAIN FOREST						■		
KAWA'ALOA BAY	●			■				
KAWĀKIU BAY	●	■						
KEPUHI BAY	●				●		●	■
KŌ'ELE (LĀNA'I)						■	●	■
MO'OMOMI BEACH	●	■						
ONE ALI'I BEACH PARK	●							
PĀPŌHAKU BEACH						■		
TWENTY-MILE BEACH	●	■						

KEY

— Major road

═ Minor road

-- Track

— Scenic route

△ Summit

The road to Kalawao on Kalaupapa Peninsula, with 'Ōkala Island and Moloka'i's northern cliffs behind

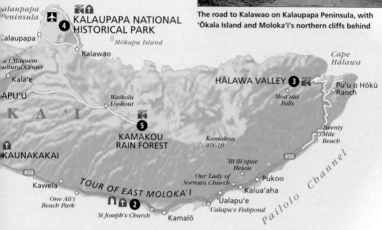

KALAUPAPA NATIONAL HISTORICAL PARK ④

Mōkapu Island

Kalaupapa Peninsula

Kalaupapa

Kalawao

'i Museum ultural Center

Kala'e

APU'U

Waikolu Lookout

KAUNAKAKAI

KAMAKOU RAIN FOREST ⑤

Kamakou △ 4961ft

HĀLAWA VALLEY ③

Cape Hālawa

Moa'ula Falls

Pu'u o Hōkū Ranch

Twenty Mile Beach

'Ili'ili'opae Heiau

Our Lady of Sorrows Church

Pukoo

Kalua'aha

Kawela

450

TOUR OF EAST MOLOKA'I ②

One Ali'i Beach Park

St Joseph's Church

Kamalō

'Ualapu'e

'Ualapu'e Fishpond

Pailolo Channel

Kalohi Channel

GETTING AROUND

Neither Moloka'i nor Lāna'i has public transportation, so renting a car is essential. Car rental firms operate at Moloka'i's Ho'olehua airport and in Lāna'i City. A 12-mile (19-km) drive west of Ho'olehua gets you to Kaluako'i, while Hālawa Valley is 35 miles (56 km) east, on a road that steadily narrows beyond Kaunakakai. Lāna'i is best explored in a four-wheel-drive vehicle since the island has only 30 miles (48 km) of paved road and more than 100 miles (160 km) of red-dirt "pine roads" and rocky trails to the sea.

Shipwreck Beach

Federation Camp

Garden of the Gods

LĀNA'I ⑩

Pu'u Mahana 4714ft

430

Kane Pu'u Forest Preserve

Kō'ele

Keōmuku

Lana'i City

MUNRO TRAIL

Hauola Gulch

one Bay

440

Luahiwa Petroglyphs

Lāna'ihale 3370ft

Lōpā

alapau Harbor

Pōka'i

Palawai Basin

Naha

Mākole Point

Kaunolū

Hulopo'e Bay

Mānele Bay

'Au'au Channel

0 kilometers _____ 10

0 miles _____ 5

Kaunakakai ❶

Maui Co. 🏘 3,500. 🅸 Ala Malama
St and Kamehameha V Hwy (Hwy 450),
(808) 553-3876. 🎭 Ka Moloka'i
Makahiki (cultural festival; late Jan).

The main town on Moloka'i,
Kaunakakai was built at the
end of the 19th century as an
administrative center and port
for the local sugar plantations.
During the 1920s, pineapple
production took over from
sugar, but these days commercial agriculture has all but

disappeared from the island,
and Kaunakakai looks its age.
The wooden boardwalks of
its principal thoroughfare, Ala
Malama Street, are lined with
false–fronted stores, such as the
Kanemitsu Bakery *(see p201)*,
famous throughout the islands
for its sweet Moloka'i bread.
Dotted along the same street,
homey diners reflect Moloka'i's
broad ethnic mix. At the
eastern end, tiny **St. Sophia's
Church** is all but obscured
behind an African tulip tree
with its orange blossoms.

About half a mile
(800 m) from the
town center, the
long stone jetty of
of **Kaunakakai
Harbor** juts out
into the ocean. It
was built in 1898
with rocks taken
from a destroyed
heiau (temple).
To the ancient
Hawaiians this
place was known

as Kaunakahakai, or "beach
landing." A break in the coral
reef made it a natural place
from which to launch canoes.
The harbor is often busy with
local fishermen and divers.

During the 1860s, Chief
Kapuāiwa, who later became
King Kamehameha V, had a
home near here. Its remains
can still be seen just west of
the road leading to the jetty.

Environs: Chief Kapuāiwa
was also responsible for planting the soaring palms of the
Kapuāiwa Coconut Grove,
sandwiched between the highway and the ocean 2 miles
(3 km) west of Kaunakakai.
Well over 1,000 in number,
the trees are a majestic sight
when silhouetted against the
setting sun. Visitors should
take care, however, not to
stand in the way of falling
nuts. Opposite the grove is
Kauanakakai's **Church Row**,
a set of small wooden chapels
belonging to different sects.

Ala Malama Street, Kaunakakai's main street

A Tour of East Moloka'i ❷

The coastal highway that nestles beneath the
peaks of eastern Moloka'i is among the most
beautiful drives in Hawai'i. Ancient sites and
picturesque churches lie tucked away amid
tropical flowers and luxuriant rain forest, while
the slopes of West Maui are visible across the
water. Few people live here now, so the
villages often feel like ghost towns.

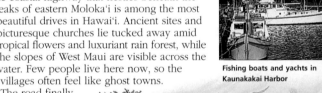

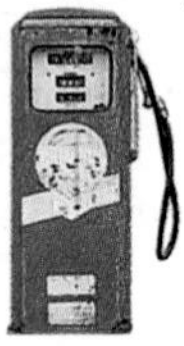

**Fishing boats and yachts in
Kaunakakai Harbor**

The road finally
twists to a halt at
ravishing Hālawa Valley, one
of Hawai'i's most stunning
"amphitheater" valleys.

**Old gas pump
en route**

KEY

🟫 Tour route

🔅 Vista

TIPS FOR DRIVERS

Tour length: 55 miles (88 km)
round trip.
Stopping-off points: Allow a full
day to visit the ancient fish ponds
and pretty churches, to have a
picnic at Twenty-Mile Beach or
One Ali'i Beach Park, and even to
fit in a hike through Hālwa Valley.

Kaunakakai

Kamehameha V Highway ④⑤⓪

**One Ali'i Beach
Park** ①
At One Ali'i
Beach Park, the
small expanse of lawn,
scattered with coconut
palms, is ideal for picnics
and also provides a perfect
launching point for kayak
trips. One Ali'i is a modern
misspelling of the ancient
Hawaiian name Oneali'i,
meaning "Royal Sands."

St. Joseph Church ②
Built in 1876 by Father Damien
(see p101), this tiny church was
painted a dazzling white in 1995 to
celebrate the return of the priest's
right hand to Kalaupapa. His statue,
permanently garlanded with fresh
lei, stands in the colorful garden.

Hālawa Valley ❸

Maui Co. End of Kamehameha V Highway (Hwy 450), 27 miles (43 km) E of Kaunakakai. ℹ *Kaunakakai, (808) 553-3876.*

Hawai'i's original Polynesian settlers were established in beautiful Hālawa Valley by AD 650, and for over 1,000 years they grew taro *(see p125)* in an elaborate network of terraced fields. The ruins of nearly 20 ancient *heiau* (temples), including two dedicated to human sacrifice, lie hidden in the undergrowth on both sides of the valley. Hālawa was all but abandoned after the 1946 tsunami, but new generations of farmers grow taro now.

Visitors get their first glimpse of Hālawa from an overlook near mile marker 26. Though its farthest reaches are often obscured by mountain mists, the dramatic shoreline lies spread out 750 ft (230 m) below. The placid, unhurried meanderings of the main stream as it approaches the ocean are in sharp contrast to the roaring surf just ahead.

Waterfall in Hālawa Valley, seen from a roadside overlook

The highway switchbacks down the hillside, reaching the valley floor at a quaint wooden chapel. A little farther along, the road ends at a low ridge of dunes, knitted together by *naupaka*, a white-flowered creeper. Surfers launch themselves into the waves from the small gray beach just beyond.

In summer, visitors wade across the river mouth to reach a nicer beach on the far side; in winter it's safer to follow the dirt road that curves from beside the chapel. Shaded by imposing palm trees and sheltered from the full force of the sea by a stony headland, the beach is idyllic for swimming.

An intermediate, spectacular two-hour trail, which involves wading through the stream, leads through the rain forest to the 250-ft (75-m) **Moa'ula Falls**. Hawaiians claim that the pool at its base is home to a *mo'o* or giant lizard. Hikers traditionally throw a *ti* leaf onto the water before swimming; if it sinks, the *mo'o* is lying in wait. The trail is accessible only by guided hikes. Contact the Moloka'i Visitors Bureau (808) 553-3876 for information.

Hālawa Valley ⑦
With its soaring walls, lush vegetation, and shimmering waterfalls, Hālawa Valley is regarded as the most scenic spot on Moloka'i.

0 kilometers 5
0 miles 3

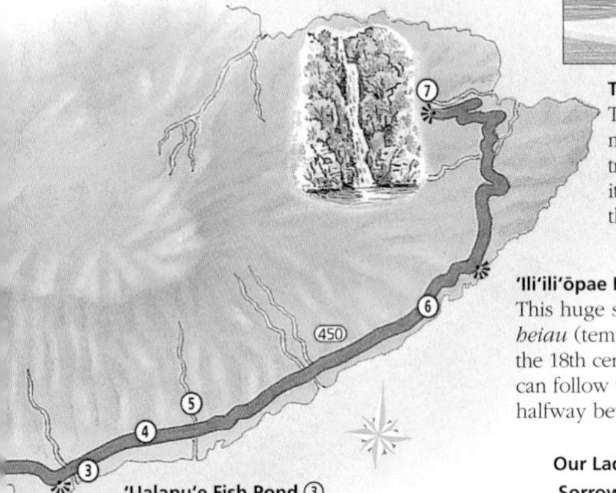

Twenty-Mile Beach ⑥
This thin strip of pristine sand at mile marker 20 is shaded by overhanging trees. Sheltered from the open ocean, it's great for snorkeling, but beyond the reef the sea can be dangerous.

'Ili'ili'ōpae Heiau ⑤
This huge structure, Hawai'i's second largest *heiau* (temple), witnessed human sacrifices in the 18th century. It is on private land, but hikers can follow the five-minute trail that runs inland halfway between mile markers 15 and 16.

'Ualapu'e Fish Pond ③
Of the 50 or so ancient fish ponds that line Moloka'i's southeast coast, 'Ualapu'e, just after mile marker 13, is one of the largest. Created by erecting a stone wall on top of a submerged reef, it encloses a vast area of shallow ocean and was used to raise mullet for the chief's table.

Our Lady of Sorrows ④
Father Damien took his first short break from Kalaupapa in 1874, to build the church of Our Lady Of Sorrows at 'Ualapu'e. Below lush mountain slopes, its red-tiled roof is shaded by the tousled coconut palms that surround it.

Kalaupapa National Historical Park ❹

A local stone landmark

Millions of years after Moloka'i emerged from the sea, a volcanic afterthought created the remote Kalaupapa peninsula (see pp18–19). In 1865, when the imported disease of leprosy seemed to threaten the survival of the Hawaiian people, the peninsula was designated a leprosy colony. Bounty hunters rounded up those with even minor skin blemishes to be exiled at the original settlement of Kalawao. In the beginning, food and medicine were in short supply, and condemnation to the peninsula was seen as a death sentence. The settlement eventually relocated to the more sheltered Kalaupapa. The last patients arrived in 1969, when the policy of enforced isolation ended. The park now serves as a permanent memorial.

View from Pālā'au State Park
Sealed off from the rest of Moloka'i by a mighty wall of cliffs, this remote peninsula was an obvious choice for a leprosy colony.

★ **Kalaupapa**
All of the peninsula's residents, consisting of aging patients who chose to live out their lives here and state and federal employees, live on its sheltered western side in the village of Kalaupapa. It has three churches and a bar – Elaine's Place.

The Moloka'i Light from Kalaupapa Lighthouse was one of the most powerful in the Pacific when it was built in 1908.

Kalaupapa airstrip

SS Kā'ala, wrecked in 1932, remains a rusting hull stranded on the reef just offshore.

The Damien Monument, a Celtic cross, was paid for by public donations in England (1890) and erected in 1893.

★ **Kalaupapa Trail**
Hikers and mule riders alike pick their way down the 26 switchbacks of this precipitous trail, enjoying stupendous views during the 3-mile (5-km) journey.

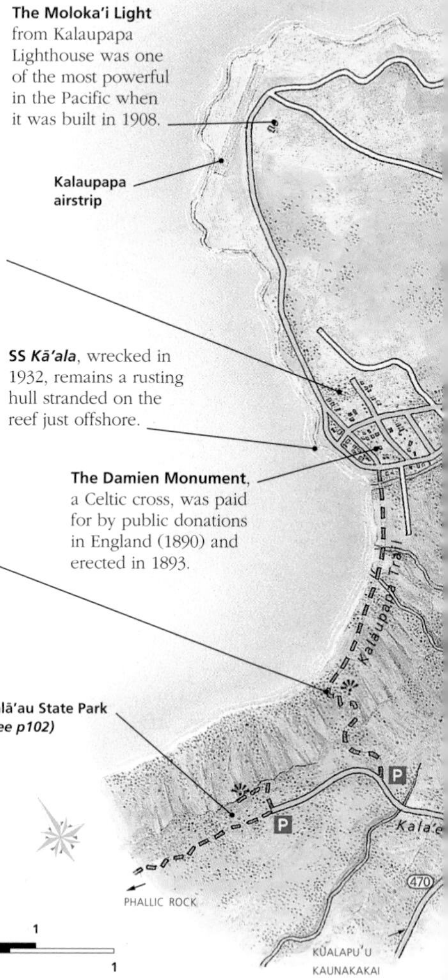

Pālā'au State Park
(see p102)

PHALLIC ROCK

Kala'e

470

KŪALAPU'U
KAUNAKAKAI

STAR SIGHTS

★ Kalaupapa

★ Kalaupapa Trail

★ St. Philomena Church

0 kilometers   1
0 miles   1

Offshore Islands
From the peninsula's exposed eastern side, small islands can be seen poking out of the sea next to staggering 2,000-ft (600-m) cliffs – the tallest sea cliffs in the world.

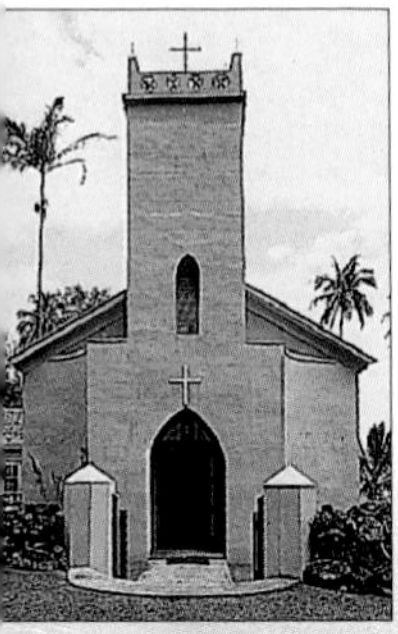

★ St. Philomena Church
The church was shipped from Honolulu in 1872 and later modified by Father (now Saint) Damien, whose grave lies nearby. In 1936 his body was returned to Belgium, but his right hand was later reinterred here.

Ancient Hawaiians used to jump off Leinaopapio Point for fun, with palm leaves as parachutes.

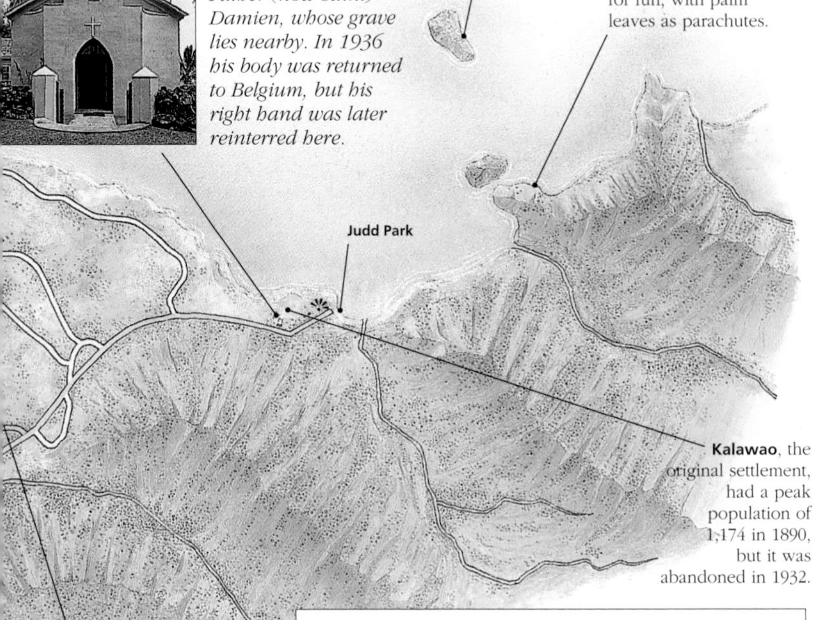

Judd Park

Kalawao, the original settlement, had a peak population of 1,174 in 1890, but it was abandoned in 1932.

Kauhakō Crater, what's left of the volcano that formed the peninsula, has an 800-ft (245-m) deep lake at its center.

KEY

═══ Minor road

══ Dirt or four-wheel-drive road

▪ ▪ Hiking trail and mule track

🅿 Parking

☼ Vista

ST. DAMIEN OF MOLOKA'I (1840–89)

Joseph de Veuster, born in Belgium, went to Hawai'i as a Roman Catholic missionary in 1864, and was ordained as Father Damien at Our Lady of Peace *(see p56)* in Honolulu. In 1873, he volunteered to serve the original leprosy colony of Kalawao, on the isolated Kalaupapa Peninsula. Hailed as a hero by the Honolulu press, he embraced his destiny willingly. He built hospitals, churches, and homes with his bare hands and nursed patients without fear for his own life. Father Damien finally succumbed to leprosy in 1889. The dedication of the "Martyr of Moloka'i" won him universal acclaim. His beatification as the "Blessed Damien" in 1995 preceded his canonization by Pope Benedict XVI in 2009.

Father Damien statue in Honolulu

Path through the dense vegetation of the Kamakou Rain Forest

Kamakou Rain Forest **❺**

Maui Co. Reached by four-wheel-drive road E of Maunaloa Hwy (Hwy 460), 4 miles (6.5 km) NW of Kaunakakai. 🛈 *Kaunakakai, (808) 553-3876.*

The remote mountain-top ridges of eastern Moloka'i preserve one of the least spoiled tracts of rain forest in Hawai'i. It is reached by four-wheel-drive vehicle or mountain bike on a rutted dirt road.

This region saw its one brief flurry of activity early in the 1800s, when native Hawaiians were sent up here in search of sandalwood to sell to foreign merchants *(see p42)*. Near the top of the island's central ridge is a grooved depression in the shape of a ship's hold. This so-called **Sandalwood Boat** was where the cut logs were piled.

The higher you climb, the wetter and lusher the forest becomes, and the more the road deteriorates. Native fauna and flora increasingly predominate, with colorful *'ōhi'a* trees erupting amid vivid green foliage. Ten miles (16 km) in, superb views open out all the way to the north shore valleys. Here, Waikolu Lookout stands above the 3,700-ft (1,150-m) drop of Waikolu Valley.

Just beyond, the Pēpē'ōpae Trail climbs along a wooden walkway through otherwise impenetrable rain forest. Every tree is festooned with hanging vines and spongy moss, while

orchids glisten in the undergrowth. This misty wonderland is the last refuge of endangered birds like the Moloka'i thrush *(oloma'o)* and Moloka'i creeper *(kākāwahie)*. After crossing an eerie, windswept bog, the trail traverses a series of gulches to emerge at an astonishing overlook above Pelekunu Valley.

Kualapu'u **❻**

Maui Co. 🏘 *1,700.* 🛈 *Kaunakakai, (808) 553-3876.*

The former plantation village of Kualapu'u is now home to Moloka'i's first coffee plantation, whose products can be tasted at the friendly, roadside espresso bar. Two miles (3 km) northeast of town, the **RW Meyer Sugar Mill** preserves the remains of the area's short-lived dabble in the sugar business. The mill machinery, now beautifully restored, was in use for just 11 years from 1878 to 1889. It now forms part of the adjoining **Moloka'i Museum**

RW Meyer Sugar Mill, the smallest in Hawai'i

and Cultural Center, an interesting little collection of artifacts that illustrates the island's varied history.

Environs: Four miles (6.5 km) northeast of Kualapu'u, Kala'e Highway (Hwy 470) comes to an end at **Palau'au State Park**, which combines superb views over the Kalaupapa Peninsula *(see pp100–1)* with a legendary site. Stop at the viewpoint to gaze eastward along the awesome cliffs to Kalaupapa village and beyond. From the vista's parking lot a hiking trail leads through the forest to **Phallic Rock**. As ancient legend has it, women who sleep beneath this outcrop will wake up pregnant. Its lifelike appearance is in part the work of human hands.

🏛 **Moloka'i Museum and Cultural Center**
Kala'e Highway (Hwy 470).
Tel *(808) 567-6436.* ☐ *10am–2pm Mon–Sat.* ⬤ *public hols.* 📷 ♿

Legendary Phallic Rock, Pālā'au State Park

Mo'omomi Beach **❼**

Maui Co. At the end of Mo'omomi Rd, 5 miles (8 km) NW of Ho'olehua.

Mo'omomi Beach, the only stretch of Moloka'i's north shore accessible to casual visitors, belongs very much to the drier western end of the island. The coastline here is made up of ancient sand dunes that have become lithified (turned to rock). The area is rich in the bones of flightless birds, which may have been hunted to extinction by the early Polynesian

The dirt road serving Mo'omomi Beach

settlers. A 5-mile (8-km) dirt road from Ho'olehua leads to Mo'omomi Bay, a surfing and fishing beach popular with local residents.

Kaluako'i ❽

Maui Co. Off Maunaloa Hwy (Hwy 460), 5 miles (8 km) NW of Maunaloa. 🚹 Kaunakakai, (808) 553-3876. 🎏 Moloka'i Ka Hula Piko (May).

The gentle slopes of Mauna Loa, Moloka'i's western volcano, have always been far too arid to sustain a significant human presence. The island's west coast was known to the ancients as Kaluako'i, "the adze pit," for its valuable basalt deposits. This area had a population of just one person in the 1970s. Since then, it has become Moloka'i's only resort, home to a large hotel and condo complexes.

Environs: The island's most spectacular expanse of sand, broad **Pāpōhaku Beach** starts about a mile (1.5 km) down the coast. Colossal waves render the beach unsafe for swimming, so it is often empty, with a splendid sense of romantic isolation.

Every May, **Pāpōhaku Beach County Park** hosts the Moloka'i Ka Hula Piko festival, which celebrates the birth of *hula* with music and dance. There are *hālau hula* (*hula* schools), contemporary musicians, and local crafts. Lectures and storytelling take place across the island in the week before the festival.

Beyond Pāpōhaku's southern end, secluded **Dixie Maru Beach** offers sheltered swimming and good snorkeling.

Maunaloa ❾

Maui Co. 🏠 400. 🚹 Kaunakakai, (808) 553-3876.

When the Moloka'i Ranch specialized in cattle and pineapples, tiny Maunaloa, on the flanks of the mountain, was the quintessential Hawaiian plantation village. From wooded groves, the timber-frame houses of its farm workers and *paniolo* (*see p143*) faced right across the ocean to Waikīkī.

In the 1970s, the ranch switched to tourism, offering luxury camping, an upscale hotel, and outdoor activities. However, it was not successful and shut down in 2008. Today, a few homespun businesses still survive on the main street, including the **Big Wind Kite Factory**. Owner Jonathan Socher is happy to show visitors around his manufacturing area and discuss the many kite designs. He also offers kite-flying lessons in the adjacent park.

Moloka'i was renowned in ancient times as *Moloka'i pule o'o* (Moloka'i of strong prayers), the home of powerful priests and sorcerers. Dreaded "poisonwood gods" lived in the forests above Maunaloa; a sliver of wood cut from their favored trees could kill any foe. However, the *'ōhi'a* woods nearby played a more benign role in Hawaiian legend. Here the goddess Laka learned the *hula* and taught it to humans. This claim to be the birthplace of *hula* is disputed. Kē'ē Beach on Kaua'i boasts the same distinction (*see p167*).

Big Wind Kite Factory
120 Maunaloa Hwy (Hwy 460). *Tel* (808) 552-2364. www.molokai.com/kites

Colorful kites at the Big Wind Kite Factory in Maunaloa

Lāna'i ⑩

Sun-baked Lāna'i was once the world's largest pineapple plantation, owned by the Dole Company, but in 1991 it underwent an historic conversion. In that year, Lāna'i's new owner, the Castle & Cooke Corporation, opened two luxury resorts and reemployed the island's farm workers as hotel staff. This identity shift left the island open for exploration of its many beaches, cliffs, and ancient ruins.

Colorful Lāna'i City house backed by Cook Island Pine trees

Exploring Lāna'i

This relatively low island is topped by the Lāna'ihale ridge. The heart of the island, rural Lāna'i City, is perched below the ridge at an elevation of 1,600 ft (490 m). Roads, more often dirt than paved, radiate outward to reach the coast at a few remote, beautiful spots.

Lāna'i City

Home to virtually all of the island's 3,200 residents, Lāna'i City offers a firsthand experience of the classic Hawaiian plantation town. Built in the early 1920s to house Dole's mostly Filipino laborers, this friendly town centers on rectangular **Dole Park**. The park is lined with frontier-style shops and the **Hotel Lāna'i**, a vintage wooden inn *(see p183)*. At the northeast corner

of the town, on the site of the former headquarters of Lāna'i Ranch (1874–1951), is **The Lodge at Kō'ele** *(see p184)*. This award-winning resort offers respite from the island's coastal heat. The attractions here include an 18-hole golf course, an orchid house, stables, and manicured grounds. The fine restaurant is open to the public.

⋔ Luahiwa Petroglyphs

Off Hō'ike Rd, 2 miles (3 km) S of Lāna'i City, near the water tower on the ridge.

The broad, softly hazy expanse of Pālāwai Basin is actually the remains of Lāna'i's extinct and worn-down volcanic crater. Its eastern wall bears one of Hawai'i's richest collections of petroglyphs. Visible from quite a distance, a cluster of 34 black boulders stands out against a steep red hillside dotted with dry white patches of *pili* grass. Some of these stones were thought to possess the *mana* (sacred power) of the rain gods Kū and Hina. Starting at least 500 years ago, Hawaiians decorated them by carving enigmatic figures representing humans and dogs. More recent images of horses, surfers, and leashed dogs were carved by students from Maui's Lahainaluna School during the 1870s. The petroglyphs are best viewed early or late, when the sun is not overhead.

⛵ Mānele and Hulopo'e Bays

End of Mānele Rd (Hwy 440), 8 miles (13 km) S of Lāna'i City.

Together, these adjacent bays form a marine life conservation district, home to Hawaiian spinner dolphins. Mānele Bay is Lāna'i's only small boat harbor. The misleadingly named **Four Seasons Lāna'i at Mānele Bay** *(see p184)* spreads over the hillside above Hulopo'e Bay, the island's best swimming and snorkeling spot. The resort, even with its interior opulence and fragrant gardens, harmonizes with its savage location. The bay is off-limits to all boats except those of Maui's oldest sailing excursion company, **Trilogy**. Camping is permitted here.

Between the bays lies **Pu'u Pehe**, or Sweetheart Rock. According to legend, lovely Pehe was kept by her jealous husband in a nearby cave until one day, while he was away, she drowned in a storm. He buried her on this rock island and then jumped to his death.

Pu'u Pehe, or Sweetheart Rock, in the waters off Mānele Bay

⋔ Kaunolū

Kaunolū Trail, a dirt track off Kaupili Rd, which leaves Mānele Rd (Hwy 440) 4.5 miles (7 km) S of Lāna'i City.

Few sites evoke the drama of ancient Hawaiian life like the ruins of this seldom-visited fishing village, abandoned in the mid-19th century. The rough drive to this naturally fortified cliff top, with its dizzying views of Lāna'i's southern coast, takes a full hour from Lāna'i City and requires a four-wheel-drive vehicle.

The early Hawaiians excelled in the art of building with un-mortared stone, and here at

The beautifully maintained grounds of The Lodge at Kō'ele in Lāna'i City

LĀNA'I'S COOK ISLAND PINE TREES

Groves of Cook Island Pine, which give the island its characteristic look, were planted in the early 1900s by New Zealander George C. Munro, the manager of what was then the Lāna'i Ranch. Freshwater is Lāna'i's most precious resource, and Munro realized that these trees increase the island's water-drawing capacities. Mountain mists collect in the trees' tightly leaved branches and drip onto the thirsty ground – on a good day, as much as 40 gallons (150 liters) of water per tree.

An impressive row of Cook Island Pines at The Lodge at Kō'ele stables

Kaunolū you can see several well-preserved examples, including the stone platform of the large **Halulu Heiau** on Kaunolū Bay's west side. On the east side there is a cliff-side platform that was once the home and fishing retreat of Kamehameha the Great. There are also ruins of a canoe house and a large fishing shrine.

One way in which ancient Hawaiians showed their bravery was by cliff-jumping, and just west of Kaunolū Bay there is a suicidal diving platform. At **Kahekili's Leap**, the former chief of Maui, Kahekili, proved his mettle by hurling himself more than 60 ft (18 m) down – clearing a 15-ft (4.5-m) wide outcrop of rocks – into water just 10 ft (3 m) deep.

🎎 The Munro Trail
Turn off Mānele Rd (Hwy 440) 5 miles (8 km) S of Lāna'i City.
This pine-studded drive along the volcanic ridge of Lāna'ihale, whose summit reaches 3,370 ft (1,050 m), offers sensational views of five of the Hawaiian islands. Because the Kō'ele end of the road can be alarmingly muddy, best taken downhill, the drive should begin at the other end. At the concrete stripe on Mānele Road just after the Pālāwai Basin, turn left onto a dirt road and then follow the most worn track up the hill. Allow at least two hours by jeep for this rugged 20-mile (32-km) jaunt.

🎎 Garden of the Gods
Polihua Rd, 6 miles (10 km) NW of Lāna'i City.
The Garden of the Gods is a visual oddity, a reddish lunar landscape dotted with boulders made of compacted sand. They range in color from reds and oranges to browns and blues, and the effect is most intense at sunset, when the rocks seem to glow. This peculiar dry and rocky landscape is reached by an easy 30-minute drive along a dirt road from Kō'ele, which passes through a hunting zone for axis, or spotted, deer and native dryland forest.

Continuing on, the road to the island's northern tip gets rougher, ending at long, wild **Polihua Beach**. At this remote strand, one hour from Kō'ele, a visitor's footprints may be the only ones of the day. The ocean currents can be dangerous.

Strange rust-red rock formations at the Garden of the Gods

🎎 Shipwreck Beach
Keōmuku Rd (Hwy 430), 8 miles (13 km) NE of Lāna'i City.
Lāna'i's northern shore is lined with an 8-mile (13-km) stretch of beach that takes its name from the rusting hulk of a World War II supply ship that is wrecked on the reef. Many other ships have come to harm in these shallow, hazardous waters, including an oil tanker that is visible 6 miles (10 km) up the beach. To reach the beach, follow Keōmuku Road (Hwy 430) until the asphalt ends; then take the dirt road on the left that rambles over sandy ground for about a mile (1.5 km). From here, a beachcomber's trek offers isolation and beautiful views of Maui and Moloka'i – a day's hike northward will bring you to Polihua Beach. Off Shipwreck Beach is an extensive reef, but swimming is dangerous here.

Shipwreck Beach, with the hulking 1940s wreck in the distance

MAUI

The second largest Hawaiian island, Maui is sparsely populated, supporting less than a tenth of the state's population. The land is verdant with sugarcane and pineapple, sprawling cattle ranches, and rain forests that descend mountain slopes to the sea. The 120 miles (195 km) of shoreline invite a host of ocean activities, from swimming, snorkeling, and diving, to world-class windsurfing.

Maui was formed by the convergence of two volcanoes at the isthmus known as the Central Valley. The green 5,788-ft (1,764-m) West Maui Mountains are the eroded slopes of a single extinct volcano, while East Maui is composed of Haleakalā, an enormous 10,023-ft (3,055-m) dormant volcano crowned by a lunar landscape.

The earliest inhabitants are thought to have arrived from the Marquesas Islands around the 4th century AD. The areas around Lahaina and Hāna were the first to be settled. Maui was split into rival chiefdoms until the 14th century, when Pi‘ilani conquered the island. This Maui chief built the massive temple of Pi‘ilanihale Heiau, whose ruins are near Hāna. In 1795 Kamehameha I conquered Maui in his quest to unite the Hawaiian Islands and in 1800 established his royal seat at Lahaina. Jean-François de Galaup, Comte de La Pérouse, was the first European to set foot on Maui, in 1786. Other foreigners followed during the 1800s, including missionaries, whalers, and contract laborers from Europe and Asia who came to work the growing sugar plantations. The communities they established retained the character of their homelands and created a multicultural heritage that is celebrated today in local holidays, customs, and food.

Visitors will see a varied landscape, from Kula's farmland, where proteas and sweet onions are grown, to the arid, eroded crater of Haleakalā and the lush, tropical vegetation on the windward coast. If you want to soak up the sun, the leeward coast offers white-sand beaches and calm waters that are the winter home of humpback whales.

Windsurfers at Ho‘okipa Beach County Park near Pā‘ia, on Maui's north shore

◁ A view of Honomanū Bay from the road to Hāna

Exploring Maui

Maui is composed of two volcanoes connected by the Central Valley, the island's population hub and the site of several attractions. The West Maui Mountains (Kahalawai) are actually a single, extinct volcano that time has carved into steep canyons, accessible at just a few places, such as 'Īao Valley. A road skirting the mountain's southern flank leads to historic Lahaina and the coastal resorts of Kā'anapali and Kapalua. Haleakalā, a dormant volcano capped by a huge crater, makes up the larger region of East Maui. Its outer slopes are covered with cattle ranches and fields of sugarcane and pineapple. The lush windward coast in the north features the plantation town of Pā'ia, Ho'okipa Beach – a windsurfers' mecca – and the little town of Hāna. The popular leeward coast enjoys a sunnier climate and calmer ocean.

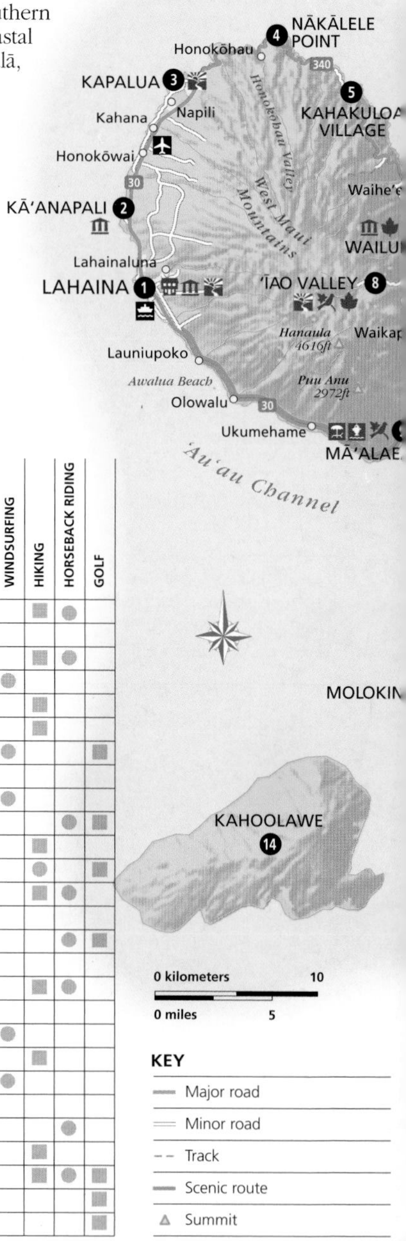

NĀKĀLELE POINT 4
Honokōhau
340
KAPALUA 3
5 KAHAKULOA VILLAGE
Kahana
Napili
Honokowai Valley
Honokōwai
30
West Maui Mountains
Waihe'e
KĀ'ANAPALI 2
WAILU
Lahainaluna
LAHAINA 1
'ĪAO VALLEY 8
Hanaula 4616ft
Waikap
Launiupoko
Awalua Beach
Puu Anu 2972ft
Olowalu
30
Ukumehame
MĀ'ALAE
'Au'au Channel
MOLOKIN
KAHOOLAWE
14
0 kilometers 10
0 miles 5
KEY
Major road
Minor road
Track
Scenic route
Summit

TOP RECREATIONAL AREAS

The places shown here have been selected for their recreational activities. Conditions, especially those of the ocean, vary depending on the weather and the time of year, so exercise caution and, if in doubt, stay out of the water or seek local advice.

	SWIMMING	SNORKELING	DIVING	BODY-SURFING	WINDSURFING	HIKING	HORSEBACK RIDING	GOLF
HALEAKALĀ NATIONAL PARK						■	●	
HĀMOA BAY	●	■		■				
HĀNA	●					■	●	
HO'OKIPA BEACH COUNTY PARK					●			
HOSMER GROVE						■		
'ĪAO VALLEY						■		
KĀ'ANAPALI AND KEKA'A POINT	●	■	●		●			■
KAHANA				■				
KANAHĀ BEACH COUNTY PARK	●				●			
KAPALUA AND HONOLUA BAY	●	■	●				●	■
KE'ANAE PENINSULA						■		
KĪHEI	●	■	●			●		■
LA PÉROUSE BAY		■	●			■	●	
LAHAINA	●	■	●					
MĀKENA	●	■	●				●	■
MOLOKINI		■	●					
'OHE'O GULCH AND KĪPAHULU	●			■		■	●	
OLOWALU		■	●					
PĀ'IA	●		●	■	●			
POLIPOLI SPRINGS RECREATION AREA						■		
SPRECKELSVILLE	●				●			
UKUMEHAME	●	■	●	■				
'ULUPALAKUA							●	
WAI'ĀNAPANAPA STATE PARK	●	■				■		
WAIHE'E	●					■	●	■
WAIKAPŪ								■
WAILEA	●	■	●					■

For additional map symbols *see back flap*

'Īao Needle, marking the confluence of
two streams in the lush 'Īao Valley

GETTING AROUND

Maui's main airport is in Kahului, but smaller airports serve
Hāna and Kapalua. Major resorts offer guests free shuttle
services to and from the airport and around the resort, but
most people explore Maui with a rental car or by tour.
There is no widespread public transit system. Some roads
are tortuous, and progress can be slow. Many highways
have bicycle lanes, and tour companies will take you up
the slope of Haleakalā to bike back down. Stables offer
horseback tours all over the island. Ferry services run
between Maui and the islands of Lāna'i and Moloka'i.

SEE ALSO

• *Where to Stay* pp188–9

• *Where to Eat* pp206–8

SIGHTS AT A GLANCE

A secluded swimming spot on the
rocky coast of the Ke'anae Peninsula

Street-by-Street: Lahaina ●

Statue outside Pioneer Inn

Stroll the streets of Lahaina, and you follow in the footsteps of scoundrels and kings. Until 1845 this small harbor town was the capital of the Kingdom of Hawai'i. By the mid-19th century, during the peak of the whaling era, it had a reputation as a rowdy port-of-call. Missionaries sometimes struggled to maintain control over the town and the souls of its inhabitants. Today, it is one of the most popular visitor attractions on Maui. Front Street, lined with pioneer-style homes and storefronts, is evocative of Lahaina's past. The Lahaina Restoration Foundation has restored a number of historic sites, and a wealth of history can be found within a small area.

Front Street, once the haunt of boisterous sailors after women and whiskey, now offers souvenir shops and colorful street stalls.

Wo Hing Temple

Masters' Reading Room

★ Baldwin Home
Maui's oldest Western-style dwelling, dating from the 1830s, has been faithfully restored with period furnishings, including several original pieces.

The Hauola Stone was believed by ancient Hawaiians to calm and heal.

★ Pioneer Inn
Built in 1901 by an Englishman, the Pioneer Inn was the first hotel to open in Lahaina. It remains a hotel to this day and is a favorite landmark in the town.

DICKENSENI STREET

FRONT STREET

MARKET ST.

PAPELEKANE ST.

KEY

– – – Suggested route

STAR SIGHTS

★ Baldwin Home

★ Banyan Tree

★ Pioneer Inn

The Old Lahaina Courthouse was built in 1859 and was intended to be a palace for King Kamehameha III, but was used instead as a post office, a courtroom and jail. It now serves as a Visitor Center and Art Society where local artists' pottery and paintings are displayed.

LAHAINA'S TRAGIC PRINCESS

Hawaiian culture once sancti-
fied royal marriages between
siblings; such alliances kept
bloodlines pure and ensured
offspring great *mana* (power).
Ancient custom was cast aside
with the arrival of Christianity,
however. When Nahi'ena'ena
and her brother Kauikeaouli
(later Kamehameha III) fell
in love, they were separated.
Nahi'ena'ena still managed to
bear their son, who lived only
hours. Sick in body and soul,
she died soon afterward.

Nahi'ena'ena, who died at 21

VISITORS' CHECKLIST

Maui Co. 🏠 9,500. 🚢 Lahaina
Harbor. 🛈 648 Wharf St,
(808) 667-9193. 🎨 Ocean
Arts Festival (Mar); 4th of July
Fireworks; Halloween in Lahaina
(Oct 31); Holiday Lighting of
the Banyan Tree (Dec).
www.visitlahaina.com

0 meters		100
0 yards		100

Chapel in the
prison grounds

Hale Pa'ahao, or "Stuck-in-
Irons House," was the new
prison built in the 1850s with
bricks from the Lahaina Fort.

Lahaina Fort was
built in the 1830s to
jail rowdy whalers, but
dismantled 20 years
later. A small part has
been reconstructed.

★ Banyan Tree

*The tree is over a century
old and is so large that
special events, including
arts and crafts fairs, are
held beneath its many
branches. The square is
named after it.*

Exploring Lahaina

Front Street is the hub of Lahaina. A low seawall opens up nearly a block of the street to scenic views of the sea and nearby islands, and makes strolling an old-fashioned pleasure. Whether you visit the historic Baldwin Home, the Old Lahaina Courthouse, or shop in the town's colorful stores, Lahaina offers a variety of interesting diversions. On most evenings, live music spills into the street from restaurants and bars.

Lahaina Harbor, against a backdrop of the West Maui Mountains

🏠 Baldwin Home
Front Street. **Tel** (808) 661-3262.
☐ 10am–4pm daily. ⬤ Jan 1,
Dec 25. 🎫 ♿ 📷 compulsory.
The four original rooms of this historic home were built in 1834 by the Reverend Ephraim Spaulding. The coral and stone walls were 24 in (60 cm) thick, perhaps a measure to minimize the sounds of revelry outside. At the height of the Pacific whaling trade, tensions often ran high between the seamen who frequented the port's brothels and grog shops and the missionaries who sought to establish Christian faith and law in the islands.

The Reverend Dwight Baldwin and his wife came to Hawai'i from the US in the early 1830s and were assigned to Lahaina's Waine'e Church. When Spaulding fell ill around 1836 the Baldwins moved into his house. As the family grew – to an eventual total of eight children – so did their home. A second-story dormitory was added in 1849, apparently to protect the daughters from the town's rowdier elements.

The first floor is open to the public. Many of the furnishings, which were donated by

the Baldwin family, date from the 1850s. Original pieces include an 18th-century sewing box, rocking chairs, and a four-poster bed made out of *koa* wood. Among the acquisitions is a quilt with a Hawaiian-flag design *(see p68)*, a gift to a Captain Born from Hawai'i's last queen, Lili'uokalani.

The two-story house next door was built around 1834 – the same time as the Baldwin Home – and was used for various mission purposes. It takes its name, the **Masters' Reading Room**, from the second floor, which was designed to offer "suitable reading rooms for the accommodation of Seamen who visit Lahaina, as well as a convenient place of retirement from the heat and unpleasant dust of the market."

The Baldwin Home, set in a shady garden

The Reading Room, once housing the Lahaina Restoration Foundation, has been preserved in its original state but is closed to the public.

🌳 Banyan Tree
Canal St or Front St.
The Banyan Tree *(ficus benghalensis)* was all of 8 ft (2.4 m) tall when it was planted by Maui sheriff William O. Smith in 1873 to mark the 50th anniversary of the founding of Lahaina's first Christian mission. Lahaina was once the capital of the Hawaiian kingdom and the whaling capital of the world, and as the town grew and developed, the tree continued to grow – and grow. Today, it measures almost one-fourth of a mile (402 m) in circumference, stands 60 ft (18 m) high and covers two-thirds of an acre (2,700 sq m) in the courtyard outside the Lahaina courthouse. There are many celebrations and festivities held underneath its branches, such as the weekly He U'i Cultural Arts Festival and the annual holiday tree lighting ceremony in December. The Banyan Tree attracts hundreds of people every day who come to take its picture and catch a glimpse of history. It has also been designated as a National Historical Landmark.

🏠 Pioneer Inn
658 Wharf St. **Tel** (808) 661-3636. ♿
Lahaina's best-known hotel was built by an Englishman called George Freeland. He had originally emigrated to Canada, where he joined the Mounties, but ended up in Lahaina in 1900, having pursued a criminal all the way to Maui. Freeland did not catch the fugitive, but stayed here, fell in love with a Hawaiian woman, and, in 1901, built a hotel. Pioneer Inn is a hotel to this day, on land still owned by the Freeland family. It has been renovated but retains many of the original features. These include whaling memorabilia and a list of house

SCRIMSHAW – THE WHALERS' ART

Life aboard a 19th-century whaling ship had its moments of excitement, but these were the exception. For the average sailor, whaling meant months of boredom, bad food, and low pay. To pass the time, sailors made scrimshaw from whale ivory – carving and etching into the surface of whale teeth and bones. Their "dot-to-dot" technique involved puncturing the surface with a knife or sail needle, applying a mixture of soot and oil, and polishing the ivory with shark's skin. The results were often exquisite works of art. A scrimshander might just decorate the ivory, or else carve it into something useful, such as spoons or gun handles. Scrimshaw fetched a high price then and still does today, in stores along Lahaina's Front Street and at Kā'anapali's Whalers Village (see p114).

Decorative scrimshaw made from whale bones

rules in the rooms, forbidding tenants from burning the beds and womanizing. You do not need to be a guest to explore the shopping arcade or enjoy the popular bar and grill overlooking the harbor.

🏛 Lahaina Courthouse
649 Wharf St. **Tel** (808) 667-9193. ◯ daily. ● Jan 1, Dec 25. ♿
Completed in 1859, the Lahaina Courthouse on Wharf Street originally contained a governor's office, a customs house, a post office, a courtroom, and a jail. It was built with stones from the earlier courthouse and palace that were destroyed by gale-force winds in 1858.

Here too is the Lahaina Visitor Center, which sells souvenirs and other goods. Archive photos in the hallway give a glimpse of how the place once looked. The galleries of the Lahaina Arts Society are located in the old jail in the basement.

🏛 Hale Pa'ahao
Prison & Waine'e Streets. **Tel** (808) 667-1985. ◯ daily. ● Jan 1, Dec 25. ♿
Sailors and missionaries who arrived in the islands in the 18th and 19th centuries introduced Hawaiians to a host of new vices – and to codes of conduct unfamiliar to them.

This jail, whose name means "Stuck-in-Irons House," was built by convicts in the 1850s, using coral stone taken from the town's demolished fort.

It was used to incarcerate foreigners and natives alike for crimes ranging from murder to riding horses on the Sabbath or violating fish taboos.

A high stone wall encloses a grassy yard and the jailhouse. Visitors can peek into one of the cells, where a "convict" (actually a mannequin lying on a straw mattress) talks about 19th-century prison life.

🏛 Wo Hing Temple
858 Front St. **Tel** (808) 661-5553. ◯ 10am–4pm daily. ● Jan 1, Dec 25.
The Chinese were among Hawai'i's earliest immigrants. They came to work on the plantations, but many later moved into commerce. The Chinese often formed mutual aid societies to help maintain ties with the homeland. One such was the Wo Hing Society, founded in 1909, which built the Wo Hing Temple in 1912.

As a museum, the temple provides a good insight into the local Chinese community. There are artifacts as well as a shrine; the altar is replenished with fresh offerings every day.

A separate cookhouse serves as a theater, showing old films about Hawai'i made by American inventor Thomas Edison in 1898 and 1906.

🏛 Hale Pa'i
End of Lahainaluna Road. **Tel** (808) 667-7040. ◯ 10am–3pm Mon–Fri. ● Jan 1, Dec 25. ♿ 🚻
The "house of printing" is situated on the grounds of the oldest high school west of the Rocky Mountains – the former Lahainaluna Seminary. When missionaries arrived in Hawai'i they lost no time in trying to convert the locals to Christianity, as well as teaching them to read.

Hawaiian papers in Hale Pa'i

The Lahainaluna Seminary was set up in 1831, and in 1834 the missionaries added the Hale Pa'i. Originally a thatched hut, the printing house was later replaced with a sturdier building made of stone and timber.

In 1982, the Hale Pa'i became a museum, tracing the history of the written word in Hawai'i. There is a working replica of the original printing press and facsimiles of early Hawaiian printing.

Taoist altar in the shrine room of the Wo Hing Temple

Locals demonstrating their courage at Pu'u Keka'a (Black Rock)

Kā'anapali ❷

Maui Co. 🚶 1,400. 🛈 Suite 1B, 2530 Keka'a Drive, (808) 661-3271. 🎏 Maui Onion Festival (early Aug), Na Mele O Maui (Dec). **www**.kaanapaliresort.com

Nestled between a 3-mile (5-km) beach and the West Maui Mountains, Kā'anapali is Maui's largest resort. It includes six beachfront hotels, five condominiums, two golf courses, 35 tennis courts, and a large shopping center.

Despite all the hotels, the resort maintains a sense of community by staging events like Na Mele O Maui ("the songs of Maui"), a celebration of Hawaiian culture, and the Maui Onion Festival, which honors the local crop.

Through the ages Kā'anapali was a special place, the site of a *heiau* (temple), a taro patch, and a royal fishpond. In the early 20th century, it became a playground for Hawaiian royalty, complete with a horse-racing track. Free tours of sites throughout the resort are conducted by hotel employees each week.

Pu'u Keka'a, better known as Black Rock, towers above long, white Kā'anapali Beach and overlooks one of the best snorkeling spots in Maui. Two centuries ago, when Maui chief Kahekili sought to encourage his troops, he would leap into the ocean from Black Rock. This involved spiritual, not physical, danger since it was believed that the dead jumped into the spirit world from here.

At the heart of Kā'anapali is **Whalers Village**, an upscale shopping center with many stores and restaurants. In addition, the **Whalers Village Museum** explores in unhappy detail the demise of the whale through the whaling trade. Displays include tools and weapons used for whaling, old photographs, models of whaling ships, and products made from the carcasses. Even more fascinating is the insight given into a young whaler's life by letters, diaries, and official accounts.

West Maui's most unusual means of transportation is the **Lahaina Kā'anapali & Pacific Railroad**, whose steam locomotives chug the 6 miles (10 km) between Lahaina and Kā'anapali. Steam engines were used in Hawai'i from the late 1800s until the 1950s to carry both sugarcane and plantation workers. Now the "Sugarcane Train" rides again, taking passengers along the same route as that used in earlier times. The scenic ride passes fields of cane and rises to cross the impressive Hahakea Trestle for a view of the ocean and the West Maui Mountains.

🏛 **Whalers Village and Whalers Village Museum**
2435 Kā'anapali Parkway. **Tel** (808) 661-5992. ⏲ 9:30am–10pm daily. ♿ **www**.whalersvillage.com

Lahaina Kā'anapali & Pacific Railroad
Lahaina Station: Limahana Place. **Ka'anapali (Pu'ukoli'i) Station:** off Pu'ukoli'i Road. **Tel** (808) 661-0080. ⏲ daily. 🎟 ♿ **www**.sugarcanetrain.com

Steam "Sugarcane Train", Lahaina Kā'anapali & Pacific Railroad

For hotels and restaurants in this region see pp184–7 and pp202–6

One of the pristine bays that line the coast at Kapalua

Kapalua ❸

Maui Co. 🏘 500. ✈ 🛈 Lahaina, (808) 669-0244. 🍷 Kapalua Wine & Food Symposium (Jul), Celebration of the Arts (March/April). www.kapaluamaui.com

Twenty minutes' drive north of Kā'anapali lies Kapalua, West Maui's second planned resort, whose luxury rooms and 54 championship fairways are surrounded by a series of exquisite crescent bays and a pineapple plantation that carpets the lower slopes of the West Maui Mountains.

Two of the bays, **Honolua** and **Mokulē'ia**, have been designated marine life conservation districts, where divers and swimmers keep company with reef fish and sea turtles. The golf courses are Audubon Society-approved bird sanctuaries, and the environmentally sensitive lands above the resort are under the stewardship of the Nature Conservancy. The resort also hosts a PGA golf championship in January, with prize money in excess of $1 million, and a wine and food symposium that attracts vintners, chefs, and connoisseurs from around the world. The resort also offers a wedding package, complete with a cake and Hawaiian performers.

Built in 1929 as a plantation general store, **Honolua Store** looks much the same today as it did when it opened. Now the merchandise is more upscale and clothing here sports the Kapalua Resort butterfly logo. A deli counter serves breakfast and lunch.

🏪 **Honolua Store**
502 Office Rd.
Tel (808) 669-6128.
🕐 6am–8pm daily.

Nakalele Point ❹

Maui Co. Hwy 30. 🛈 Maui VB, Wailuku, (808) 244-3530.

This is the most northerly point on Maui and the site of Hawai'i's first lighthouse. Vivid red-hued cliffs drop to the ocean and the trails along the bluffs offer terrific ocean views. When the surf is right here, sea water is forced as high as 100 ft (30 m) into the air through a hole in the shoreline lava tube. The blowhole is a short walk down the hill from the road, though you can see it from the top. Be careful if you approach it, as both the waves and the geysers are unpredictable.

Kahakuloa Village and Head ❺

Maui Co. 🏘 25. 🛈 Maui VB, Wailuku, (808) 244-3530.

For nearly 1,500 years families have inhabited Kahakuloa, growing taro (see p125) on stone terraces and using aqueducts to irrigate their crops from mountain streams. One of the most isolated villages on Maui, it has no gas stations or restaurants, and the most prominent building is a lovely small church. East of the village, the monolithic 636-ft (194-m) Kahakuloa Head rises majestically from the water's edge.

HUMPBACK WHALES

Once the hub of the Pacific whaling trade, Maui County is today an official sanctuary for humpbacks. The whales spend the winter here, bearing their young in the warm, shallow waters. Newborns are 10–12 ft (3–4 m) long and weigh a svelte 1–2 tons. Adults may reach 45 ft (14 m) in length and weigh 30 to 40 tons. In the mating season, males produce a hauntingly beautiful "song" – a series of whistles, groans, creaks, and screeches that are thought to help establish territory or attract females. Although regulations forbid boats from moving too close, these intelligent creatures may approach a boat, as passengers on Maui's whale-watching cruises (see p224) are often thrilled to discover.

The unforgettable sight of a humpback whale breaching

Plants cultivated at Maui Tropical Plantation and Country Store

Wailuku ❻

Maui Co. 🏠 12,000. ✈ ℹ MVB, 1727 Wili Pā Loop, (808) 244-3530.

Tucked into the foothills of the West Maui Mountains, Wailuku was in ancient times a royal center and the scene of many important battles. Today, it is a county seat and a thriving community. It has an intriguing mix of architectural styles, with several notable buildings along High Street. These include **Wailuku Library**, whose main structure was designed by noted Hawaiian architect C.W. Dickey, the old **Wailuku Courthouse**, the **Territorial Building**, and **Wailuku Union Church**. Also of interest is Market Street, with its antique stores, art galleries, cafés, boutiques, and the historic **ʻIao Theater**.

🏛 Bailey House Museum

2375A Main St. **Tel** (808) 244-3326. ⏰ 10am–4pm Mon–Sat. 🚫 Jan 1, Thanksgiving, Dec 25. 🌐 www.mauimuseum.org

Headquarters of the Maui Historical Society, this museum is a time capsule of mission life in 19th-century Hawaiʻi. From 1837 to 1849, the building housed the Wailuku Female Seminary, where New England missionary Edward Bailey and his wife, Caroline, taught. When the seminary closed, Bailey bought the house. Today, the museum contains a large collection of local artifacts, including *kapa* (tree bark) cloth, stone utensils, carvings, *lei* (see p29), and Bailey's own paintings of Maui.

Carving at Bailey House Museum

🏠 Kaʻahumanu Church

103 S. High Street. **Tel** (808) 244-5189. 🕐 9am Sun.

This Wailuku landmark was originally constructed in 1832 and is listed on the National Register of Historic Places. After several attempts at rebuilding, the New England-style structure and steeple we see today were erected in the 1880s. It is named for an important early convert to Christianity, Queen Kaʻahumanu, the powerful wife of Kamehameha I. The church was designed by the Protestant missionary Edward Bailey, whose home next door is now the Bailey House Museum. At this church, the Sunday services are conducted in the Hawaiian language and visitors are welcome to attend.

🌿 Maui Tropical Plantation and Country Store

1670 Honoapiʻilani Hwy (Hwy 30), 2 miles (3 km) S of Wailuku. **Tel** (808) 244-7643. ⏰ daily. 🚋 tram only. ♿

Some of the tropical plants displayed here, such as banana, coconut, breadfruit, and taro, were brought to the Hawaiian islands by the ancient Polynesians. Others were introduced more recently, such as orchids from Africa, papaya from South America, starfruit from Southeast Asia, and macadamia nuts from Australia. An informative open-air tram tour circles about half of the plantation's 112 acres. Various plants are sold in the shop.

🏛 Halekiʻi-Pihana Heiau State Monument

Hea Place, off Kūhiō Place, accessed from Waiehu Beach Rd. ⏰ daily.

Important religious and civic affairs were conducted here, at the most significant pre-contact *heiau* (temple) in the Central Valley. Halekiʻi ("the House of Images") was probably a compound for chiefs. During religious ceremonies, *aliʻi* (royalty) would reside in thatched houses whose walls are still visible on the temple's eastern face. A reconstructed section of wall is all that remains of Pihana ("Fullness"), a *luakini heiau* (temple used for human sacrifices). Kamehameha I conducted a sacrifice here in order to give thanks for his victory in ʻIao Valley in 1790.

Aerial view of Kahului harbor

Kahului ❼

Maui Co. 🏠 20,000. ℹ MVB, Wailuku, (808) 244-3530.

Kahului is the commercial and industrial center of Maui. The island's biggest airport and principal shipping harbor are located here. It also offers beaches, large parks, historic sites, and cultural attractions.

The **Alexander and Baldwin Sugar Museum** is located 2 miles (5km) west of Kahului. Across from the Puʻunēnē Sugar Mill, built in 1902 by Alexander and Baldwin (see p123), the old supervisor's residence has been transformed into a museum about the industry that dominated Hawaiʻi's economy for more than half a century. It features historical exhibits, narrated displays, and a model of a cane-crushing mill.

The **Kanaha Pond State Wildlife Sanctuary**, once a royal fish pond, is home to many migratory and native birds. These include two endangered species, the slender, pink-legged Hawaiian stilt (*ae'o*) and the gray-black, ducklike Hawaiian coot (*'alae keoke'o*). To access the walking trails, visitors must obtain a permit from the **State Department of Natural Resources**. There is an observation pavilion on the ocean side of Hāna Highway.

🏛 Alexander and Baldwin Sugar Museum
3957 Hansen Rd. *Tel (808) 871-8058.* ⬜ *9:30am–4:30pm daily.* ⬛ *Jan 1, Thanksgiving, Dec 25.* 📷 🔊 www.sugarmuseum.com

✈ Kanaha Pond State Wildlife Sanctuary
Off Hāna Hwy, between Kahului Airport and Kahului town. *Tel (808) 984-8100.*

State Department of Natural Resources
Division of Forestry and Wildlife, 54 S High St, Room 101.

ʻĪao Valley **8**

Maui Co. 📍 *MVB, Wailuku, (808) 244-3530.*

The ʻĪao Valley Road leads into the West Maui Mountains, winding beneath sheer cliffs as it follows a river hidden by trees. As the road begins to climb, the air becomes cooler, and traffic noise is replaced by the green of ʻĪao Valley, one of Maui's most sacred and historic sites. At one time, the bones of kings were buried here. In this valley in 1790, equipped with Western knowledge and weaponry, the forces of Kamehameha the Great trapped and annihilated those of Kahekili, the last independent chief of the island.

In a beautiful setting, about 2 miles (3 km) up the valley from Wailuku, you will find

Kepaniwai Heritage Gardens, a lovely county park with shaded picnic tables used by local families. Scattered about the park are smaller-than-life models showing the architectural styles brought to the islands by various ethnic and racial groups. A thatched Hawaiian *hale* (house), a Portuguese dwelling with its outdoor oven, a simple Japanese home, and a prim New England cottage are some of the structures that reflect Hawaiʻi's people – immigrants who come from the four corners of the world.

Statue of Japanese workers at Kepaniwai Heritage Gardens

Adjacent to the gardens, the **Hawaiʻi Nature Center** offers hikes and other outdoor activities for young and old. "Mud Scientists," "Tremendous Trees," and "Slugfest" are a few of the hands-on educational offerings for budding scientists as young as three years old. In 1997, the center opened a new building called the ʻĪao Valley Interactive Science Arcade, an innovative museum featuring games and displays that serve to educate visitors about the plant and animal life that has reached these islands.

The paved road ends at **ʻĪao Valley State Park**, at the foot of ʻĪao Needle, a pinnacle of rock that towers 1,200 ft (365 m) above the valley floor. The Needle is a hard, volcanic rock that remained when softer rocks around it eroded away. Trails continue into the valley, but this is one of the wettest places on earth, and hiking here can be dangerous when heavy rains create flash-flood conditions.

🌿 Kepaniwai Heritage Gardens
ʻĪao Valley Road. *Tel (808) 270-7230.* ⬜ *daily.* 🔊

✈ Hawaiʻi Nature Center
ʻĪao Valley Road. *Tel (808) 244-6500.* ⬜ *10am–4pm daily.* ⬛ *Jan 1, Thanksgiving, Dec 25.* 📷 🔊 www.hawaiinaturecenter.org

📷 ʻĪao Valley State Park
ʻĪao Valley Road, 3 miles (5 km) W of Wailuku. ⬜ *7am–7pm daily.*

Māʻalaea **9**

Maui Co. 🏠 *500.* 📍 *MVB, Wailuku, (808) 244-3530.*

Nestled along the shoreline off Honoapiʻilani Highway, Māʻalaea has oceanfront condominiums, several restaurants, a shopping plaza, a few attractions, and a small boat harbor. Many snorkel and fishing boat charters depart from Māʻalaea Harbor and facilities here include an activity booth and a US Coast Guard station. Māʻalaea Bay, is a favorite of surfers and windsurfers. In the winter, humpback whales (*see p115*) frequent the bay and can easily be seen from shore.

On the seafront, **Maui Ocean Center**, a huge aquarium and marine park, has more than 60 indoor and outdoor displays, where it is possible to see marine life up close without getting wet. Exhibits include the Living Reef, Turtle Lagoon, and the Open Ocean. The Discovery Pool is an interactive exhibit, where visitors can handle creatures that inhabit tide pools, like sea stars and sea cucumbers. For a thrilling experience, try The Underwater Journey, on which visitors walk through a transparent tunnel set inside a 750,000-gallon tank that is teeming with colorful fish, sharks, rays, and other marine life.

✈ Maui Ocean Center
192 Māʻalaea Rd. *Tel (808) 270-7000.* ⬜ *9am–5pm daily.* 📷 www.mauioceancenter.com

Diving with spotted eagle rays, Maui Ocean Center

Kīhei ⓾

Maui Co. 🚶 17,000. 🚌 🛈 MVB,
Wailuku, (808) 244-3530.

One of the most populated
areas on Maui, Kīhei lies on
the island's sunny southern
shore and boasts a vast
stretch of sparkling white-
sand beaches. Some of the
island's best beaches for
swimming, windsurfing, and
snorkeling are found here,
including Kalama Park and
Kama'ole I, II, and III Parks.
Just south of Kama'ole III,
there is a boat ramp from
which many ocean activity
charters depart.

The **Hawaiian Islands
Humpback Whale National
Marine Sanctuary**
encompasses most of the
ocean around Hawai'i, but its
administrative center is
located in Kīhei, at the edge
of an ancient fishpond. Here
there is an observation deck
with a large viewing scope,
allowing visitors to enjoy
whale watching at a safe and
nonintrusive distance.

Covering 1.1 sq miles
(2.8 sq km) of some of the
last remaining natural wetland
habitat in Hawai'i, **Kealia
Pond National Wildlife Refuge**
has wet and dry periods. It is
home to more than 30 species
of birds. Neighboring it is
Kealia Beach, a nesting
ground for the endangered
hawksbill turtle.

🛫 **Hawaiian Islands
Humpback Whale National
Marine Sanctuary**
726 S Kīhei Road. **Tel** (808) 879-
2818. ⬚ 10am–3pm Mon–Fri.
www.hihwnms.nos.noaa.gov

🛫 **Kealia Pond National
Wildlife Refuge**
Off Mokulele Hwy near Mile
Marker 6. **Tel** (808) 875-1582.

Mākena ⓫

Maui Co. 🚶 5,700. 🛈 MVB,
Wailuku, (808) 244-3530.

At Mākena, Big Beach is
separated from Little Beach
by a rock outcropping that
you have to climb over. When
conditions are right, both
beaches are good spots for

An alluring stretch of golden sand at Little Beach, Mākena

body surfing, boogie boarding,
snorkeling, swimming, and
sunbathing. Big Beach is the
nickname of the long, white-
sand, crescent-shaped Oneloa
Beach, which lies to the south
of Wailea Marriott Resort
(see p187). Facilities in the
area are few so arrive
prepared. Unofficially, Little
Beach is known as a "clothing
optional" beach.

The white, steepled
Keawala'i Church stands beside
the ocean in a tranquil, palm-
tree-fringed cove. The spectacular setting of this quaint
church make it a popular
venue for weddings. Built in
1855, it has had a continuous
and active congregation,
which has lovingly renovated
the building over the years.
The church welcomes visitors,
but asks that they remove
their shoes before entering.
Sunday services are held in
the Hawaiian language.

🛈 **Keawala'i Church**
190 Makena Road. **Tel** (808) 879-
5577. **www**.keawalai.org

Ahihi Kina'u
Natural Area
Reserve ⓬

Maui Co. At the end of Mākena
Alanui, 5 miles (8 km) past Wailea.
⬚ daily.

About a mile and a half
south of the Makena Beach
and Golf Resort (see p186),
this preserve is unique in
Hawai'i in that it protects both
land and sea environments.
The section on dry land is a
dramatic lava landscape

created by the last eruption
of Haleakalā (see pp128–9)
in 1790. Hiking trails cross
the lava and lead to natural
pools and archaeological
sites. Underwater, fantastic
snorkeling and diving is
on offer. Because this area
is protected, it is illegal to
damage or remove any of
the natural habitat.

La Pérouse Bay ⓭

Maui Co. 🛈 MVB, Wailuku,
(808) 244-3530.

South of Mākena, this bay
was named for the first
European to set foot on Maui,
French explorer Jean Francis
Gallup Comte de La Pérouse,
who arrived in 1786. There is
a monument marking the spot
on the *mauka* (mountain)
side of the road. When La
Pérouse returned in 1790, he
found that the communities
he had visited before were
abandoned and covered with
lava. Today the bay is known
for its fantastic kayaking,
snorkeling, and diving.

Kayaking in the crystal clear waters
of La Pérouse Bay

Kaho'olawe ⓮

Maui Co. No general access.

A dry, uninhabited island less than 11 miles (18 km) long, Kaho'olawe has at different times been host to exiled convicts, sheep and goats who eroded the soil, and the United States Navy, who used it for target practice. In the 1970s, native Hawaiians began a campaign to regain the island, and in 1994 the US ceded it to the state of Hawai'i. Hundreds of ancient sites have been found here, and although access is strictly limited, Hawaiians have begun to reclaim their heritage.

The tiny island of Molokini, popular for underwater exploration

Molokini ⓯

Maui Co. 🚢 from Mā'alaea Harbor. 🛈 MVB, Wailuku, (808) 244-3530.

An almost completely submerged volcano, Molokini rises just 160 ft (50 m) above the sea. The exposed rim is rocky and barren, but below the surface this marine reserve teems with pelagic (open-sea) fish that are comfortable with people, thanks to the many boats that anchor here for snorkeling and scuba diving.

'Ulupalakua Ranch and Tedeschi Winery ⓰

Maui Co. Hwy 37. **Tel** (808) 878-1202. 🕐 9am–5pm daily. 🖼
www.ulupalakuaranch.com & **www**.mauiwine.com

High up on the slopes of Haleakalā, where this ranch and winery are located, the air is cooler and the scenery panoramic. In the 19th century this area was known as Rose Ranch because of the many rose gardens planted

here by the then owner's wife. Some of the trees that she planted still stand shading the grounds today. What is today known as 'Ulupalakua Ranch is a working ranch and the site of Maui's only winery, at the Tedeschi Vineyards. The winery's tasting room is located in King's Cottage, which was built in 1874 for King David Kalakaua, a frequent visitor. Here you can sample and purchase the fruits of the winery's labor. Two free tours of the winery are offered daily.

Upcountry Farms ⓱

Maui Co. Kula District. 🛈 MVB, Wailuku, (808) 244-3530.

Upcountry is the term used to describe the verdant western slopes of Haleakalā. At these higher elevations, the views are breathtaking, the scenery is magnificent, the cool and misty air is invigorating, and the volcanic soil is fertile. Here you will find most of the island's farms and ranches, where an intriguing array of flowers, vegetables, fruits, and livestock flourish. Many welcome visitors to enjoy their beauty and their bounty.

O'o Farm is run by the owners of two leading Lahaina restaurants, Pacific'O and I'o (see p204), who are the first in the state to own and operate a farm for the sole purpose of supplying their restaurants. Their farm features orchards where citrus fruits, tropical fruits, stone fruits, and apples are cultivated, as well as

extensive herb and vegetable gardens. Visitors may tour the farm with a culinary specialist, handpicking items for a one-of-a-kind lunch, with a choice of fresh fish or vegetarian fare. You are welcome to bring wine to enjoy with your lunch.

Fragrant and pastoral, **Ali'i Kula Lavender** farm cultivates 45 different varieties of lavender. Stroll through the gardéns or take a 90-minute guided tour that offers information about the history, health benefits, and culinary attributes of lavender. In addition to the walking tour, a visit to this farm can include lunch and various seasonal tours, some with wreath-making and others with cooking demonstrations.

So named because there are surfboards in the pens and the goats stand on them, the **Surfing Goat Dairy** produces more than 20 different varieties of goat's cheese. The dairy offers daily tours that include information about cheese making and cheese sampling. During the "Evening Chores and Milking" tour you can help bring in the herd, feed them, and even try out your skills at hand milking the goats.

O'o Farm
Kula. **Tel** (808) 667-4341 🖼 🖼

Ali'i Kula Lavender
1100 Waipoli Road, Kula.
Tel (808) 878-3004. 🕐 9am–4pm daily. 🖼 🖼 **www**.maui kulalavender.com

Surfing Goat Dairy
3651 Omaopio Road, Kula.
Tel (808) 878-2870 🖼 🖼
www.surfinggoatdairy.com

Fertile upcountry farmland on the misty western slopes of Haleakalā

A Tour of Upcountry Maui ⑱

Sign outside the Tedeschi Winery

Between Maui's coastal towns and the mountaintop wilderness of Haleakalā, the air is cool, scented by eucalyptus groves that give way to the rolling hills of 'Ulupalakua and Haleakalā ranches. Here, roads wind through long stretches of countryside and often ascend into cloud banks, meanwhile offering stupendous views of Central Maui, the West Maui Mountains, and the surrounding island-dotted seas. While the scenery alone is worth the drive, any bend in the road can reveal a surprising bit of history – a European-style winery, a park paying homage to Chinese immigrants, or a church shaped like the Queen of Portugal's crown.

Baldwin Avenue ⑧
From Makawao to the coast at Pā'ia, this scenic road makes a pleasant drive and is used by bicycle tours descending from Haleakalā National Park (*see pp128–9*).

Church of the Holy Ghost ①
Built in the mid-1890s by Maui's Portuguese community, this Catholic church has an octagonal shape based on a crown worn by Queen Isabella of Portugal. Inside, opposite an exquisite wood and gold altar, sits a replica of a crown given to the church by Portugal.

Kēōkea ②
Little Kēōkea has a colorful church and charming country stores. Beyond it, the road twists through pastureland offering expansive views of West Maui and the islands of Lāna'i, Moloka'i, Kaho'olawe, and tiny Molokini.

Sun Yat-sen Memorial Park ③
In this now overgrown park, stone lions guard the statue of the revolutionary Dr. Sun Yat-sen, first president of the Republic of China (1911), whose brother was among the many Chinese immigrants who settled in Kēōkea. Sun Yat-sen hid his family here during the Chinese Revolution (1911–12).

Tedeschi Winery ④
Set in the heart of 'Ulupalakua Ranch, this winery has picnic tables under grand old trees. The tasting room is in a cottage once used by King Kalākaua.

lling hills and open spaces,
pical upcountry landscape

TIPS FOR DRIVERS

Tour length: *48 miles (77 km).*
Stopping-off points: *Plan half a day to accommodate a tour of Tedeschi Winery, a walk through Kula Botanical Gardens, and a stroll around Makawao. There are good restaurants in Makawao and Hāli'imaile (north of Makawao) (see pp202–6); alternatively, there are various good picnic spots along the way.*

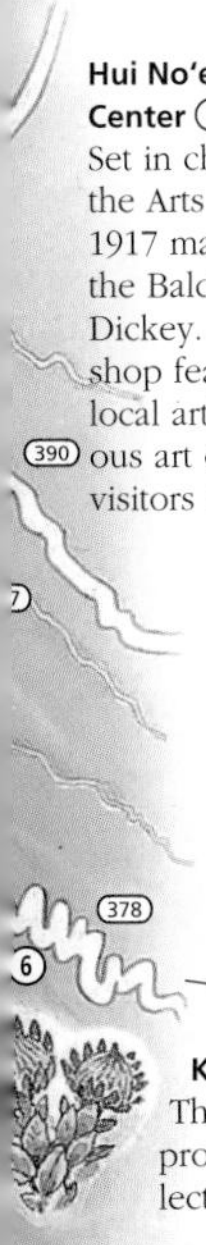
390
7
378
6
HALEAKALĀ
NATIONAL PARK

Hui No'eau Visual Arts Center 7
Set in charming grounds, the Arts Center occupies a 1917 mansion designed for the Baldwin family by C.W. Dickey. A gallery and gift shop feature pieces by local artists, and the various art classes welcome visitors on a drop-in basis.

KEY

- Tour route
- Other roads
- Vista

0 kilometers 5
0 miles 3

Small Upcountry Farms 6
Proteas and sweet Maui onions are the principal crops here. Several walk-through farms and gardens admit visitors and sell cut proteas.

Kula Botanical Gardens 5
These lush, cool gardens display hydrangeas, proteas, and other delights. There is also a collection of the world's most poisonous plants.

HENRY PERRINE BALDWIN

Maui's verdant "lawn" of cane fields is due largely to the vision of H.P. Baldwin (1842–1911), the son of prominent Lahaina missionaries. In 1876, he and his partner S.T. Alexander trumped their sugar competitors by digging the Hāmākua Ditch, an innovative 17-mile (27-km) irrigation system that carried up to 40 million gallons (150 million liters) of upcountry water a day to their dry fields east of Pā'ia. "HP" went on to develop a highly profitable sugar company and build modern Maui's top business power (Alexander & Baldwin). In effect, he ruled Maui during its transition from monarchy to annexation *(see pp43–4)*.

"HP" (right) and associate at Hāmākua Poko Mill in 1898

UCK
244-67

Bronco-riding at the Makawao Rodeo, an annual extravaganza

Makawao 19

Maui Co. 👥 *6,500.* ℹ *MVB, Wailuku, (808) 244-3530.* 🎉 *Makawao Rodeo (Jul 4).*

The false-front wooden buildings, the annual rodeo, and the cattle ranches that surround the town give Makawao a distinctly Old West flavor. It has been a cowboy town since the mid-19th century, but gradually the *paniolo (see p143)* have made way for an "alternative" culture catering to a growing artistic community.

Trendy art galleries showing local creations cluster around the crossroads at the town center. Glassblowing can be seen throughout the day at **Hot Island Glass** on Baldwin Avenue. Alternatively, you can sit in a café to watch town life go by, or stroll into **Komoda Store and Bakery** (also on Baldwin Avenue) for pastries and old-Maui ambience.

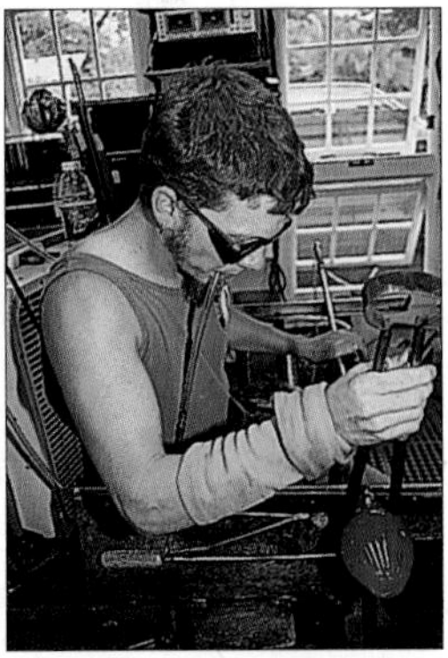

A glassblower demonstrating his skills at Hot Island Glass

Windsurfers at Hoʻokipa Beach County Park

Pāʻia ⑳

Maui Co. 🏠 *2,500.* ℹ️ *MVB, Wailuku, (808) 244-3530.*

Today, Pāʻia is a bohemian beach town with offbeat stores, an international surfing reputation, and good, rustic restaurants. Back in the 1930s, though, this little sugar town was the island's biggest population center. No longer in use, the sugar mill that once supported the town is located on Highway 390, a mile (1.5 km) southeast of Pāʻia's only traffic light. The **Mantokuji Buddhist Temple**, just east of town beside Hāna Highway (Hwy 36), speaks eloquently of those who came to work the plantations.

Environs: To the west of town, **HA Baldwin Beach County Park** is good for bodysurfing and popular with locals. Ten minutes east of Pāʻia on Hāna Highway is the world-famous windsurfing spot, **Hoʻokipa Beach County Park**. Unique conditions allow windsurfers to perform spectacular aerial maneuvers over the breaking waves. This is not a swimming beach, but with five surf breaks it is certainly a spectators' spot, especially in the afternoon when the wind blows strongly.

Keʻanae Peninsula and Wailua Valley ㉒

Maui Co. ℹ️ *MVB, Wailuku, (808) 244-3530.*

Between Mile Markers 16 and 20, drivers cross an area deemed by the state a "cultural landscape." The star attraction, the ancient *loʻi* or taro ponds, can be seen from overlooks at mile markers 17 and 19. It is said that the Keʻanae Peninsula was just lava rock until the local chief, jealous of his neighbors in Wailua, sent people to bring soil down from the hills.

Wailua's Coral Miracle Church, site of **Our Lady of Fatima** shrine, was built in 1860 with sea-coral. A freak storm deposited the coral on a nearby beach. The locals gathered what they needed to build the church; later, another storm swept the unused coral back out to sea.

The Road to Hāna ㉑

MILE 1

360

Mile marker

Not until 1926 did the "Hāna Belt Road" connect the rest of Maui to its rain-forested eastern shores. The drive itself is pure fun, somehow being as suited to Jeeps as to convertible BMWs. The road is notoriously twisting and narrow, and road-handling commands every second of your attention. At the same time, the scenery demands that you stare in awe. This is one of the earth's rainiest coasts; the terrain is sliced with waterfalls and gulches choked with tropical vegetation.

Waikamoi Ridge Trail ①
An unmarked but obvious rest stop between mile markers 9 and 10 offers a picnic area, barbecues, and an easy nature walk. On the trail, labels identify the flora, which includes species of eucalyptus and bamboo.

Keʻanae
PĀʻIA
Wailua
Hana Hi.

Honomanū Bay ②
This dramatic bay with its rocky, black-sand beach is a popular surfing spot, but swimming in the turbulent waters can be risky.

0 kilometers   5

0 miles   5

KEY

▭ Tour route

═ Other road

🌿 Viewpoint

Keʻanae Arboretum ③
These public gardens just before mile marker 17 provide a close-up look at working taro fields as well as a pleasant trail amid a variety of tropical flora from around the world.

Hāna [23]

Maui Co. 👥 700. ✈ ℹ MVB, Wailuku, (808) 244-3530. 🎉 East Maui Taro Festival (Mar/Apr).

Often called Hawai'i's most Hawaiian town, Hāna continues to lag lazily behind the tempo of modernity, and everyone here seems to think that this is just fine. Its perfect round bay and dreamy climate have made Hāna a prized settlement since time immemorial. Kings of Maui and Hawai'i Island fought to possess the district, using **Ka'uiki Head**, the large cinder cone on the right flank of the bay, as a natural fortification. A cave at the base of the cone was the birthplace of Queen Ka'ahumanu *(see p42)*.

Tiny **Hāna Cultural Center** presents a *kauhale* (residential compound) in the precontact style once unique to this area. Exhibited artifacts give a sense of local history. **Wānanalua Church**, beside Hāna Highway (Hwy 360), was constructed from blocks of coral in 1838. Missionaries built it on top of an existing *heiau* (temple), thus symbolizing the triumph of Christianity over paganism.

Sugar cultivation took root in Hāna in the 1860s and continued until 1944, when San Francisco capitalist Paul Fagan closed the mill and converted the area to cattle. Three years later he built Hotel Hāna-Maui on a plot once used by early missionaries. Today, Fagan's influence is still felt, and his large memorial cross looms on the hillside above the bay.

TARO IN HAWAI'I

The purplish-gray root (corm) of *Colocasia esculenta* was the staff of life in ancient Hawai'i. It was believed that taro and humans had the same parents and that the gods had ordered the plant to care for humans, its siblings. This it did by providing nutrition, mostly in the form of *poi*, a pounded paste. It also acted as a symbol of the ideal *'ohana* (family): the plant grows in clumps of *'ohā* (stems), with the younger stems, like children, staying near the older core.

The taro plant, a traditional source of food in Hawai'i

🏛 **Hāna Cultural Center**
Uakea Road. ***Tel*** *(808) 248-8622.*
🕐 *10am–4pm daily.* ● *Jan 1, Dec 25.* 🎫 ♿ **www.**hookele.com

...nihale Heiau [4]
...beautifully preserved ...nihale Heiau is ...ai'i's largest ancient ...le. It is well worth ...king your journey ... closer look.

Wai'ānapanapa State Park [5]
Plan a stop here to explore sea caves, rocky cliffs, the black-sand beach, and the ancient "King's Trail," which follows the spectacular coastline from here to Hāna.

Ka Iwi o Pele [6]
This large cinder cone beyond mile marker 51 is the site of mythical struggles involving Pele, the goddess of volcanoes. Nearby, the excellent Kōkī and Hāmoa beaches face the waters where Maui the demigod is said to have fished the islands out of the sea.

'Ohe'o Gulch [7]
The pools in this lovely stream are perfect for swimming, but beware of sudden flooding. A 2-mile (3-km) trail leads through a forest to Waimoku Falls, one of Maui's highest waterfalls.

Palapala Ho'omau Congregational Church [8]
The famous US aviator Charles Lindbergh is buried at this beautifully preserved 1864 church, along with fellow flyer Sam Pryor.

TIPS FOR DRIVERS

Tour length: *70 miles (110 km) round trip.*
Stopping-off points: *Start early, allowing a day for the drive. There are no gas stations from Pā'ia to Hāna, where most facilities close at dusk. Hāna has a few restaurants (see p202) and hotels (see p184); there are camping facilities at Wai'ānapanapa State Park (permit required) and 'Ohe'o Gulch (very basic). For tours of Pi'ilanihale Heiau, phone (808) 248-8912.*

Breathtaking waterfall at Kīpahulu

Kīpahulu ㉔

Maui Co. Highway 31.
🛈 Haleakalā National Park, (808)
248-7375. **www**.nps.gov/hale

Reached on the winding Hāna
Highway, in the Kīpahulu
District of Haleakalā National
Park *(see pp128–9)*, is
'Ohe'o Gulch, popularly but
incorrectly called The Seven
Sacred Pools. In Hawai'i all
water is considered sacred
and there are many more
than seven pools here, all
formed by the waterfalls
rushing seaward from the
top of Haleakalā.

About 10 miles (16 km) past
Hāna you will drive over a
small concrete bridge that
spans the pools. A few curves
after the bridge is a parking
lot on your left, which is the
site of the ranger station. An
admission fee ($10 per car) is
charged. There are restrooms,
but no food, gas, or drinking
water are available.

This lush, tropical area is
great for hiking, swimming,
and camping. The pools below
the road are easy to reach
along the short Kuloa Point
Loop Trail that begins in the
parking area. More adven-
turous visitors can search out
the upper pools along the
Waimoku Falls Trail. This trail
begins across the road from
the ranger station, climbs
through a meadow and winds
along the stream through the
rainforest. After ascending
for a while, it passes the
magnificent Falls at Makahiku,

an 181-ft (55-m)
waterfall, where
you can stop for a
breathtaking view
down the cascading
falls and pools to the
ocean. Continuing for
another 2 miles (3 km),
beyond a fantastic
bamboo forest, the
trail ends at a shallow
pool at the base of
Waimoku Falls, which
spill 400 ft (120 m)
over the high cliff
ledge. It is possible
to swim or wade in
the refreshing water
here. Always be alert
to the weather as flash
flooding is common
throughout this area.

A mile (1.5 km) past 'Ohe'o
Gulch, on the ocean side of
the road, stands the small,
white **Palapala Ho'omau
Congregational Church**, built
in 1857. It is the final resting
place of the famed American
aviator Charles Lindbergh
(1902–74), the first person
to fly a plane solo across
the Atlantic. He spent his
last days in peaceful Hāna.
Next to the cemetery is
**Kīpahulu Lighthouse Point
County Park**, perched on the
edge of the cliff. There are
shaded picnic tables here.

Kaupo ㉕

Maui Co. 8 miles (13 km) past
'Ohe'o Gulch on Highway 31.
🛈 Maui VB, (808) 244-3530.

From 'Ohe'o Gulch, the Hāna
Highway winds in and out of
valleys with steep rock walls
and on blind curves hugging
the ocean cliffs, to arrive at
Kaupo. Kaupo means

"Landing at Night" and could
refer to travelers from other
islands, who arrived by canoe
at night. Established in the
mid-1920s, the quaint **Kaupo
Store** was the last of the Soon
family stores. These were set
up by the son of an indentured
Chinese laborer, Nick Soon,
who also built the first electric
generator in the area. The
store sells cold beverages and
local snacks like marlin jerky
and shave ice. Opening times
are erratic but if it is closed,
stop and peruse the bulletin
board by the door, which is
plastered with business cards
from all over the world.

Before the first Europeans
arrived on Maui, thousands of
people lived in the villages
along this coast, sustaining
themselves through farming the
fertile land and fishing in the
bountiful sea. The missionary
churches that still stand here,
such as **St. Joseph's Church**
(built in 1862), give a clue to
the large Hawaiian population
they once served. Built in
1859, **Huialoha Church** fell
into disrepair during the last
century. However, volunteers
worked to renovate the
building and it was reopened
in 1978, adding extra meaning
to its name Huialoha,
"meeting of compassion".

From Kaupo, the landscape
turns to dry desert as this
area is in the lee of Haleakalā
and gets little rain. The impressive **Kaupo Gap** is visible
from the road. It was created
when an erupting Haleakalā
blew away a large section of
the mountain's rim.

Eventually, the highway
leads to the verdant uplands
of 'Ulupalakua *(see p121)*,
offering spectacular scenery
and serenity.

Spectacular scenery surrounding Huialoha Church, Kaupo

Beaches of South Maui

From the small harbor town of Māʻalaea to the solidified lava flows of La Pérouse Bay, South Maui's leeward coast is a playground for activities in, on, and near the water. Haleakalā's towering bulk shelters the region from trade winds and rain, while the proximity of neighboring islands and shallow waters create generally mild ocean conditions. All the beaches on Maui are public, and these along South Maui's leeward coast are particularly fine for swimming, snorkeling, scuba diving, and kayaking.

Mai Poina ʻOe la'u *is a long, narrow sandy beach whose south end is popular with windsurfers, while children play on the north end. It is a great spot for whale watching in the winter.*

Keawakapu, *the beach lying between Kīhei and Wailea, offers good swimming and body boarding, a great view of nearby islands, and freshwater showers.*

Maluʻaka, *the wide beach fronting the Makena Beach and Golf Resort (see p186), is sheltered and safe for small children.*

KEY

▬▬▬	Major road
▬▬▬	Minor road
🏌	Golf course
☀	Vista

0 kilometers   3

0 miles   2

Haleakalā National Park 26

The land mass of East Maui is really the top of an enormous shield volcano that begins more than 3 miles (5 km) below sea level. Haleakalā ("House of the Sun") is thought to have last erupted some 200 years ago and is still considered to be active, although not currently erupting. Its summit depression is 7.5 miles (12 km) long and 2.5 miles (4 km) wide, formed by erosional forces acting on volcanic rock. This natural wonder is preserved as part of the national park, which includes Kīpahulu valley and 'Ohe'o Gulch on the coast *(see p109)*. In under two hours, motorists drive from sea level to the 10,023-ft (3,055-m) summit, rising from one ecosystem to the next while temperature and oxygen levels fall dramatically.

Nēnē living on Haleakalā

Hosmer Grove campground has an easy, informative nature hike.

At Leleiwi Overlook it may be possible to see your shadow on the clouds in the valley below, encircled by a rainbow.

MAKAWAO

Hōlua Cabin

Park headquarters

Haleakalā Crater Road

378

★ Pu'u'ula'ula Summit

Standing on Pu'u'ula'ula (Red Hill) is a breathtaking experience because of both the altitude – this is the highest point on Maui – and the view of the entire volcano. A glassed-in shelter provides relief from the bitterly cold winds.

Haleakalā Observatories

This off-limits, science fiction-style cluster of research stations is set in the summit's lunar landscape. Data from here help scientists map movements of the Earth's crust.

Visitor center

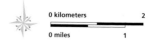

0 kilometers 2

0 miles 1

STAR SIGHTS

- ★ Pu'u'ula'ula Summit
- ★ Silversword Loop
- ★ Sliding Sands Trail

Summit Depression

At one time, Haleakalā was much higher than it is now. Water eroded the peak, formed the basin you see today, and drained away through two huge gaps in the rim. Later volcanic activity filled in the valley floor and created the cinder cones.

Halemau'u Trail

This trail incorporates switchbacks and sharp drops, plus fine views, often to the ocean. The hike from the trailhead on Haleakalā Crater Road to Hōlua Cabin and back is a good but tough day trip.

★ Silversword Loop

The Haleakalā Silversword, one of the world's rarest plants, thrives here under the most hostile conditions the volcano can offer: hot days, cold nights, and porous ash soil. The soft silvery hairs on its incurved leaves protect the plant from sunlight and draft. It takes up to 50 years to flower, when it raises a spectacular spike of purplish flowers.

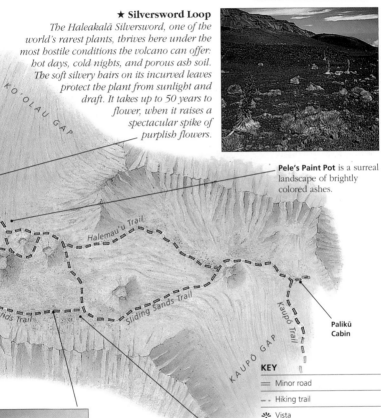

KO'OLAU GAP

'u Trail

Halemau'u Trail

Pele's Paint Pot is a surreal landscape of brightly colored ashes.

Sliding Sands Trail

ng Sands Trail

Kaupō Trail

KAUPŌ GAP

Palikū Cabin

KEY

═══ Minor road

‒ ‒ Hiking trail

☀️ Vista

★ Sliding Sands Trail

The only way to really appreciate the scale and varied terrain here is to descend 3,000 ft (900 m) into the volcano. The 10-mile (16-km) Sliding Sands Trail takes you from the visitor center through scenery that ranges from a barren cinder desert to an alpine shrubland.

Kapalaoa Cabin

One of three primitive cabins in the volcano – so popular that you must reserve well in advance.

HAWAI'I ISLAND

To understand fully the culture and spirit of the Hawaiian islands, travelers must venture to the island of Hawai'i itself – commonly called "the Big Island." This is the site of some of the earliest Polynesian settlements as well as the last *heiau* (temple) to be built. Here, Captain Cook met his demise, Kamehameha the Great rose to power, and the first Christian missionaries set foot on Hawaiian soil.

Being a relatively young island (a million years old, compared with Kaua'i's five million) not yet ringed with sandy beaches, Hawai'i has wisely placed its tourist-industry focus on the preservation of cultural sites. An amazing number of these are accessible to the traveler.

Spreading over 4,035 sq miles (10,450 sq km), Hawai'i Island is more than twice the size of all the other islands combined. Its bulk includes the earth's most massive mountain, Mauna Loa, which rises over 30,000 feet (9,150 m) from its base on the sea floor and is still growing. It also includes the state's tallest peak, the often snow-capped Mauna Kea, and three other mountains: Hualālai, which blocks the moist trade winds from dry north Kona; Kohala, the soft hump of the Waimea area's northern ranch lands; and Kīlauea, the

most active volcano on earth. A new mountain called Lō'ihi, currently forming 20 miles (32 km) off the southeast coast, should emerge from the sea thousands of years from now. Hawai'i Island's great bulk offers travelers the chance to see a variety of ecosystems, from alpine heights to barren desert.

Today, with only ten percent of the state's population, the Big Island is one of Hawai'i's sleepiest, most scattered communities. Hilo, its main town, was pushed into the economic background by devastating tsunamis in 1946 and 1960, and in the 1990s the island's sugar industry collapsed. Now tourism plays a big role, especially in sunny Kona. Visitors will find a land of open space, quiet towns, and a population that is friendly in the traditional Hawaiian way.

Paniolo (Hawaiian cowboys) at the Parker Ranch in the Waimea area

◁ A cluster of astronomical domes on Mauna Kea, Hawai'i Island's tallest mountain

Exploring Hawai'i Island

Both East and West Hawai'i Island provide good bases for touring. Hilo is well situated for excursions to the Hāmākua Coast, Mauna Kea, the Puna district, and Hawai'i Volcanoes National Park – a highlight on any visitor's itinerary, with Kīlauea Caldera and its active lava rifts. Hilo itself is charming but very rainy, averaging 130 in (330 cm) per year. Travelers who prefer their days bone dry head for Kailua-Kona on the island's burgeoning west side. From here there is access to the South Kohala resorts to the north, the Parker Ranch country of Waimea, Kona coffee country to the south, and many well-preserved ancient sites, including Pu'uhonua O Hōnaunau.

Traditional canoe at Pu'uhonua O Hōnaunau National Historical Park

Mo'okini Heiau
HĀWĪ **13**
KAPA'A
LAPAKAHI STATE HISTORICAL PARK **12**
250
KOHALA MOUNTAIN ROAD
270
Kawaihae
PU'UKOHOLĀ HEIAU NATIONAL HISTORIC SITE **11**
HĀPUNA BAY **10**
MAUNA LANI **8**
WAIKOLOA COAST **7**   Waik Villa
Kīlolo Bay
19
Makalawena
190
KEKAHA KAI STATE PARK **6**
Honokōhau
KAILUA-KONA **1**   180   Hualālai 8,271ft
Kailua Bay   **2** HŌLUALOA
Keauhou
Honalo
Kealakekua   Captain C
KEALAKEKUA BAY **3**
PU'UHONUA O HŌNAUNAU NATIONAL HISTORICAL PARK   **5**   **4** HO'OK
Kauhakō Bay
11
Miloli'i
Hawaii O View Est

TOP RECREATIONAL AREAS

The places shown here have been selected for their recreational activities. Conditions, especially those of the ocean, vary depending on the weather and the time of year, so exercise caution and, if in doubt, stay out of the water or seek local advice.

	SWIMMING	SNORKELING	DIVING	BODY-SURFING	WINDSURFING	HIKING	HORSEBACK RIDING	GOLF
AHALANUI BEACH PARK	●							
'ANAEHO'OMALU BAY	●	●	●	●	●			
HĀPUNA BAY	●	●	●	●				●
HAWAI'I VOLCANOES NATIONAL PARK						●		
HILO	●	●	●	●			●	●
HONOKA'A								●
HO'OKENA	●							
KA LAE						●		
KAHALU'U BEACH COUNTY PARK	●	●	●					
KAILUA-KONA	●	●	●	●			●	●
KALŌPĀ STATE RECREATION AREA						●		
KAPA'AU						●		
KAWAIHAE HARBOR					●			
KEALAKEKUA BAY	●	●	●			●		
KEKAHA KAI STATE PARK	●	●	●			●		
KOLEKOLE BEACH COUNTY PARK	●							
LAPAKAHI STATE HISTORICAL PARK	●	●	●					
MAUNA KEA						●	●	
MAUNA LANI	●	●					●	●
PĀHALA								●
PEPE'EKEO SCENIC DRIVE						●		
PUAKŌ		●						
PUNALU'U BEACH COUNTY PARK	●	●	●					
PU'UHONUA O HŌNAUNAU	●	●	●					
SPENCER BEACH COUNTY PARK	●	●	●	●				
VOLCANO VILLAGE								●
WAIKOLOA							●	●
WAIMEA							●	
WAIPI'O VALLEY	●					●	●	

0 kilometers   25
0 miles   20

SEE ALSO

• **Where to Stay** pp188–9

• **Where to Eat** pp206–8

KEY

— Major road

== Minor road

-- Track

— Scenic route

△ Summit

SIGHTS AT A GLANCE

WAIPI'O VALLEY **16**
Kukuihaele
HONOKA'A **17**
HĀMĀKUA COAST
19
WAIMEA
Kalōpā Forest State Park
18
Laupāhoehoe
Kolekole Beach County Park
MAUNA KEA **21**
'AKAKA FALLS STATE PARK **22**
WORLD BOTANICAL GARDENS **19**
Honomū
PEPE'EKEO SCENIC DRIVE **23**
Hilo Bay
SADDLE **20** ROAD
200
HILO **25**
Hilo Bay
Kea'au
Mauna Loa Observatory
11
130
KAPOHO
Lava Tree State Monument
27 Cape Kumukahi
PĀHOA **26**
Abalanui Beach Park
24
MAUNA LOA
Kīlauea Caldera
VOLCANO **29** VILLAGE
HAWAI'I VOLCANOES NATIONAL PARK
32 Napau Crater
MacKenzie State Recreation Area
28 PUNA LAVA FLOWS
Kalapana Kehena Beach
Hawai'i Volcanoes National Park
11
Pāhala
KA'Ū DISTRICT
Punalu'u
30 Punalu'u Beach Park
i'ōhinu Whittington Beach Park
Na'ālehu
Sands Beach
31
LAE

Ka Lae, the southernmost point in the United States

GETTING AROUND

Travelers can fly into Hilo Airport or Kona International Airport, north of Kailua-Kona. From there, a rented car is essential as bus services are minimal. The island is encircled by the Hawai'i Belt Road. Its northern stretch (Hwy 19 and continuing on Hwy 190) crosses from Hilo via Waimea to Kailua-Kona, taking about two hours. The southern route (Hwy 11) crosses the vast Ka'ū district in about three hours. Saddle Road, a shorter middle route passing between Mauna Kea and Mauna Loa, has narrow, rutted stretches that make progress slow. Recent lava flows have split Highway 130 into two sections: an eastern route into the Puna area, and Chain of Craters Road, which offers a close-up view of Kīlauea's eruptions.

Aerial view of the coastline south of Kailua-Kona

Kailua-Kona ❶

Hawai'i Co. 🎟 9,500. ✈ 🚌
🛈 Big Island VB, (808) 961-5797.
🎭 Ironman Triathlon (Oct: Sat
closest to full moon).

Referred to locally as "Kona", this town is the center of the island's "Gold Coast". Within a two-block span along ocean-front Ali'i Drive are sites that played a role in some of the most important moments in Hawai'i's history, from the unification of the islands to the advent of Christianity. Kailua-Kona's tourist strip does little to obscure these vivid reminders of Hawaiian history.

Built out into Kailua Bay is **Ahu'ena Heiau**, an ancient temple dedicated to the god Lono. It was restored by Kamehameha the Great, whose residence was next to the temple. Adjoining it is **King Kamehameha Kona Beach Hotel** (see p188) – the lobby has Hawaiian artifacts: tools, handicrafts, and a feather cape.

Idyllic Kahalu'u Beach

In 1820, the first party of missionaries landed at Kailua-Kona. They built the original **Moku'aikaua Church** on Ali'i Drive. The present lofty, granite church dates from 1837. A modest museum at the rear offers a scale model of the missionaries' brig, *Thaddeus*. Across the street, **Hulihe'e Palace** was built at the same time of similar rough-stone construction. In 1885, King Kalākaua beautified the little building, which now serves as a museum. It takes a candid look at the lifestyle of the monarchy in its heyday.

Kailua-Kona, so named to distinguish it from Kailua on O'ahu, is synonymous with sportfishing. Charter boats offer year-round opportunities to fish for marlin and other ocean giants. In October the town is overrun by endurance athletes who compete in the grueling Ironman Triathlon. The sunny coastline is dotted with small beaches good for swimming, snorkeling, and diving. **Kahalu'u Beach**, 4.5 miles (7 km) south of Kailua, provides snorkelers with the island's finest natural aquarium.

🔒 **Moku'aikaua Church**
75-5713 Ali'i Drive. **Tel** (808) 329-0655. ◯ daily. ♿

🏛 **Hulihe'e Palace**
75-5718 Ali'i Drive. **Tel** (808) 329-1877. ◯ daily. ◉ public hols. 🎫

Hōlualoa ❷

Hawai'i Co. 🎟 6,100. 🛈 Big Island VB, West Hawai'i, (808) 886-1655. 🎭 Kona Coffee Cultural Festival (2nd week of Nov).

A 15-minute drive up the winding and scenic Hualalai Road from Highway 19, on the slopes of Mount Hualalai, lies Hōlualoa. Set in the heart of the Kona coffee belt, coffee is its main focus, as attested by the annual Kona Coffee Cultural Festival. Artists also add their flavor to the town.

Long before tourism took hold, many immigrants settled here to work on the coffee plantations and vegetable farms and Hōlualoa was a thriving town full of hotels, restaurants, and general stores to provide for their needs. Some of these stores still operate today. **Kimura Lauhala Shop** began as a general store in 1915, but became famous for its *lauhala* hats woven from the leaves of the pandanus tree. The Kimura family still runs the store.

Hōlualoa's main street is lined with galleries that present works by many of the island's most well known artists. **Studio 7** showcases the creations of Hiroki and Setsuko Morinoue. He is known for his large watercolors and woodblock prints; she is a ceramist. The studio also displays works by other artists, including turned bowls, wooden bracelets, and silk-screen prints. The pottery and paintings of Matthew and Mary Lovein are on show at their **Hōlualoa Gallery**, along with jewelry, sculptures, and glass works by other artists.

35th Annual
KONA COFFEE CULTURAL FESTIVAL
NOVEMBER 4–13, 2005

Honoring Kona's Pioneer Spirit

Kona Coffee Cultural Festival poster

🏠 **Kimura Lauhala Shop**
Mamalahoa Highway and Hualalai Road. **Tel** (808) 324-0053.

🏠 **Studio 7**
76-5920 Mamalahoa Highway.
Tel (808) 324-1335.

🏠 **Holualoa Gallery**
76-5921 Mamalahoa Highway.
Tel (808) 322-8484.

For hotels and restaurants in this region see pp188–9 and pp206–8

Kona Coffee

For over a century the upward slopes of the Kona district have been home to the United States' only coffee-growing region. The massive bulk of Mauna Loa, an enormous shield volcano (see p147), creates a localized weather pattern that favors the crop. Sunny mornings are followed by cloudy, humid afternoons that often drench the rich, volcanic soil with rain. Over 500 independent small farms cultivate this world-class, gourmet coffee, producing a crop of about 2 million pounds (900,000 kg) a year. Roadsides are dotted with cafés, mills, and farms, and the Hawai'i Visitors and Convention Bureau in Kailua-Kona offers a driving map of the area. Every year, in the second week of November, the district celebrates its coffee with the Kona Coffee Cultural Festival.

HOW COFFEE IS HARVESTED

Coffee beans grown in the rich soil of the Kona district are picked by hand, ensuring only the best beans go into making coffee.

"Kona snow" *is the local term for the white, fragrant spring flowers. The first Coffea arabica plants were introduced to the area in 1828 by the American missionary Samuel Ruggles.*

Coffee cherries *ripen in waves, from August until March, so they must be laboriously hand-harvested. The cherries start out green in color and turn red as they ripen.*

A kuriba *(pulping mill) separates the flesh of the cherry from its hard, parchment-covered bean. After soaking and washing, beans in the "wet parchment" stage are left to dry in the sun.*

A hoshidana *is a drying deck with a wheeled cover that is rolled over the beans whenever the mountain rains move in. Beans are raked three or four times a day for up to two weeks.*

Milling *removes two outer layers from the hard beans - the tough parchment and the filmy "silver skin." Raw beans, called green coffee, are then graded and ready for roasting.*

IMMIGRANT WORKERS

The success of Kona's coffee owes as much to its people as to its weather. In the late 19th century, after decades of control by the large plantations, the crop began to be cultivated tenaciously on small-scale family farms. Many of these farmers were Japanese immigrants who fled slavelike conditions on the plantations to work their own farms. Today, their descendents continue the coffee tradition.

Kona coffee beans *are known throughout the gourmet coffee world for their rich, highly aromatic flavor. The roasting process brings out the flavor: beans that are roasted longer and at higher temperatures are darker with a more intense taste. Additional flavorings, such as chocolate or macadamia nuts, may be added immediately after roasting.*

Roasted coffee beans

The colorful interior of St. Benedict's Painted Church in Hōnaunau

Kealakekua Bay ❸

Hawai'i Co. Nāpō'opo'o Road,
4 miles (6 km) S of Captain Cook.
🚆 Captain Cook. 🚹 Big Island VB,
(808) 961-5797.

In 1778, Captain Cook sailed
into this deep, protected bay,
"discovering" Hawai'i. He
was honored as the returning
Hawaiian god Lono, but less
than a month
later was killed
here *(see p41)*.
Hikiau Heiau,
where Cook was
honored, is at
the road's end. A
monument marks
where he died.

The bay, a
State Marine Life
Preserve with an
abundance of
fish, sea turtles,
and spinner
dolphins, offers
excellent diving,
snorkeling, and kayaking.

ENVIRONS: The bay sits at the
heart of Kona coffee country,
with its rustic farms and mills.
In the town of **Kealakekua**,
the **Kona Historical Society**
gives interpretive tours of its
headquarters in the 1870s-
vintage **Greenwell Store** and
of neighboring **Uchida Farm**,
a restored 1930s coffee farm.
The entire district invites
exploration, from Hōnaunau
in the south up to Hōlualoa
(see p134) in the north. In
Hōnaunau, **St. Benedict's
Painted Church** is brightly
illuminated with biblical scenes
executed by a Belgian priest
in the early 20th century.

🏛 **Kona Historical Society**
81-6551 Māmalahoa Hwy
(Hwy 11). **Tel** (808) 323-3222.
◯ 9am–3pm Mon–Fri. ◉ public
hols. 🖼 donation requested. ♿
🚪 **St. Benedict's
Painted Church**
Painted Church Road, off Hwy 160
near mile marker 1. **Tel** (808) 328-
2227. ◯ daily. ♿

Ho'okena ❹

Hawai'i Co.
🚹 Big Island VB,
West Hawai'i, (808)
886-1655.

In 1889, when
author Robert
Louis Stevenson
asked to see a
classic Hawaiian
village, King
Kalākaua sent him
to Ho'okena. In
those days, the
town could boast
churches, a school, a courthouse, and a pier from which

Ho'okena's Kauhakō Bay,
which is lined with a beach
of gray sand

cattle were shipped to market
in Honolulu. Today, besides
weather-beaten houses and
beach shacks, only lava walls
and the ruined pier survive
as reminders of its more
prosperous past.

The center of life, then as
now, is beautiful **Kauhakō
Bay** with its gray-sand beach
backed dramatically by long
cliffs. The water teems with
sea life, and there is excellent
snorkeling and diving. However, the surf can be rough,
and wearing foot protection
is recommended.

Pu'uhonoua O Honaunau National Historic Park ❺

See pp138–9.

Kekaha Kai State Park ❻

Hawai'i Co. Off Queen Ka'ahumanu
Highway (Hwy 19), 9 miles (14 km) N
of Kailua-Kona. **Tel** Division of State
Parks, (808) 974-6200. ◯ Thu–Tue.

North of Kailua, the road
runs through barren lava
fields, the aftermath of an
1801 eruption of Mount
Hualālai. In places, road and
landscape are distinguishable
only by their relative smooth-
ness. The state park, with its
picnic shelters and sinuous
beach of salt-and-pepper sand,
is an oasis in this distorted
wasteland. It is an excellent
spot for swimming, snorkeling, diving, and, when the
conditions are right, surfing.

Green sea turtle swimming in the waters off the beach at Makalawena

Just before the park entrance, a dirt road on the right leads 1.5 miles (2.5 km) to isolated **Makalawena**, a beautiful beach with dunes and coves for snorkeling. Turtles, dolphins, and seals frequent these waters, as well as whales.

Waikoloa Coast ❼

Hawai'i Co. W of Queen Ka'ahumanu Highway (Hwy 19), 24 miles (39 km) N of Kailua-Kona. 🈯 *Kohala Coast Resort Association, (808) 885-6414.*

Waikoloa Beach Resort has built itself around one of this coast's best family recreational areas, coconut-rimmed **'Anaeho'omalu Bay**. The beach at "A-Bay" is calm, with a gradual, sandy bottom. Watersports equipment, including kayaks and sailboats, can be rented from the beach hut, and lessons in windsurfing and scuba diving are offered. Boat dives and cruises are also available.

From the beach, coastal trails lead to fish ponds, caves, and natural pools in which salt and fresh water mix to form unique ecosystems.

A short walk north of the beach is **Hilton Waikoloa Village Resort** (*see p189*), a 62-acre fantasy resort built in 1988 at a cost of $360 million. Silent monorails and canal boats provide transportation around the resort. Visitors can view the impressive art collection and explore the artificial beach, lagoon, and waterfall. At the dolphin pool, both guests and visitors can swim with the resort's trained dolphins. Also within the resort, the Waikoloa Beach Marriott Resort (*see p189*) fronts ancient fishponds along A-Bay and is a short walk from a restored *heiau* (temple).

Hilton Waikoloa Village Resort
69-425 Waikoloa Beach Drive. *Tel* (808) 886-1234. 🔲 *daily.* 👤 www.hiltonwaikoloavillage.com

Vacationers enjoying the lagoon at Hilton Waikoloa Village Resort

Mauna Lani ❽

68–140 Mauna Lani Dr. *Tel* (808) 885-6622. 🔲 *daily.* 👤 www.maunalani.com

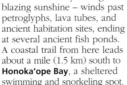
Petroglyph figure

The vast resort at Mauna Lani includes two luxury hotels, a couple of award-winning golf courses, several tennis courts, and small, white-sand beaches. It also encloses sites of cultural importance. **Kalāhuipua'a Trail** – a 20-minute hike, usually through blazing sunshine – winds past petroglyphs, lava tubes, and ancient habitation sites, ending at several ancient fish ponds. A coastal trail from here leads about a mile (1.5 km) south to **Honoka'ope Bay**, a sheltered swimming and snorkeling spot.

At the northern end of the resort, a shorter shady trail leads to the **Puakō Petroglyphs**. These are an expanse of crusty red lava plates that were engraved with more than 3,000 symbols between AD 1000 and 1800. Wear sturdy shoes.

Waimea ❾

Hawai'i Co. 🏠 6,000. ✈ 🔲
🈯 *Waimea Visitor Center, Main St, (808) 885-6707.* 🎡 *Parker Ranch Rodeo (Jul 4).*

Waimea's setting amid sprawling pasture land at a cool elevation of 2,700 ft (820 m) is a startling contrast to Hilo's rainforest and the Kona Coast's lava flats. By Hawai'i Island standards, Waimea is a large, modern town. On the edge of town is the **Keck Observatory Center**, with the world's most powerful telescopes (*see p147*).

In the middle of town, the **Parker Ranch Visitor Center** offers a short video and an eloquent collection of artifacts that tells the history of *paniolo* (cowboy) culture and provides an insight into the tempestuous and influential Parker family.

The **Historic Parker Ranch Homes** include Puopelu, a ranch house with a Regency interior and a respectable collection of European art, and Mānā Hale, the Parkers' original home, which has a display of family photographs.

🏛 **Keck Observatory Center**
65-1120 Māmalahoa Hwy (Hwy 19). *Tel* (808) 961-2120. 🔲 8am–4:30pm Mon–Fri. ⬤ public hols. 👤 www.keckobservatory.org

🏛 **Parker Ranch Visitor Center**
Parker Ranch Shopping Center, Māmalahoa Hwy (Hwy 19). *Tel* (808) 887-1046. 🔲 9am–5pm Mon–Sun. ⬤ public hols. 📷 👤

🏠 **Historic Parker Ranch Homes**
Off Māmalahoa Hwy (Hwy 190). *Tel* (808) 885-5433. 🔲 9am–5pm Mon–Sat. ⬤ Sun, public hols. 📷 👤 (partial access only.) www.parkerranch.com

The façade of Puopelu, one of the Historic Parker Ranch Homes

Pu'uhonua O Honaunau National Historical Park

From the 11th century on, social interactions were regulated by the *kapu* (taboo) system *(see p40)*. Violent death was the consequence of infractions, which ranged from stepping on a chief's shadow to women eating bananas. Lawbreakers could escape punishment, however, by reaching a *pu'uhonua* (place of refuge). The greatest of these was at Hōnaunau, a 6-acre temple compound dating from the 16th century that offered absolution to all who managed to run or swim past the chief's warriors. The sanctuary was stripped of power in 1819, after the fall of the *kapu* system. Partially restored, it now provides a glimpse into precontact Hawai'i.

Heleipālala Fish Ponds
These two ponds were stocked with fish reserved for the royal table.

Hālau
Thatched A-frame structures were used for storage and as work sheds.

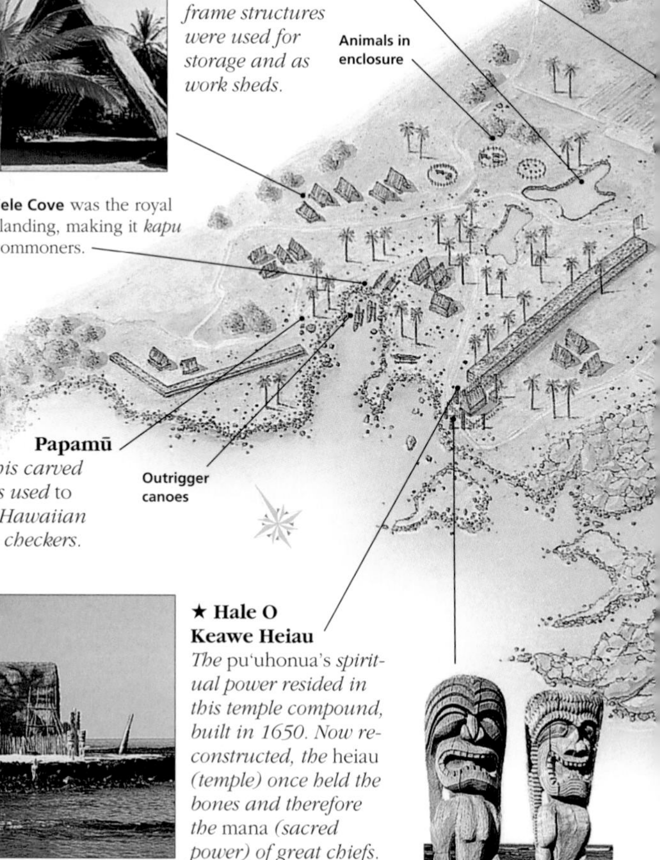

Worker in a field

Animals in enclosure

Keone'ele Cove was the royal canoe landing, making it *kapu* to all commoners.

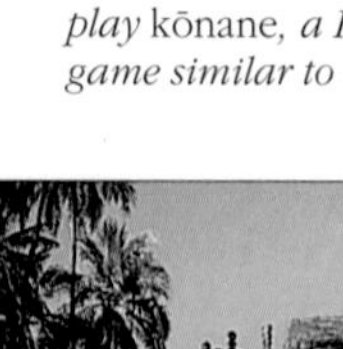

Papamū
This carved stone board was used to play kōnane, *a Hawaiian game similar to checkers.*

Outrigger canoes

★ **Hale O Keawe Heiau**
The pu'uhonua's spiritual power resided in this temple compound, built in 1650. Now reconstructed, the heiau *(temple) once held the bones and therefore the* mana *(sacred power) of great chiefs.*

STAR SIGHTS

★ Hale O Keawe Heiau

★ The Great Wall

Wooden Ki'i
These carved images of gods outside Hale O Keawe Heiau are copies based on drawings and descriptions of the originals.

'Āle'ale'a Heiau
predates the 16th-century Great Wall. It served as the focus of spiritual power until the construction of Hale O Keawe.

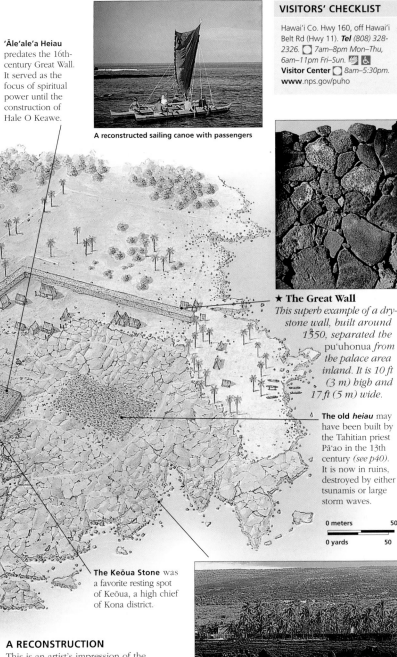

A reconstructed sailing canoe with passengers

VISITORS' CHECKLIST

Hawai'i Co. Hwy 160, off Hawai'i Belt Rd (Hwy 11). **Tel** (808) 328-2326. 7am–8pm Mon–Thu, 6am–11pm Fri–Sun. **Visitor Center** 8am–5:30pm. www.nps.gov/puho

★ **The Great Wall**
This superb example of a dry-stone wall, built around 1550, separated the pu'uhonua *from the palace area inland. It is 10 ft (3 m) high and 17 ft (5 m) wide.*

The old *heiau* may have been built by the Tahitian priest Pā'ao in the 13th century *(see p40)*. It is now in ruins, destroyed by either tsunamis or large storm waves.

0 meters 50
0 yards 50

The Keōua Stone was a favorite resting spot of Keōua, a high chief of Kona district.

A RECONSTRUCTION
This is an artist's impression of the *pu'uhonua* when the ruling chief of the district lived here along with his court and attendants. Some elements have been reconstructed by the National Park Service, and visitors may see artisans at work.

Exposed Peninsula of Black Lava
The peninsula's jagged shoreline made it difficult for kapu-*breakers to approach from the sea.*

The popular white-sand beach at Hāpuna Bay, on Hawaiʻi Island's south Kohala Coast

Hāpuna Bay ⑩

Hawaiʻi Co. Off Queen Kaʻahumanu
Highway (Hwy 19), 7 miles (11 km)
N of Waikoloa Coast.

An expanse of white sand,
both broad and deep,
makes Hāpuna Bay the most
popular beach on Hawaiʻi
Island. With its clean, sandy
bottom, the bay offers excellent
swimming, snorkeling, and
diving conditions. When the
waves are active, surfers and
body-boarders flock here, and
it is generally a good spot for
beginners to acquire some
wave-riding skills. The water
should be approached with
caution, however; strong currents have resulted in several
drownings. On the beach,
there are places to rent snorkel
sets and boogie boards, and
posts staffed by life guards
throughout the day.

**Hāpuna Beach State
Recreation Area**, which surrounds the beach, provides
cabins for overnight stays, as
well as a snack bar and picnic
tables at which visitors can
enjoy their own food.

About 1 mile (1.5 km) north
of the bay, accessed via the
Mauna Kea Beach Hotel *(see
p189)*, is the lovely, crescent-
shaped **Kaunaʻoa Beach**, with
fine conditions for swimming
and snorkeling most of the
year. One of the most photo-
graphed beaches on the
island, this stretch of sand
was once the playground of
aliʻi (Hawaiian royalty).

🏊 **Hāpuna Beach State
Recreation Area**
Around Hāpuna Beach. **Tel** *Division of
State Parks, (808) 974-6200.* ⭕ *daily.*

Puʻukoholā Heiau National Historic Site ⑪

Hawaiʻi Co. Off Akoni Pule Hwy (Hwy
270), 1 mile (1.5 km) S of Kawaihae.
Tel *(808) 882-7218.* ⭕ *7:30am–
4pm daily.* ♿ *visitor center only.*

In 1790, Kamehameha I had
reached an impasse in his
drive to unify the island chain.
On the advice of an oracle,
he undertook the construction
of **Puʻukoholā Heiau**, dedicated to Kūkāʻilimoku, his
family war god, which was
destined to become the last
such temple ever built. For
the dedication ceremonies,
the crafty king invited his
rival Keoua, the chief of Kaʻū.
As Keoua stepped out of his

canoe, he was slaughtered
and carried to the new altar
to serve as its first sacrifice.

Today, the massive monu-
ment stands undamaged on a
hilltop overlooking Kawaihae
Bay. Below it are the ruins
of **Mailekini Heiau**, built for
Kamehameha's ancestors.
A third *heiau*, **Haleokapuni**,
dedicated to shark gods, is
believed to lie submerged in
the waters below. Sacrifices left
here would soon have become
shark fodder. An easy trail
runs down past the first two
heiau from the visitor center.

Immediately south of
the *heiau* is **Spencer Beach
County Park**, a popular spot
for camping, snorkeling, and
diving. The clean white beach
and calm waters make it an
excellent area for children.
Operated by the National
Park Service, it includes a
visitor center where park
rangers provide information
and you can pick up a map
of points of interest.

Traditional ceremony at Puʻukoholā Heiau National Historic Site

Lapakahi State Historical Park ⑫

Hawai'i Co. Off Akoni Pule Hwy (Hwy 270), 12 miles (19 km) N of Kawaihae. *Tel (808) 974-6200.* ◯ *daily.* ⬤ *public hols.*

The ruins of this large settlement provide a glimpse into the daily life of an old Hawaiian fishing village. Established in the 14th century, the village was inhabited for 500 years – until a falling water table and changing economic conditions caused the natives to abandon their homes.

Some thatched walls and roofs are gone; others have been restored to their original appearance. The lava foundations, *hālau* (canoe sheds), *kū'ula ko'a* (fishing shrines), and a *kōnane* stone board-game remain undamaged.

Hāwī ⑬

Hawai'i Co. 🏠 950. 🛈 *Big Island Visitors Bureau, (808) 961-5797.*

The town of Hāwī had its heyday during the era of "King Cane," when five sugar plantations brought prosperity to Kohala, the island's northern district. After the mills closed in 1975, Hāwī was left to dwindle to its present size. These days it is a pleasant town to wander through, with its wooden sidewalks and brightly painted storefronts. Hāwī's grassy, windswept surroundings and relaxed

A traditional hale (grass hut) at Mo'okini Heiau

charm now attract a new breed of citizen – the town currently offers a health-food store and a handful of trendy eateries.

Environs: Reached by a rutted dirt road, lichen-covered **Mo'okini Heiau** is one of the oldest temples on the islands, possibly dating from the 5th century AD. In 1250 it was re-dedicated as a *luakini heiau* (for human sacrifice). Legend says the temple was built in one night using stones that were passed hand to hand by a human chain of 18,000 men from Pololu Valley 14 miles (23 km) away. In 1963, Mo'okini Heiau was the first Hawaiian site to be listed in the National Historical Site Registry. Today, visitors to this massive *heiau* will discover a remote and peaceful ruin.

⛩ Mo'okini Heiau
Off Akoni Pule Highway (Hwy 270) at mile marker 20, then left at airfield.

Restored thatched dwelling, Lapakahi State Historical Park

Kapa'au ⑭

Hawai'i Co. 🏠 1,100. 🛈 *Big Island Visitors Bureau, (808) 961-5797.*

The small town of Kapa'au contains the original statue of Kamehameha the Great, a much-photographed replica of which stands in front of Ali'iōlani Hale in Honolulu (see *p54*). King Kalakaua commissioned the bronze sculpture in 1878. Cast in Paris, France, the statue was thought lost when the ship carrying it to Hawai'i sank. A new statue was commissioned and cast and this is the one that now stands in Honolulu. However, the original statue was found and arrived in the islands a few weeks after the first was installed on O'ahu. So it was brought to Kapa'au, historically known as the birthplace of Kamehameha I.

A large boulder labeled **Kamehameha Rock** can be found on the roadside heading east of town. Legend has it that the big chief once carried it to prove his strength; whole road crews have failed to move it since! Nearby, the intricately painted **Tong Wo Society** building is the last of its kind on Hawai'i Island. Immigrant Chinese communities once relied on clubs like this to provide social cohesion.

Environs: At the end of Highway 270, a lookout focuses the gaze on idyllic **Pololū Valley.** Isolated by lush canyon walls, the valley's wide floor meets the ocean at a black-sand beach. It is a 20-minute walk down the steep trail to the beach.

Kapa'au's Tong Wo Society building, part of Hawai'i's immigrant heritage

Some of the dramatically varied terrain along Kohala Mountain Road

Kohala Mountain Road ⑮

Hawai'i Co. Highway 250. 🏠 BIVB, East Hawai'i, (808) 961-5797.

The 20-mile (32-km) drive from Hāwī to Waimea follows the western ridge of low, worn Kohala Mountain. It is a beautiful, cool and breezy drive. This narrow, twisting, tree-lined road provides breathtaking vistas and constantly changing scenery. The landscapes range from lush green hills and rolling pastures to black lava rock and distant beaches. A good place to stop and enjoy the dramatic panoramic views of the entire North Kohala coastline is at the Kohala Mountain Road lookout which gives a sense of the awesome size of Hawai'i island. This is ranch land, and the scenic drive gives views of elegant ranch houses, cattle and horses grazing in deep grass, and occasional vistas of the north Kohala Coast.

Parker Ranch is the largest operation in this area, and, in fact, the largest privately owned cattle ranch in the United States. Its origins date right back to the early years of Western discovery and a young American adventurer named John Palmer Parker. In 1809, Parker befriended Kamehameha I and eventually married one of the king's granddaughters. He established a small dynasty that shaped the history of the Kohala district. Today, the ranch covers a tenth of the island and supports 50,000 head of cattle.

Waipi'o Valley ⑯

Hawai'i Co. 🏠 Big Island Visitors Bureau, (808) 961-5797.

If any particular spot could be designated the spiritual heartland of ancient Hawai'i, it would have to be Waipi'o, or the "Valley of the Kings." The largest of seven enormous amphitheater valleys that punctuate this windward stretch of coast, Waipi'o measures 1 mile (1.5 km) wide at the sea and extends nearly 6 miles (10 km) inland. Its steep walls, laced with waterfalls, including the stupendous Hi'ilawe cascade, rise as high as 2,000 ft (600 m). Waipi'o Stream slices the lush valley floor, courses through fertile taro fields, and empties into the rough sea across a wide black-sand beach.

The road from the stunning lookout at the end of Highway 240 down to the valley floor is only a mile (1.5 km) long, but its steepness limits access to four-wheel-drive vehicles; on foot the trip takes about 30 minutes. Shuttle tours, even one in a mule-drawn surrey, are available at the tiny village of Kukuihaele, and nearby stables offer horseback trips.

In precontact days, Waipi'o supported a population of over 10,000. A sacred place, the valley contained important *heiau*, including a *pu'uhonua* (place of refuge) equal to that at Hōnaunau *(see pp138–9)*. The valley was Kamehameha the Great's boyhood playground. It was here that he received the sponsorship of his terrifying war god Kūkā'ilimoku, and that he defeated his cousin and rival Keoua. Today, Waipi'o's few inhabitants cultivate taro, lotus, avocado, breadfruit, and citrus, and earnestly protect Hawai'i's ancient spirit.

Isolated Waipi'o Valley, historically a sacred site and now a favorite of hikers and nature lovers

For hotels and restaurants in this region see pp188–9 and pp206–8

Honoka'a ⑰

Hawai'i Co. 🏢 🛖 2,350.
🛈 Big Island VB, East Hawai'i, (808) 961-5797.

A 15-mile (24-km) drive from Waipi'o Valley, this quaint rural town is actually one of the largest on the Hāmākua Coast. It has one hotel, bed and breakfast accommodations, shops, boutiques, and restaurants. The town also boasts art galleries, antique stores, a macadamia nut factory, a movie theater, and a nine-hole golf course.

This small community is home to The **Honoka'a People's Theater**. Built in 1930 on the town's main thoroughfare, Mamane Street, the renovated theater now shows movies on a big screen and also hosts the Hawai'i International Film Festival (*see p218*) and the **Hāmākua Music Festival**. Held each fall, the music festival features renowned Jazz, Classical, and Hawaiian folk musicians such as Eric Marienthal, Gene Harris, Ray Brown, and Kenny Burrell.

📷 **Hāmākua Music Festival**
PO Box 1757, Honoka'a.
Tel (808) 775-3378.
www.hamakuamusicfestival.com
The Honoka'a People's Theater
Mamane Street, Honoka'a.
Tel (808) 775-0000.

Hāmākua Coast ⑱

Hawai'i Co. (Hwy 19), Waipi'o Valley to Hilo. 🏢 Honoka'a, Laupāhoehoe, Honomū, and Pepe'ekeo. 🛈 BIVB, East Hawai'i, (808) 961-5797.

The verdant cliffs lining the island's windward coast are stunning company on the drive along the Hawai'i Belt Road (Hwy 19). With dozens of side roads begging investigation, you can easily spend a day traveling the 55 miles (89 km) between Waimea and Hilo.

This stretch has been designated the Hilo-Hāmākua Heritage Coast due to the area's historic and cultural significance. Look out for brown-and-white signs on the Hawai'i Belt Road as these indicate specific points of interest situated along the way.

High in the hills south of Honoka'a is **Kalōpā State Recreation Area**. This has a native forest nature trail and a small arboretum of Hawaiian and introduced plants. Twelve miles (19 km) farther on is **Laupāhoehoe Point**, a lush lava outcrop that juts into the pounding sea, providing stupendous views along the coast. A sizable village once existed here but was destroyed by the 1946 tsunami (*see p149*).

At **Kolekole Beach County Park**, south of mile marker 15, a delightful stream tumbles into the ocean, making this a popular picnic and swimming spot.

🥾 **Kalōpā State Recreation Area**
Off Hawai'i Belt Rd (Hwy 19), 2 miles (3 km) S of Honoka'a.
Tel (808) 974-6200. ◷ daily. ⛺

PANIOLO CULTURE

When George Vancouver brought eight cattle to Hawai'i Island in 1794, the sight of the huge beasts sent the natives running in terror. Fifty years later, herds of wild cattle had become such a scourge that Kamehameha III hired three Mexican *vaqueros* (cowboys) to control them. The *vaqueros* introduced their own customs, which evolved into the tradition of the *paniolo* (from *español*). They also

A paniolo astride his horse

brought the guitar and the fundamental sound of popular Hawaiian music. There are now ranches all over the state. Hawai'i Island has annual rodeos at Honoka'a, Waimea, Nā'ālehu, and Waikoloa. Maui's *paniolo* host a parade and rodeo on July 4 in Makawao (*see p123*).

World Botanical Gardens ⑲

Hawai'i Co. Off Highway 19 near mile marker 16. ***Tel*** (808) 963-5427. ◷ 9am–5:30pm daily.
📷 www.wbgi.com

World Botanical Gardens, just north of Hilo on an expanse of former sugarcane fields, is Hawai'i's largest botanical garden. Featuring 5,000 species, it includes the spectacular three-tiered 300-ft (90-m) Umauma Falls. The viewing area for Umauma Falls is reached by a short walk through the rainforest along a flower-lined path that follows a stream.

Although only in development since 1995, the site is abundant with fruits, flowers, trees, medicinal plants, and lush greenery. There is also a large children's maze.

The sheer, green cliffs of the stunning Hāmākua Coast

Spectacular lava flow from Kīlauea Volcano, Hawai'i Island ▷

The route serving Mauna Loa weather station, off Saddle Road

Saddle Road ⑳

Hawai'i Co. Hwy 200 from Waimea to Hilo. **i** *BIVB, East Hawai'i, (808) 961-5797.*

To drive the 55-mile (89-km) Saddle Road linking Hilo and Waimea is to drive along the shoulders of giants. The jumbled peaks of **Mauna Kea** rise to the north, while broad **Mauna Loa** looms to the south, the road following the trough where the two mountains collide. Some car rental companies ban drivers from taking the Saddle Road, an "unimproved" two-lane highway, but the road is better than they make out. As long as you drive at a reasonable speed, and in daylight, this is not a hazardous trip.

Drivers get a close-up look at the ecological forces at work on the island's interior – the cool rain forests of Hilo district, dominated by *'ōhi'a* trees, *koa*, and huge ferns; the subalpine lava fields at the road's 6,500-ft (2,000-m) summit; and the vast, parched grasslands on the Waimea side. Much of the traffic is generated by two sizable military installations.

The highest vantage point from which to view the imposing terrain is a weather station situated 11,000 ft (3,350 m) above sea level. It is reached along a narrow paved road that begins near the summit of Saddle Road and climbs for 17 miles (27 km) up Mauna Loa. The 45-minute drive is hard work (loosening the gas tank cap helps to prevent vapor lock at this altitude), but the reward is the spectacular view across Saddle Road to Mauna Kea. Starting at the weather station, an extremely rugged trail – a four- to six-hour hike – leads to the crater on the summit of Mauna Loa, at 13,677 ft (4,169 m).

Mauna Kea ㉑

Hawai'i Co. Off Saddle Road (Hwy 200) at mile marker 28. **i** *BIVB, East Hawai'i, (808) 961-5797.*

Midway between Hilo and Waimea, an unmarked but well-paved road climbs up Mauna Kea, winding through a native *māmane* forest that has been severely damaged by the predations of wild goats and sheep. The road rises so steeply that most cars crawl up the 15-minute drive to the **Onizuka Center for International Astronomy**.

Here, a small visitor center, named after the Kona-born astronaut who died in the 1986 explosion of the space shuttle *Challenger*, offers the solace of shelter with refreshments. It also has informative displays about the ecology of Mauna Kea and a video about its observatories. There are impressive views, too, but the panorama is better still from the summit. Driving to the very top of Mauna Kea is impossible, however, without a four-wheel-drive vehicle. The alternative is to go on foot. The 4,600-ft (1,400-m) climb is a tough 6-mile (10-km) hike.

The route to the summit takes in several remarkable sites: the **Mauna Kea Ice Age Natural Area Reserve**, with a quarry where the ancient Hawaiians obtained the rock used for making their axlike tools, or adzes; **Moon Valley**, where *Apollo* astronauts practiced driving their lunar rover in the 1960s; **Lake Waiau**, the third-highest lake in the US; and **Pu'u Poli'ahu**, the legendary abode of Pele's sister Poli'ahu, the goddess of snow.

Mauna Kea is crowned with a cluster of astronomical domes, including the **W.M. Keck Observatory**. Research teams from the US, Canada, France, and the UK are based here, collecting new information about the cosmos.

🏛 **Onizuka Center for International Astronomy**
6 miles (10 km) N of mile marker 28 off Saddle Road (Hwy 200). **Visitor Center** *Tel (808) 961-2180.* ◯ *9am–10pm daily.* ♿ ◲

Mauna Kea, a giant post-shield stage volcano *(see pp18–19)*, viewed from Mauna Loa weather station

THE W.M. KECK OBSERVATORY

Mauna Kea, due to its elevation, the clear air, and the absence of light and air pollution, is the best observatory site in the world – enabling the telescopes at its summit to observe the universe with minimal distortion. Keck I (built in 1992) and Keck II (1996), sitting like a pair of huge eyes on the mountain top, have four times the imaging power of the world's next largest telescope in California. Instead of just one monolithic mirror, each observatory has a mosaic of flexible mirror segments computer-guided to focus in unison.

The twin globes of the W.M. Keck Observatory on Mauna Kea

'Akaka Falls State Park ㉒

Hawai'i Co. Highway 220, 3.5 miles (5.5 km) W of Honomū. 🚉 Honomū. **Tel** Division of State Parks, (808) 974-6200. ◯ daily.

Two of the state's most hypnotic waterfalls have been packaged for easy viewing at 'Akaka Falls State Park, in the hills above the Hāmākua Coast. A loop trail, taking less than half an hour, links the 400-ft (120-m) **Kahūnā Falls** to **'Akaka Falls**, an unbroken cascade of 420 ft (130 m). At the main lookout, the roar of water almost drowns out the incessant clicking of cameras. At the edge of the path you can see the entire length of the falls from top to bottom, including the pool below, yet not get wet from the spray.

The waterfalls apart, the breezy 66-acre park alone is worth the visit. Paths wind through a rich blend of trees, vines, bamboo, ginger, orchids, and other exotic plants, accompanied by the cooling sounds of rushing streams.

The access road veers off Highway 19 at the welcoming old sugar town of **Honomū**, which has dwindled from its 1930s population of 3,000 to just over 500 today. The

residents have kept the small main street alive, with the **Ishigo General Store and Bakery** (established 1910) and several other weathered wooden buildings serving as cafés and gift shops. The **Honomū Henjoji Mission**, a temple of the Buddhist Shingon Esoteric sect, was founded in the 1920s and has a sanctuary richly ornamented in black lacquer and gold. The signs inviting visitors to come in are sincerely meant.

🛕 **Honomū Henjoji Mission**
28-1668 Government Main Road, Honomū. **Tel** (808) 963-6308. ◯ call ahead for details.

Gracefully cascading 'Akaka Falls, set back above the Hāmākua Coast

Pepe'ekeo Scenic Drive ㉓

Hawai'i Co. Off Hawai'i Belt Road (Hwy 19), 4 miles (6.5 km) N of Hilo. 🚉 Pepe'ekeo. 🛈 BIVB, East Hawai'i, (808) 961-5797.

This 4-mile (6.5-km) scenic detour off the Hawai'i Belt Road plunges into tropical growth, crossing waterfall-fed streams and shaded by vine-draped palms and mango, banana, and *hala* trees. Halfway along the drive, at beautiful Onomea Bay, the **Hawai'i Tropical Botanical Garden** has trails meandering through a patch of rainforest that includes a lily pond and a vast array of tropical plants.

🌺 **Hawai'i Tropical Botanical Garden**
2 miles (3 km) from either end of the drive. **Tel** (808) 964-5233. ◯ 9am–4pm daily. ● Jan 1, Thanksgiving, Dec 25. 📵 www.htbg.com

Mauna Loa ㉔

Hawai'i Co. 🛈 BIVB, East Hawai'i, (808) 961-5797.

Mauna Loa, or "Long Mountain", is the largest volcano on earth and one of the most active. One of five volcanoes that form Hawai'i Island, it covers the entire southern half of the island. It is 60 miles (95 km) long and 30 miles (50 km) wide and rises to 13,677 ft (4,169 m) above sea level. Mauna Loa's summit is protected as part of Hawai'i Volcanoes National Park *(see pp152–3)*.

Since its first documented eruption in 1843, Mauna Loa has erupted more than 33 times, most recently in 1984. It is a shield volcano, with gently sloping inclines that have been created from successive lava flows oozing from the earth's crust. The caldera at the summit, Moku'aweoweo, is more than 3 miles (5 km) long and 1.5 miles (2.5 km) wide, with towering 600-ft (180-m) walls.

Kilauea *(see pp152–3)*, an extremely active volcano with areas of continually moving lava, lies on Mauna Loa's southeast flank.

Hilo ㉕

With 38,000 residents, significant shipping and fishing industries out of its large bay, and a campus of the University of Hawai'i, Hilo rightfully deserves its designation as the state's second city. In spirit, though, "rainy old Hilo" couldn't be more different from sunny, urban Honolulu. The downtown buildings, many of them beautifully restored, were mostly constructed in the early 1900s; the streets are quiet, the pace is slow, and the atmosphere is low-key. Local attractions include gardens, a waterfall, beach parks, and fish ponds.

Exploring Hilo

Nature itself has checked the city's progress in two ways: the fact that rain falls 278 days of the year has not endeared Hilo to sun-worshiping vacationers; and, as though even more water were needed, the sea pounded Hilo with two destructive tsunamis in 1946 and 1960. The city has since retreated from the sea, turning the waterfront area into enormous green parks.

The Hawaiian Telephone Company building

Hilo has a friendly, relaxed, and ethnically diverse personality. The population is largely Japanese and Filipino in ancestry, and the stores and eating places reflect that heritage. The Merrie Monarch Festival, the state's most prestigious *hula* competition, takes place here every year in the week following Easter. The plentiful rain makes Hilo a natural garden, suited to orchids and anthuriums. This is a city not so much for "tourists" as for visitors.

Downtown

Many of the brightly colored, restored buildings of the old business district, clustered next to the Wailuku River, are listed with the National Register of Historic Places. Look out for the **Hawaiian Telephone Company building**, which combines aspects of the traditional Hawaiian house *(hale)* and Californian mission architecture; its designer, C.W. Dickey, is credited with developing Hawaiian Regional Architecture. A walking tour brochure is available from the Hawai'i Visitors and Convention Bureau and Lyman House.

🏛 Farmers' Market

Corner of Mamo St and Kamehameha Ave. ⭕ Wed & Sat.
On two mornings a week the junction of Mamo Street and Kamehameha Avenue turns into a multilingual open-air marketplace. Farmers bring exotic produce such as squash blossoms, ice cream bananas, cut orchids, and mats woven from *lauhala* (leaves of the pandanus plant). Stroll around and pick up a fresh breakfast.

🏛 Pacific Tsunami Museum

130 Kamehameha Ave. **Tel** (808) 935-0926. ⭕ 9am–4pm Mon–Sat. ● public hols. 📷
www.tsunami.org
This museum is located in the historic First Hawaiian Bank Building, designed by C.W. Dickey. Built in 1930, it survived both the 1946 and 1960 tsunamis and was donated to the museum in 1970. Exhibits focus on how tsunamis (often called tidal waves) are formed.

🏛 Mokupāpapa Discovery Center

308 Kamehameha Ave, Suite 109.
Tel (808) 933-8195. ⭕ 9am–4pm Tue–Sat. ● public hols. **www.** papahanaumokuakea.gov
The natural science, culture and history of the remote northwest Hawaiian islands, and that of the surrounding marine environment, is explained at this free exhibition center. A 2,500-gallon salt-water aquarium provides a home for some of the fish that inhabit the region's coral reef.

🏛 Wailoa Center

In Wailoa River State Park, Piopio St. **Tel** (808) 933-0416. ⭕ 8:30am–4:30pm Mon–Fri, noon–4:30pm Wed. ● public hols. ♿
This octagonal gallery sits on a wide lawn where the Japanese quarter used to be – the town refused to rebuild here after the tsunami of 1960. Downstairs there is a photographic display showing the appalling destruction caused by the giant waves. The rest of the gallery hosts temporary exhibitions.

🏛 Lyman Museum and Mission House

276 Haili St. **Tel** (808) 935-5021. ⭕ 10am–4:30pm Mon–Sat. ● Jan 1, Jul 4, Thanksgiving, Dec 25. 📷 ♿ museum only.
www.lymanmuseum.org
Once the home of the Reverend David and Sarah Lyman, missionaries who settled in Hilo in the early 1830s. It is well preserved with household items like a cradle and quilts. The complex also includes a

People and produce at the lively Farmers' Market

For hotels and restaurants in this region see pp188–9 and pp206–8

TSUNAMIS IN HILO

In 1946 an Alaskan earthquake triggered a tsunami that hit the unsuspecting Hawaiian Islands on the morning of April 1. Waves 56 ft (17 m) high tore Hilo's bayfront buildings off their foundations and swept them inland, killing 96 people. In 1960, another tsunami struck with a vengeance. Originating off the coast of Chile, it slammed Hilo on May 23 with three successive waves, causing damage worth $23 million. In spite of warnings, many locals refused to retreat, and 61 died.

Great devastation in the aftermath of the 1946 tsunami

modern museum housing a varied collection of Hawaiiana, including a display of volcanic geology and artifacts from the years of immigration, such as a *braginha* – the Portuguese precursor to the *ukulele*.

♣ Waiākea Peninsula
Banyan Drive.

Jutting into Hilo Bay, Waiākea Peninsula supports a nine-hole golf course, a row of high-rise hotels, and the 30-acre

Lili'uokalani Gardens. The latter is a Japanese park that blends fish ponds with small pagodas and arched bridges. A footbridge crosses to tiny **Coconut Island**, now a park and popular fishing spot but once a place of healing; the Hawaiians called it Moku Ola (Island of Life). **Banyan Drive** loops the peninsula under the dense shade of huge banyans planted by celebrities such as Amelia Earhart and Babe Ruth.

VISITORS' CHECKLIST

Hawai'i Co. 38,000. 3 miles (5 km) E. Kamehameha Ave, near Mamo St, (808) 961-8744. BIVB, 250 Keawe St, (808) 961-5797. Merrie Monarch Festival (Mar or Apr).

Rainbow Falls
Waiānuenue Avenue, 2 miles (3 km) W of Downtown.

Rainbow ("Waiānuenue") Falls earns its name when the morning sun filters through the mist generated by the 80-ft (24-m) waterfall, creating beautiful rainbows. The hollow at the base of the falls is the legendary home of Hina, Maui's mother. The surrounding trails provide a range of lookouts.

The Eastern Beaches
Kalaniana'ole Ave.

Kalaniana'ole Avenue, which follows the east side of Hilo Bay, passes a number of beach parks interlaced with large fish ponds. **James Kealoha Beach Park** (also called Four Mile Beach) offers excellent snorkeling and swimming on its sheltered eastern side; fishermen often cast their nets on the Hilo side, which is also a popular but challenging winter surfing hangout. Another good swimming spot is **Richardson Ocean Park**, which nature has sculpted into protected, lagoonlike pools.

A fisherman throwing his net into the rough waters off James Kealoha Beach Park

Pāhoa's old Akebono Theater, now a popular spot for concerts

Pāhoa ㉖

Hawai'i Co. 🏘 *1,100.* 🚌 ℹ️ *BIVB, East Hawai'i, (808) 961-5797.*

The main strip of Pāhoa, the central town of the Puna district, offers a double surprise – "Wild West"-style buildings with raised boardwalks and low awnings that have been reinterpreted along psychedelic themes. Shops sell hemp products, espresso coffee, and New Age books. The popular **Akebono Theater** (built in 1917) has been kept alive to host a busy schedule of rock and reggae concerts.

Three miles (5 km) southeast of Pāhoa, a state-sponsored geothermal energy project has attempted to derive electricity from the heat of the world's most active volcano. However, a public outcry over environmental damage has embroiled the project in legal controversy.

Kapoho ㉗

Hawai'i Co. ℹ️ *BIVB, East Hawai'i, (808) 961-5797.*

In 1960, the town of Kapoho was destroyed by lava that spewed from a fire fountain 2,600 ft (795 m) wide. Today, the eerie devastation can be crossed on a 2-mile (3-km) cinder road leading to **Cape Kumukahi**, where a light-tower was inexplicably spared when the flow parted. Volcanic activity in Kapoho is a source of local legends: one tells of a

local chief who challenged a beautiful young woman to a sled race down Kapoho Crater and found to his shock that he was competing with the volcano goddess, Pele, riding on a wave of lava.

In 1790, one such wave surged through a nearby forest, leaving 'ōhi'a trunks sheathed in black stone. Today, only the hollowed-out casts, or "lava trees," remain, but new trees have grown back. Together they make up the **Lava Tree State Monument**, a shady park with a trail around the casts. This serene spot will be best enjoyed if you bring your mosquito repellent.

Lava tree cast

🌳 Lava Tree State Monument
Highway 132, 2.5 miles (4 km) E of Pāhoa. *Tel Division of State Parks, (808) 974-6200.* ⬜ *daily.* ♿

Clidemia hirta (Koster's curse) growing in a lava tree cast

Puna Lava Flows ㉘

Hawai'i Co. Hwy 137 SW of Kapoho for 14 miles (23 km). ℹ️ *County Parks & Recreation, (808) 961-8311.*

Narrow highway 137 traces the Puna coastline along the base of Kīlauea's East Rift Zone. Here, the dense foliage occasionally breaks into solidified lava flows, mute reminders that Puna residents live by the grace of Madam Pele's fury.

At **Ahalanui Beach Park**, a natural thermal spring in a coconut grove has been adapted into a 60-ft (18-m) wide seaside swimming pool. With a sandy bottom and waves crashing against the pool's edge, this is the best place to swim in the district.

Isaac Hale Beach Park features camping, a small boat ramp, and a rugged beach with a respectable surf break. **MacKenzie State Recreation Area**, a clifftop campsite set in an ironwood forest, gives access to an old Hawaiian coastal trail and a long lava tube.

Southwest of here the Puna coastal road ends with shocking abruptness where the roadway, and indeed the entire countryside, has been obliterated by congealed piles of lava. In 1990, this flow erased the town of Kalapana and a much-loved black-sand beach called Kaimū.

🏖️ Ahalanui Beach Park
Hwy 137, 1 mile (1.5 km) NE of junction with Pāhoa-Pohoiki Rd. ⬜ *daily.*

🏖️ Isaac Hale Beach Park
Junction of Hwy 137 and Pāhoa-Pohoiki Rd. ⬜ *daily.*

🌳 MacKenzie State Recreation Area
Hwy 137, 2 miles (3 km) S of junction with Pāhoa-Pohoiki Rd. ⬜ *daily.*

Volcano Village ㉙

Hawai'i Co. 🏘 *1,500.* 🚌 ℹ️ *BIVB, East Hawai'i, Hilo, (808) 961-5797.*

Cut into the 'ōhi'a rain forest of Mauna Loa's high windward slopes, this village lies just a mile (1.5 km) outside the entrance to **Hawai'i**

For hotels and restaurants in this region see pp188–9 and pp206–8

The beautiful black beach at Punalu'u Beach Park, southwest of Pāhala

Volcanoes National Park *(see pp152–3).* The village has a general store and a gas station (the only one in the area) and makes a good provisioning stop before entering the park.

ENVIRONS: Just 2 miles (3 km) west of the park entrance, a small road leads northwest to **Volcano Golf and Country Club**, which has an 18-hole public golf course and an inexpensive restaurant. At the end of the road a winery *(see p211)* gives tastings of its unique wines, which include a guava Chablis.

A short drive east of Volcano Village are **Akatsuka Orchid Gardens**, where visitors can take a self-guided tour.

🌺 **Akatsuka Orchid Gardens**
Hawai'i Belt Rd (Hwy 11), 5 miles (8 km) E of Volcano Village. *Tel (808) 967-8234.* ⬤ 8:30am–5pm daily. ⬤ public hols. ♿

Ka'ū District 🟥

Hawai'i Co. 🚌 Pāhala, Punalu'u, Nā'ālehu and Wai'ōhinu. 🚹 County of Hawai'i, (808) 961-8311.

The long southern arc of the Hawai'i Belt Road (Hwy 11) between Volcano Village and Kailua-Kona traverses the vast and sparsely populated Ka'ū district. Three very small towns are located here. Agricultural **Pāhala**, where macadamia nuts, sugarcane, and oranges are grown, is a quiet place where the only commotion might be the occasional crowing of roosters. **Nā'ālehu**, the most southerly town in the United States, is Ka'ū's largest town, with a few small shops. Tiny **Wai'ōhinu** is known for a monkeypod tree that Mark Twain planted in 1866. The original tree fell in a storm in 1957 but has since grown again

NAALEHU
SOUTHERNMOST COMMUNITY
IN THE U.S.A.
Road sign in Nā'ālehu

from shoots. The gem of the south coast is **Punalu'u Beach Park**, where a pure black sand beach is crowded with coconut trees. Visitors may camp here and at **Whittington Beach Park**, 5 miles (8 km) farther south.

🚧 **Punalu'u Beach Park**
Off Hwy 11, 5 miles (8 km) SW I of Pāhala. ⬤ daily. *Tel Dept of Parks and Recreation, Hilo, (808) 961-8311.*

Ka Lae 🟥

Hawai'i Co. S Point Rd, off Hwy 11, 6 miles (10 km) W of Wai'ōhinu. 🚹 BIVB, East Hawai'i, Hilo, (808) 961-5797.

Also known as South Point, Ka Lae is as far south as you can travel in the United States. Constant fierce winds drive against a battered grass-land that gives way finally to a rocky shoreline. Halfway along the 11-mile (18-km) access road, three rows of enormous, propeller-driven electricity generators emit a repetitive music of almost maddening whistles. It all feels suitably like the ends of the earth.

Although the powerful waves are daunting, these have long been prime fishing grounds. The mooring holes that ancient Hawaiians drilled into the coastal rocks so that they could keep their canoes safe while they went fishing are still visible – providing some of the earliest recorded evidence of Polynesian settlement.

A four-wheel-drive road runs 2.5 miles (4 km) northeast, to **Green Sands Beach**, which is composed of olivine sand.

Wind-powered electricity generators along the road to Ka Lae

Hawai'i Volcanoes National Park ❷

Petroglyph at Pu'u Loa, near the coast

The national park encompasses about a quarter of a million acres, including the 13,677-ft (4,169-m) summit of Mauna Loa, 150 miles (240 km) of hiking trails, and vast tracts of wilderness that preserve some of the world's rarest species of flora and fauna. But it is Kīlauea Caldera and the lava flows of its furious East Rift Zone that draw most visitors. Two roads – Crater Rim Drive, which loops around the caldera, and Chain of Craters Road, which descends through the recent outpourings – form a gigantic drive-through museum. The present eruption started in 1983. Check for viewing conditions before you visit; since lava flow, sulfur dioxide gas, and other hazards may restrict access. You should also stay out of closed areas. It is unkown how long the flow will continue or when it will next erupt.

Lava fountains spewing from Kīlauea during the 1983 eruption

Kīlauea Overlook

Hawai'i Belt Road

KIPUKA PUAULU

MAUNA LOA

Crater Rim Drive

Crater Rim Trail

Jaggar Museum

NA'ALEHU

KĪLAUEA CALDERA

★ **Halema'uma'u Overlook**
Once a boiling lake of lava, the crater below still steams with sulfurous fumes. This is the home of Pele, the volcano goddess (see p24).

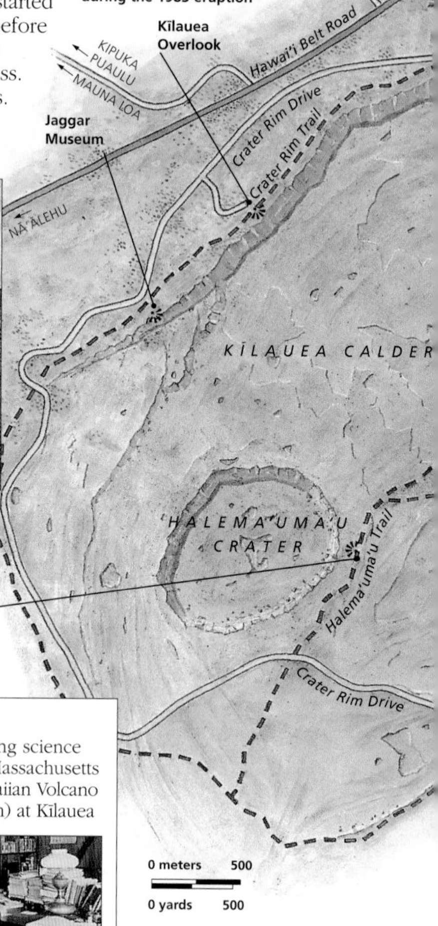

HALEMA'UMA'U CRATER

Halema'uma'u Trail

Crater Rim Drive

PROFESSOR JAGGAR (1871–1953)

Thomas A. Jaggar was a pioneer in the young science of volcanology. A professor of geology at Massachusetts Institute of Technology, he founded the Hawaiian Volcano Observatory (now part of the Jaggar Museum) at Kīlauea Caldera in 1912. Four years later, he and Honolulu publisher Lorrin Thurston persuaded Congress to preserve the area as a national park. Professor Jaggar developed techniques for collecting volcanic gases and measuring ground tilt, seismic activity, and lava temperatures. The work he initiated has made Kīlauea one of the best understood volcanoes in the world.

Professor Jaggar working at his desk in 1916

0 meters   500

0 yards   500

STAR SIGHTS

★ Halema'uma'u Overlook

★ Thurston Lava Tube

Kīlauea Iki Overlook

In 1959 the crater below this overlook filled with bubbling lava, shooting fire fountains 1,900 ft (580 m) into the air. Today a hiking trail crosses the cool crater floor to give a close-up view.

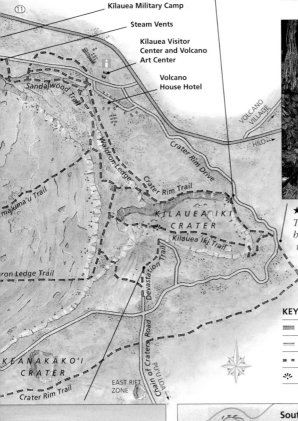

Kīlauea Military Camp
Steam Vents
Kīlauea Visitor Center and Volcano Art Center
Volcano House Hotel

Sandalwood Trail
Waldron Ledge
Crater Rim Drive
Crater Rim Trail
ʻamaumaʻu Trail
KĪLAUEA IKI CRATER
Kīlauea Iki Trail
Devastation Trail
ron Ledge Trail
KEANAKĀKOʻI CRATER
EAST RIFT ZONE
Chain of Craters Road
PUʻU LOA
Crater Rim Trail
VOLCANO VILLAGE
HILO

★ **Thurston Lava Tube**
This huge tunnel was left behind when a subterranean river of lava drained away. An easy trail runs through the tube and a grove of giant ferns.

KEY

▬▬ Major road
═══ Minor road
▪ ▪ Hiking trail
🌿 Vista

Devastation Trail
This short walk passes through the ghostly remains of a rain forest wiped out by ash falling from Kīlauea Iki's 1959 eruption.

Southern Extent of the Park

Kīlauea Caldera
Puʻu ʻŌʻō
Makaopuhi Crater
Nāpau Crater
Nāpau Crater Trail
Chain of Craters Road
Kalapana Trail
Hilina Pali Road
Keauhou Trail
HILINA PALI
HŌLEI PALI
Hilina Pali Trail
Puʻu Loa
Hōlei Sea Arch
Puna Coast Trail

0 kilometers   7
0 miles   5

Exploring Hawai'i Volcanoes National Park

The impressive volcanic terrain of Hawai'i Volcanoes National Park supports diverse climates and ecosystems that range from sea level to the summit of Mauna Loa, the largest volcano on earth. The park is also the site of Kīlauea – the world's most active volcano. This dramatic volcanic landscape, including sulfur banks, steam vents, lava tubes, fern forests, lava deserts, and endangered plants and animals, attracts millions of visitors each year. Numerous hiking paths and scenic drives lead visitors from one awe-inspiring panoramic scene to another. Over half of the park is designated wilderness and, in recognition of its outstanding natural wonders, the area has been recognized as an International Biosphere Reserve and as a World Heritage Site.

Lava fountain erupting from Kīlauea

Kīlauea Visitor Center building

Kīlauea Visitor Center

Hwy 11. **Tel** *(808) 985-6000.*
◯ *7:45am–5pm daily.* ♿
The visitor center presents an informative overview of the environmental, historical, and cultural features of the park. Exhibits give information about island formation, ecosystems, invasive species, and resource protection. A 25-minute film about geology and volcanism, "Born of Fire, Born of the Sea", is shown throughout the day. Trail and lava viewing conditions can change rapidly so check with the park rangers at the center for the latest information. Overnight visitors must register here and permits are issued on a first-come basis.

Volcano Art Center

Crater Rim Dr. **Tel** *(808) 967-8222.*
◯ *8:30am–5pm daily.* ◉ *Dec 25.*
♿ ⬛ **www.**volcanoartcenter.org
The Volcano Art Center preserves and promotes Hawaii's rich culture and traditions through *hula* performances, exhibitions,

and concerts. The center's Volcano Art Center Gallery is housed in the nearby 1877 Volcano House Hotel, listed in the National Register of Historic Places as Hawai'i's oldest visitor accommodation. The gallery features works by over 300 prominent local artists inspired by Hawaii's environmental and cultural heritage. The displays embrace a variety of media including paint, glass, metal, ceramic, fiber, wood, and photography. The center also offers classes and workshops on Hawaiian music, dance, crafts, writing, and language as well as sponsoring a performing arts season.

Earthquake Trail (Waldron Ledge)

A section of the Crater Rim Loop Trail along Waldron Ledge, this is an easy trail that is wheelchair and stroller accessible over a paved road surface. It begins to the left of the Volcano House Hotel and follows a section of the road that was cracked and destroyed by a devastating magnitude 6.6 earthquake in 1983 on Mauna Loa. The earthquake caused many rockfalls along the caldera walls and damaged trails and roads in the park. It takes approximately 45 minutes to complete the one mile (1.6-km) roundtrip. The trail features interesting earthcracks, a rich variety of plants, birds, and insects, and spectacular views of Kīlauea Caldera and Mauna Loa.

Panorama of Kīlauea Caldera from Waldron Ledge

For hotels and restaurants in this region see pp188–9 and pp206–8

Halema'uma'u Crater

On the floor of the enormous expanse of the Kīlauea Caldera, Halema'uma'u Crater is 3,000 ft (914 m) across and 300 ft (90 m) deep. The many fumaroles found both in the crater and along the rim continue to spew a large quantity of sulphur dioxide daily so those with respiratory problems should beware. The challenging 7-mile (11-km) Halema'uma'u Trail that leads to the crater can take three to six hours to complete. It begins by the Volcano House Hotel, descends 400 ft (120 m) through lush rain forest to the barren floor of the caldera, and crosses old lava flows to the southern edge of the crater. The trail passes Halema'uma'u Overlook which offers direct views of the crater pit.

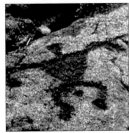

Ancient Hawaiian petroglyph depicting a human figure

Pu'u Loa Petroglyphs

This coastal trail crosses old lava flows to reach an extensive petroglyph field located on the southern flank of Kīlauea. It is an easy to moderate 2-mile (3.2-km) roundtrip hike, beginning at mile marker 16 on Chain of Craters road, that takes about one and half hours to complete. Hikers walk across rough basaltic lava to reach a wooden boardwalk that surrounds in excess of 23,000 petroglyph images etched on to the abundant lava surface. The majority of the images in this extensive field depict stylized human forms but there are also representations of the moon, canoes, ships, insects, fish, and spears. Circles, spirals, dots, and other geometric designs are also common features.

Thurston Lava Tube Trail

Thurston Lava Tube can be accessed via an easy 15-minute loop trail. The paved trail begins with a steep descent into the rain forest, dense with towering green ferns. The trail then leads visitors in to a pit crater where it is possible to enter the lava tube. Formed when the exterior of a lava flow cooled to a crust while the still-molten interior magma flowed out, the tube resembles a giant tunnel. Walking through the 600-ft (180-m) winding passage takes about ten minutes. Signs posted along the trail provide information about plants and animals that can be seen in the area.

Native *elepaio* bird

Kīlauea Ike Trail

Descending 400 ft (120 m) through tropical rain forest, this trail crosses the Kīlauea Iki Crater floor, passes Pu'u Pua'i cinder cone, and returns along the crater's rim. It is a moderate to challenging 4-mile (6.4-km) loop that takes two to three hours to hike. The trail allows visitors to explore features resulting from the 1959 Kīlauea Iki eruption, such as steam vents and cinder cones. Beginning at the Thurston Lava Tube parking lot on Crater Rim Drive, it takes 2-3 hours to complete. The contrast between the lush vegetation found on the crater rim and the barren rocky terrain of the crater floor is striking.

Devastation Trail

This easy paved trail winds through a forested area recovering from the devastating effects of the 1959 eruption of Kīlauea Iki. The eruption produced huge fountains of lava that shot up to 1,900 ft (580 m) in the air and covered the densely forested area with black pumice and falling cinder. In addition to the ghostly remains of the trees, the one-mile (1.6-km) trail features a variety of native plants, birds, tree molds, and cinder and spatter cones.

Kipuka Puaulu

A kipuka is a forested island untouched by surrounding lava flow. Vegetation has been spared by the lava flows and is therefore older and richer here. The lush green woodlands of Kipuka Puaulu bird park are home to one of the richest concentrations of rare native plants and bird life in Hawai'i. The 1-mile (1.6-km) loop trail takes about one hour to complete. It begins with a gentle hike on an unpaved forest path, surrounded by recent lava flows from Mauna Loa. Native *koa* and *'ōhi'a lehua* trees (*see p20*) grow here. It is possible to glimpse endemic birds such as the 'elepaio or 'apapane as well as other species including finches and Japanese white eyes. A bulletin board at the start of the trail provides descriptions of the diverse birds and plants species that are found here.

Kipuka Puaulu, dense forest land on the barren slopes of Mauna Loa

KAUA'I

*I*t is no coincidence that the oldest of the major Hawaiian islands is also the most beautiful. Wind and water have had six million years to carve Kaua'i into a stunning array of pleated cliffs and yawning chasms, while the rich topsoil of the "Garden Island" is cloaked in a spectacular mantle of emerald green vegetation. With its sandy beaches and large coral reefs, Kaua'i is Hawai'i's most irresistible destination.

The outline of the volcano that created Kaua'i has all but vanished, leaving a roughly circular island on which no place is more than a dozen miles (19 km) from the ocean. Although its highest point barely exceeds 5,000 ft (1,500 m), the interior remains a forbidding, water-logged wilderness, and Kaua'i's 55,000 inhabitants are distributed fairly evenly around the coastal lowlands.

Settled by a separate wave of Polynesian voyagers – possibly the small, legendary *Menehune (see p161)* – and never conquered by the other islands, Kaua'i has its own proud history. It was here that Captain Cook first landed, and here too that the sandalwood and sugar industries were established. A trail of ancient temples can still be seen along the Wailua River on the east shore, and former plantation towns from Hanalei in the north to Hanapēpē in the south lend the island a small-town charm.

The capital Līhu'e is surprisingly sleepy, while resorts such as Princeville and Po'ipū are rare pockets of modern luxury in an otherwise timeless rural landscape.

Scenery is Kaua'i's greatest attraction. The North Shore, in particular, is stunning, with a succession of gorgeous beaches to the east and the soaring Nā Pali Coast to the west. High above lies Kōke'e State Park, where trails command views of the valleys and lace through the rain-soaked Alaka'i Swamp, home to rare flora and fauna. The road to the park climbs the flanks of mighty Waimea Canyon, an ever-changing panoply of colors.

Visitors are both intrigued by Kaua'i's fascinating history and awed by the vast array of scenic beauty that it offers. Exotic, enchanting, and welcoming, the "Garden Isle" is a memorable place to stay.

Workers picking taro, a traditional Hawaiian crop cultivated in Kaua'i's Hanalei Valley

◁ The soaring cliffs of the Nā Pali Coast, accessible only by rugged trail, or by boat or helicopter tour

Exploring Kaua'i

Tourist facilities on Kaua'i are concentrated in three main areas. Po'ipū in the south is a classic family resort, with beautiful beaches and modern hotels. On the east coast, from Līhu'e to Kapa'a, the beaches are equally stunning, and the hotels are cheaper and well placed for sightseeing. Līhu'e also has a couple of grand plantation-era mansions, while the back roads behind Kapa'a offer glimpses of both ancient history and scenic wilderness. Finally, the lush North Shore is a playground for active travelers, with surfing and golf at Hanalei and Princeville, plus hiking and canoeing on the magnificent Nā Pali Coast. No visitor should leave Kaua'i without taking in the dramatic splendor of Waimea Canyon and the breathtaking views from Kōke'e State Park.

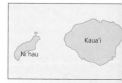

NI'IHAU LOCATOR MAP
See p173

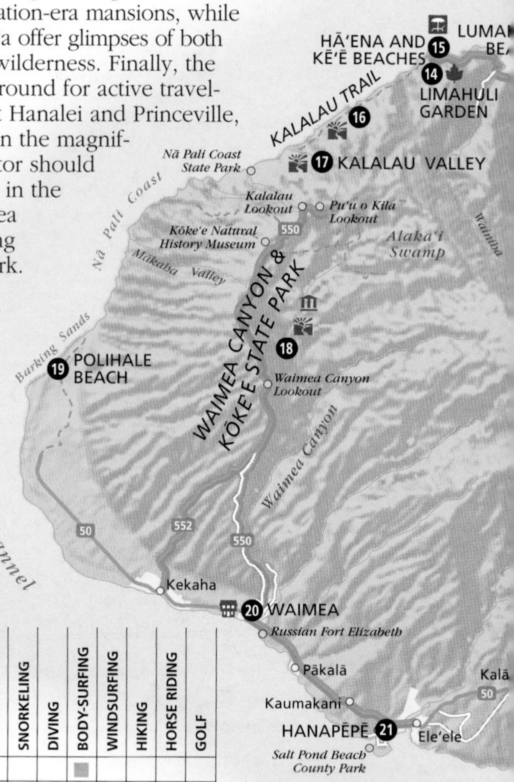

TOP RECREATIONAL AREAS

The places shown here have been selected for their recreational activities. Conditions vary depending on the weather and the time of year, so exercise caution and, if in doubt, stay out of the water or seek local advice.

	SWIMMING	SNORKELING	DIVING	BODY-SURFING	WINDSURFING	HIKING	HORSE RIDING	GOLF
ANAHOLA BAY	●			■				
'ANINI BEACH	●		●					
HANALEI BAY	●			■				
KALAPAKĪ BEACH	●	■		■	●			
KALIHIWAI BEACH	●			■				
KEĀLIA BEACH				■				
KĒ'Ē BEACH	●	■						
KŌKE'E STATE PARK						■		
LUMAHA'I BEACH						■		
LYDGATE STATE PARK	●	■						
NĀ PALI COAST STATE PARK		■				■		
PALI KE KUA (HIDEAWAYS) BEACH		■						
PO'IPŪ BEACH COUNTY PARK	●	■	●	■	●			■
PRINCEVILLE	●	■					●	■
PU'UPŌĀ BEACH	●	■						
SALT POND BEACH COUNTY PARK		■				●		
SECRET BEACH						■		
TUNNELS BEACH	●	■	●					

GETTING AROUND

Kaua'i's major highway is prevented from completing a loop around the island by the Nā Pali cliffs. Known as Kūhiō Highway (Hwy 56) north of Līhu'e, and Kaumuali'i Highway (Hwy 50) to the west, it is served by the regular, inexpensive Kaua'i Bus (large suitcases and backpacks not allowed). To explore the island in detail, however, rent a car at either Līhu'e or Princeville airport. You can drive anywhere in Kaua'i in three hours or less, so you can see the whole island from a single base.

Map labels:

HĀ'ENA AND KĒ'Ē BEACHES 15 · LUMA... BE... · LIMAHULI GARDEN 14 · KALALAU TRAIL 16 · KALALAU VALLEY 17 · Nā Pali Coast State Park · Kalalau Lookout · Pu'u o Kila Lookout · Kōke'e Natural History Museum 550 · Alaka'i Swamp · Mākaha Valley · WAIMEA CANYON & KŌKE'E STATE PARK · 18 · Waimea Canyon Lookout · Barking Sands · POLIHALE BEACH 19 · Kaulakahi Channel · 50 · 552 · 550 · Kekaha · WAIMEA 20 · Russian Fort Elizabeth · Pākalā · Kaumakani · HANAPĒPĒ 21 · Ele'ele · Salt Pond Beach County Park · Kalā · 50

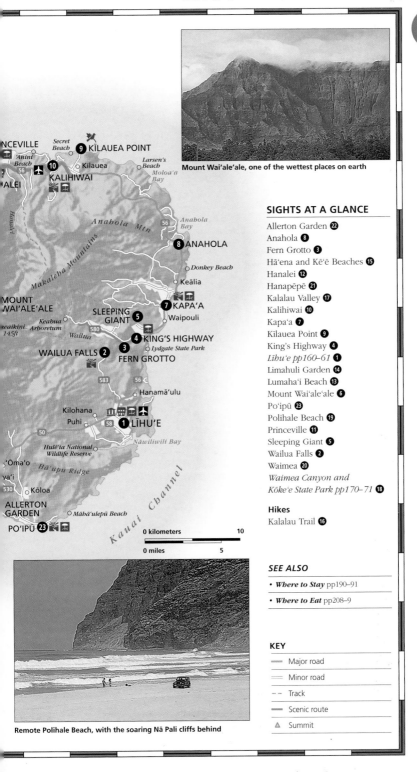

Mount Waiʻaleʻale, one of the wettest places on earth

NCEVILLE

Secret Beach

9 KĪLAUEA POINT 🚶

ʻAnini Beach

10 🏩

Kilauea

Larsen's Beach

Moloaʻa Bay

ʻALEI

KALIHIWAI 🏞🏖

Anaholo Mtn

56

Anahola Bay

8 ANAHOLA

Makaleha Mountains

Donkey Beach

Keālia

MOUNT WAIʻALEʻALE

waikini 145ft

Keahua Arboretum

SLEEPING GIANT 5

580

Wailua

7 KAPAʻA 🏖🏩

Waipouli

4 KINGʻS HIGHWAY 🚉

3

WAILUA FALLS 2 🏞

Lydgate State Park

FERN GROTTO

583

56

Hanamāʻulu

Kilohana

Puhi

🏛🏞🚉🏩 **1 LĪHUʻE**

50

58

Nāwiliwili Bay

Huleʻia National Wildlife Reserve

ʻŌmaʻo

Haʻupu Ridge

ʻya'i

530

Kōloa

Māhāʻulepū Beach

ALLERTON GARDEN

POʻIPŪ 23 🏖🏩

Kauai Channel

0 kilometers   10

0 miles   5

SIGHTS AT A GLANCE

SEE ALSO

• *Where to Stay* pp190–91

• *Where to Eat* pp208–9

KEY

——	Major road
══	Minor road
- -	Track
——	Scenic route
△	Summit

Remote Polihale Beach, with the soaring Nā Pali cliffs behind

Līhu'e ❶

Līhu'e is Kaua'i's administrative and business center, and site of the island's main air and sea ports. It was built in the mid-19th century to serve the Līhu'e Sugar Mill, whose rusting machinery still dominates the downtown area. Līhu'e's multi-ethnic heritage, which stems from plantation days, is reflected in some of the shops and restaurants here. Within a few miles of central Līhu'e lie several more attractive areas. The oceanfront district, now recovered from the hammering it took from Hurricane Iniki in 1992, is especially appealing. Though the Kaua'i Marriott Resort dominates Kalapakī Beach, visitors can also enjoy a safe swim or a surfing lesson.

Hamura Saimin Stand, an Oriental diner in central Līhu'e *(see p209)*

Exploring Līhu'e

The outskirts of town offer hidden delights. To the west, Hulē'ia Stream is a wildlife sanctuary, overlooked by a splendidly forbidding ridge of green mountains. To the east lies the barely distinct community of Hanamā'ulu, where a pleasant little beach, sadly too polluted for swimming, lines a sweeping crescent bay.

🏛 Kaua'i Museum

4428 Rice St. *Tel (808) 245-6931.* ⬤ *10am–5pm Mon–Sat.* ⬤ *Jan 1, Labor Day, Jul 4, Thanksgiving, Dec 25.* 🔲 🔳 *www.kauaimuseum.org*

This two-part museum relates the island's history. The Wilcox Building centers on a collection of traditional artifacts gathered by the missionary Wilcox family, including huge *koa*-wood bowls and *kāhili*, feathered standards once used as a sign of royalty in Hawai'i. The newer Rice Building tells *The Story of Kaua'i*, with displays ranging from ancient weapons to videos on geology. Dioramas show how the island might have looked before European contact, and the arrival of immigrants from around the world is chronicled, with an emphasis on the harsh conditions endured by early plantation workers. A gift shop sells books and crafts, and the museum has its own café.

🏚 Grove Farm Homestead

Nāwiliwili Rd. *Tel (808) 245-3202.* ⬤ *Mon, Wed & Thu.* ⬤ *public hols.* **Donation.** 🔳 *by appointment.*

No settlement existed on the site of modern Līhu'e until 1864, when George Wilcox, the son of early missionaries, established the Grove Farm Plantation. Hawai'i's sugar business was then in its first boom, and although water was scarce, Wilcox prospered by developing a network of irrigation channels that reached deep into the mountains.

He lived on until the 1930s, content with a humble cottage. It was his heirs who built the imposing mansion, paneled throughout in dark, heavy *koa*-wood, that now forms the centerpiece of the Grove Farm Homestead. As well as the rather formal house and cramped servants' quarters, the two-hour guided tour takes in Wilcox's lush and beautifully scented private orchard. Phone a week in advance for a place on the tour; you will not be let in without a reservation.

🏖 Kalapakī Beach

Off Wa'apā Road (Hwy 51), at Kaua'i Marriott Resort & Beach Club.

Līhu'e became Kaua'i's main port during the 1920s, when a new deepwater harbor was dredged in Nāwiliwili Bay. While the breakwaters and harbor installations appeal only to avid fishermen, the gently sloping white sands of Kalapakī Beach just to the east are highly inviting.

The safest beach in the area, it is one of the finest for family use on the entire island, and as such is home to the top-class Kaua'i Marriott Resort & Beach Club *(see p191)* and a handful of restaurants. Expert surfers swirl right out into the bay, but the inshore waters are sheltered enough for children. The western limit of the beach is marked by the mouth of Nāwiliwili Stream. On the far side, the palm-fringed lawns of Nāwiliwili Beach County Park are ideal for picnics.

🏚 Kilohana Plantation

3-2087 Kaumuali'i Hwy (Hwy 50), 1.5 miles (2.5 km) W of Līhu'e. *Tel (808) 245-5608.* ⬤ *9:30am–9:30pm daily.* 🔳 *ground floor.* *www.kilohanakauai.com*

The grand house known as Kilohana Plantation was, like Grove Farm Homestead, built

The shady *koa*-wood veranda at Grove Farm Homestead

Late 19th-century carriage used for tours at Kilohana Plantation

Wilcoxes. Dating from the 1930s, its resemblance to an English country estate makes it the perfect home for one of Kaua'i's most elegant restaurants (see p175), as well as a small mall of expensive craft shops and galleries. Hurricane Iniki cleared away many of the trees on the property so that the mansion now commands superb views of Kilohana mountain inland. Horse-drawn carriages tour the adjacent cane fields, and you can take longer wagon tours into the backcountry.

🎏 Menehune Fish Pond

Lookout Hulemalū Rd, 1.5 miles (2.5 km) S of Līhu'e. 🚫 to the public.

West of Nāwiliwili Harbor, a minor road ascends a small headland to enter an idyllic pastoral landscape that comes as a surprise so close to Līhu'e. Beneath a highway lookout, the tranquil Hulē'ia Stream makes a sharp right-angle turn. Ancient Hawaiians exploited this natural bend by constructing a 900-ft (275-m) dam of rounded boulders to create the Alakoko ("Rippling Blood") Fish Pond. Skilled fish farmers,

the Hawaiians used it to fatten mullet for the royal table; as the fish grew, they could no longer pass through the latticed sluices that had allowed them to enter the enclosure.

This ancient structure is more commonly referred to as the Menehune Fish Pond, its prehistoric stonemasonry being credited, as so often in Hawai'i, to the little *Menehune*. These mythical figures are described by popular legend as hairy dwarfs already hard at work in Hawai'i when the first Polynesian settlers arrived. Now privately owned, the fish pond can be seen only from afar.

Unless you rent a kayak, the same goes for the **Hulē'ia National Wildlife Refuge** just upstream, where former taro and rice terraces are set aside for the exclusive use of a raucously grateful population of waterbirds.

Wailua Falls ❷

Kaua'i Co. Mā'alo Road (Hwy 583), 5 miles (8 km) N of Līhu'e. 🚌 Līhu'e.

Sugarcane still grows in an unbroken swath north from central Līhu'e, as far as the south fork of the Wailua River. The one winding road through the fields, which branches left from the main highway a mile (1.5 km) north of Līhu'e, leads directly to the 80-ft (24-m) Wailua Falls.

From the roadside parking lot you can admire the white cascade as it tumbles from a sheer ledge. After heavy rain the river also bursts from a couple of natural tunnels hollowed into the rock wall below. Reaching the pool below the falls is difficult and dangerous because the hillside is all but vertical and very muddy. The intrepid will find a slippery path lined with knotted ropes five minutes' walk back down the road.

The twin cascade of Wailua Falls, seen from a roadside overlook

The ruins of Poli'ahu Heiau, a sacrificial temple on the King's Highway

beach. Only vestiges survive here of the mighty stone walls of the **Hikinaakalā Heiau** (the name means "Rising of the Sun"), where worshipers would greet the dawn. Across the highway farther inland, Kaua'i's largest temple, **Malae Heiau**, lies buried beneath a tree-covered mound.

North of the river, a short way up Kuamo'o Road (Hwy 580), **Holoholokū Heiau** was, by contrast, so small that it could be entered only on all fours. Even so, it was the site of Kaua'i's first human sacrifices. Farther up the road lies a pair of boulders known as the **Birthing Stones**; only chiefs whose mothers gave birth while wedged between them could ever rule Kaua'i. A mile (1.5 km) farther up Kuamo'o ("lizard") Ridge, on a flat promontory with wide views, the stone walls of **Poli'ahu Heiau** remain in place, guarded by swaying coconut palms.

Half a mile (800 m) more and the ground to the right drops away to swift 'Ōpaeka'a ("rolling shrimp") Stream, which tumbles over the broad **'Ōpaeka'a Falls**. It is a fine spectacle, but do not go closer than the roadside lookout.

Lydgate State Park
Leho Drive, off Kūhiō Hwy (Hwy 56), just S of Wailua River.

Fern Grotto ❸

Kaua'i Co. Wailua River.
Smith's Motor Boat Service, (808) 821-6895. Waipouli.
daily. www.smithskauai.com

Although a bridge makes it impossible to sail up the Wailua River from the ocean, a constant procession of pleasure barges sets out from a marina upstream for the 2-mile (3-km) excursion to the Fern Grotto. This large cave behind a fern-draped rock face is famous for its beauty. A paved path, lined with lush foliage, leads up to the grotto, where you may end up being serenaded with the *Hawaiian Wedding Song* – about three couples per day get married here. The hour-long narrated cruise up the longest navigable river in Hawai'i gives you a chance to enjoy some attractive scenery; the riverbanks are covered in palm-like pandanus plants and piri grass. There's a singalong on the return trip.

King's Highway ❹

Kaua'i Co. Waipouli.
KVB, Līhu'e, (808) 245-3971.

The Wailua Valley was the seat of power in ancient Kaua'i, and the nearby shoreline remains the island's main population center. A trail of sacred sites known as the King's Highway ran from the ocean to the remote peak of Mount Wai'ale'ale. It started just south of the Wailua River in what is now **Lydgate State Park**, a deservedly popular

Sleeping Giant ❺

Kaua'i Co. 1.5 miles (2.5 km) NW of Wailua. Waipouli.

The east shore's principal residential district nestles 3 miles (5 km) in from the ocean, behind the undulating ridge of Nounou Mountain.

Sleeping Giant ridge, its profile reminiscent of a reclining figure

This long, low hillock is more commonly known as Sleeping Giant, thanks to an outline resembling a huge human figure lying flat on its back.

Three distinct hiking trails climb from its east, west, and south sides. They are reached from Kūhiō Highway (Hwy 56), Kāmala Road (Hwy 581), and Kuamo'o Road (Hwy 580) respectively. They converge to follow the alarmingly narrow crest, arriving at a meadow-like clearing in the forest at the top. This prime picnic spot offers panoramic views up and down the coastline, as well as westward to the sequence of parallel ridges that stretch inland. You can continue up the giant's head from here, but be extremely careful; the ridge is very steep in places and prone to rock slides.

Mount Wai'ale'ale 6

Kaua'i Co.
11 miles (18 km) W of Wailua.

Within spitting distance of Kapa'a's sunny beaches lies one of the wettest places on earth – Mount Wai'ale'ale, or "overflowing water." An average of 440 in (1,100 cm) of rain each year cascades in huge waterfalls down its green-velvet walls. The summit, wreathed in almost perpetual mists, was the last call on the sacred King's Highway; the ancients would follow knife-edge ridges to reach a mountaintop *heiau* (temple).

These days, unless you take a helicopter tour, you can glimpse Wai'ale'ale only from below. Follow Kuamo'o Road (Hwy 580) past 'Ōpaeka'a Falls and the Keahua Forestry Arboretum, and if the clouds clear you will be confronted by astonishing views of a sheer, pleated cliff face. Dirt roads lead through the forest to its base, where the Wailua River thunders down from the 5,148-ft (1,570-m) peak. These roads are dangerous, if not impassable, after heavy rain.

1920s rain gauge once used on Mt. Wai'ale'ale

The curving expanse of Donkey Beach, popular with nudists and surfers

Kapa'a 7

Kaua'i Co. 8,200.
KVB, Līhu'e, (808) 245-3971.

Tourist development along Kaua'i's East Shore, also known as the Coconut Coast, is mostly concentrated into the 5-mile (8-km) coastal strip that stretches north of the Wailua River. Maps mark distinct communities at Wailua and Waipouli, but the only real town here is Kapa'a, farther north, home of the Coconut Festival (see p35). Most of the false-front buildings that line its wooden boardwalks now hold tourist-related businesses such as restaurants, souvenir stores, or equipment rental outlets, but Kapa'a still maintains the look of a late 19th-century plantation village. The fringe of sand at the ocean's edge is divided into a number of beach parks.

ENVIRONS: The first of the more appealing beaches north of Kapa'a is tucked out of sight half a mile (800 m) from the highway and is reached by a forest trail that drops to the right not far past mile marker 11. This uncrowded, pretty stretch of sand is known as **Donkey Beach**, thanks to the beasts of burden that used to work in the adjacent sugar fields and were turned loose to graze along the beach's edges in the evenings. In their absence, wildflowers have flourished. There are no trees to provide shade for sunbathers, many of whom take advantage of this remote spot to go entirely naked. The surf is generally too rough to allow swimming, but is a rendezvous for expert surfers.

Anahola 8

Kaua'i Co. 1,200.
KVB, Līhu'e, (808) 245-3971.

The small, scattered village of Anahola overlooks the sweeping, palm-fringed curve of Anahola Bay, an ancient surfing site. North of town, just inland of the highway, is the picturesque **Anahola Baptist Church**. Set against a beautiful mountain backdrop, the church makes a lovely photograph.

Nearby Anahola Beach is often relatively empty, despite its combination of beautiful setting, safe swimming, and convenient access. Reached by a spur road that loops down from Kūhiō Highway (Hwy 56) shortly after mile marker 13, the beach faces the most sheltered section of Anahola Bay. The area nearest the showers is reserved for family swimming, while the slightly more turbulent waters farther north are enjoyed by local surfers.

Hawaiian activists have sometimes staged protests on the beach, arguing that the state has failed to meet its obligation to provide native Hawaiians with affordable housing in the area. However, their campaigns have not been directed against tourists.

An inviting stretch of golden sand at secluded Secret Beach, near Kīlauea Point

Kīlauea Point ❾

Kaua'i Co. Kīlauea Road, off Kūhiō Highway (Hwy 56), 10 miles (16 km) NW of Anahola. 🚌 *Kīlauea.* ℹ️ *KVB, Līhu'e, (808) 245-3971.*

The Hawaiian name Kīlauea ("much spewing") applies not only to the southernmost volcano on Hawai'i Island but also to the northernmost spot on the Hawaiian archipelago, Kaua'i's Kīlauea Point. Here the name refers not to spouting lava, but rather to the raging waves that foam around the base of this rocky promontory.

Together with a couple of tiny offshore islets, the splendidly windswept cliff top has been set aside as the **Kīlauea Point National Wildlife Refuge**, a sanctuary for Pacific seabirds. Displays in the refuge's well-equipped visitor center enable amateur birdwatchers to pick out frigatebirds, Laysan albatrosses, and various tropic birds.

A short walk beyond the visitor center leads to the red and white **Kīlauea Lighthouse**, which marks the beginning of Kaua'i's North Shore. When erected in 1913, the lighthouse held the largest clamshell lens in the world, but that has now been supplanted by a much smaller and barely noticeable structure on its far side. As you approach the tip of the headland, extensive views open up to the west beyond Secret Beach and Princeville to the Nā Pali cliffs. The exposed oceanfront slopes to the east, meanwhile, are flecked with thousands of white seabirds and can be explored on ranger-led walking tours.

Environs: The most dramatic views of Kīlauea Lighthouse and, in winter especially, of the mighty waves that pound northern Kaua'i, are from the vast but little-visited shelf of glorious yellow sand known as **Secret Beach**. To reach it, turn right onto Kalihiwai Road, half a mile (800 m) west of the Kīlauea turn-off, then follow a red-dirt track that cuts away almost immediately to the right. From its far end, a narrow trail zigzags through the woods, coming out after ten minutes at a luscious tropical cove. Even in the summer, when the mile (1.5 km) of coarse sand at least doubles in width, the sea tends to be too rough for swimming.

HAWAII VISITORS BUREAU MARKER

KILAUEA LIGHTHOUSE

Colorful official marker for the lighthouse

However, it is worth walking the full length of the beach to see the white surf as it crashes against the black lava rocks that poke from the sand, and the glorious waterfall at the far end, nearest the lighthouse.

🦅 Kīlauea Point National Wildlife Refuge
Kīlauea Point. *Tel* (808) 828-1413. 🕙 *10am–4pm Mon–Fri.* 🔴 *Jan 1, Thanksgiving, Dec 25.* 📷 ♿

Kalihiwai ❿

Kaua'i Co. 👥 *450.* ℹ️ *KVB, Līhu'e, (808) 245-3971.*

From Kūhiō Highway (Highway 56), two successive turnings, a mile and a half (2.5 km) apart, are called Kalihiwai Road. The two parts of the road through this small settlement were connected until a tsunami washed away the bridge over the Kalihiwai River in 1957. The last few hundred yards of the eastern segment, just before the mouth of the river, run alongside the lovely **Kalihiwai Beach**. Shielded behind a grove of ironwood trees, this beach offers fine surfing and bodysurfing as well as swimming. Kūhiō Highway crosses the river about half a mile (800 m) back from the ocean; glance inland from the bridge at this point to spot the beautiful, wide **Kalihiwai Falls**.

Environs: The second (western) segment of Kalihiwai Road quickly dead-ends at the Kalihiwai River, with no beach on this side. However, an unmarked spur road to the left, halfway down this segment, leads to quiet **'Anini Beach**. Here, between 3 miles (5 km) of golden sand and the coral reef that lies 200 yds (180 m) offshore, shallow turquoise waters provide the safest swimming on Kaua'i's North Shore. There is also excellent snorkeling on the coral reef itself, as well as an idyllic campsite set among the trees. The large lawns on the inland side of the road host polo matches on summer Sunday afternoons, often with boisterous crowds cheering on the players.

The mouth of the Kalihiwai River with Kalihiwai Beach behind

The Princeville Hotel, set amid golf courses and ocean views

Princeville ⓫

Kaua'i Co. 1,250. ✕ 🏢
ℹ️ KVB, Līhu'e, (808) 245-3971.

The former sugar plantation and livestock ranch of Princeville, set on the rolling meadows of a headland above Hanalei Bay, was sold off in the 1960s to be developed as Kaua'i's most exclusive resort. Its centerpiece, the opulent **Princeville Hotel** *(see p191)*, occupies a prime site near the remains of an earthwork fort built by the German adventurer George Schäffer in 1816 *(see p172)*. Its long-range views of the North Shore mountains are now shared by two golf courses, as well as several more hotels, condominiums, vacation homes, and a small shopping mall.

Below the bluffs, Princeville boasts some delightful little beaches. The best of the bunch, **Pu'upoā Beach**, is reached by trails that drop from both the Princeville Hotel and the Hanalei Bay Resort next door. Its wide sands offer dramatic views across Hanalei Bay, as well as over the wetlands to the peaks that tower behind Hanalei *(see p166)*, and there's excellent family swimming in the shallow waters. Pu'upoā Beach stretches as far as the mouth of the Hanalei River, so rented kayaks can easily be paddled upstream. Princeville-based surfers and snorkelers flock to **Pali Ke Kua Beach**, also known as Hideaways Beach, by way of a trail down from the tennis courts of the Pali Ke Kua condominiums.

KAUA'I IN THE MOVIES

The fabulous scenery of Kaua'i has served as an exotic backdrop in countless Hollywood blockbusters, from a Caribbean paradise in *Islands in the Stream* (1977) to South America in *Raiders of the Lost Ark* (1981) and Vietnam in *Uncommon Valor* (1983). Ever since Esther Williams performed one of her trademark aquatic ballets in Hanalei Bay in *Pagan Love Song* (1950), the island has starred alongside the big screen's biggest names. Frank Sinatra's war-torn Pacific-island beach in *None but the Brave* (1965) was Pīla'a Beach, east of Kīlauea. Meanwhile, Elvis Presley's greatest box-office hit, *Blue Hawaii* (1961), climaxed with a gloriously kitsch wedding ceremony at the Coco Palms Resort. The remote Honopū Valley on the Nā Pali coast stood in as Skull Island in the 1977 remake of *King Kong* and, before Hurricane Iniki put an abrupt end to proceedings, much of *Jurassic Park* (1993) was shot in Hanapēpē Valley. Kaua'i is probably best remembered, however, for its role in the smash-hit Rodgers and Hammerstein musical *South Pacific* (1958). Of the movie's show-stopping songs, *Some Enchanted Evening* was filmed at Hanalei Bay, and, most famous of all, Mitzi Gaynor sang *I'm Gonna Wash That Man Right Out of My Hair* at Lumaha'i Beach.

Publicity poster of Elvis Presley in *Blue Hawaii*

Hanalei ⑫

Kaua'i Co. 🏠 500.
🚌 ℹ️ KVB, Līhu'e,
(808) 245-3971.

Only one spot in all the islands bears the name Hanalei, or "crescent bay." Nowhere deserves it more than the placid half-moon inlet, fringed with golden sand and cradled by soaring green cliffs, that lies just west of Princeville.

The taro fields of Hanalei Valley, seen from a highway overlook

The flat valley floor of the Hanalei River was in ancient times a prime area for growing taro. Later turned into a patchwork of rice paddies by Chinese settlers, it is once again dominated by taro, planted under the auspices of the **Hanalei National Wildlife Refuge** to re-create the preferred habitat of the state's increasingly endangered waterbirds. Crisscrossed by irrigation channels and scattered with inaccessible islands that poke from the mud, it is home to an ever-changing population of coots, herons, stilts, and transient migratory birds. The valley's lush, green landscape is best seen from a lookout on Kūhiō Highway (Hwy 56), just west of the Princeville turnoff.

The slender bridge across the Hanalei River is the first of a series of one-lane bridges that slow North Shore traffic to a virtual crawl, thereby helping to protect the region from the ravages of overdevelopment. The village of **Hanalei** on the far side is a relaxed place, still recognizably a plantation settlement but kept busy these days catering to the needs of a year-round community of surfers and Nā Pali adventurers.

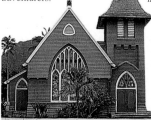

The striking facade of Wai'oli Hui'ia Church

A trio of awe-inspiring mountains forms a magnificent backdrop – Hīhīmanu to the east, Māmalahoa to the west, and, in the center, the sublime Nāmolokama, furrowed with over 20 waterfalls that combine to form Wai'oli Stream.

At first glance **Hanalei Bay** might look like an ideal harbor, but so many ships have come to grief on its submerged reefs that only shallow-draft pleasure yachts now use the old jetty on its eastern side. Conditions for swimmers using the 2-mile (3-km) strand east of the jetty depend on the state of the reef; although there are several attractive spots for sunbathing or camping, swimming is only really advisable from Waikoko Beach at the western end, beyond the mouth of the Wai'oli Stream. Expert surfers, untroubled by these issues, set off from Wai'oli Beach, or "Pinetrees Park," nearer the center of the bay, to practice their art amid the waves that break at the bay's entrance.

Hanalei's most visible relic of the past is the missionary complex, set on landscaped lawns west of the town center and backed by high, tree-clad mountains. The town's earliest Christian edifice, **Wai'oli Church**, was put up in 1841. Dwarfed beneath a tall, sloping roof, this large wooden structure now functions as a social hall, set back to the right of its successor, the 1912-vintage **Wai'oli Hui'ia Church**. With its vivid green shingles, shimmering stained glass, and gray-capped belfry, all nestled beneath a spreading palm tree, Wai'oli Hui'ia is without a doubt the loveliest building on Kaua'i. Tucked away behind it, the **Wai'oli Mission House** was home to several generations of two missionary families, including the Wilcoxes (see p160), whose descendants lived here until the late 1970s. Although some of the original furnishings have gone, period replacements provide a sense of 19th-century Hanalei.

🏛️ **Wai'oli Mission House**
Kūhiō Hwy (Hwy 56). **Tel** (808) 245-3202. 🕐 9am–3pm Tue, Thu & Sat. 🔴 public hols. **Donation**. ♿ ground floor only.

Lumaha'i Beach ⑬

Kaua'i Co. Off Kūhiō Highway (Hwy 56), 2 miles (3 km) W of Hanalei. 🚌 Hanalei.

Immediately beyond Hanalei Bay, a small roadside pull-off marks the top of a steep, muddy trail down to the spell-binding Lumaha'i Beach. Thanks to its appearance in the movie South Pacific (see p165), this has a reputation as the most romantic beach in all Hawai'i. Its golden sands always seem to hold at least one pair of lovers, but the beaches are long and broad enough to maintain the illusion of privacy. Except on very calm days, rolling in the surf is not a good idea.

The mountain peak of Bali Hai may have dominated the beach on screen, but that was due to technical trickery; in fact it's a tiny outcrop called Makana at the end of a ridge, 4 miles (6.5 km) farther west.

Limahuli Garden ⑭

Kaua'i Co. Kūhiō Hwy (Hwy 56), 6 miles (10 km) W of Hanalei. **Tel** (808) 826-1053. ☐ 9:30am–4pm Tue–Fri & Sun. ● Jan 1, Thanksgiving, Dec 25. 📷 📹 **www.**ntbg.org

The lush Limahuli Garden is located a quarter of a mile (400 m) before the end of Kūhiō Highway, in a steep, high valley. In ancient times, the Limahuli Valley was part of a self-sufficient *ahupua'a* (a wedge-shaped division of land running from mountain to sea). Since then, it has barely been occupied, with the exception of the notorious "Taylor Camp," an ocean-front commune that survived from 1969 to 1977 on land owned by Elizabeth Taylor's brother.

Part of the valley remains in sufficiently pristine condition to have been set aside as a botanical sanctuary, protecting both indigenous Hawaiian plants and species brought to the islands by early Polynesian settlers. The preserve is run by the National Tropical Botanical Garden, whose aim is to preserve the native species and increase their numbers.

Visitors can explore only a 17-acre portion that begins at the road and stretches inland,

Hibiscus at Limahuli Garden

supporting reconstructed ancient taro terraces that climb the hillside. A network of trails allows one to meander through a mixed forest of unusual trees, such as the Polynesian-introduced *kukui* or candlenut, once prized for its oil, and the native *'ōhi'a 'ai* or mountain apple. The higher slopes command wonderful views of the coastline below, as well as giving glimpses of the jagged Nā Pali cliffs to the west. Inland, the strangely eroded mountains loom above slender Limahuli Stream, overshadowing the off-limits Limahuli Preserve.

Hā'ena and Kē'ē Beaches ⑮

Kaua'i Co. Off Kūhiō Hwy (Hwy 56), 7 miles (11 km) W of Hanalei.

Two separate beach parks with similar names are located near the end of the highway along the North Shore. The first one, **Hā'ena Beach County Park**, offers a pleasant campsite in a coconut grove where the shoreline is too exposed for safe swimming. Ten minutes' walk east from here is **Tunnels Beach**, whose extensive reef is one of Kaua'i's most popular snorkeling sites. The name refers not to the beautiful coral formations but to the tubular waves that lure the surfers here in winter.

Immediately west of here, the second park, **Hā'ena State Park**, is mostly inaccessible to

Snorkeling at Tunnels Beach

casual visitors, having been set aside more to spare this section of coast from development than to make it available for public use. **Kē'ē Beach**, at the end of the road but still within the state park, is one of the most beautiful of all the North Shore beaches, its glowing yellow sands all but engulfed by rampant tropical vegetation. The turquoise inshore lagoon provides an irresistible cooling-off spot for hikers back from the Kalalau Trail *(see pp168–9)*, as well as a much-loved swimming and snorkeling site. However, the often-turbulent waters around and beyond the reef hold perils for the unwary.

Many legends attach themselves to this remote beach, including one that identifies it as the original birthplace of *hula*. Pele the volcano goddess *(see p24)* is said to have been enticed here in a dream by the sweet music of the young Kauaian warrior Lohi'au. Upon waking, she sent her sister Hi'iaka to bring Lohi'au to her, but these two promptly fell in love. Beneath the undergrowth, near the start of the Kalalau Trail, crumbling walls mark the site of Lohi'au's home, while the raised headland just west of the beach holds the remains of Hawai'i's first *hālau hula* (*hula* school). Here, Hi'iaka passed on the art of *hula* to eager devotees from all the islands.

Limahuli Garden's taro terraces, where the crop is grown in the traditional way

Kalalau Trail ⑯

The precipitous cliffs of the Nā Pali Coast make it impossible for the road to continue west of Kē'ē Beach, but hardy hikers can follow the narrow Kalalau Trail 11 more miles (18 km) to isolated Kalalau Valley. One of the most dramatic hikes in the world, it threads its way through a landscape of almost primeval vastness and splendor. While this is not an expedition to undertake lightly, a half-day round trip to Hanakāpī'ai Valley is within most capabilities and provides an unforgettable wilderness experience. The trail gets progressively drier as it heads west, so the initial stretches are the muddiest, with the densest vegetation. Negotiating this tangled forest of *hala* (pandanus) trees often requires scrambling over rock falls, or picking your way among slippery tree roots.

Start of the trail ①
The trail climbs steeply from the trailhead at the end of Kūhiō Highway, affording spectacular views of the rugged coastline.

Makana Peak ②
On special occasions, the ancient Hawaiians tossed flaming logs into the night sky from this peak. Crowds would gather in boats on the sea below to watch this early form of fireworks.

Ke Ahu A Laka ③
This was once Hawai'i's most celebrated *hālau hula* (*hula* school), where students could spend several years learning their art. The ancient temple nearby is thought to have been used for graduation ceremonies.

Hanakāpī'ai Valley ④
In summer, a pristine sandy beach replaces the pebbles found in winter at the mouth of Hanakāpī'ai Valley. Swimming and wading are not recommended due to dangerous rip currents.

End of the trail ⑨
For the last 5 miles (8 km), the trail clings perilously to a sandstone cliff that turns to dust at every step, thanks to the goats that have eaten the vegetation that should bind the soil together. The view of Kalalau Valley is the reward for the long hike.

TIPS FOR HIKERS

There is no food or safe drinking water along the trail. To camp in Hanakāpī'ai, Hanakoa, or Kalalau valleys, you must obtain permission in advance from the State Parks office, 3060 'Eīwa St, Līhu'e, HI 96766, (808) 274-3444. It is also possible to enjoy the North Shore coastline by boat or helicopter. For a full list of tour operators, contact the KVB, Līhu'e, (808) 245-3971.

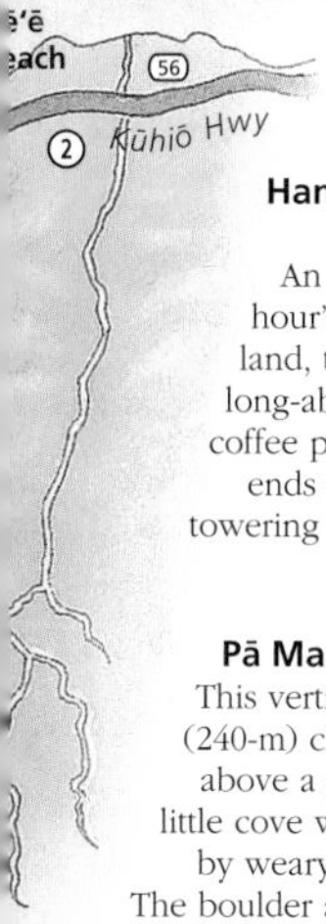

Hanakāpī'ai Falls 5
An energetic hour's hike inland, through a long-abandoned coffee plantation, ends up at this towering waterfall.

Pā Ma Wa'a 6
This vertical 800-ft (240-m) cliff stands above a protected little cove welcomed by weary canoers. The boulder at the top marks the highest point on the Kalalau Trail.

Hanging Valleys 7
Between Hanakāpī'ai and Hanakoa, the trail dips into a number of "hanging valleys," where the streams have yet to ut their way down to sea level.

nakoa Valley 8
campsite here is set amid ruins of ancient taro terraces p125), with no access to the The mighty 2,000-ft (600-m) cade at the head of the valley ist 600 yds (550 m) away – hort but muddy climb.

0 kilometers 2
0 miles 1

EY
Hiking trail
Road
Vista

Ko'olau the Leper (far right) with his family

Kalalau Valley 17

Kaua'i Co. ℹ *KVB, Līhu'e, (808) 245-3971.*

Unless you persevere through the last difficult stretch of the Kalalau Trail, the majestic amphitheater of Kalalau Valley can be seen only from afar. Most visitors view it by boat or helicopter tour, or from the two lookouts at the end of Kōke'e Road *(see pp170–71)*.

For well over 1,000 years this isolated valley was home to a thriving community of taro farmers. In the years after European contact, however, disease and the lure of the city thinned out the population, the last permanent inhabitant leaving in 1919. Later, Kalalau became a cattle ranch and was then briefly colonized by hippies who sneaked in during the 1960s. Attempts to evict them resulted in the creation of the Nā Pali Coast State Park, which now controls access and limits places at Kalalau's idyllic camp site.

The valley's pinnacles made a perfect refuge for the infamous Ko'olau the Leper, as immortalized by Jack London *(see p25)* in his story of the same name. Ko'olau, a cowboy from Waimea, fled into the valley in the 1890s rather than face exile and death at Moloka'i's dreaded leper colony *(see pp100–1)*. Ko'olau's wife eventually left Kalalau alone, after both her husband and son had died of leprosy.

BIRDS OF KAUA'I

The tiny *'anianiau*

The innermost recesses of the Nā Pali valleys, and the bogs and ravines that stretch across the top of Kaua'i, are cloaked with dense rain forest. This unique environment is the last natural sanctuary for the island's native flora and fauna. Before human contact with Hawai'i, only a handful of bird species lived here – probably descendants of wind-blown stragglers lucky to find dry land. Encountering endemic plants with curved flowers, many birds developed curved bills for sipping nectar; others acquired short, strong beaks for crushing seeds and nuts. Forest birds extinct elsewhere in the state still cling to life in the *'ōhi'a* forests of the Alaka'i Swamp. Honeycreepers abound here, the most common being the bright-red *'i'iwi*, with its black wings and salmon-colored sickle-shaped bill; the *'apapane*, similarly colored but with a short, black bill; and the diminutive yellow *'anianiau*. Also conspicuous is the gregarious rust-colored *'elepaio*, which follows hikers through the forest.

Red-billed tropicbird

Most prominent on the Nā Pali Coast are the soaring tropicbirds, while in the drier Kōke'e State Park, honking *nēnē* appear at the lookouts together with Kaua'i's most ubiquitous bird, the *moa*, or red jungle fowl – a showy wild chicken.

***Moa*, red jungle fowl**

Waimea Canyon and Kōke'e State Park ⑱

Waimea Canyon, known as the "Grand Canyon of the Pacific," was created by earth movements that almost split Kaua'i in two. Over time, heavy rains have helped form a gorge 3,000 ft (915 m) deep that is still being eroded today, as occasional landslides slash away layers of rich green vegetation and the Waimea River carries the red mud into the ocean. Most visitors see the canyon from the lookouts dotted along the rim, along Kōke'e Road, but hiking trails enable the more adventurous to explore in greater depth. At the north end of Waimea Canyon is Kōke'e State Park, laced through by more hiking trails and including the most accessible part of the daunting Alaka'i Swamp. The road finally ends at two stunning overlooks 4,000 ft (1,220 m) above the Nā Pali Coast.

View from Waimea Canyon Drive showing eroded, exposed earth

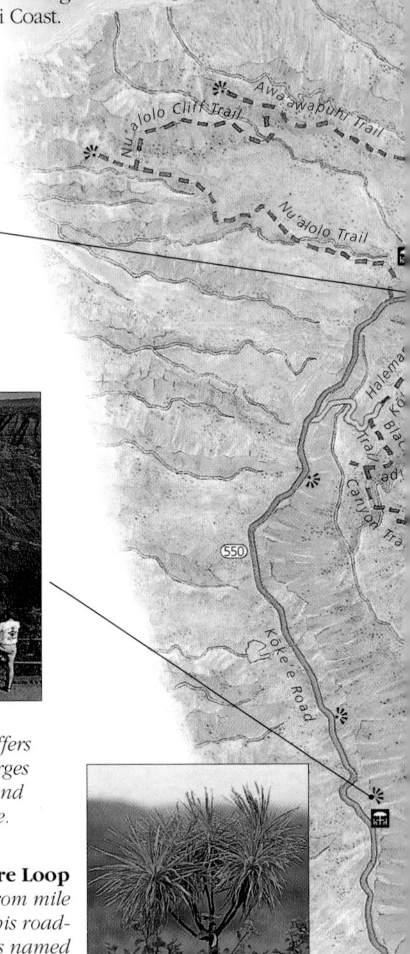

Kōke'e Natural History Museum
Displays on wildlife and local history are featured in the museum, while the shop has hiking information, books, and trail maps.

★ Waimea Canyon Lookout
Despite being the lowest of the lookouts, this offers the definitive canyon views: north into the gorges cut by the Waiahulu and Po'omau streams, and south to Waimea itself on the distant shoreline.

STAR SIGHTS

- ★ Alaka'i Swamp
- ★ Pu'u O Kila Lookout
- ★ Waimea Canyon Lookout

Iliau Nature Loop
Reached from mile marker 9, this roadside trail is named after the iliau plant, which is endemic to this part of Kaua'i. Native plants along the loop are labeled.

WAIMEA

Kalalau Trail
(see pp142–3)

Kalalau Lookout

VISITORS' CHECKLIST

Kauaʻi Co. Kōkeʻe Rd (Hwy 550).
Tel Kauaʻi Division of State Parks,
(808) 274-3444. **Kōkeʻe State
Park** ☐ daily. **Kōkeʻe Museum
Tel** (808) 335-9975. **Donation.**
☐ 10am–4pm daily. ☐ **Kōkeʻe
Lodge Tel** (808) 335-6061. ☐
Cabins available for rent.

★ **Puʻu O Kila Lookout**
*The main body of the magnificent Kalalau Valley
(see p169) opens out at this spectacular lookout.
The shore is inaccessible from here.*

Pihea Trail switchbacks down for 4
miles (6.5 km) to emerge at an exposed
headland high above Nuʻalolo Valley.

Alakaʻi Swamp Trail is a makeshift
boardwalk leading to the cliffs above
Wainiha Valley, with views to Hanalei.

KILOHANA
LOOKOUT

Kaluapuhi Trail

Valley Trail

Ditch Trail

Mōhini Trail

Kohua Ridge Trail

Koaʻe Canyon Trail

Waimea Canyon Trail

★ **Alakaʻi Swamp**
*This bowl-like depression is drenched by up to 500
in (1,270 cm) of rain per year. Much of that water
goes to feed Kauaʻi's myriad waterfalls, but the rest
is trapped by an underlying layer of nonporous
volcanic rock. Part rain forest, part mist-draped
bog, the Alakaʻi Swamp boasts some of Hawaiʻi's
rarest birds, such as the ʻiʻiwi, or honeycreeper.*

Kukui Trail
*An extension of the
Iliau Nature Loop,
this trail heads
sharply down into
the canyon as far as
the Waimea River
– a relatively easy,
rewarding trip.*

NA ALA HELE
Hawaiʻi Trail & Access System
STATE OF HAWAII
DEPARTMENT OF LAND & NATURAL RESOURCES
DIVISION OF FORESTRY & WILDLIFE

KUKUI TRAIL
↑ START →

WAIMEA

0 kilometers ——————— 2
0 miles ——————— 1

KEY

▬▬▬	Major road
═══	Minor road
═══	Dirt or four-wheel-drive road
▪ ▪ ▪	Hiking trail
~~	River
☙	Vista
⛏	Picnic area

Polihale Beach ⑲

Kaua'i Co. 5 miles (8 km) beyond the end of Kaumuali'i Hwy (Hwy 50).

The westernmost region of Kaua'i, shielded from the ocean winds in the rain shadow of the central mountains, is characterized by long, flat expanses of sand. A sizable chunk has been taken over by the US military, whose sophisticated installations include systems that would give early warning of another attack on Pearl Harbor.

Skirt the security fences by following the dirt roads inland, and 15 miles (24 km) northwest of Waimea you come to the vast expanse of Polihale Beach. The surf is far too ferocious for swimming, but it's a wonderful place for a walk, with the cliffs of the Nā Pali Coast rising to the north. Head west from the end of the road and you'll reach the dunes known as the **Barking Sands**, whose hollow grains are said to groan and howl when disturbed by wind or a heavy footfall.

Waimea ⑳

Kaua'i Co. 🏠 1,900. 🚍 ℹ️ KVB, Lῑhu'e, (808) 245-3971.

Waimea is among Kaua'i's more historic towns. It was here in 1778 that the crewmen of Captain Cook's third Pacific voyage – after pausing to shoot a Hawaiian – became the first Europeans to set foot on Hawaiian soil. Cook stated that "I never saw Indians so much astonished," while he himself was amazed to find the natives speaking a Polynesian language similar to those in the far-off South Seas. A statue of Cook graces the town center.

However, perhaps mindful of the mixed results of Cook's visit, including rampant venereal disease, the beach where he landed is named not in his honor but after Lucy Wright, Waimea's first native teacher. Situated west of the Waimea ("reddish water") River, it is

made up largely of mud washed down from Waimea Canyon. A plaque marks the site of Cook's first landfall.

Just across Waimea River, a headland holds what's left of **Russian Fort Elizabeth**. This star-shaped edifice was built by an adventurer, George Schäffer, in 1816. A German doctor, pretending to be a naturalist but working as a spy for the Russian-American Company, he had gained the confidence of Kaumuali'i, the chief of Kaua'i, and decided to double-cross his employers. He and Kaumuali'i hatched a plot to conquer the archipelago and divide it between the Tsar of Russia and the chief. Within a year, fooled into thinking that the US and Russia were at war, Schäffer fled the islands. His fort served the government for 50 more years but is now dilapidated.

Statue of Captain Cook in Waimea

Hanapēpē ㉑

Kaua'i Co. 🏠 1,400. 🚍 ℹ️ KVB, Lῑhu'e, (808) 245-3971.

Halfway between Waimea and Po'ipū, Hanapēpē makes an intriguing detour off Kaumuali'i Highway (Hwy 50). Although taro was once grown in the valley, the village owes its late 19th-century look to the Chinese laborers who farmed rice here after serving out their contracts on sugar plantations.

Later Hanapēpē was all but abandoned, but several of its timber-frame buildings have now reopened as galleries and craft shops, and there are several attractive restaurants.

Allerton Garden ㉒

Kaua'i Co. **Tel** (808) 332-7324. ◯ daily. ⬤ public hols. 📷 ♿ with prior notification. 🎫 by appointment, at visitor center across from Spouting Horn parking lot, Lāwa'i Road, Po'ipū. **www**.ntbg.org

Lāwa'i Valley stretches back from the pretty little cove of Lāwa'i Kai, 2 miles (3 km) west of Po'ipū. Occupied in antiquity by taro farmers and later used by Chinese immigrants to grow rice, the valley became Queen Emma's favorite retreat in the 1870s. In the 1930s, it was bought by the Allertons, a Chicago banking family, and a plot near the sea was exquisitely landscaped to create Allerton Garden.

Bequeathed to the National Tropical Botanical Garden by the last of the Allertons in 1987, the valley was devastated by Hurricane Iniki in 1992. Both the Allertons' oceanfront home and Queen Emma's cottage have been fully restored, and the Allerton Garden is once more a showpiece. Unlike its counterpart at Limahuli (see p167), it aims to delight the eye rather than concentrate on native plants.

Visitors are transported from the visitor center near Po'ipū to the otherwise inaccessible

The pool and pavilion of the Diana Fountain at Allerton Garden

site in low-roofed, open-sided vintage limousines known as Hilo sampans, and from there tour the garden on foot. The Allertons conceived the design as a series of separate "rooms," and each section, such as the serene Diana Fountain or the Italianate Art Deco Mermaid Fountain, has its own character. The plants are the real stars, however, from heliconias and bromeliads to assorted tropical fruits in the orchards. Species familiar as house plants in chillier climes run riot, while graceful palms line the placid stream that glides through the heart of the valley.

Serious botanists will appreciate the chance to see rare species in the nursery, including *Kanaloa kahoolawensis*, a woody shrub whose only two known wild specimens were first identified on Kahoʻolawe *(see p121)* during the 1980s. Prior reservation is required for the tour, and children under five are not admitted. A visitor center, surrounded by 10 acres of gardens near the parking lot, was opened in 1997.

Poʻipū ㉓

Kauaʻi Co. 🏠 *1,000.* 🚌 *2 a day.* ℹ️ *KVB, Līhuʻe, (808) 245-3971.*

Sprawling to either side of the mouth of the Waikomo Stream, at the southern tip of Kauaʻi, Poʻipū remains the island's most popular beach

Spouting Horn sending up a jet of water

resort. In 1992, Hurricane Iniki ripped the roofs off its plush oceanfront hotels and filled their lobbies with sand and ruined cars. Give or take the odd derelict property, Poʻipū is now back to normal: a strip of hotels, condos, and restaurants.

The prime spot in the center of the beach is **Poʻipū Beach Park**, complete with vigilant lifeguards and a kids' playground. There's safe swimming directly offshore, and great snorkeling around the rocks at its western end. To the east, **Brennecke's Beach** is more of a haunt for young surfers, while farther along, beyond Makahūʻena Point, the shoreline becomes a wilderness of sand dunes. The fossilized

bones of long-extinct flightless birds known as Māhāʻulepū have been found in this area, and several native plant species survive here and nowhere else.

Environs: Poʻipū itself is a modern creation, but the rudimentary jetty at the mouth of Waikomo Stream has been in use since the mid-19th century. Known as Kōloa Landing, it was built to serve Hawaiʻi's first sugarcane plantation, established 2 miles (3 km) inland at **Kōloa** in 1835. Kōloa now plays second fiddle to Poʻipū, but with its wooden boardwalks and false-fronted stores, it's a pleasant place for a stroll. A huge sugar mill dominates the area a mile (1.5 km) east of town. Built in 1913, it finally shut down in 1996.

The coastal road west of Poʻipū ends after only a mile (1.5 km) at **Spouting Horn**, a natural blow-hole in a ledge of black lava a few steps back from the sea. The waves that break against the rock are channeled underground and then forced up in fountains of white spume that can reach a height of 50 ft (15 m) before raining down onto the usual crowd of spectators. It is very dangerous to approach closer than the roadside lookout.

NIʻIHAU, THE "FORBIDDEN ISLAND"

Lying 15 miles (24 km) southwest of Kauaʻi, but just visible from the coast at Waimea, Niʻihau is the smallest populated island in the chain, with 250 inhabitants. Owned by the Robinson family – descendants of Elizabeth Sinclair, who paid Kamehameha V $10,000 for the island in 1864 – it is little affected by tourism. You can visit only by a costly helicopter tour that avoids the inhabited areas *(see p243)*. It has no hotel, airport, or cars.

Although Niʻihau's original inhabitants were furious at the sale of their homeland to an outsider, the isolation has since turned the island into the last stronghold of Hawaiian culture – Hawaiian is still the first language here. When not tending cattle for the Niʻihau Ranch, locals support themselves with fishing, farming, and threading necklaces of the delicate *pūpū* (shells) that wash up on the beaches.

With annual rainfall of just 12 in (300 mm) Niʻihau is able to support only minimal agriculture. The only town, Puʻuwai ("heart"), is on the west coast, a grid of dirt roads dotted with bungalows and colorful gardens.

Niʻihau's west coast and the tiny town of Puʻuwai

TRAVELERS' NEEDS

WHERE TO STAY

From thousand-room, oceanfront mega-resorts to a treehouse for two in Hawai'i Island's Waipi'o Valley, the accommodation possibilities in Hawai'i are as numerous as they are diverse. The price range, too, is vast. As the beach is the main attraction for most visitors, the hotels closest to the ocean are considered most desirable and are usually the most pricey. Air-conditioning is

Bellhop at Mauna Lani

standard, though some smaller and older properties provide ceiling fans instead. In addition to resort hotels, there are many dozens of smaller hotels, condominiums, inns, and bed & breakfasts, all with lower rates. Many of the inns and B&Bs are charming and distinctive and stress personalized service; some, like the Old Wailuku Inn at Ulupono on Maui, are historic properties.

CHAIN AND BOUTIQUE HOTELS

Most of Hawai'i's large resort hotels are run by well-known chains such as **Hilton**, **Hyatt**, and **Sheraton**. Some are so self-contained and offer such a variety of activities that many visitors choose never to leave the property. If you prefer elegance and gracious service, however, head for gems like the Halekūlani in Waikīkī *(see p180)* or Maui's Four Seasons Resort *(see p187)*.

Less expensive options include local chains such as **Aston Hotels**, **Outrigger Hotels Hawai'i**, and **Castle Resorts**, as well as smaller, individual establishments that stress service over amenities. The latter, known as "boutique" hotels, are popular with inter-island travelers.

CONDOMINIUMS

A condominium unit or "condo" – an apartment, really – is an ideal choice for a family or travelers who would prefer to spend their money

on sightseeing and activities rather than on accommodations and dining. On O'ahu, they are mostly in high-rise buildings *mauka* (inland) of Waikīkī. On the neighboring islands, they are generally in low-rise complexes often located on or near the beach.

Condos range in size from studios to three-bedroom units suitable for up to eight adults or a family. They have kitchens and are stocked with everything from china to beach towels. Most condo units are privately owned and may be booked directly, through companies such as **Sunquest Vacations** on Hawai'i Island, and **Destination Resorts Hawai'i** on Maui. Condos in smaller complexes can be booked through the building's resident manager. Housekeeping service varies, but is normally provided every three or four days.

Twist Lounge, Sheraton Waikīkī *(see p180)*

INNS AND B&BS

Hawai'i's few inns are worth seeking out as an alternative to the big hotels. Because they are small and do not offer the amenities of the resorts, their staff pride themselves on service and attention to detail. Maui's Lahaina Inn, a restored Victorian-era masterpiece, is a stunning example *(see p186)*.

Nowadays there are hundreds of B&Bs (bed & breakfasts) all over Hawai'i. Many are just a room in someone's home; others are charming cottages. If a B&B suits your needs, there are two reservation services you can use, **Hawai'i's Best Bed & Breakfasts**, which represents the top 100 in the state, and **All Islands Bed & Breakfast**.

CAMPING AND HOSTELS

Campsites range in setting from beachfront park to volcanic crater. All county and state parks require permits, available for a small fee from **County Departments of Parks and Recreation** or the **State Department of Land and Natural Resources**. Some parks have basic cabins, which are inexpensive, but usually

Aston Waimea Plantation Cottages *(see p191)*

◁ Vacationers enjoying the sea and sun at one of Hawai'i's golden sand beaches

Idyllic seaside camp site at 'Anini Beach on Kaua'i's North Shore

booked months in advance, especially on weekends. The main islands also have hostels, with dormitory accommodations and some private rooms. Contact the Hawai'i Visitors and Convention Bureau for more information (see p235).

PRICES AND BOOKING

Hawai'i has accommodations to match every desire and wallet. Prices are highest from December to April, and lowest in May, June, September, and October. One of the more economical options is to stay in a condo. A one-bedroom unit, which can easily fit a family of four, costs between $150 and $250 per night. Some inns and B&Bs have double rooms for under $100 a night.

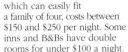
Cabin in Haleakalā National Park

It is simplest to book accommodations through your travel agent. The Hawai'i Visitors and Convention Bureau can help, as can resort and B&B reservation services. You can book directly over the Internet; check for good deals and packages. Most accommodations' phone numbers are toll-free in the US.

Oceanfront bungalow at the Four Seasons Resort Hualalai (see p189)

HIDDEN EXTRAS

All accommodations are subject to a combined sales and room tax of 11.42 percent. Most places allow children to share with parents at no extra charge, but check beforehand. Phone calls and faxes from hotel rooms are more expensive than normal rates, and many hotels in Honolulu charge a daily rate for parking. Extra costs can include things like towel "rental" and items from your minibar. To avoid surprises at checkout, ask beforehand. Tipping is not mandatory, but average tips for staff are as follows: $2–3 a day for housekeepers; $1–2 for bellmen and parking attendants.

VISITORS WITH DISABILITIES

All hotels and many smaller properties have at least some rooms with disabled access; many ensure access to public areas as well. The Disability and Communication Access Board website (see p237) provides an up-to-date list of the most accessible hotels.

TRAVELING WITH CHILDREN

Families with children should choose a large resort with children's activities, or a condo. Most of the hotels with activities charge for the care, but some of the top hotels offer a fantastic service at no additional charge.

DIRECTORY

HOTEL CHAINS

Hilton Hotels
Tel (800) 445-8667.
www.hilton.com

Hyatt Hotels & Resorts
Tel (800) 233-1234.
www.hyatt.com

Castle Resorts
Tel (800) 367-5004.
www.castleresorts.com

Outrigger Hotels Hawai'i
Tel (800) 688-7444.
www.outrigger.com

Aston Hotels
Tel (877) 997-6667.
www.astonhotels.com

Sheraton Hotels & Resorts
Tel (800) 325-3535.
www.sheraton.com

CONDOMINIUM RESERVATIONS

Destination Resorts Hawai'i
Tel (866) 384-1365.
www.drhmaui.com

Sunquest Vacations
Tel (800) 367-5168.
www.sunquest-hawaii.com

BED & BREAKFAST BOOKING SERVICES

All Islands Bed & Breakfast
Tel (800) 542-0344.
www.all-islands.com

Hawai'i's Best Bed & Breakfasts
Tel (800) 262-9912.
www.bestbnb.com

CAMPING

County Departments of Parks and Recreation
Hawai'i Co. *Tel (808) 961-8311.*
www.hawaii-county.com
Honolulu Co. *Tel (808) 523-4525.*
www.co.honolulu.hi.us/parks
Kaua'i Co. *Tel (808) 241-4460.*
www.kauai.gov
Maui Co. *Tel (808) 270-7230.*
www.co.maui.hi.us/parks

State Department of Land and Natural Resources
Tel (808) 587-0300.
www.hawaii.gov/dlnr

Choosing a Hotel

The hotels in this guide have been selected across a wide price range for their good value, facilities, and location. These listings highlight some of the factors that may influence your choice. Entries are listed by island, beginning with Honolulu and Waikiki. For information on restaurants in the area, see pages 196–209.

PRICE CATEGORIES
For a standard double room per night in high season, with all unavoidable extra charges including service and tax.
$ under $100
$$ $100-$200
$$$ $200-$300
$$$$ $300-$450
$$$$$ over $450

HONOLULU AND WAIKĪKĪ

WAIKĪKĪ Aston Waikīkī Joy Hotel $$

320 Lewers St, 96815 **Tel** (808) 923-2300 **Fax** (808) 924-4010 **Rooms** 47   **Map** 4 D4

One of the smaller boutique hotels, this has pleasant rooms and interesting extras, including Jacuzzis, state-of-the-art stereo systems, and soundproofing. Complimentary continental breakfast is served on the tropical veranda off the lobby. It is within walking distance of Waikīkī Beach, shopping, dining, and activities. **www.astonhotels.com**

WAIKĪKĪ Aston Waikīkī Sunset $$

229 Paoakalani Ave, 96815 **Tel** (808) 922-0511 **Fax** (808) 923-8580 **Rooms** 435   **Map** 4 F4

Just a block from the beach and two from the zoo, this all-suite hotel has a pool, a sauna, and a tennis court. Dining and shopping are a step away. Decorated in tropical style, the one- and two-bedroom suites have kitchens and private *lānai* (verandas) with views of the ocean, mountains, or Diamond Head. **www.waikikisunset.com**

WAIKĪKĪ The Breakers Hotel $$

250 Beach Wlk, 96815 **Tel** (808) 923-3181 **Fax** (808) 923-7174 **Rooms** 64   **Map** 4 D4

A 1950s-vintage, Hawaiian-style oasis amid towering neighbors, this hotel prides itself on real Hawaiian hospitality. A patio with tropical flowers surrounds the pool, which has a bar and grill right next to it. Every room overlooks the shady courtyard and has a kitchenette, air-conditioning, television, and telephone. **www.breakers-hawaii.com**

WAIKĪKĪ Diamond Head Bed & Breakfast $$

3240 Noela Dr **Tel** (808) 923-3360 **Fax** (808) 923-3360 **Rooms** 3   **Map** 4 F5

On the side of Kapi'olani Park *(see pp72–3)* farthest from Waikīkī, Joanne Trotter has been welcoming guests into her home for two decades. Her tasteful house, with its big *lānai* (veranda), is filled with heirlooms. One room features a carved bed that once belonged to a Hawaiian princess. Breakfast is included. **www.diamondheadbnb.com**

WAIKĪKĪ Ewa Hotel Waikīkī $$

2555 Cartwright Rd, 96815 **Tel** (808) 922-1677 **Fax** (808) 922-8538 **Rooms** 92   **Map** 4 F5

Tucked between Kalākaua and Kūhiō Avenues, the attractions here are a check-in time of 2pm (the usual is 3pm), particularly good kitchen facilities in many rooms, and low rates. One block from the beach, it is as close to Kapi'olani Park *(see pp72–3)* as you can get. **www.ewahotel.com**

WAIKĪKĪ Queen Kapi'olani Hotel $$

150 Kapahulu Ave, 96815 **Tel** (808) 922-1941 **Fax** (808) 922-2694 **Rooms** 315   **Map** 4 F5

Overlooking Kapi'olani Park *(see pp72–3)* and Diamond Head, this simple high-rise is good value. Named for the wife of Hawai'i's last king, it has an ambience that recalls the grandeur of her era. As well as being across the street from Kapi'olani Park, it is a short walk to the beach and close to other major attractions. **www.queenkapiolani.com**

WAIKĪKĪ Ramada Plaza Waikīkī $$

1830 Ala Moana Blvd, 96815 **Tel** (808) 955-1111 **Fax** (808) 947-1799 **Rooms** 199   **Map** 3 B4

This 17-story hotel is at the gateway to Waikīkī, two blocks from the beach. Rooms have telephones with voicemail. A pool and sundeck, complimentary fitness equipment, laundry facilities, business services, and a gift shop are all on site. The China Buffet Restaurant offers bountiful, affordable Asian fare. **www.ramadaplazawaikiki.com**

WAIKĪKĪ Royal Garden at Waikīkī $$

440 Olohāna St, 96815 **Tel** (808) 943-0202 **Fax** (808) 945-7407 **Rooms** 220   **Map** 4 D4

This boutique hotel is a luxurious breath of fresh air. Located on a peaceful, tree-lined street, a half block from the Ala Wai Canal, it is quiet and beautifully appointed. Rooms have one king, one queen, or two twin beds, a small refrigerator, and Internet access. There is a pool, a sauna, and a restaurant. **www.royalgardens.com**

WAIKĪKĪ Aqua Bamboo & Spa $$$

2425 Kūhiō Ave, 96815 **Tel** (808) 922-7777 **Fax** (808) 922-9473 **Rooms** 90   **Map** 4 E4

A block from Waikīkī Beach, this deluxe boutique hotel offers stylish rooms with kitchen facilities. Complimentary continental breakfast is served daily. The Aqua Spa, in a cabana by the pool, offers Swedish, Hawaiian *lomi-lomi*, and hot-stone massages. Shopping, dining, and attractions are within walking distance. **www.aquaresorts.com**

Key to Symbols *see back cover flap*

WAIKĪKĪ Aqua Island Colony 🍴🏊🎿📺🔊🅿 $$$

445 Seaside Ave, 96815 **Tel** *(808) 923-2345* **Fax** *(808) 921-7105* **Rooms** *347* **Map** *4 E4*

This condo hotel is on a busy street off Kalākaua Avenue, near the Ala Wai Canal. Although small, units have private *lānai* (verandas). Studio units have kitchenettes and one-bedrooms have full kitchens. The great views are of either Diamond Head and the ocean, or nearby mountains. **www.aquaresorts.com**

WAIKĪKĪ Aqua Waikīkī Beachside Hotel 🅿 $$$

2452 Kalākaua Ave, 96815 **Tel** *(808) 931-2100* **Fax** *(808) 931-2129* **Rooms** *79* **Map** *4 E5*

This elegant boutique hotel is lavishly furnished with art and antiques reflecting the many influences that shape the islands' culture. Guest rooms are decorated in oriental style and feature luxurious private bathrooms. Continental breakfast is included. The hotel is just across the street from Waikīkī Beach. **www.aquaresorts.com**

WAIKĪKĪ Aqua Waikīkī Marina 🏊📺🔊🅿 $$$

1700 Ala Moana Blvd, 96815 **Tel** *(808) 942-7722* **Fax** *(808) 942-1873* **Rooms** *103* **Map** *3 B4*

This 40-story high-rise offers affordable condominium accommodations within walking distance of the Hawai'i Convention Center and Ala Moana Shopping Center. Guest rooms have kitchenettes and panoramic views of the Pacific Ocean, Honolulu, Waikīkī Beach, or Diamond Head. Tennis courts are available. **www.aquaresorts.com**

WAIKĪKĪ Coconut Waikīkī Hotel 🏊🎿🔊🅿 $$$

450 Lewers St, 96815 **Tel** *(808) 923-8828* **Fax** *(808) 923-3473* **Rooms** *80* **Map** *4 D4*

A favorite of inter-island business travelers, this boutique hotel is just 10 miles (16 km) from Honolulu Airport. Near the Ala Wai waterway, it is ideal for a scenic early morning walk or jog. There are hotel rooms, studio rooms, and suites, most with kitchenettes. **www.aquaresorts.com**

WAIKĪKĪ Hilton Waikīkī Prince Kūhiō 🍴🏊🎿📺🔊🅿 $$$

2500 Kūhiō Ave, 96815 **Tel** *(808) 922-0811* **Fax** *(808) 921-5507* **Rooms** *601* **Map** *4 E4*

A block from the beach and two from Kapi'olani Park *(see pp72–3)*, this hotel nevertheless seems a long way from the Waikīkī crowds. Rooms offer high-speed Internet access, work areas, refrigerators, and telephones with voicemail. There is a fitness center. **www.princekuhiohotel.com**

WAIKĪKĪ Ilima Hotel 🏊🎿📺🔊🅿 $$$

445 Nohonani St **Tel** *(808) 923-1877* **Fax** *(808) 924-2617* **Rooms** *98* **Map** *4 E4*

Many believe this condominium-style hotel offers the best value in Waikīkī. All the studios, one-, two-, and three-bedroom suites are spacious, with kitchens and *lānai* (verandas). HBO, The Disney Channel, and even local calls are included in the low prices. There is a pool, an exercise room, a sauna, and limited free parking as well. **www.ilima.com**

WAIKĪKĪ 'Ohāna East 🍴🏊🎿📺🔊🅿 $$$

150 Ka'iulani Ave, 96815 **Tel** *(808) 922-5353* **Fax** *(808) 954-8800* **Rooms** *441* **Map** *4 E4*

'Ohāna means family in Hawaiian and this is a good choice for family vacations. Standard hotel rooms, and studios with kitchenettes, are available. The Nintendo games in each room will keep the kids busy when you are not out or using the pool or restaurants. It is a short walk to the beach, shopping, and attractions. **www.ohanahotels.com**

WAIKĪKĪ 'Ohāna Waikīkī Beachcomber Hotel 🍴🏊🎿🔊🅿 $$$

2300 Kalākaua Ave, 96815 **Tel** *(808) 922-4646* **Fax** *(808) 923-4889* **Rooms** *494* **Map** *4 E5*

The main attractions here are proximity to the beach, live entertainment, and shopping. The hotel has modern decor throughout and hosts the dazzling Magic of Polynesia. Macy's department store occupies the ground floor and The Royal Hawaiian Shopping Center is across the street. **www.ohanahotels.com**

WAIKĪKĪ Outrigger Reef on the Beach 🍴🏊🎿📺🔊🅿 $$$

2169 Kālia Rd, 96815 **Tel** *(808) 923-3111* **Fax** *(808) 924-4957* **Rooms** *858* **Map** *4 D5*

This beachfront hotel is a good mid-price option; with oustanding decor in the guest rooms, reception and communal areas. Guests from nearby Outrigger hotels share the amenities, including restaurants, a pool, a spa, a fitness center, wedding planning services, and beach activities. **www.outrigger.com**

WAIKĪKĪ Outrigger Waikīkī on the Beach 🍴🏊🎿📺🔊🅿 $$$

2335 Kalākaua Ave, 96815 **Tel** *(808) 923-0711* **Fax** *(808) 921-9749* **Rooms** *530* **Map** *4 E5*

This flagship of the Outrigger chain has a prime oceanfront location and plenty of amenities. It has five restaurants and three lounges, some with popular live entertainment nightly. Rooms are large and views determine prices. The hotel offers a wide range of Hawaiian cultural programs, displays, and workshops. **www.outrigger.com**

WAIKĪKĪ Outrigger Waikīkī Shore 🎿🅿 $$$

2161 Kālia Rd, 96815 **Tel** *(808) 922-3871* **Fax** *(808) 922-3887* **Rooms** *37* **Map** *4 D5*

The only resort condominium on Waikīkī Beach has studio units with kitchenettes and one- and two-bedroom units with full kitchens; all have washer-dryers. Guests can make use of the amenities at the Outrigger Reef on the Beach *(see p179)* next door, including the pool, restaurants, Serenity Spa Hawai'i, and weekly activities. **www.outrigger.com**

WAIKĪKĪ Pacific Beach Hotel 🍴🏊🎿📺🔊🅿 $$$

2490 Kalākaua Ave, 96815 **Tel** *(808) 922-1233* **Fax** *(808) 922-8061* **Rooms** *837* **Map** *4 F5*

The main attraction at this twin-tower hotel is the three-story Oceanarium, containing nearly 400 marine creatures. It is possible to dine beside the Oceanarium at all three restaurants. Every room has a private *lānai* (veranda) with a panoramic view, digital telephone, Internet access, and video games. **www.pacificbeachhotel.com**

WAIKĪKĪ Sheraton Princess Ka'iulani

120 Ka'iulani Ave, 96815 **Tel** *(808) 922-5811* **Fax** *(808) 931-4577* **Rooms** *1147*   **Map** *4 E4*

$$$

Named for Hawai'i's last princess (her royal estate was located here), this comfortable hotel has all the advantages of a Sheraton without the oceanfront prices. Every room has a *lānai* (veranda). A huge swimming pool, shops, restaurants, and the popular cocktail-dinner show "Creation - A Polynesian Journey" are on offer. **www.princess-kaiulani.com**

WAIKĪKĪ Sheraton Waikīkī Hotel

2255 Kalākaua Ave, 96815 **Tel** *(808) 922-4422* **Fax** *(808) 931-8883* **Rooms** *1764*   **Map** *4 D5*

$$$

Sleek and modern, this towering 1,764-room hotel has a prime location on the beach at Waikīkī. Most rooms have fantastic ocean views. An exterior glass elevator rises up to the Hanohano Room, from which, at night, guests can view the sparkling lights of the city below. A pool, fitness center, and shops are on site. **www.sheraton-waikiki.com**

WAIKĪKĪ Waikīkī Sand Villa Hotel

2375 Ala Moana Blvd, 96815 **Tel** *(808) 922-4744* **Fax** *(808) 926-7587* **Rooms** *214*   **Map** *4 E4*

$$$

Near Waikīkī Beach, this ten-story hotel has affordable, good-sized rooms and studio apartments. The kidney-shaped swimming pool is the setting for the complimentary continental breakfast. Each room has free unlimited high-speed Internet access and there is also an Internet center. **www.waikikisandvillahotel.com**

WAIKĪKĪ Hyatt Regency Waikīkī Resort & Spa

2424 Kalākaua Ave, 96815 **Tel** *(808) 923-1234* **Fax** *(808) 923-7839* **Rooms** *1230*   **Map** *4 E5*

$$$$

Located in the center of Waikīkī, this impressive resort consists of two 40-story towers joined by an elaborate atrium with an intriguing waterfall. There are lots of things to do at the Hyatt, including working out at the fitness center in the Na Ho'ola Spa, using the pool that overlooks Waikīkī Beach, and, for the kids, Camp Hyatt. **www.hyatt.com**

WAIKĪKĪ Moana Surfrider

2365 Kalākaua Ave, 96815 **Tel** *(808) 922-3111* **Fax** *(808) 924-4799* **Rooms** *791*   **Map** *4 E5*

$$$$

This stunning "First Lady of Waikīkī," whose central section was built in 1901, combines modern comforts with high elegance. The hotel has retained many of its Victorian features, such as the *porte-cochère*, or replicated them, as in the case of the ornate plasterwork. On-site acitivites include a children's program. **www.moana-surfrider.com**

WAIKĪKĪ Waikīkī Beach Marriott Resort & Spa

2552 Kalākaua Ave, 96815 **Tel** *(808) 922-6611* **Fax** *(808) 921-5255* **Rooms** *1310*   **Map** *4 F5*

$$$$

Once the site of Queen Liliu'okalani's summer homes, this large resort is next to Kūhiō Beach in the heart of Waikīkī. Two towers house attractively decorated rooms and many amenities. The resort includes several restaurants, two swimming pools, and a spa created by world-famous hairstylist Paul Brown. **www.marriottwaikīkī.com**

WAIKĪKĪ Waikīkī Parc

2233 Helumoa Rd, 96815 **Tel** *(808) 921-7272* **Fax** *(808) 923-1336* **Rooms** *297*   **Map** *4 D5*

$$$$

This friendly, intimate hotel offers affordable luxury in a great location. Guests here enjoy privileges at the Halekulani, the Waikīkī Parc's sister hotel, which is right across the street on Waikīkī Beach. The Parc's comfortable rooms have sitting areas, desks, and *lānai* (verandas), with either ocean, mountain, or city views. **www.waikikiparc.com**

WAIKĪKĪ Aston Waikīkī Beach Tower

2470 Kalākaua Ave, 96815 **Tel** *(808) 926-6400* **Fax** *(808) 926-7380* **Rooms** *98*   **Map** *4 F5*

$$$$$

These one- and two-bedroom suites, with kitchens and washer-dryers, are well-furnished and have spacious *lānai* (verandas) overlooking Waikīkī Beach. A twice daily maid service is provided. Amenities include a heated outdoor pool, jet spa, paddle tennis court, and billiards area. Complimentary valet parking is a plus. **www.waikiki-beach-tower.com**

WAIKĪKĪ Halekulani

2199 Kālia Rd, 96815 **Tel** *(808) 923-2311* **Fax** *(808) 926-8004* **Rooms** *456*   **Map** *4 D5*

$$$$$

The Halekulani is the epitome of elegance. Everything is perfect: the impeccable service, the manicured tropical grounds, the tasteful decor, the spacious rooms, the luxurious spa, and the superb cuisine at La Mer *(see p197)*. The hotel stands on extensive grounds on Waikīkī Beach Front and almost all rooms face the ocean. **www.halekulani.com**

WAIKĪKĪ The Royal Hawaiian

2259 Kalākaua Ave, 96815 **Tel** *(808) 923-7311* **Fax** *(808) 931-7098* **Rooms** *528*   **Map** *4 D5*

$$$$$

This elegant Waikīkī hotel, affectionately known as the Pink Palace of the Pacific, has been restored to its original grandeur. Right on the beach and surrounded by lush tropical gardens, the hotel has been a Waikīkī landmark since 1927, hosting movie stars and heads of state. **www.royal-hawaiian.com**

WAIKĪKĪ Trump International Hotel & Tower

223 Saratoga Rd, 96815 **Tel** *(808) 683-7401* **Rooms** *462*   **Map** *4 D5*

$$$$$

The first luxury property to be built in Waikīkī in many years, Trump Waikīkī has almost all the high-end amenities imaginable. The 38-story tower provides magnificent views from sumptuously appointed studio, one-, two- and three-bedroom suites. The term "Ritzy" may now be replaced by "Trumpy." **www.trumpwaikikihotel.com**

GREATER HONOLULU Aloha Bed & Breakfast

909 Kahauloa Pl, 96825 **Tel** *(808) 395-6694* **Fax** *(808) 396-2020* **Rooms** *3*   **Map** *4 F5*

$

Comprised of three guest rooms with a shared bath, this affordable B&B in residential, upscale Hawai'i Kai has panoramic ocean views. One room has a king-sized bed, one a queen, and one two twin beds. It is a 15-minute drive from Waikīkī Beach Front and close to local dining and shopping. **http://home.roadrunner.com/~alohaphyllis**

Key to Price Guide *see p178* **Key to Symbols** *see back cover flap*

GREATER HONOLULU J&B's Haven Bed & Breakfast 🚭 [P] $

Kahena St, 96825 **Tel** *(808) 396-9462* **Rooms** *2* **Map** *4 F5*

In Hawai'i Kai, 15 minutes east of Waikīkī Beach Front, this lovely home is close to Haunama Bay, Sea Life Park, shopping, and dining. One bedroom is large; both have private bathrooms. Daily continental breakfast is included. In addition to the wonderful hosts, there are friendly dogs living here. **http://home.roadrunner.com/~jnbshaven**

GREATER HONOLULU Doubletree Alana Hotel-Waikīkī 🍴 🏊 👪 🏋 ❄ [P] $$

1956 Ala Moana Blvd, 96815 **Tel** *(808) 941-7275* **Fax** *(808) 949-0996* **Rooms** *268* **Map** *3 C4*

This small boutique hotel located at the gateway to Waikīkī has a reputation for hospitality and offers the amenities of a luxury hotel at affordable prices. These include a poolside fitness center, a business center, room service, and in-room massage. Guest rooms are compact, but well equipped. **http://doubletree1.hilton.com**

GREATER HONOLULU Manoa Valley Inn [P] $$

2001 Vancouver Dr, 96822 **Tel** *(808) 947-6019* **Fax** *(808) 946-6168* **Rooms** *9* **Map** *4 D1*

Set in beautiful grounds just minutes from Waikīkī, this 1912 home retains its old-fashioned charm. There are seven rooms and also one cottage. Each is distinctively decorated and named for a prominent Hawaiian historical figure. Some rooms share a bath. Rates include continental breakfast. **www.manoavalleyinn.com**

GREATER HONOLULU Pagoda Hotel and Floating Restaurant 🍴 🏊 ❄ [P] $$

1525 Rycroft St, 96814 **Tel** *(808) 941-6611* **Fax** *(808) 955-5067* **Rooms** *360* **Map** *3 A3*

The Pagoda offers rooms that are unadorned but good value. Close to shopping at the Ala Moana Center, this hotel is a favorite with local residents. Accommodations are standard, studios, and suites. Facilities include free parking, laundry facilities, and a shop. The floating restaurant and water gardens are notable. **www.pagodahotel.com**

GREATER HONOLULU Ala Moana Hotel 🍴 🏊 👪 🏋 ❄ [P] $$$

410 Atkinson Dr, 96814 **Tel** *(808) 955-4811* **Fax** *(808) 944-6839* **Rooms** *1058* **Map** *3 A4*

Set near the popular Ala Moana Beach Park, the Hawai'i Convention Center, and the Ala Moana Shopping Center, this 36-story hotel offers many amenities at reasonable prices. These include three restaurants, a nightclub, a good fitness center, a swimming pool, and direct access to the Ala Moana Shopping Center. **www.outrigger.com**

GREATER HONOLULU The Lotus at Diamond Head ♿ 🍸 🍴 🏊 👪 ❄ [P] $$$

2885 Kalākaua Ave, 96815 **Tel** *(808) 922-1700* **Fax** *(808) 923-2249* **Rooms** *51* **Map** *4 F5*

Situated at the base of Diamond Head, this small boutique hotel is only a few minutes away from the activities and attractions of Waikīkī. Each guest room has views of Diamond Head or the ocean. Amenities include high-speed Internet access, cable television, video games, and CD/DVD player. **www.castleresorts.com**

GREATER HONOLULU The New Otani Kaimana Beach Hotel 🍴 🏋 ❄ [P] $$$

2863 Kalākaua Ave, 96815 **Tel** *(808) 923-1555* **Fax** *(808) 922-9404* **Rooms** *125* **Map** *4 F5*

On beautiful San Souci beach, across from Kapi'olani Park *(see pp72–3)*, this boutique hotel has small, but nicely appointed rooms. Choose from tasteful rooms and suites, or studios and one-bedroom suites with kitchenettes. Two seaside restaurants include a Japanese one. Honolulu Zoo and other attractions are nearby. **www.kaimana.com**

GREATER HONOLULU Diamond Head Beach Hotel 👪 [P] $$$$

2947 Kalākaua Ave **Tel** *(808) 922-1928* **Fax** *(808) 924-8980* **Rooms** *45* **Map** *4 F5*

No frills here, but the serene oceanfront setting away from the crowds of Waikīkī makes up for the simplicity. Rooms come with refrigerators and coffee makers; one-bedroom suites have full kitchens. All are air-conditioned and many have large private *lānai* (verandas). Kalākaua Avenue is a short walk away. **www.obrhihotel.com**

GREATER HONOLULU Hawai'i Prince Hotel Waikīkī 🍴 🏊 👪 🏋 ❄ [P] $$$$

100 Holomoana St, 96815 **Tel** *(808) 956-1111* **Fax** *(808) 946-0811* **Rooms** *578* **Map** *3 A4*

Every room at this marina-front hotel has a panoramic ocean view, but only a few have a *lānai* (veranda). There are two award-winning restaurants, a day spa, a fitness center, a business center, and tennis courts. Located near the Ala Moana Shopping Center, the hotel is also close to Waikīkī and downtown Honolulu. **www.princeresortshawaii.com**

GREATER HONOLULU Ilikai Hotel & Suites 🍴 🏊 👪 🏋 ❄ [P] $$$$

1777 Ala Moana Blvd, 96815 **Tel** *(808) 949-3811* **Fax** *(808) 947-0892* **Rooms** *696* **Map** *3 B4*

This hotel is convenient for Waikīkī beaches, the Ala Moana Shopping Center, and Beach Park. Its main attractions are Sarento's Top of the I Restaurant, a fitness center, and a tennis court. Most of the rooms have *lānai* (verandas) and kitchens. All have televisions with on-demand movies and Internet access. **www.ilikaihotel.com**

GREATER HONOLULU Hilton Hawaiian Village Beach Resort & Spa 🍴 🏊 👪 🏋 ❄ [P] $$$$$

2005 Kālia Rd, 96815 **Tel** *(808) 949-4321* **Fax** *(808) 951-5458* **Rooms** *3886* **Map** *3 C4*

More like a small city than a hotel, the Hilton has it all: a beach, five pools, 100 shops, a spa, a wedding chapel, tropical gardens, and penguins and other wildlife in the lobby. There are 22 lounges and restaurants. Rooms, in six towers, are equipped with cable television and *lānai* (verandas). **www.hiltonhawaiianvillage.com**

GREATER HONOLULU The Kahala Hotel & Resort 🍴 🏊 👪 🏋 ❄ [P] $$$$$

5000 Kahala Ave, 96816 **Tel** *(808) 739-8888* **Fax** *(808) 739-8800* **Rooms** *338* **Map** *4 F1*

Set in an upscale district, this modern, stylish hotel is fronted by a great swimming beach. There are six restaurants, notably Hoku's, a state-of-the-art fitness center, and a full spa. The property is famous for its lagoon, where guests can get up close and personal with six Atlantic bottlenose dolphins. **www.kahalaresort.com**

O'AHU

HALE'IWA North Shore Vacation Homes   🏃 P $$
66-250 Kamehameha Hwy, 96712 **Tel** *(808) 637-3507* **Fax** *(808) 637-8881* **Rooms** *4*

You will feel like a local at a Hawaiian-style beach house in this quiet North Shore neighborhood. These furnished rentals have large *lānai* (verandas), spectacular sunset views, and all the comforts of home. The fabled surf of Sunset Beach and Waimea Bay is nearby as are shopping, dining, golf, and other attractions. **www.teamrealestate.com**

HALE'IWA Kē Iki Beach Bungalows   🏃 P $$$
59-579 Kē Iki Rd, 96712 **Tel** *(808) 638-8829* **Fax** *(808) 637-6100* **Rooms** *11*

These modest, yet clean and comfortable beach cottages occupy their own stretch of white sand between the famous surfing beaches of Waimea Bay and Banzai Pipeline. Run by a local resident, they have televisions and kitchens. Outdoors, there are barbecues and hammocks; tennis courts are nearby. **www.keikibeach.com**

KAHUKU Turtle Bay Condominiums   🏢 🏃 P $$
55-565 Kamehameha Hwy, 96731 **Tel** *(808) 293-0600* **Fax** *(808) 293-2169* **Rooms** *52*

About an hour away from the bustle of Waikīkī, these large one- and two-bedroom condominium units have full-size kitchens, washer-dryers, telephones, and cable television, making them perfect for families. They are on the golf courses in the Turtle Bay Resort, near famous surfing beaches and major North Shore attractions. **www.turtlebay-rentals.com**

KAHUKU Turtle Bay Resort   🍴 🏢 🏃 🛏 P $$$
57-091 Kamehameha Hwy, 96731 **Tel** *(808) 293-6000* **Fax** *(808) 293-9147* **Rooms** *448*

Stretching for 5 miles (8 km) along the coastline, this is the only full-service resort on the North Shore. Amenities include a spa, a fitness center, two championship golf courses, a tennis complex, riding, and water sports. All luxury guest rooms, suites, beach cottages, and villas have ocean views and *lānai* (verandas). **www.turtlebayresort.com**

KAILUA Kailua Beachside Bungalows   P $$
204 S. Kalaheo Ave, 96734 **Tel** *(808) 230-8019* **Rooms** *3*

Close to beautiful windward-side beaches and a short drive from activities, these one-and two-bedroom bungalows have island-style decor. All have kitchens, barbecues, phones, and cable television. Units can be combined for large families. Guests enjoy the use of boogie boards and diving and tennis gear. **www.beachsidebungalows.com**

KAILUA Lanikai Bed & Breakfast   P $$
1277 Mokolua Dr, 96734 **Tel** *(808) 261-7895* **Fax** *(808) 262-2181* **Rooms** *2*

In a chic neighborhood across from Lanikai Beach, this bed and breakfast has warm and knowledgeable hosts. The upstairs apartment has a kitchenette, living-dining area, and den. There is also a small, secluded room with a kitchenette. Beverages, breakfast pastries, and chairs and coolers for the beach are provided. **www.lanikaibeachrentals.com**

KAILUA Pat's Kailua Beach Properties   P $$
204 S. Kalāheo Ave, 96734 **Tel** *(808) 261-1653* **Fax** *(808) 261-0893* **Rooms** *34*

The O'Malley's have island-style homes in the beautiful residential areas of Kailua and Lanikai. Ranging from fully-furnished studios to four-bedroom units, they are perfect for families and sleep up to eight people. Some have ocean views and some are beachfront. Weekly rentals are preferred; three nights is the minimum stay. **www.patskailua.com**

KAILUA Hawaii's Hidden Hideaway   P $$$
1369 Mokolea Dr, 96734 **Tel** *(808) 262-6560* **Fax** *(808) 262-6561* **Rooms** *3*

A short walk from Lanikai and Kailua beaches, this privately-owned house is comfortable and well equipped. Choose between a suite with an ocean view and private outdoor Jacuzzi and a studio with a garden view. Both have private entrances, baths, kitchenettes, and televisions. A minimum three-night stay is required. **www.ahawaiibnb.com**

KAILUA Ingrid's Place   P $$$
571 Pauku Street **Tel** *(808) 262-8133* **Fax** *(808) 262-5030* **Rooms** *1*

Located in a residential neighborhood just a mile from Kailua Beach, this one-bedroom apartment is decorated in dramatic Japanese style. It has a kitchenette complete with dishwasher, a television, high-speed Internet access, and a large deck. Rates include continental breakfast. A minimum five-night stay is required. **www.bestbnb.com**

KĀNE'OHE Ali'i Bluffs Windward Bed & Breakfast   P $
46-251 Iki Iki St, 96744 **Tel** *(808) 235-1124* **Fax** *(808) 236-4877* **Rooms** *2*

This European-style bed and breakfast is a short drive from Oahu's best beach. Overlooking Kāne'ohe Bay, it offers two double bedrooms, each with private bath. The Victorian Room is in period style, while the Circus Room has antique circus toys and posters. Continental breakfast and afternoon tea are included. **www.hawaiiscene.com/aliibluffs**

KĀNE'OHE Schrader's Windward Country Inn   P $$
47-039 Llihikai Dr, 96744 **Tel** *(808) 239-5711* **Fax** *(808) 239-6658* **Rooms** *22*

In a rural setting on a peninsula 30 minutes from Waikīkī, these modest cottages include complimentary snorkeling and kayaking expeditions. One-, two-, three-, and four-bedroom accommodations with kitchenettes are available. Picnic tables, barbecues, and a pool set the scene for a fun vacation. **www.schradersinn.com**

WAI'ANAE JW Marriott 'Ihilani Resort & Spa at Ko Olina Resort 🏠🏖️🏃🏾📺🅿️ $$$$
92-1001 Olani St Tel (808) 679-0079 Fax (808) 679-0080 Rooms 423

This enormous, sprawling property is the only resort on the island's leeward side. The rooms are large and luxurious, with marble baths and high-tech systems to control the interior environment. There is an 18-hole championship golf course with clubhouse. The resort's huge spa offers massages, facials, soaks, and scrubs. **www.ihilani.com**

WAI'ANAE Ko Olina Beach Villas Resort 🛏️🍸🏖️🏃🏾📺🅿️ $$$$$
92-106 Waiali'i Pl, 96707 Tel (808) 225-5590 Fax (808) 469-3624 Rooms 270

These two- and three-bedroom villa suites are situated within the luxurious Ko Olina Resort. The kitchens are custom-designed by master chef Roy Yamaguchi, featuring high-end appliances, separate living and dining areas, and spacious private *lānai*. The resort includes a marina, a golf course, and a spa. **www.koolinabeachvillasresort.com**

MOLOKA'I AND LĀNA'I

EAST END (MOLOKA'I) Wavecrest 🏖️🚭🅿️ $$
Kamehameha V Hwy, Mile Marker 13 Tel (808) 553-8334 Fax (808) 553-8332 Rooms 126

In the lush East End of the island, 13 miles (21 km) past Kaunakakai, are these waterfront condominiums with a pool, cabanas, and tennis courts. Units are individually owned, and reservations are made through an agency. Laundry facilities and Internet access are available on site. **www.molokai-vacation-rental.net**

EAST END (MOLOKA'I) Aloha Beach House 📺🅿️ $$$$
Kamehameha V Hwy, Mile Marker 19, 96770 Tel (808) 828-1100 Fax (808) 828-2199 Rooms 2

This Hawaiian-style beach house sits right on Waialua's white sand, in the lush East End. It has two bedrooms, an open living-dining area, a complete kitchen (including a dishwasher), a DVD with video library, and beach toys. Its location close to the neighborhood store is a plus on this remote side of the island. **www.molokaivacation.com**

KALUAKO'I (MOLOKA'I) Kaluako'i Villas 🏃🏾🅿️ $$
1131 Kaluakoi Rd, 96770 Tel (808) 552-2721 Fax (808) 552-2201 Rooms 22

These studio and one-bedroom condos are set in the Kaluakoi Resort on the west coast of Moloka'i. Each has a spacious private *lānai* (veranda) and kitchenette. Guests can sunbathe on the glistening white-sand beach, or stroll in the beautifully landscaped grounds. **www.castleresorts.com**

KALUAKO'I (MOLOKA'I) Ke Nani Kai Resort 📺🏖️🅿️ $$
50 Kepuhi Pl, 96770 Tel (808) 533-3666 Fax (808) 533-3867 Rooms 57

This complex of low-rise condominiums lies along the fairways of the old golf course, within the planned Kaluakoi Resort. Every unit has a private *lānai* (veranda), color television, telephone, kitchen, and washer-dryer. Amenities include a free-form pool, heated whirlpool, tennis courts, and barbecue area. **molokai-beachfront-condos.com**

KALUAKO'I (MOLOKA'I) Paniolo Hale 🏖️🚭🅿️ $$
Lio Pl, 96770 Tel (808) 553-8334 Fax (808) 552-2288 Rooms 15

Situated within the Kaluako'i Resort, these studio, one- and two-bedroom condominiums are individually owned but booked through a rental pool. All are fully furnished and most have a *lānai* (veranda). Tropical landscaping and a pool add island flavor. It is a short walk to the 3-mile (5-km) Papohaku Beach. **molokai-beachfront-condos.com**

KAUNAKAKAI (MOLOKA'I) Hotel Moloka'i 🏠🏖️🏃🏾🅿️ $
Kamehameha V Hwy, 96748 Tel (808) 553-5347 Fax (808) 553-5047 Rooms 45

Not fancy, but right on the water and affordable, this is the only centrally located hotel on the island. The oceanfront dining room, Hula Shores (*see p201*), provides a gathering place for local residents on Friday nights, when everyone brings their 'ukuleles and joins in a Hawaiian jam session by the pool. **www.hotelmolokai.com**

KAUNAKAKAI (MOLOKA'I) Dunbar Beachfront Cottages 📺🅿️ $$
Kamehameha V Hwy, just past Mile Marker 18, 96748 Tel (808) 558-8153 Fax (808) 558-8153 Rooms 4

The two green and white plantation-style cottages sit right at the water's edge on their own secluded beach. Each has two bedrooms, a kitchen, television with VCR, and ceiling fans. Their large decks have views of the nearby islands of Maui, Lāna'i, and Kaho'olawe. They are truly idyllic and peaceful. **www.molokai-beachfront-cottages.com**

KAUNAKAKAI (MOLOKA'I) Moloka'i Shores 🏖️🏃🏾🅿️ $$
Kamehameha V Hwy, 96748 Tel (808) 553-5954 Fax (808) 553-3241 Rooms 102

A few minutes outside of Kaunakakai are these comfortable but basic oceanfront condominiums. One- and two-bedroom units, they have full kitchens and large living rooms. The great view from the swimming pool and barbecue area makes this a perfect whale-watching spot. There are no phones and no air-conditioning. **www.castleresorts.com**

LĀNA'I CITY (LĀNA'I) Dreams Come True 🅿️ $$
547 12th St Tel (808) 565-6961 Fax (808) 565-7056 Rooms 4

Built in 1925 in picturesque Lānai City, this bed and breakfast is shaded by papaya, banana, lemon, and avocado trees. The hosts, both jewelers, decorated it with the Asian antiques they collected on their travels. There are four bedrooms and a common area that overlooks the garden. Continental breakfast is included. **www.dreamscometruelanai.com**

LĀNA'I CITY (LĀNA'I) Hotel Lāna'i

828 Lāna'i Ave, 96763 **Tel** *(808) 565-7211* **Fax** *(808) 565-6450* **Rooms** *11*

Built in 1923 as a home for plantation executives, this hotel has simple, plantation-style Hawaiian architecture, and tall Cook pines still stand out front. The rooms in this charming rustic place are small, but clean and comfortably furnished. All have private baths. There is an excellent hotel restaurant and a full bar. **www.hotellanai.com**

LĀNA'I CITY (LĀNA'I) Four Seasons Resort Lanai, The Lodge at Ko'ele

1 Keomuku Hwy, 96763 **Tel** *(808) 565-4000* **Fax** *(808) 565-4561* **Rooms** *102*

Here at the edge of Lānai City, 1,700 ft (520 m) above sea level and 8 miles (13 km) from the nearest beach, the air is cool and misty. Rooms have an upcountry elegance and spacious bathrooms. The hotel offers restaurants, two 18-hole championship golf courses, horseback riding, and sporting clays. **www.fourseasons.com/koele**

LĀNA'I CITY (LĀNA'I) Captain's Retreat

504 Nininiwai Circle, 96763 **Tel** *(808) 565-7519* **Rooms** *4*

Surrounded by towering Cook pine trees in the misty cool air of Lānai City, this two-story cedar home has an upstairs master suite with private bath, and three bedrooms and two bathrooms downstairs. A fireplace, big-screen television, stereo, and VCR are in the living room. Outside, there is a large redwood deck with barbecue. **www.lanairental.com**

MĀNELE BAY (LĀNA'I) Four Seasons Lānai at Mānele Bay

1 Mānele Bay Rd, 96763 **Tel** *(808) 565-2000* **Fax** *(808) 565-2483* **Rooms** *236*

This hotel commands the sparkling crescent beach at Mānele Bay. Averaging a spacious 700 sq ft (65 sq m), rooms have *lānai* (verandas), LCD televisions, and high-speed Internet access. Bathrooms offer Four Seasons amenities: plush bathrobes, a marble double basin, deep-soaking tub, and separate shower. **www.fourseasons.com/manelebay**

MAUI

HAIKU Maui Vacation Hideaway

240 N Holokai Rd, 96708 **Tel** *(808) 572-2775* **Fax** *(808) 573-2775* **Rooms** *3*

Surrounded by lush tropical vegetation, these uniquely decorated units have kitchens and Wi-Fi. The hostess lives on-site and provides an eco-friendly environment by not using chemicals or pesticides on the property. Gentle breezes and a saltwater pool fed by a waterfall add to the natural experience. **www.mauivacationhideaway.com**

HAIKU Pu'u Koa

66 Pu'ukoa Place, 96708 **Tel** *(808) 573-2884* **Rooms** *7*

With a great location for access to the North Shore waves, these affordable studio and one-bedroom apartments in a shady garden setting are a short drive from Pā'ia and Baldwin Beach. The large studios have kitchenettes; the one-bed units have fully equipped kitchens. Haiku town is close by for groceries and restaurants. **www.puukoa.com**

HĀNA Hāna Kai Maui

1533 Uakea Rd, 96713 **Tel** *(808) 248-8426* **Fax** *(808) 248-7482* **Rooms** *18*

These studio and one-bedroom condominiums are set in a sheltered cove overlooking a black-sand beach. The spacious furnished units have fully equipped kitchens, private *lānai* (verandas), and come with a daily maid service. Children aged six or younger stay free. Discounts are also offered for stays of at least seven nights. **www.hanakaimaui.com**

HĀNA Hotel Hāna-Maui

5031 Hāna Hwy, 96713 **Tel** *(808) 248-8211* **Fax** *(808) 248-7202* **Rooms** *69*

Maui's most secluded resort is a magical getaway on the lush east end of the island. Its luxury accommodations are situated in one-story buildings and cottages scattered around the tropical grounds. The hotel also has a fitness center, a full-service spa, and a fine-dining restaurant. Horseback riding and tennis are available. **www.hotelhanamaui.com**

HONOKŌWAI Aston at Papākea Resort

3543 Lower Honoapi'ilani Rd, 96761 **Tel** *(808) 669-4848* **Fax** *(808) 665-0662* **Rooms** *463*

Five four-story beachfront condominiums offer simple studios to luxurious two-bedroom suites. Amenities include two pools, two huge Jacuzzis, two saunas, floodlit tennis courts, a putting green, and a barbecue area. There are *koi* ponds and tropical gardens that meander down to the beach. It is great for families. **www.astonhotels.com**

KĀ'ANAPALI Kā'anapali Beach Hotel

2525 Kā'anapali Pkwy, 96761 **Tel** *(808) 661-0011* **Fax** *(808) 667-5978* **Rooms** *430*

Right on the beach in the Kā'anapali Resort, this is known as Maui's most Hawaiian hotel. Rooms and suites are furnished island-style and have *lānai* (verandas) looking onto a lush tropical garden. The six-story Maui, Lāna'i, and Kaua'i wings have elevators; the three-story Moloka'i does not. Hawaiian cultural activities abound. **www.kbhmaui.com**

KĀ'ANAPALI Aston Kā'anapali Shores

3445 Honoapi'ilani Hwy, 96761 **Tel** *(808) 667-2211* **Fax** *(808) 661-0836* **Rooms** *463*

All studios and suites offer fully equipped kitchens; washer-dryers are available in one- and two-bedroom suites. Guests can enjoy the Ocean Pool and Beach Club Restaurant, the Garden Pool (ideal for kids), three tennis courts, a fitness-massage center, two jet spas, complimentary scuba lessons, and a beautiful beach. **www.astonhotels.com**

Key to Price Guide *see p178* **Key to Symbols** *see back cover flap*

KĀ'ANAPALI Kā'anapali Ali'i 🏊 👪 🌳 🏋 [P] $$$$

50 Nohea Kai Dr, 96761 ***Tel*** *(808) 667-1400* ***Fax*** *(808) 661-5686* ***Rooms*** *264*

This elegant property right on the beach offers one- and two-bedroom condominium units. They are spacious, with full kitchens and sometimes two bathrooms. Nicely furnished, all have air-conditioning, washer-dryers, and a daily maid service. There are tennis courts, a pool, an exercise room, and a beach activity center. **www.kaanapalialii.com**

KĀ'ANAPALI Marriott's Maui Ocean Club 🍴 🏊 👪 🌳 🏋 [P] $$$$

100 Nohea Kai Dr, 96761 ***Tel*** *(808) 667-1200* ***Fax*** *(808) 667-8300* ***Rooms*** *442*

One of the first hotels on Maui to spend millions on renovations in order to become vacation ownership properties, the Maui Marriott is a great place to take the kids, with fully equipped apartments, resort amenities, and one of the best locations on Kā'anapali Beach. **www.marriott.com**

KĀ'ANAPALI Royal Lahaina Resort 🍴 🏊 👪 🌳 🏋 [P] $$$$

2780 Keka'a Dr, 96761 ***Tel*** *(808) 661-3611* ***Fax*** *(808) 661-6150* ***Rooms*** *516*

The first hotel built in the Ka'anapali resort in 1962, this property offers up-to-date hotel rooms in high-rise towers, low-rise plantation-style cottages, and a budget inn. Its poolside restaurant serves *mai tais* in an oceanfront setting. Guests can also enjoy a nightly *lu'au* and an 11-court tennis ranch on the property. **www.hawaiihotels.com**

KĀ'ANAPALI The Westin Maui 🍴 🏊 👪 🌳 🏋 [P] $$$$

2365 Kā'anapali Pkwy, 96761 ***Tel*** *(808) 667-2525* ***Fax*** *(808) 661-5764* ***Rooms*** *758*

The rooms are small, but well-appointed at this opulent oceanfront hotel. Asian artwork is found throughout the public areas and the lush tropical grounds, which also have a collection of exotic birds. There are five pools and a huge waterslide, along with restaurants, exclusive boutiques, beach activities, and a spa. **www.westinmaui.com**

KĀ'ANAPALI The Whaler on Kā'anapali Beach 🏊 👪 🌳 🏋 [P] $$$$

2481 Kā'anapali Pkwy, 96761 ***Tel*** *(808) 661-4861* ***Fax*** *(808) 661-8315* ***Rooms*** *360*

This luxury condominium is situated next to Whalers Village Shopping Center. All suites have fully equipped kitchens and are generously sized. A beachfront swimming pool, five tennis courts, a fitness-massage center, and the beautiful beach are at hand. Fine shops, galleries, and restaurants are in nearby Whalers Village. **www.astonhotels.com**

KĀ'ANAPALI Hyatt Regency Maui Resort & Spa 🍴 🏊 👪 🌳 🏋 [P] $$$$$

200 Nohea Kai Dr, 96761 ***Tel*** *(808) 661-1234* ***Fax*** *(808) 667-4497* ***Rooms*** *806*

The impressive beachfront grounds feature works of art, tropical flowers and plants, exotic birds, a meandering pool with waterfalls, a swinging rope bridge, and an underwater grotto bar. An upscale shopping arcade, restaurants, spa and nightly *lu'au*, are also on site. Rooms have a sitting area and a private *lānai* (veranda). **www.maui.hyatt.com**

KĀ'ANAPALI Sheraton Maui 🍴 🏊 👪 🌳 🏋 [P] $$$$$

2605 Kā'anapali Pkwy, 96761 ***Tel*** *(808) 661-0031* ***Fax*** *(808) 661-0458* ***Rooms*** *510*

Kā'anapali's first luxury resort hotel sits above Black Rock, but the original 1950s-style decor is gone. Now the furnishings are reminiscent of Hawai'i's plantation era, using natural materials and pastel shades. Almost all guest rooms face the ocean and have air-conditioning, a *lānai* (veranda), and small refrigerator. **www.sheraton-maui.com**

KAHANA Kahāna Sunset 🏊 👪 🏋 [P] $$

4909 L Honoapi'ilani Hwy, 96761 ***Tel*** *(808) 669-8700* ***Fax*** *(808) 669-4466* ***Rooms*** *90*

Kahana Sunset has a great location on a white-sand beach surrounded by tropical gardens. Six two- and three-story buildings house 90 units, with modern kitchens, cable television, washer-dryers, and VCRs. Each has a *lānai* (veranda) linked to those of its neighbors. A heated pool, barbecues, and Internet access are on site. **www.kahanasunset.com**

KAPALUA Kapalua Villas 🏊 👪 🌳 🏋 [P] $$$$

500 Office Rd, 96761 ***Tel*** *(808) 669-8088* ***Fax*** *(808) 669-5234* ***Rooms*** *280*

These spacious one- and two-bedroom condominiums offer oceanfront, ocean-view and fairway-view units in three complexes: The Bay Villas, The Ridge, and the Golf Villas. Guests have full use of Kapalua golf and resort amenities, such as complimentary tennis and discounts in resort shops and restaurants. **www.outrigger.com**

KAPALUA The Ritz-Carlton Maui 🍴 🏊 👪 🌳 🏋 [P] $$$$$

1 Ritz-Carlton Dr, 96761 ***Tel*** *(808) 669-6200* ***Fax*** *(808) 669-2028* ***Rooms*** *490*

This Ritz is set apart by its Hawaiian cultural program, including hands-on activities, entertainment, special events, seminars, and exhibits. Elegance abounds in the guest rooms and sumptuous Residential Suites. Spa, golf course, a variety of cafés, bars and restaurants, and stunning ocean views complete the picture. **www.ritzcarlton.com**

KĪHEI Mana Kai Maui Resort 🍴 🏊 👪 [P] $$

2960 S Kīhei Rd, 96753 ***Tel*** *(808) 879-2778* ***Fax*** *(808) 879-7025* ***Rooms*** *132*

This high rise is on beautiful, white-sand Keawakapu Beach, right before Wailea. The accommodations are not spectacular, but the location is. One- and two-bedroom condos have kitchens and private *lānai* (verandas). Hotel rooms have baths. An open-air restaurant, general store, and beauty shop are on site. **www.crhmaui.com**

KĪHEI Maui Coast Hotel ❄ 🍴 🏊 🌳 [P] $$

2259 S Kīhei Rd, 96753 ***Tel*** *(808) 874-6284* ***Fax*** *(808) 875-4731* ***Rooms*** *265*

The only full-service hotel in Kīhei offers a reasonably priced alternative to Wailea. Just across the street from a 6-mile (9-km) stretch of sandy beach parks, it has a restaurant, pool, tennis courts, and laundry facilities. Rooms are small, but have fridges, coffee makers, Internet access, air-conditioning, and *lānai* (verandas). **www.mauicoasthotel.com**

KĪHEI Punahoa 🖼️ P $$$

2142 Ili'ili Rd, 96753 Tel (808) 879-2720 Fax (808) 875-9147 Rooms 15

All these individually owned studio, one-, and two-bedroom condominium units are oceanfront. Each has one bathroom, a kitchen, a big *lānai* (veranda), cable television, and DVD or VCR. The units are in a four-story building with an elevator and laundry facilities. Kama'ole and Kalama Parks flank the property. **www.punahoabeach.com**

KĪHEI Hale Hui Kai 🏊🏃 P $$$$

2994 S Kīhei Road, 96753 Tel (808) 879-2727 Fax (808) 875-8242 Rooms 59

With two-bedroom, two-bath units in a Hawaiian-style condominium right on the beach, this property is great for families. Units have kitchens and cable television. Laundry facilities on each floor, shuffleboard, a putting green, barbecues, and a recreation area are provided. Dining, shopping, and golf are nearby. **www.halehuikaimaui.com**

KĪHEI Kama'ole Sands Condominiums 🏊🏃 P $$$$

2695 S Kīhei Rd, 96753 Tel (808) 874-8700 Fax (808) 879-3273 Rooms 315

Across the street from the popular Kama'ole Beach Park, this complex offers studios and one-, two-, and three-bedroom suites. All units have a kitchen and *lānai* (veranda). Four tennis courts, a swimming pool, a sun deck, two jet spas, and barbecue areas are set in vast tropical gardens, with ponds, fountains, and waterfalls. **www.castleresorts.com**

KUAU The Inn at Mama's Fish House 🍴 P $$$

Pono Place, off Hana Highway, 96779 Tel (808) 579-9764 Rooms 9

These comfortable, tropical one- and two-bedroom cottages are well appointed with retro Hawaiian-style rattan furniture, local artworks, and fully equipped kitchens. They are situated in a quiet oceanfront neighborhood right next to one of the island's best and most popular restaurants, Mama's Fish House. **www.mamasfishhouse.com**

KULA Kula Lodge 🍴 P $$$

15200 Haleakalā Hwy, 96790 Tel (808) 878-1535 Fax (808) 878-2518 Rooms 5

Not what you would expect on a tropical island, this rustic lodge is set in cool, upcountry Maui, where nights can be chilly – two units have gas fireplaces. There's a restaurant with scenic views and an art gallery on site. It's a long ride to the beach, but Kula Lodge is a great romantic getaway. **www.kulalodge.com**

LAHAINA Lahaina Inn 🍴 P $$

127 Lahainaluna Rd, 96761 Tel (808) 661-0577 Fax (808) 667-9480 Rooms 12

This small boutique hotel in the heart of Lahaina has nine rooms and three parlor suites lovingly decorated with authentic Victorian furnishings. There are no televisions in the rooms. The Lahaina Grill restaurant *(see p204)* occupies the first floor; the ocean is half a block away. **www.lahainainn.com**

LAHAINA The Makai Inn P $$

1415 Front St, 96761 Tel (808) 662-3200 Fax (808) 661-9027 Rooms 18

A quiet retreat on the edge of Lahaina town, this good-value inn sits right on the beach. The Makai has modest one-bedroom units with kitchens. Shops, restaurants, and the action of Front Street are just a few blocks away. Clean and comfortable, if not luxurious (there are no TVs or air-conditioning in the rooms). **www.makaiinn.net**

LAHAINA The Pioneer Inn 🍴🏊🏃 P $$

658 Wharf St, 96761 Tel (808) 661-3636 Fax (808) 667-5708 Rooms 34

The Pioneer Inn's colorful history dates back to 1910, when a Canadian Mountie came to Maui to catch his man. Now managed by Best Western, its rooms are not deluxe, but the location is: right at the water's edge in scenic Lahaina Harbor. Rooms are on the second floor. There is a pool, a rowdy bar, and a restaurant. **www.pioneerinnmaui.com**

LAHAINA The Plantation Inn 🍴🏊 P $$

174 Lahainaluna Rd, 96761 Tel (808) 667-9225 Fax (808) 667-9293 Rooms 19

Steps from the waterfront, this charming inn combines plantation style with modern convenience. Romantic island-style guest rooms have *lānai* (verandas); suites have kitchenettes. Breakfast is served around the pool, a delightful garden oasis in hot Lahaina town. Gerard's Restaurant *(see p204)* is on the first floor. **www.theplantationinn.com**

LAHAINA Lahaina Shores Beach Resort 🏊🏃 P $$$

475 Front St, 96761 Tel (808) 661-4835 Fax (808) 661-4696 Rooms 200

This hotel is right on the beach and offers great value. Accommodations include studios, one-bedroom, and penthouse suites with full kitchens, *lānai* (verandas), and ocean or mountain views. Right next to the 505 Front Street shopping village, with restaurants and boutiques, the hotel is a short walk from the center of town. **www.lahainashores.com**

MAKAWAO Banyan Tree House 🖼️🏊 P $$

3265 Baldwin Ave, 96768 Tel (808) 572-9021 Fax (808) 573-5073 Rooms 7

Accommodations here are in a classic Hawaiian pineapple plantation home and four cottages. The historic main house has three bedrooms and three baths. The cottages have bathrooms and phones; some have kitchens. Between Pā'ia and Makawao, the location offers sweeping views of the ocean and nearby islands. **www.banyantreehouse.com**

MĀKENA Mākena Beach & Golf Resort 🍴🏊🏃🍸🏋️ P $$$$

5400 Mākena Alanui, 96753 Tel (808) 874-1111 Fax (808) 879-8763 Rooms 291

Standing alone in Mākena, this gleaming, wing-shaped hotel fronts a big, beautiful beach. The guest rooms are stylishly simple in their design. Some are oceanfront and all have an ocean view. Three restaurants, two pools, six tennis courts, and 36 holes of championship golf are some of the amenities on offer. **www.makenaresortmaui.com**

Key to Price Guide *see p178* **Key to Symbols** *see back cover flap*

NĀPILI Outrigger Napili Shores Resort

5315 Lower Honoapi'ilani Rd, 96761 **Tel** *(808) 669-8061* **Fax** *(808) 669-5407* **Rooms** *152*

Perched at one end of crescent-shaped Napili Bay, these studio and one-bedroom units have *lānai* (verandas) and full kitchens. There is a restaurant and a grocery store, along with two pools, an adult hot tub, a croquet lawn, and a barbecue area. This is a great location for viewing sunsets and seasonal whale watching. **www.outrigger.com**

NĀPILI Napili Kai Beach Resort

5900 Lower Honoapi'ilani Rd, 96761 **Tel** *(808) 669-6271* **Fax** *(808) 669-0086* **Rooms** *161*

This older, spacious and graceful property commands one of the best beach locations on the island. It offers hotel rooms, studios and one- and two-bedrooms suites, almost all with ocean views. There are four pools, a Jacuzzi, putting greens, an exercise room, and an oceanfront restaurant in the lush, tropical grounds. **www.napilikai.com**

WAILEA Grand Champions

151 Wailea Iki Pl, 96753 **Tel** *(808) 879-1595* **Fax** *(808) 874-3554* **Rooms** *188*

The exclusive country club atmosphere of these luxury condominiums is due to their proximity to the world-class Wailea Tennis Club and Wailea Golf Courses. Condos range from one to three bedrooms, all with two baths and European-style kitchens. Within walking distance of beaches, the village has resort amenities. **www.drhmaui.com**

WAILEA Palms at Wailea

3200 Wailea Alanui, 96753 **Tel** *(808) 879-5800* **Fax** *(808) 874-3723* **Rooms** *150*

These spacious one- and two-bedrooms condominium units in the upscale resort of Wailea offer great value. Each is well decorated, has a big kitchen, washer-dryer, comfortable living and dining areas, and a private *lānai* (veranda). There are verdant tropical gardens and a pool. The beach is a short downhill walk away. **www.outrigger.com**

WAILEA 'Ekahi, 'Elua and 'Ekolu

3750 Wailea Alanui, 96753 **Tel** *(808) 879-1595* **Fax** *(808) 874-3554* **Rooms** *594*

Many of these individually owned condominium units (managed by Destination Resorts Hawaii) in upscale Wailea offer contemporary furnishings and custom appliances. All have air-conditioning, high-speed Internet, and daily housekeeping. A good-value option in this pricey resort community. **www.drhmaui.com.com**

WAILEA The Fairmont Kea Lani Maui

4100 Wailea Alanui, 96753 **Tel** *(808) 875-4100* **Fax** *(808) 875-2250* **Rooms** *450*

With its stark, onion-domed exterior, it looks like a castle from the Arabian Nights. Inside, it has a cool, luxurious island ambience. All rooms are suites with sitting rooms and huge marble bathrooms. There are 37 oceanfront one-, two-, and three-bedroom villas, each with a private pool. Three restaurants and a spa are here, too. **www.kealani.com**

WAILEA Four Seasons Resort Maui

3900 Wailea Alanui, 96753 **Tel** *(808) 874-8000* **Fax** *(808) 891-7086* **Rooms** *301*

Huge guest rooms, imposing furnishings, elegant decor, and incredible service: all trademarks of Four Seasons resorts are available on a sparkling beach in Wailea. There are three restaurants, including Spago *(see p206)*, a spa, and a beauty salon. At the two pools, an attendant will, on request, cool your face with a water spritz. **www.fourseasons.com**

WAILEA Wailea Beach Marriott Resort & Spa

3700 Wailea Alanui, 96753 **Tel** *(808) 879-1922* **Fax** *(808) 875-4878* **Rooms** *423*

Set on a rocky promontory between two sparkling white-sand beaches, this sprawling property has restaurants, pools (infinity and children's), and a spa. Rooms are quite large, with refrigerators, cable television, and an ocean view in most cases. An oceanfront *lu'au* rounds out the resort experience here. **www.marriott.com**

WAILEA Grand Wailea Resort, Hotel & Spa

3850 Wailea Alanui, 96753 **Tel** *(808) 875-1234* **Fax** *(808) 874-2411* **Rooms** *780*

Grand is the word for this opulent beachfront resort, a fantasy land of art and ambience set in sprawling tropical grounds with awesome water features: waterfalls, streams, rapids, slides, reflecting pools, swimming pools, and a saltwater lagoon. Rooms are on a grand scale too, as are the bathtubs. The spa is legendary. **www.grandwailea.com**

WAILEA Mākena Surf

96 Mākena Alanui, 96753 **Tel** *(808) 891-6249* **Fax** *(808) 874-3554* **Rooms** *107*

Managed by Destination Resorts Hawai'i, these one, two-, three-, and four-bedroom condominiums are big, have huge *lānai* (verandas), and feel secluded. They offer all the comforts of home, including pleasant furnishings and full kitchens, plus extras such as a wet bar and a daily housekeeping service. **www.drhmaui.com**

WAILUKU Banana Bungalow

310 N Market St, 96793 **Tel** *(808) 244-5090* **Rooms** *26*

The Banana Bungalow offers probably the least expensive accommodation on Maui. It has both private and dorm rooms. Kitchen facilities, a Jacuzzi, and high-speed Internet are available on-site. Not large or luxurious, but excellent value. Daily free tours are offered to Hana, beaches, and Haleakala. **www.mauihostel.com**

WAILUKU Old Wailuku Inn at Ulapono

2199 Kaho'okele St, 96793 **Tel** *(808) 244-5897* **Fax** *(808) 242-9600* **Rooms** *10*

Built in 1924 by a wealthy banker as a wedding gift for his daughter, this historic home has been lovingly restored by hosts Tom and Janice Fairbanks. The ambience of an earlier gracious time is prevalent throughout. This cool, open, and airy house has guest rooms named for Hawaiian flowers, with quilts to match. **www.mauiinn.com**

HAWAI'I ISLAND

HILO Hilo Hawaiian Hotel
71 Banyan Dr, 96720 **Tel** *(808) 935-9361* **Fax** *(808) 961-9642* **Rooms** *286*

The views from the guest rooms here are the best in Hilo. All have air-conditioning, televisions, on-demand movies, coffee makers, and baths. Suites offer good value for families as they include a kitchen and living-dining area. Guest services include a laundromat, free parking, a pool, restaurants, and a day spa. **www.castleresorts.com**

HILO Hilo Seaside Hotel
126 Banyan Dr, 96720 **Tel** *(808) 935-0821* **Fax** *(808) 969-9195* **Rooms** *135*

Rooms here are not fancy, but affordable, clean, and well kept; all have refrigerators, televisions, air-conditioning, ceiling fans, and *lānai* (verandas). The pretty tropical gardens include *koi* ponds and colorful flowers, and there is a pool. It is a 45-minute drive from Hawai'i Volcanoes National Park *(see pp152–5)*. **www.seasidehotelshawaii.com**

HILO Naniloa Volcanoes Resort
93 Banyan Dr, 96720 **Tel** *(808) 969-3333* **Fax** *(808) 969-6622* **Rooms** *318*

This affordable resort is a Hilo landmark. Rooms are air-conditioned and have TVs and refrigerators. There are two pools, a spa, and a restaurant on the property. Right on Hilo Bay, it is well placed for a trip to Hawai'i Volcanoes National Park *(see pp152–5)*. **www.hottours.us**

HILO Uncle Billy's Hilo Bay Hotel
87 Banyan Dr, 96720 **Tel** *(808) 935-0861* **Fax** *(808) 935-7903* **Rooms** *143*

Uncle Billy's is the least expensive place to stay on Hilo Bay. The rooms have televisions and air-conditioning; some have kitchenettes. The on-site general store offers deli-style food, souvenirs, sundries, and resort apparel. There is a *hula* show nightly in the restaurant. This is the place for a fun, island-style experience. **www.unclebilly.com**

KAILUA-KONA King Kamehameha Kona Beach Hotel
75-5660 Palani Rd, 96740 **Tel** *(808) 329-2911* **Fax** *(808) 329-4602* **Rooms** *460*

This hotel has a fabulous location, with its own beach in downtown Kailua-Kona. This is an old property with modern amenities including a restaurant and an outdoor bar with Hawaiian entertainment, a pool, Jacuzzi, tennis courts, a shopping arcade, and a Hawaiian cultural activity center. **www.konabeachhotel.com**

KAILUA-KONA Outrigger Royal Sea Cliff Resort
75-6040 Alii Dr, 96740 **Tel** *(808) 329-8021* **Fax** *(808) 326-1887* **Rooms** *148*

Rising high above a lava rock bluff looking out toward the sea, the terraced design here provides uninterrupted ocean views from balconies that are a feature of the one- and two-bedroom villas. Units have kitchens and washer-dryers. The lush tropical grounds include a cascading water feature and two oceanfront pools. **www.outrigger.com**

KAILUA-KONA Royal Kona Resort
75-5852 Ali'i Dr, 96740 **Tel** *(808) 329-3111* **Fax** *(808) 329-2230* **Rooms** *436*

Perched oceanfront on Kailua Bay, there are the usual resort amenities to enjoy, such as a multi-level swimming pool and a saltwater lagoon. Guest rooms have granite countertops and marble showers; all have *lānai* (verandas). Don the Beachcomber restaurant is on the property. **www.hawaiihotels.com**

KAILUA-KONA Aston Kona By The Sea
75-6106 Alii Dr, 96740 **Tel** *(808) 327-2300* **Fax** *(808) 327-2333* **Rooms** *56*

Situated along a rocky shoreline, this four-story condominium complex has an oceanfront swimming pool and Jacuzzi. Redecorated to reflect a casual Hawaiian style, the large one- and two-bedroom suites have kitchens and *lānai* (verandas) with ocean views. Golf, tennis, shops, and restaurants are nearby. **www.astonhotels.com**

KAILUA-KONA Kona Village Resort
Queen Ka'ahumanu Hwy, 96740 **Tel** *(808) 325-5555* **Fax** *(808) 325-5124* **Rooms** *125*

Indulge yourself at this exquisite resort. Bungalows have thatched roofs, a bedroom, bathroom, and *lānai* (veranda). Some have outdoor hot tubs and a room with a single bed; none have televisions, air-conditioning or phones. All meals are included. Historic sites and cultural programs add to the Polynesian feel. **www.konavillage.com**

KEAUHOU Outrigger Keauhou Beach Resort & Spa
75-6740 Ali'i Dr, 96740 **Tel** *(808) 332-3441* **Fax** *(808) 322-3117* **Rooms** *309*

This hotel sits right on the ocean and has easy-to-explore tidepools full of fascinating marine life, such as reef fish and sea turtles. There are interesting spots on land, too, such as the remains of three Hawaiian *heiau* (ancient temples) and a replica of King David Kalākaua's summer cottage. Resort amenities include a spa. **www.outrigger.com**

KEAUHOU Outrigger Kanaloa at Kona
78-261 Manukai St, 96740 **Tel** *(808) 322-9625* **Fax** *(808) 322-3818* **Rooms** *166*

These oceanfront apartments range in size from one bedroom to two bedrooms with a loft. They are roomy and have open-beamed ceilings, family-sized kitchens, washer-dryers, and covered *lānai* (verandas). There are three pools, two tennis courts, and barbecue grills. Golf and shopping are available nearby. **www.outrigger.com**

Key to Price Guide *see p178* **Key to Symbols** *see back cover flap*

KEAUHOU Sheraton Keauhou Bay Resort & Spa

🏨 🏊 🎿 📺 🍴 🅿️ $$$$

78-128 Ehukai St **Tel** *(808) 930-4900* **Fax** *(808) 930-4800* **Rooms** *522*

Perched on an old lava flow, this resort has modern rooms and the latest amenities: a fantasy pool with the island's largest waterslide, a spa, golf, tennis, restaurants, and children's programs. Just about everything is modern, but in time honored tradition the manta rays still come for their nightly visits. **www.sheratonkeauhou.com**

KOHALA COAST Hilton Waikoloa Village Resort

🏨 🏊 🎿 📺 🍴 🅿️ $$$

69-425 Waikoloa Beach Dr **Tel** *(808) 886-1234* **Fax** *(808) 886-2902* **Rooms** *1,240*

Set in extensive and beautiful grounds, this is the giant among Kohala's resorts. There are the usual activities – tennis, golf, and a pool – and a program in which guests can swim with Atlantic bottlenose dolphins. The resort transportation takes the form of Swiss-made trams and mahogany boats. **www.hiltonwaikoloavillage.com**

KOHALA COAST Hāpuna Beach Prince Hotel

🏨 🏊 🎿 📺 🍴 🅿️ $$$$

62-100 Kaunaoa Dr, 96743 **Tel** *(808) 880-1111* **Fax** *(808) 880-3142* **Rooms** *350*

This stylish, low-key resort nestles beside the island's best beach. Guest rooms face the ocean and have private *lānai* (verandas), entertainment centers, refrigerators, and bathrobes. Amenities include a spa, golf, tennis courts, five restaurants, plus access to facilities at the Mauna Kea Beach Hotel next door. **www.princeresortshawaii.com**

KOHALA COAST Mauna Kea Beach Hotel

🏨 🏊 🎿 📺 🍴 🅿️ $$$$

62-100 Mauna Kea Beach Dr, 96743 **Tel** *(808) 882-72222* **Fax** *(808) 882-5700* **Rooms** *258*

The Big Island's first big resort, the Mauna Kea is still one of the best in Hawai'i. It has been extensively renovated and upgraded with fewer, more spacious rooms. Rooms have *lānai* (verandas), and residents can enjoy the remarkable collection of museum-quality Pacific and Asian art and artifacts. **www.princeresortshawaii.com**

KOHALA COAST Mauna Lani Bay Hotel & Bungalows

🏨 🏊 🎿 📺 🍴 🅿️ $$$$

68-1400 Mauna Lani Dr, 96743 **Tel** *(808) 885-6622* **Fax** *(808) 885-1484* **Rooms** *355*

The rooms here are large and all but 27 have ocean views. Every room has a *lānai* (veranda), air-conditioning, robes, coffee, and other high-end touches. Amenities include five restaurants, a spa, a sports and fitness club, tennis courts, two golf courses, water sports, a Hawaiian cultural program, and a children's camp. **www.maunalani.com**

KOHALA COAST Waikoloa Beach Marriott Resort

🏨 🏊 🎿 📺 🍴 🅿️ $$$$

69-275 Waikoloa Beach Dr, 96738 **Tel** *(808) 886-6789* **Fax** *(808) 886-7852* **Rooms** *555*

The location of this resort on 'Anaeho'omalu Bay (or A-Bay, as it is known locally) is its most outstanding feature. The beach is good for swimming, snorkeling, diving, kayaking, windsurfing, and exploring ancient royal fish ponds. This hotel is not as luxurious as some of its Kohala Coast neighbors, but lower room rates reflect this. **www.marriott.com**

KOHALA COAST Fairmont Orchid Hawaii

🏨 🏊 🎿 📺 🍴 🅿️ $$$$$

1 North Kanikū Dr, 96743 **Tel** *(808) 885-2000* **Fax** *(808) 885-5778* **Rooms** *483*

The spacious rooms in this luxury hotel have big *lānai* (verandas), sitting areas, and marble bathrooms, each with a double sink and separate shower. Active travelers will love the outdoor spa, fitness center, oceanfront pool, canoe paddling, 36 holes of championship golf, 10 tennis courts, and many cultural activities. **www.fairmont.com/orchid**

KOHALA COAST Four Seasons Resort Hualalai

🏨 🏊 🎿 📺 🍴 🅿️ $$$$$

72-100 Ka'upulehu Dr, 96740 **Tel** *(808) 325-8000* **Fax** *(808) 325-8053* **Rooms** *243*

Luxurious oceanfront accommodations are available here in bungalows that surround three swimming pools. There are five pools on the property; one of them is a saltwater pond containing colorful reef fish. An award-winning spa and further luxurious resort amenities pamper the guests at this beautiful resort. **www.fourseasons.com/hualalai**

VOLCANO VILLAGE Chalet Kīlauea – The Inn at Volcano

🎿 🍴 🅿️ $$$

Wright Rd & Laukapu Rd, 96785 **Tel** *(808) 967-7786* **Fax** *(808) 967-8660* **Rooms** *5*

The rooms at this charming, affordable place are individually decorated and have names such as Out of Africa. They are adorned with art and memorabilia from the travels of the chalet's owners. Guests begin their day with the sounds of the rain forest, and enjoy afternoon tea in the living room. **www.volcano-hawaii.com**

VOLCANO VILLAGE Kīlauea Lodge

🏨 🎿 $$$

19-3948 Old Volcanco Rd, 96785 **Tel** *(808) 967-7366* **Fax** *(808) 967-7367* **Rooms** *17*

Built as a YMCA camp in 1938, this refurbished lodge is just a mile (1.6 km) from Hawai'i Volcanoes National Park *(see pp152–5)*. There are 12 rooms and three vacation cottages. Some rooms have fireplaces or wood-burning stoves; stained-glass windows feature throughout. Cottages have kitchens and two bedrooms. **www.kilauealodge.com**

WAIMEA Kamuela Inn

🎿 🍴 🅿️ $$

65-1300 Kawaihae Rd, 96743 **Tel** *(808) 885-4243* **Fax** *(808) 885-8857* **Rooms** *31*

At this tranquil, private bed and breakfast, old-world charm is combined with all the modern conveniences of home. Rooms and suites have private baths; some have kitchenettes. The inn's location in the quaint town of Waimea is 30 minutes from the island's finest white-sand beaches and 10 minutes from golf courses. **www.hawaii-bnb.com/kamuela**

WAIMEA Waimea Gardens Cottages

📋 🅿️ $$

Mamalahoa Hwy **Tel** *(808) 265-3100* **Fax** *(808) 962-6560* **Rooms** *4*

Three cozy cottages set alongside a meandering stream on rolling pasture land. The Waimea Wing has a fireplace; the Kohala Wing a Japanese-style soaking tub and a private enclosed garden. Both are furnished with antiques and come with plenty of special touches, such as plush robes, bedside mints, and fresh flowers. **www.waimeagardens.com**

KAUA'I

HANALEI Hanalai Colony Resort $$$
5-7130 Kūhiō Hwy, 96714 **Tel** *(808) 826-6235* **Fax** *(808) 826-9893* **Rooms** *52*

This seaside village of two-bedroom condominium units on Kaua'i's north shore offers a peaceful retreat: there are no private phones or televisions. These are, however, available in an oceanfront community room, along with computers and Internet access. Complimentary weekly breakfasts and *mai tai* cocktail parties are held, too. **www.hcr.com**

KALĀHEO Classic Vacation Cottages $$
2687 Onu Pl, 96741 **Tel** *(808) 332-9201* **Fax** *(808) 332-7645* **Rooms** *9*

These reasonably priced, nicely furnished studios, cottages, and homes are set in the quaint town of Kalāheo, just a few minutes' drive from Po'ipū Resort. Studios have kitchenettes; other units have full kitchens. Guests can make use of tennis racquets, golf clubs, and snorkel gear to enjoy nearby recreational facilities. **www.classiccottages.com**

KALĀHEO Kalāheo Inn $$
4444 Paplina Rd, 96741 **Tel** *(808) 332-6023* **Fax** *(808) 332-5242* **Rooms** *15*

These one-, two-, and three-bedroom suites are decorated in comfortable island style. They are situated in lush, tropical landscaping, with fruit trees and colorful flowers. Each unit has an equipped kitchenette, television, and DVD. There are laundry facilities and free on-island phone calls. It is a 10-minute drive to Po'ipū beaches. **www.kalaheoinn.com**

KAPA'A Kaua'i Sands $
420 Papaloa Rd, 96746 **Tel** *(808) 822-4951* **Fax** *(808) 822-0998* **Rooms** *200*

Offering spartan, yet clean beachfront accommodations, this is part of the only Hawaiian-owned hotel chain in the world. Its grounds feature native plants and a walking-jogging path extends for a mile (1.6 km) along the white-sand beach. Golf, tennis, and shopping are nearby. There are self-service laundry facilities. **www.kauaisandshotel.com**

KAPA'A Aston Kaua'i Beach at Makaiwa $$
4-484 Kūhiō Hwy, 96746 **Tel** *(808) 822-3455* **Fax** *(808) 822-1830* **Rooms** *311*

Within walking distance of three major shopping centers and popular island activities, this resort is situated on a beautiful oceanfront site, amid a historic grove of swaying palm trees that evoke the essence of traditional Hawai'i. There are lots of activities and amenities, including high-speed Internet access in every room. **www.astonhotels.com**

KAPA'A Hotel Coral Reef $$
4-1516 Kūhiō Hwy, 96746 **Tel** *(808) 822-4481* **Fax** *(808) 822-7705* **Rooms** *48*

One of the first hotels built on Kauai's spectacular Royal Coconut Coast, the Coral Reef has been remodeled and offers affordable accommodations. The tropical oceanfront setting on white sandy beaches in the heart of charming Kapa'a is only 10 miles (16 km) from Līhue International Airport. **www.hotelcoralreefresort.com**

KAPA'A Kapa'a Sands Resort $$
380 Papaloa Rd, 96746 **Tel** *(808) 822-4901* **Fax** *(808) 822-1556* **Rooms** *20*

This affordable oceanfront property offers individually owned studio and two-bedroom condominium units. All are fully furnished and have telephones, televisions, microwaves, and ceiling fans. Shops and restaurants at nearby shopping plazas, hiking trails, waterfalls, and outdoor activities are all close by. **www.kapaasands.com**

KAPA'A Aloha Beach Resort $$$
3-5920 Kūhiō Hwy, 96746 **Tel** *(808) 823-6000* **Fax** *(808) 823-6666* **Rooms** *216*

Situated on Wailua Bay, this resort is convenient for the airport and many Kaua'i attractions. An affordable full-service, family oriented property, it has rooms, suites, and cottages, plus several restaurants, a spa, a fitness room, two pools, and more. It is close to Lydgate State Park *(see p162)* and a playground. **www.alohabeachresortkauai.com**

KAPA'A Kaua'i Coast Resort at the Beachboy $$$$
4-484 Kūhiō Hwy, 96746 **Tel** *(808) 822-3441* **Fax** *(808) 822-0843* **Rooms** *108*

Fronting a long beach, this property offers one- and two-bedroom units, each with a *lānai* (veranda), full kitchen, washer-dryer, air-conditioning, telephone, and television. Studio units have a mini-bar and coffee maker. Choose from the heated pool or the oceanside Jacuzzi. There are shopping and dining options nearby. **www.shellhospitality.com**

KŌKE'E Kōke'e State Park Lodge $
3600 Kōke'e Road (Hwy 550), 96796 **Tel** *(808) 335-6061* **Fax** *(808) 335-3519* **Rooms** *12*

Located in Kōke'e State Park *(see pp170–71)*, the Kōke'e Lodge contains a gift shop and restaurant and maintains a dozen cabins. Reservations for the cabins are a must and should be made months in advance. They accommodate up to six and come with bed linens, cooking utensils, and wood for the woodstoves. **www.thelodgeatkokee.net**

KŌLOA Kaua'i Condominiums at Po'ipū Kai Resort $$
1941 Poipu Rd, 96756 **Tel** *(808) 742-7400* **Fax** *(808) 742-9121* **Rooms** *200*

Set amid extensive tropical gardens, these condominium units have *lānai* (verandas), kitchens, washer-dryers, cable television, stereos, CD players, and telephones with voicemail. Tennis courts, a swimming pool, Jacuzzi, and restaurant are on the resort. Brennecke and Shipwreck beaches are easily accessible. **www.suite-paradise.com**

Key to Price Guide *see p178* **Key to Symbols** *see back cover flap*

LĪHU'E Garden Island Inn

P $$

3445 Wilcox Rd, 96766 **Tel** *(808) 245-7227* **Fax** *(808) 245-7603* **Rooms** *21*

This economically priced inn is conveniently located in the heart of Kaua'i's bustling Kalapakī Beach–Nāwiliwili Harbor area, minutes from Līhu'e Airport and only a two minute stroll from Kalapakī Bay. All rooms come with air-conditioning, refrigerators, microwaves, wet bars, cable television, and a daily maid service. **www.gardenislandinn.com**

LĪHU'E Kaha Lani Resort

🏖 🛄 P $$$

4460 Nehe Rd, 96766 **Tel** *(808) 822-9331* **Fax** *(808) 822-2828* **Rooms** *35*

Oceanfront in the heart of Līhue, surrounded by miles of white sandy beaches and lush tropical gardens, these one- and two-bedroom units feature kitchens, views of the Pacific Ocean, and the comforts of home. The resort has barbecue areas, putting greens, tennis, and a pool. Shops and dining are a short drive away. **www.castleresorts.com**

LĪHU'E Kaua'i Beach Resort

🍴 🏖 🛄 📺 🚻 P $$$$

4331 Kauai Beach Dr, 96766 **Tel** *(808) 245-1955* **Fax** *(808) 246-3956* **Rooms** *351*

Fronting 3 miles (5 km) of beautiful beach on the east coast of Kaua'i, this plantation-style resort set in its own lush grounds boasts spa, fitness centre, four pools – including two lagoons with waterfalls, and a lava tube waterslide – and much else besides. **www.kauaibeachresorthawaii.com**

LĪHU'E Kaua'i Marriott Resort & Beach Club

🍴 🏖 🛄 📺 🚻 P $$$$

3610 Rice St, 96766 **Tel** *(808) 245-5050* **Fax** *(808) 245-5049* **Rooms** *345*

This resort stretches along a white-sand beach, just a mile (1.6 km) from Līhue Airport. A spectacular pool, two Jack Nicklaus-designed golf courses, and several restaurants, including the casual Duke's Canoe Club *(see p209)*, are available to guests. In-room amenities include a mini-refrigerator and cable television. **www.marriott.com**

PO'IPŪ Aston at Po'ipū Kai

🏖 🚻 P $$$

1775 Po'ipū Rd, 96756 **Tel** *(808) 742-7424* **Fax** *(808) 742-8798* **Rooms** *350*

This resort complex is set on vast grounds in sunny Po'ipū. Accommodations are in five individual communities, each with its own style. All suites are tropically decorated and have kitchens and *lānai* (verandas). Shopping, dining, activities, and sightseeing are nearby. Brennecke and Shipwreck Beaches are a stroll away. **www.astonhotels.com**

PO'IPŪ Outrigger Kiahuna Plantation

🍴 🏖 🛄 📺 🚻 P $$$

2253 Po'ipū Rd, 96756 **Tel** *(808) 742-6411* **Fax** *(808) 742-1698* **Rooms** *204*

Comfortable and spacious one- and two-bedroom units, in quaint wooden apartments reminiscent of Hawai'i's 19th-century past, are set on an historic expanse of former sugar cane plantation. Units have *lānai* (verandas), fully equipped kitchens, and daily maid service. Shopping and championship golf are nearby. **www.outrigger.com**

PO'IPŪ Sheraton Kauai Resort

🍴 🏖 🛄 📺 🚻 P $$$

2442 Ho'onani Rd, 96756 **Tel** *(808) 742-1661* **Fax** *(808) 742-9777* **Rooms** *394*

Commanding a premier location on famous Po'ipū Beach, and no taller than the coconut trees on the property, this resort offers a full array of services and amenities in a beautiful tropical setting. Hawaiian culture is showcased in the art work dotted around and in activities such as *lei* making and *hula* lessons. **www.sheraton-kauai.com**

PO'IPŪ Grand Hyatt Kauai Resort & Spa

🍴 🏖 🛄 📺 🚻 P $$$

1571 Po'ipū Rd, 96756 **Tel** *(808) 742-1234* **Fax** *(808) 742-1557* **Rooms** *600*

Grand is the key word at this elegant and luxurious large oceanfront resort. The lush, tropical grounds include three pools (one with waterfalls), water slides, and meandering saltwater swimming lagoons. A full-service spa, championship golf, tennis, and several restaurants add to the experience. **www.kauaihyatt.com**

PRINCEVILLE Hanalei Bay Resort & Suites

🏖 🚻 📺 🛄 P $$$

5380 Honoiki Rd, 76722 **Tel** *(808) 826-6522* **Fax** *(808) 826-6680* **Rooms** *182*

Perched above Hanalei Bay, this resort has all the tropical amenities one would want, including fabulous views, lagoon pools with waterfalls, open-air restaurants, tennis courts, and superb golf. The rooms are light and airy, with tropical furnishings, *lānai* (verandas), air-conditioning, telephones, and a daily maid service. **www.hanaleibayresort.com**

PRINCEVILLE Princeville Bed & Breakfast

P $$$

3875 Kamehameha Rd, 96722 **Tel** *(808) 826-6733* **Fax** *(808) 826-1558* **Rooms** *4*

This bed and breakfast is located on the fairway at the Prince Golf Course. Its biggest room is the penthouse suite, with a semi-private entrance and large whirlpool tub. All rooms have televisions and mini-refrigerators. Continental breakfast is served. Guests get discounts at the golf course. Children are not allowed to stay. **www.kauai-bandb.com**

PRINCEVILLE Princeville Hotel & Resort

🍴 🏖 🛄 📺 🚻 P $$$$$

5520 Ka Haku Rd, 96722 **Tel** *(808) 826-9644* **Fax** *(808) 826-1166* **Rooms** *252*

This elegant resort, built on a bluff above Hanalei Bay, offers exquisite panoramas, spacious rooms, and splendid dining. Uniquely, the lobby is up on the ninth floor and the buildings terrace down to the beach. The views are of waterfalls cascading down verdant cliffs and the sparkling blue Pacific Ocean. **www.princeville.com**

WAIMEA Waimea Plantation Cottages

🍴 🏖 🚻 🛄 P $$$

9400 Kaumuali'i Hwy, 96796 **Tel** *(808) 338-1625* **Fax** *(808) 338-2338* **Rooms** *47*

Step back into old Hawai'i at these wonderful seaside plantation cottages, set in a coconut grove at the gateway to Waimea Canyon. Situated on the western coast of Kauai, these cottages have all been individually restored, with period-inspired furnishings, kitchens, and a front porch overlooking the grassy lawn. **www.waimea-plantation.com**

WHERE TO EAT

From local-style drive-ins to elegant dining rooms, the opportunities for eating well in Hawai'i are endless. In addition to hundreds of restaurants of every description, there are informal outlets – such as street stalls, delis, and coffeehouses – that sell delicious, cheap food, which is perfect for a quick bite between bouts of sightseeing. In large shopping malls, food courts offer a wide,

Colorful sign in Kaua'i

surprisingly good array of ethnic and American food, and for those with late-night cravings, some supermarkets and convenience stores offer food 24 hours a day. There are many open-air restaurants, and indoor places are usually air-conditioned. Unless you stick to the mainstream fast-food outlets, you cannot fail to taste the full range of exotic flavors that influence cooking in Hawai'i.

Beach Bar at the Sheraton Moana Surfrider Hotel *(see p180)*

MEAL TIMES

Some visitors to Hawai'i may be surprised by the state's early meal times. You will find places open for breakfast at 5am; lunch starts at 11am; and dinner begins at 5pm and is often over by 9pm. Many local-style establishments do not serve dinner and close by 2pm.

Cocktail hour begins early, too, around 4pm. Most hotels and restaurants serve *pūpū* (Hawaiian-style hors d'oeuvres) with the drinks, sometimes at no additional charge.

Many restaurants are closed on Sunday or Monday, but hours and closing days often change. You should phone if you have your heart set on a particular restaurant (it is a good idea to book anyway).

HAWAI'I REGIONAL CUISINE

The days of Hawai'i as a gastronomic wasteland are long gone – thanks, in no small part, to the advent of the Hawai'i Regional Cuisine

movement. Peter Merriman *(see p208)* is widely acknowledged as the leader of a pack of chefs who were determined to put Hawai'i on the culinary map. Other chefs, including Roy Yamaguchi on O'ahu *(see p198)* and Bev Gannon at Joe's Bar & Grill on Maui *(see p206)*, quickly followed suit – until a core group of 12 chefs formed a nonprofit organization dedicated to the promotion of Hawai'i Regional Cuisine.

The cuisine takes its ingredients directly from local farms and the surrounding Pacific, but its influences come from the many ethnic groups that make up Hawaiian society. The results – dishes such as breadfruit vichyssoise, tempura of Keāhole baby lobster, and Kona coffee cheesecake, as well as the upsurge of interest in Hawaiian cooking – have been of benefit to everyone,

from local producers to the dining public. Whichever name you use – Hawai'i Regional, Island Regional, East Meets West, or Pacific Rim – this new cuisine makes the most of what the islands have to offer.

LOCAL FOOD

Those dishes collectively known as "local food" are as diverse as the population that has created them. This style of cooking is filling, inexpensive, and unbeatable in the eyes of local people and those who acquire a taste for it.

The "plate lunch" is the most traditional local-style meal and consists of a meat or poultry main course – such as teriyaki beef, two scoops of sticky rice, and a scoop of macaroni or potato salad heaped onto a paper plate or molded tray. These lunches are dispensed from street carts or diners,

Chef Roy Yamaguchi at his restaurant in Honolulu *(see p198)*

The oceanfront Pacific'O in Lahaina (see p204)

and there are often dozens of food choices – of Japanese, Chinese, Korean, Filipino, and even American origin. Expect to pay in the region of $5–8.

Poi (a gray paste made from pounded taro root and definitely an acquired taste); *kālua* pork (from a whole pig baked in leaves, especially at *lū'au*); sweet potato; *limu* (seaweed); and *laulau* (fish, pork, and taro leaf stems wrapped in *ti* leaves and then steamed) are all easy-to-find Hawaiian staples.

You will see sushi everywhere, and *bento* is a Japanese version of the plate lunch, served cold. *Saimin*, a Japanese-style bowl of broth brimming with pork, fish cake, green onions, and noodles, is popular for breakfast, lunch, or dinner. Another common dish is *manapua*, the local version of Chinese steamed buns filled with seasoned pork.

Local sweet treats include shave ice (or "snow cones"), shavings of ice flavored with syrup, and crack seed – dried fruits and chewy candies seasoned with Chinese five-spice known as *li hing mui*.

FAST FOOD AND TAKE-OUT MEALS

Hawai'i is part of the United States, after all, so don't be surprised to find Burger King, McDonald's, Pizza Hut, Taco Bell, and the rest. However, you will find things on the menu that are particular to Hawai'i: most notably *saimin*, sticky rice and Portuguese sausage. Local-style fast food is sold at numerous drive-ins throughout Hawai'i, and at the many branches of Zippy's on O'ahu; most of the Zippy's outlets are open 24 hours. Another local company, L & L Drive-In, is expanding fast and has many outlets on O'ahu, too.

Mock-Victorian Burger King, Waikīkī

Few restaurants will not do food to take out. Many groceries and supermarkets have delis and salad, Chinese food, or *bento* bars offering take-out meals. Health food stores often have food bars, too. All these places are good for picnic food – Hawai'i being ideal picnicking territory.

Delivery, on the other hand, is rarely available in Hawai'i. Your choices will be limited to large chains like Pizza Hut and Domino's Pizza.

COFFEEHOUSES

Just like on the US mainland, coffeehouses have opened up all over the islands. The difference in Hawai'i is that they are not chains, and they feature aromatic home-grown Kona coffee *(see p135)*.

Most coffeehouses sell delicious pastries, mostly home-baked, and many provide light meals as well.

ALCOHOL

Most restaurants have bars and wine lists offering a good choice from around the world. Restaurants without a bar will usually allow patrons to bring in their own beer or wine, and there is rarely a charge for opening the bottle.

VEGETARIANS

Although there are only a few vegetarian restaurants in Hawai'i, many places have a vegetarian section on their menu and will accommodate vegetarians with a plate of steamed vegetables and rice or a vegetarian pasta dish. All you have to do is ask.

CHILDREN

Hawai'i is an extremely child-friendly place, and the only restaurants that do not welcome children with open arms are the few very formal dining rooms – mostly located in fancy resort hotels. But even here, children should never be turned away.

Many restaurants provide a children's menu, with small portions of the food kids love, such as pizzas and burgers.

ETIQUETTE

Smoking is prohibited in restaurants in Hawai'i, so those wanting to light up during a meal will have to step outside before doing so.

A standard restaurant tip is 15 percent of the check. Depending upon the service and style of restaurant, you may wish to tip more or less than this.

Casual dress is acceptable in all but the most formal of Hawai'i's restaurants, and then jackets are usually requested rather than required.

Local-style diner on Hawai'i Island

The Flavors of Hawai'i

The diet of ancient Hawaiians consisted of fish, shellfish, pork, fresh fruit – mostly bananas – tubers like sweet potatoes, and, most importantly, taro *(kalo)*. Since the migration of many ethnic groups to Hawai'i in the 1820s, island food has evolved to embrace various new recipes and ingredients. The fusion of these traditional cuisines has brought delicious modern offerings with a Hawaiian twist. Although Hawaiian food is often modified to appeal to Western palates, it is still possible for visitors to experience truly authentic local dishes at a *lū'au*.

Macadamia nuts

Worker tending plants in a taro field, Maui

TRADITIONAL HAWAIIAN FOOD

Hawaiians once got everything they needed from ancient land divisions that ran from mountain to sea known as *ahupua'a*. These plots of land provided them with sweet potatoes, bananas, dozens of types of *limu* (seaweed), fish and seafood from fresh, brackish, and ocean water, and of course taro, of which there were also dozens of varieties. Many foods were eaten raw, but ancient Hawaiians had several ingenious cooking methods including the *'imu*, or underground oven, which is still widely used today. In this, everything from a whole pig to individual sweet potatoes are slow-cooked at a very low temperature. The heat is generated from extremely dry, hot rocks that fill the pit. The rocks are covered with banana stalks and *ti* leaves onto which the food is laid. It is then covered with more leaves and earth and left to bake. A whole pig takes about nine hours to cook and "the opening of the *'imu*" is a ceremony enjoyed to this day by *lū'au* guests.

Papaya **Pineapple** **Mango** **Bananas**
Coconut **Passion fruits**
Lychees **Kiwi fruits**

Lusciously ripe tropical fruits from the Hawaiian islands

THE HAWAIIAN LŪ'AU

Traditional Hawaiian *lū'au* (feasts) are still held to mark special occasions with friends and family, as they have been for centuries. It is not unusual to have in excess of 400 guests at a wedding, family reunion, or baby's first birthday. The *lū'au* was originally a spiritual event when islanders thanked the gods for bountiful harvests whilst enjoying traditional entertainment, such as *hula* performances. It takes its name **Breadfruit** from the taro tops served at the feast. The main event is the preparation of the *kālua* pig, but certain dishes are also central, including *laulau*, *lomi lomi* salmon, chicken long rice, *haupia*, and, most important of all, *poi*. This thick, purple-gray paste is made from steamed and pounded taro root *(kalo)*. *Poi* is the absolute staple of the Hawaiian diet and is meant to be eaten with the fingers.

Laulau *Meat or fish, plus taro tops, are wrapped in* ti *leaves and baked in the* 'imu, *often served with* poi.

Colorful haul of typical Hawaiian fish

Despite so much culinary integration there are still many ethnic restaurants, so visitors can sample everything from sashimi and sushi to Portuguese sausage, bean soup, and sweet bread – and even some pretty great all-American hamburgers.

Over the last two decades, top island chefs have gathered to promote the use of locally grown and produced ingredients. They have pioneered modern Hawaiian regional cuisine, emphasizing creative methods and presentation.

HAWAIIAN FOOD TODAY

Mix traditional Hawaiian produce and preparations with foods from Japan, China, Portugal, Korea, the Philippines, Europe, and the mainland United States, and you get what can best be described as today's "local" food. These diverse ethnic groups began arriving in Hawai'i in the mid- to late 19th century, bringing their traditional foods with them. Perhaps the most obvious example of the resulting combinations is that ubiquitous local staple, the "plate lunch". From lunch wagons to beachside kiosks and neighborhood eateries, plate lunch ingredients are unmistakable – meat or fish, plenty of carbohydrate (usually two scoops of white sticky rice), and a scoop of macaroni salad. However, in the interests of a healthier lifestyle, the protein may now be tofu, the white rice may be replaced by brown, and the macaroni salad by a fresh green salad.

Roasted *kālua* pig, the highlight at a traditional *lū'au*

WHAT TO DRINK

From colorful cocktails festooned with orchids and paper parasols, to tropical fruit juices and world-renowned Kona coffee, there are many beverages that are synonymous with Hawai'i.

Perhaps the most ubiquitous of the Polynesian cocktails is the Mai Tai. Many claim to have invented this potent rum concoction, the name of which means "good" in Tahitian. Other favorites include the Blue Hawai'i, Chi-Chi, and Banana Daiquiri.

Freshly-squeezed tropical juices, like pineapple, papaya, lychee, mango, and coconut, are a perfect start to breakfast on the *lanai* (veranda).

In addition to Kona coffee, other islands – notably Maui, Molokai, and Kauai – grow, roast, and sell their own high-end, "estate" coffees. All are rich and delicious, and make an ideal gift or souvenir.

Lomi lomi salmon *Finely sliced raw salmon is marinated with green onions and tomatoes.*

Chicken long rice *A cross between a stew and a soup. The "rice" is actually long cellophane noodles.*

Haupia *A simple coconut-flavored custard pudding – the dessert of choice at every* lū'au.

Choosing a Restaurant

The restaurants in this guide have been selected across a wide price range for their exceptional food, good value, and location. These listings highlight some of the factors that may influence your choice, such as whether you can eat outdoors or if the venue offers live music. Entries are alphabetical within each price category.

PRICE CATEGORIES
For a three-course meal for one, a glass of wine, and all unavoidable extra charges including service and tax.
$ under $15
$$ $15–$30
$$$ $30–$55
$$$$ $55–$80
$$$$$ over $80

HONOLULU AND WAIKĪKĪ

DOWNTOWN HONOLULU Gordon Biersch Brewery Restaurant $$
1 Aloha Tower Dr, 96813 **Tel** *(808) 599-4877*   **Map** *1 A3*

A popular after-work hangout, Gordon Biersch has the distinction of being Hawai'i's very first brewpub, producing its own lagers on the premises. The food is good bar fare, such as garlic fries and drunken *poki* (raw fish). Located in the Aloha Tower Marketplace, it provides the option of dining in or out. There is live entertainment on weekends.

DOWNTOWN HONOLULU Legend Seafood Restaurant $$
100 N Beretania St, 96817 **Tel** *(808) 532-1868*   **Map** *1 A2*

Choices are plentiful when it comes to a weekend dim-sum brunch in Chinatown. Many in-the-know locals consider this to be the best. Servers circulate trolleys stacked high with dozens of different bite-sized delicacies, ranging from egg custard to pork hash cups. An extensive à la carte lunch and dinner menu is also available.

DOWNTOWN HONOLULU Indigo Eurasian Cuisine $$$
1121 Nu'uanu Ave, 96813 **Tel** *(808) 521-2900*   **Map** *1 A2*

This place started the culinary transformation of Honolulu's Chinatown. Its series of rooms brings the tropical outdoors inside in a very real way. The menu features an exotic blend of Asian cuisines and the food is artistically served, as is fitting in this district full of galleries. The bartenders mix a mean martini.

DOWNTOWN HONOLULU Ruth's Chris Steakhouse $$$$
500 Ala Moana Blvd, 96813 **Tel** *(808) 599-3860*   **Map** *1 B4*

Ruth's Chris Steakhouse is located in Restaurant Row, in the heart of Honolulu's business district, near the Hawaiian Convention Center. Steaks are, unsurprisingly, the specialty of the house. Choose between filet, ribeye, New York strip, or Porterhouse – they're all as fabulous as they are expensive. Dinner only.

WAIKĪKĪ Wailana Coffee House $$
1860 Ala Moana Blvd, 96815 **Tel** *(808) 955-1764*   **Map** *3 B4*

This 24-hour diner provides both locals and tourists with reliable food and fast service. The inexpensive but hearty meals, especially breakfast, are great for families and those traveling on a budget. The jamboree breakfast costs under $6 and features all the pancakes you can eat. There is also a cocktail lounge with karaoke.

WAIKĪKĪ Duke's Canoe Club $$$
2335 Kalākaua Ave, 96815 **Tel** *(808) 922-2268*   **Map** *4 E5*

Named after famed Hawaiian surfing champion Duke Kahanamoku, this is a good spot for live Hawaiian music and spirited crowds at sunset. Located on the beach at the Outrigger Waikīkī *(see p180)*, it is a steak-and-seafood restaurant, and offers breakfast as well as lunch and dinner, and a light, inexpensive menu at its Barefoot Bar.

WAIKĪKĪ Hiroshi Eurasion Tapas $$$
500 Ala Moana Blvd **Tel** *(808) 533-4476*   **Map** *1 B4*

A calm and comfortable space, this restaurant puts the distinctive fusion cuisine of award-winning chef Hiroshi Fukui into the spotlight. Although based on traditional Japanese techniques and flavors, it is the modern European twists that make the food memorable. This downtown hot spot features a menu of small plates designed for sharing.

WAIKĪKĪ Keo's in Waikīkī $$$
2028 Kūhiō Ave, 96815 **Tel** *(808) 951-9355*   **Map** *3 C4*

Although he is Laotian, Keo Sananikone's name is synonymous in Hawai'i with Thai food. His restaurants are award winning: *Bon Appetit* magazine voted Keo's America's Best Thai Restaurant and *Gourmet* named it one of America's top tables. Specialties include the stir-fried shrimp with peanut sauce. Usefully, dishes are rated for spiciness.

WAIKĪKĪ Sansei Seafood Restaurant & Sushi Bar $$$
2552 Kalākaua Ave, 96815 **Tel** *(808) 931-6286*   **Map** *4 F5*

Million-dollar views of world-famous Waikīkī Beach, and the expansive space it shares with d.k. Steak House, make this Sansei dining experience unforgettable. Dozens of signature dishes – from creative New-Wave sushi sporting surprise ingredients like foie gras to award-winning contemporary Japanese specialties – draw a steady crowd.

Key to Symbols *see back cover flap*

WAIKĪKĪ Ciao Mein ♿ 🚸 🍸 [P] [$][$][$][$]

Hyatt Regency Waikīkī, 2424 Kalākaua Ave, 96815 ***Tel*** *(808) 923-2426* ***Map*** *4 E5*

This clever and lovely restaurant deliciously resolves the classic clash between those diners who adore Italian food and those who crave Chinese. Both cuisines are skillfully represented on a menu that offers individual dishes and a wonderful assortment of set menus served family style. Dinner only.

WAIKĪKĪ d.k. Steak House ♿ 🚸 🌳 🍸 [P] ★ [$][$][$][$]

2552 Kalākaua Ave, 96815 ***Tel*** *(808) 931-6280* ***Map*** *4 F5*

This restaurant is named for, and owned and run by, one of Hawai'i's most celebrated chef-restauranteurs, DK Kodama. With the island's only dry-aging room, the restaurant's signature is a huge rib-eye steak. The menu is classic American steak house, with an Asian twist. The service is pure class and the view incredible.

WAIKĪKĪ La Mer at Halekulani ♿ 🍸 [P] [$][$][$][$][$]

2199 Kālia Rd, 96815 ***Tel*** *(808) 923-2311* ***Map*** *4 D5*

Choose this elegant, romantic, and expensive French restaurant when you are in the mood to savor each exquisite bite. Dishes are impeccably prepared. On the second floor of the Halekulani *(see p180)*, it has a magnificent ocean view and is one of the best places in Waikīkī for watching the sun set. Gentlemen are required to wear jackets.

GREATER HONOLULU Eggs 'n' Things 💳 🚸 [P] [$]

343 Saratoga Rd, 96815 ***Tel*** *(808) 923-3447* ***Map*** *3 C4*

Boasting some of the best omelets, pancakes and waffles on the island, this popular Honolulu institution is still the best place to satisfy your cravings. Locals line up happily, newspapers in hand, to wait. The staff are very friendly and the food is simple yet delicious.

GREATER HONOLULU Helena's Hawaiian Food 💳 ♿ [$]

1240 N School St, 96817 ***Tel*** *(808) 845-8044* ***Map*** *1 A1*

These days octogenarian Helen Chock is at the cash register rather than the stove in this Kalihi eatery. Grandson Craig Katsuyoshi continues the tradition of smoking *pipikaula*-style spare ribs. Always buzzing, it serves its trademark *'opihi* (short ribs), hard to find elsewhere. The *kālua* pork and cabbage are straight from grandma's kitchen.

GREATER HONOLULU Makai Market Food Court 💳 ♿ 🍸 [P] [$]

1450 Ala Moana Blvd, 96816 ***Tel*** *(808) 955-9517* ***Map*** *3 A4*

The huge seating area at the Ala Moana Center *(see p214)* is surrounded by kiosks offering every conceivable type of food: from pizzas to Korean barbecue fare; sub sandwiches to Japanese *bentos*; and salads to ice cream. The variety illustrates the multi-ethnic mix of Hawai'i. Almost everything you can order is under $10.

GREATER HONOLULU Ono Hawaiian Foods 💳 🚸 [$]

726 Kapahulu Ave, 96816 ***Tel*** *(808) 737-2275* ***Map*** *4 F2*

This eatery is always busy serving delicious Hawaiian dishes such as *poi* (taro paste), *laulau* (leaf-wrapped meat or fish bundles), and *lomi-lomi* salmon. You know it is genuinely Hawaiian because the combo plates come with a small cup of raw onion and Hawaiian *'alaea* salt. This restaurant is clean, basic, and inexpensive. It is closed on Sundays.

GREATER HONOLULU Assaggio ♿ 🍸 [P] [$][$]

1450 Ala Moana Blvd, 96814 ***Tel*** *(808) 942-3446* ***Map*** *3 C4*

Italian favorites are the specialties of the house at Assaggio, and the menu features a wide selection of tasty pasta dishes, in addition to fresh fish and chicken options, all offered at reasonable prices. Located inside the Ala Moana Shopping Center. Open daily.

GREATER HONOLULU California Beach Rock n' Sushi ♿ 🍸 [P] [$][$]

404 Ward Ave, 96814 ***Tel*** *(808) 597-8000* ***Map*** *2 D4*

California Beach Rock n' Sushi serve traditional and new wave sushi at reasonable prices, in a friendly, casual atmosphere. Tempura Combo meals include miso soup, salad, and rice. For a real deal, drop by between 5 and 6:30pm for early-bird specials. The Ward Center is nearby, with movies and shopping.

GREATER HONOLULU California Pizza Kitchen ♿ 🚸 🍸 [P] [$][$]

4211 Wai'alae Ave, 96816 ***Tel*** *(808) 737-9446* ***Map*** *4 E1*

Pizzas topped with everything from barbecue chicken to pear and Gorgonzola cheese are on offer here in the Kahala Mall. This chain began in California and now has more than 180 outlets. Salads that are large, fresh, and delicious, sandwiches, and other non-pizza choices round out a superb menu, with something to satisfy everyone.

GREATER HONOLULU The Contemporary Café ♿ 🚸 🌳 [P] [$][$]

2411 Makiki Heights Dr, 96822 ***Tel*** *(808) 523-3362* ***Map*** *2 F1*

A perfect complement to the world-class Contemporary Museum *(see p71)*, this café has a short menu of tasty and good-value soups, salads, and sandwiches. Ask for the popular daily specials menu. You can dine inside or out surrounded by inspiring artworks. It is closed for dinner and on Mondays.

GREATER HONOLULU Hale Vietnam Restaurant ♿ 🍸 [P] [$][$]

1140 12th Ave, 96816 ***Tel*** *(808) 735-7581* ***Map*** *4 F2*

Steaming noodle soups are the highlight of the menu at this simple restaurant in Kaimuki. It offers no frills, but the service is fast and friendly and the atmosphere pleasant. Authentic Vietnamese vegan and vegetarian dishes are the fare. If it is available, try the *bun* (cold noodles heaped with sliced vegetables and herbs).

GREATER HONOLULU Little Village Noodle House $$
1113 Smith St, 96817 **Tel** *(808) 545-3008*   *Map 1 A2*

Not too long ago this fabulous Chinatown restaurant was a local secret, but it became so popular that it has expanded to twice its original size. Fans typically use the same words to describe the food – clean and fresh, with brilliant flavors. All the noodle and fresh vegetable dishes are musts.

GREATER HONOLULU The Ranch House $$
449 Kapahulu Ave, 96815 **Tel** *(808) 737-4461*   *Map 4 F4*

Home-style cooked dishes like prime rib, meatloaf, and catch of the day, along with local-style comfort food including *kalbi* (marinated) ribs, *huli huli* (spit roasted) chicken, chili and rice, and beef stew, top the extensive menu at this family style restaurant. Portions are large but the price is not.

GREATER HONOLULU Mariposa $$$
1450 Moana Blvd, 96814 **Tel** *(808) 951-3420*   *Map 2 F4*

Located on the third level of the Neiman Marcus store in the Ala Moana Shopping Center, this restaurant offers sophisticated dining and really good service. Lunch and dinner are served daily, brunch on the weekends, and tea in the afternoons. Outdoor seating provides ocean views of Ala Moana Beach Park.

GREATER HONOLULU Side Street Inn $$$
1225 Mopaka St, 96814 **Tel** *(808) 591-0253*   *Map 3 A4*

The Side Street Inn might look like just another bar with neon beer signs and a TV playing sports, but this is where Honolulu's best chefs gather after they close their own restaurants to enjoy great food in a funky setting. Highlights on the menu include blackened ahi and barbecued baby back ribs. Closed for lunch Saturdays and Sundays.

GREATER HONOLULU Singha Thai Cuisine $$$
1910 Ala Moana Blvd, 96815 **Tel** *(808) 941-2898*   *Map 3 C4*

Award-winning Singha Thai is an exotic haven, its atmosphere heightened by original Thai artwork, fresh orchids, and colorful silk-clad Royal Thai dancers performing every evening. The magnificent dishes served at this Thai-Hawaiian fusion restaurant make use of local ingredients, alongside those of traditional Thai cuisine.

GREATER HONOLULU 3660 on the Rise $$$$
3660 Wai'alae Ave, 96816 **Tel** *(808) 737-1177*   *Map 4 F1*

This unassuming restaurant in a refurbished building was one of the original pioneers in the gentrification of the Kaimuki neighborhood. Now a popular spot, 3660 offers creative island cuisine with a European twist. Ahi katsu is the restaurant's signature dish.

GREATER HONOLULU Alan Wong's Restaurant $$$$
1857 King St, 96826 **Tel** *(808) 949-2526*   *Map 3 B2*

Considered by many to be the best restaurant in town, this place is owned by one of Hawai'i regional cuisine's original chefs, Alan Wong. Innovative dishes are fashioned out of traditional Hawaiian ingredients. The contemporary menu changes periodically, but is always great. The friendly staff make up for the restaurant's odd location.

GREATER HONOLULU Chai's Island Bistro $$$$
1 Aloha Tower Dr, 96813 **Tel** *(808) 585-0011*   *Map 1 A3*

Owned and run by one of Hawai'i's most beloved chefs, Chai Chaowasaree, this bistro combines his Thai heritage and delicious local ingredients to create his own signature style. The entertainment is as good as the food, and as lovely as the atmosphere. Hawai'i's top contemporary entertainers all perform regularly at Chai's.

GREATER HONOLULU Chef Mavro $$$$
1969 S King St, 96826 **Tel** *(808) 944-4714*   *Map 3 B2*

Mavro is an award-winning chef, originally from France, who is known for his culinary creativity. In his restaurant you can dine prix-fixe or à la carte, with or without wine pairings. Menus change to take advantage of the freshest local seasonal ingredients. This is an expensive option, but worth it. It is closed for lunch and on Mondays.

GREATER HONOLULU Kincaid's Fish, Chop & Steakhouse $$$$
1050 Ala Moana Blvd, 96814 **Tel** *(808) 591-2005*   *Map 2 D5*

A terrific place at which to take a break from shopping in Ward Warehouse, Kincaid's offers excellent food along with first-rate service. The menu is varied, with choices across a wide price range. At the end of the work day, this is a lively party bar, and it also gets extremely busy around noon.

GREATER HONOLULU Nick's Fishmarket Restaurant $$$$
2070 Kalākaua Ave, 96815 **Tel** *(808) 955-6333*   *Map 3 C4*

This is the spot for classic fare: escargot, Oysters Rockefeller, lobster tail, crab, veal, rack of lamb, steaks, and more. A wine cellar housing thousands of bottles provides fine vintages from Italy, France, California, and Germany. The decor may be 1980s, but the service is timeless. There is live entertainment and dancing after dinner.

GREATER HONOLULU The Pineapple Room $$$$
1450 Ala Moana Blvd, 96814 **Tel** *(808) 945-6573*   *Map 3 A4*

The third floor of Macy's Department Store at the Ala Moana Center *(see p214)* is not a place you would expect to find a great restaurant, but chef Alan Wong's Pineapple Room is, some say, one of the best in town. Inviting yet elegant, it offers the world-renowned chef's excellent Hawai'i regional cuisine.

Key to Price Guide *see p196* **Key to Symbols** *see back cover flap*

GREATER HONOLULU Roy's Restaurant

6600 Kalaniana'ole Hwy, 96825 **Tel** *(808) 396-7697*

Map *4 F5*

The first of chef Roy Yamaguchi's restaurants in Hawai'i (there are more than 20 worldwide) serves his signature Euro-Asian cuisine in a characteristically loud, busy atmosphere. This restaurant is extremely popular and menus offer Roy's classics, which are longtime favorites, as well as daily specials and a nightly prix-fixe selection.

GREATER HONOLULU Sam Choy's Breakfast, Lunch, and Crab

580 N Nimitz Hwy, 96817 **Tel** *(808) 545-7979*

Map *1 A1*

A big chef needs a big restaurant: this former warehouse now serves up several varieties of fresh crab, all manner of local fish dishes, and Sam's signature style of local cuisine. At breakfast, make sure someone at the table orders the fried rice. Portions are generous. Sam also brews beer on the premises and his brewpub is open nightly.

O'AHU

AIEA Champa Thai

98-199 Kamehameha Hwy, 96701 **Tel** *(808) 488-2881*

This award-winning Thai restaurant in Pearl Kai Shopping Center has a dozen types of curry and in excess of 20 vegetarian choices on the menu. Dishes are made as spicy as you want them: either hot, medium, or mild. Everyone loves the steamed rice served in woven baskets.

HALE'IWA Kua-Aina Sandwich

66-214 Kamehameha Hwy, 96712 **Tel** *(808) 637-6067*

Try this humble surfer hangout on O'ahu's North Shore. It is a popular local landmark with some of the best food around, especially if you love chargrilled burgers and shoestring French fries. If it is too crowded, take your food to the beach and enjoy it there.

HALE'IWA Shave Ice Shops: Matsumoto's and Aoki's

Kamehameha Hwy, 96712 **Tel** *(808) 637-4827, (808) 637-7017*

These neighboring places serve sweet, drippy shave ice. A legacy from the days when ice was shipped to Hawai'i from Alaska, the chipped ice flavored with fruit syrups is a local favorite. Matsumoto's (66-087 Kam Hwy) and Aoki's (66-117 Kam Hwy) are still there. Join the shortest line and enjoy.

HALE'IWA Ted's Bakery

59-024 Kamehameha Hwy, 96712 **Tel** *(808) 638-8207*

This is the source of heavenly cream pies sold all over the island. The chocolate-*haupia* (coconut) pie is Ted's signature creation. Stop by from 7am to pick up fresh pastries and coffee. There are inexpensive breakfasts and a selection of sandwiches and plate lunches, too. Food is take-out only. Ted's closes at 2pm.

HALE'IWA Coffee Gallery

66-250 Kamehameha Hwy, 96712 **Tel** *(808) 637-5355*

This North Shore eatery has a classic surf-beach atmosphere. Popular with surfers and local residents, its breakfasts are legendary. The huge omelets have surf-lingo names like Off the Wall and Off the Lip. There is also an espresso bar featuring a large selection of fresh roasted gourmet coffee, including Kona and organically grown beans.

HALE'IWA Hale'iwa Joe's Seafood Grill

66-011 Kamehameha Hwy, 96712 **Tel** *(808) 637-8005*

The original Hale'iwa Joe's is a lively North Shore spot, with a terrific view of the Hale'iwa harbor and glorious sunsets. A surf-and-turf restaurant, it specializes in fresh fish and seafood, and steaks. There is a full bar and live music on weekends. The outdoor seating takes advantage of the scenery.

HALE'IWA Jameson's by the Sea

62-540 Kamehameha Hwy, 96712 **Tel** *(808) 637-6272*

At the north end of Hale'iwa, this is a good place for cocktails and sashimi. The outdoor deck is perfect for watching the sun set and indoor dining is romantic, too. The more expensive upstairs dining room serves fresh fish and *filet mignon*; the pub on the lower level does sandwiches. Reservations are recommended: ask for a window seat.

HAU'ULA Papa Ole's

54-316 Kamehameha Hwy, 96717 **Tel** *(808) 293-2292*

A great place for families, this casual eatery serves burgers and sandwiches, but the local favorites offered at breakfast, lunch, and dinner are what really draw people here. The plate lunches (two scoops of rice, macaroni salad with meat or fish) are huge and satisfying. Try to save room for the freshly baked desserts.

HAWAI'I KAI Cha Cha Cha Salsaria

377 Keahole St, 96825 **Tel** *(808) 395-7797*

The fare here is predominantly Mexican, with some Caribbean dishes thrown in. Nightly specials, homemade desserts, big margaritas, and a good happy hour are all plus points. The live entertainment often features Hawaiian "slack key" *(see p34)* as well as acoustic guitar.

HAWAI'I KAI Kona Brewing Co   💰💰
7192 Kalaniana'ole Hwy, 96825 **Tel** *(808) 394-5662*

The Hawai'i Island-based Kona Brewing Company opened this O'ahu brewpub in the Koko Marine Center, adorned with the company's beer logos and brewing equipment. Besides the handcrafted ales and lagers, there are imported and specialty beers. The menu includes hand-tossed pizzas, burgers, salads, and other casual fare.

KAHALA Chin's Kahala   💰💰
4230 Wai'alae Ave, 96816 **Tel** *(808) 739-8760*

The Chin in Chin's Kahala is owner Chin Tsai, who started his first restaurant in Honolulu in the 1970s before moving to San Diego, where Chin's has grown into a small chain. The typically expansive menu offers classic Szechwan and Cantonese fare alongside more unusual signature dishes, like salt and pepper quail, and roast cognac pigeon.

KAHALA Hoku's   💰💰💰💰
5000 Kahala Ave, 96816 **Tel** *(808) 739-8760*

Hoku's is about as good as a restaurant gets – especially a hotel restaurant. The food is consistently fantastic, the service is exactly what people expect of Hawaiian hospitality, and the ocean views are gorgeous. Sunday brunch is a particular treat. The incredible desserts are truly mouthwatering. The dress code prohibits shorts and T-shirts.

KAHUKU 21 Degrees North   💰💰💰💰
Turtle Bay Resort, 57-091 Kamehameha Hwy, 96712 **Tel** *(808) 293-8811*

Without question, the best evening dining on this side of the island is to be had here. The East-West fusion cuisine is innovative and focuses on fresh seasonal ingredients. Overlooking the sparkling water of Turtle Bay, this restaurant is quite romantic and a perfect place to watch the sun set. Diners are asked to dress up a little.

KAILUA Buzz's Original Steakhouse   💰💰
413 Kawailoa Rd, 96734 **Tel** *(808) 261-4661*

A few feet from Kailua Beach Park, this Buzz's is the original of the chain. It is the quintessential surf (or, in this case, windsurf) fine-dining restaurant: shirt and shoes are required. Burgers are served at lunch and steaks at dinner. Not unexpectedly, everything is chargrilled. Credit cards are not accepted.

KAILUA Lucy's Grill 'n Bar   💰💰💰💰
33 Aulike St, 96734 **Tel** *(808) 230-8188*

Casual, with a lovely open-air bar and outdoor seating, this is one of the most popular restaurants in Kailua. A truly Pacific Rim restaurant, Lucy's offers an eclectic menu of well-prepared East-West fusion dishes. When local residents want a night out, they come here to dine on the fresh fish, seafood, and curries. It is open for dinner only.

KANE'OHE Koa Pancake House   💰
46-126 Kahuhipa, 96744 **Tel** *(808) 235-5772*

Bring the paper on Sunday morning and have a leisurely read while you wait in line for stacks of light, fluffy pancakes. They come with a variety of toppings including bananas, blueberries, strawberries, and whipped cream; the orange syrup is homemade. The omelets are amazing, too. Once you get in, the service is fast and friendly.

KANE'OHE Hale'iwa Joe's   💰💰💰
46-336 Haiku Rd, 96744 **Tel** *(808) 247-6671*

Overlooking a botanical garden with colorful foliage and lily ponds, this steak-and-seafood restaurant serves fresh local fish and beef from the Hawai'i Island's Parker Ranch *(see p137)*. There are bar specials and a *pūpū* (appetizer) menu, too. Seating is on a first-come, first-served basis; no reservations are accepted. It is open for dinner only.

KO OLINA Azul   💰💰💰
92-101 Olani St, 96707 **Tel** *(808) 679-0079*

This is the fine-dining signature restaurant at the JW Marriott 'Ihilani Resort *(see p183)* outside of Honolulu. The lovely, cool space opens onto a tropical lagoon. The Mediterranean menu manages to be both refined and rustic, and is complemented by a wonderful wine list. Evening resort attire is suggested. It is open for dinner only.

PEARL CITY Gyotaku Japanese Restaurant   💰💰
98-1226 Ka'ahumanu St, 96782 **Tel** *(808) 487-0091*

This bright, casual restaurant offers a wide range of authentic Japanese dishes such as sushi, tempura, and teriyaki. It is the perfect place for the uninitiated to try their first taste of Japanese cuisine (with or without chopsticks). For those in a hurry, there are sushi and *pūpū* (appetizer) platters to take out.

PEARL HARBOR Shiro's Saimin Haven & Family Restaurant   💰
98-020 Kamehameha Hwy 96701 **Tel** *(808) 488-4834*

This shrine to Japanese-style noodle soup, and immense local plate lunches, has to be seen to be believed. Founder and patriarch Shiro Matsuo has lined the walls with scribbled notes expressing his philosophy of life. A cultural icon, he is best known as "Mistah Saimin". Hawai'i's governor titled him Statesman of Goodwill of Hawai'i.

WAIMĀNALO Keneke's   💰
41-857 Kalaniana'ole Hwy 96795 **Tel** *(808) 259-9811*

Next to the 7-Eleven and post office, this is part fast-food joint and part youth center. Ignore the shabby look as the people are pleasant and the food superb and inexpensive. Plate lunches, burgers, sandwiches, shave ice, and smoothies are all offered through the window. It is a favorite with the local crowd.

Key to Price Guide *see p196* **Key to Symbols** *see back cover flap*

MOLOKA'I AND LANA'Iİ

KAUNAKAKAI (MOLOKA'I) Kanemitsu Bakery
79 Ala Malama St, 96748 **Tel** *(808) 553-5855*

Famous for its Molokai sweet bread, this bakery offers an array of fresh baked goods, snacks, and beverages. In the adjoining coffee shop, local-style breakfasts and lunches are served. You can take out, or eat in at a 1950s booth table. On Friday nights a line forms for the hot French bread stuffed with cream cheese, jam, and cinnamon butter.

KAUNAKAKAI (MOLOKA'I) Moloka'i Burger
3 Kamehameha V Hwy, 96748 **Tel** *(808) 553-3533*

The first and only drive-through restaurant on Moloka'i serves up great-tasting, fresh hamburgers, French fries, and milk shakes. A teenager's heaven, it makes a nice change from all the offerings of local, island-style *grindz* (food) found in Kaunakakai.

KAUNAKAKAI (MOLOKA'I) Moloka'i Drive-In
Kamehameha V Hwy, 96748 **Tel** *(808) 553-5655*

The Moloka'i Drive-In has the 1950s ambience that pervades downtown Kaunakakai. It is a drive-up eatery serving the favorite foods of teenagers – floats, shakes, chili dogs, burgers, and honey-dipped chicken, as well as an island delicacy, fresh *akule* (mackerel). Clean and affordable, it is open from 6am to 10pm.

KAUNAKAKAI (MOLOKA'I) Outpost Natural Food Store & Juice Bar
Ala Malama St, 96748 **Tel** *(808) 553-3377*

The juice bar at this quaint country-style store provides wholesome and nutritious all-vegetarian burritos, salads, sandwiches, and smoothies. The store sells fresh local produce, natural foods, and vitamins, and is a good place to get groceries for your stay on the island. The juice bar is closed on weekends; the store is closed on Saturdays.

KAUNAKAKAI (MOLOKA'I) Hula Shores
Mile Marker 2, Kamehameha V Hwy, 96748 **Tel** *(808) 553-5347*

Right on the ocean at the Hotel Moloka'i *(see p183)*, this restaurant also fronts the swimming pool. The ribs and the coconut shrimp are divine. On Friday evenings, cowboys, grandmas, and everyone in between tune up their 'ukuleles and get down for a good old-fashioned *kanikapila* (Hawaiian jam session).

KAUNAKAKAI (MOLOKA'I) Moloka'i Pizza Café
Wharf Rd, 96748 **Tel** *(808) 553-3288*

This bright, efficiently run restaurant is perfect for families: salads and ice-cream treats round out a mostly pizza menu. There are ethnic daily specials, such as Mexican on Wednesdays and Hawaiian on Thursdays. You can eat in, take out, or have your food delivered.

PUKO'O (MOLOKA'I) Mana'e Goods and Grindz
Near Mile Marker 16, close to Puko'o, 96729 **Tel** *(808) 558-8498*

The lunch counter at this convenience store serves breakfasts as well as lunches. There are shady picnic tables for enjoying the local favorite ethnic and vegetarian dishes available here. The store is the only place where it is possible to get groceries on the east end of the island.

LĀNA'I CITY (LĀNA'I) Blue Ginger Café
409 7th St, 96763 **Tel** *(808) 565-6363*

Probably the most popular restaurant on the island, Blue Ginger Café is reminiscent of a simpler time, with its oilcloth table coverings and home cooking. Casual and inexpensive, it offers a full breakfast menu, local favorites at lunch, and varying specials at dinner. It is a great alternative to the island's hotel restaurants.

LĀNA'I CITY (LĀNA'I) Café 565
408 Eighth St, 96763 **Tel** *(808) 565-6622*

There are outdoor tables with umbrellas at this colorful eatery, which is named after Lāna'i's phone prefix. The pizzas are cooked in special pizza ovens on the premises and the sub sandwich rolls are baked fresh every day. Salads and plate lunch specials are also available. It is closed on Saturdays and Sundays.

LĀNA'I CITY (LĀNA'I) Canoes
419 7th St, 96763 **Tel** *(808) 565-6537*

This casual spot offers big breakfasts such as omelets, pancakes, and fried rice. The lunch specials include fresh fish and baby back ribs. Canoes was formerly Tanigawa's, a local restaurant that had been a landmark since the 1920s. It is not fancy or stylish, but good value and charming, with lots of friendly Hawaiian spirit.

LĀNA'I CITY (LĀNA'I) Pele's Other Garden
811 Houston St, 96763 **Tel** *(808) 565-9628*

Lunch and dinner are available at this popular deli by day and bistro by night. Offerings are predominantly vegetarian, with daily soup and menu specials. Outdoor tables with umbrellas and tablecloths at dinner are unexpected luxuries. You can bring your own wine. Pele's Garden is the health food store next door.

LĀNA'I CITY (LĀNA'I) Lāna'i City Grille   🚹♫🅿⭐ $$$
828 Lāna'i Ave, 96763 **Tel** *(808) 565-4700*

Celebrity chef Bev Gannon, one of the original founders of the Hawai'i Regional Cuisine movement, is lending her talents to this restaurant. The atmosphere is relaxed and the food is Pacific fusion, featuring fresh local fish, prime meats, and rotisserie chicken. Reservations recommended. Open for dinner only; closed Mon, Tue.

MĀNELE (LĀNA'I) Hulopo'e Court   🚹🏃🚽🍽🅿 $$$
Four Seasons Lāna'i at Mānele Bay, 1 Mānele Bay Rd, 96763 **Tel** *(808) 565-2290*

The more casual of two fine-dining restaurants at the Four Seasons Lānai at Mānele Bay *(see p184)*, Hulopo'e Court serves breakfast and dinner. The high ceilings, rows of colonnades, and open-air feel give this graceful restaurant a Classical, yet island-style ambience. The menus feature contemporary Hawai'i regional cuisine.

MĀNELE (LĀNA'I) 'Ihilani Dining Room   🚹🚽🅿 $$$$
Four Seasons Lāna'i at Mānele Bay, 1 Mānele Bay Rd, 96763 **Tel** *(808) 565-2296*

At the most luxurious restaurant on Lāna'i everything is impeccable – the gourmet food, the service, and the ambience. The menu draws from contemporary Italian favorites, using fresh seafood and local produce. The view of the bay and the beach is magnificent. Dining here is formal, and jackets are required for men. Open for dinner only.

MAUI

HA'IKŪ Colleen's at the Cannery   🚹🍽🅿 $$
810 Ha'iku Rd, 96708 **Tel** *(808) 575-9211*

Two miles off Hāna Highway in the small center of Ha'ikū, this casual bistro is popular with local residents and visitors staying in north-shore rentals. Juicy burgers, fresh fish and salads top the menu at lunch. For dinner, choose from a menu including filet mignon, pan-seared *ahi*, or wild mushroom ravioli.

HA'IKŪ Hāna Hou   🚹🏃🚽♫🍽🅿⭐ $$$
810 Ha'iku Rd, 96708 **Tel** *(808) 575-2661*

About 2 miles (3 km) off the Hāna Highway, this is one of few places on Maui to serve Hawaiian foods like *kālua* pork, *poi* (taro paste), and *laulau* (leaf-wrapped meat or fish bundles). A good mix of ethnic dishes, like pasta and sashimi, are also featured. There are shady outdoor tables. Live music may be Hawaiian, folk, or bluegrass.

HĀLI'IMAILE Hāli'imaile General Store   🚹🏃🍽🅿 $$$$
900 Hāli'imaile Rd, 96768 **Tel** *(808) 572-2666*

Smack in the middle of a pineapple plantation, this restaurant is located in a historic building that was once the plantation's general store. Beverly Gannon renovated it and is now the chef and manager here. Her superb Hawai'i regional cuisine, with international influences, ensures that this is a trek well worth making.

HĀNA Waianu Fruit Stand   📋🚹🏃🅿 $
Mile Marker 18, Hāna Hwy, 96713

Usually open daily, this roadside stand is typical of the low-key island-style stops along the curvy Hāna Highway. Here you can stock up on snacks, fresh island fruit, and soft drinks for the rest of the drive to Hāna. It is just a casual thing and very old-style Hawai'i, so stop by to get some refreshments and enjoy the local feeling.

HĀNA Hāna Ranch Restaurant   🚹🏃🚽🅿 $$$
5301 Hāna Hwy, 96713 **Tel** *(808) 248-8255*

Opposite the bank and post office, in what passes for the hub of Hāna town, the Ranch Restaurant offers hearty servings of wholesome food in a fittingly rustic setting. Lunch includes salads and sandwiches; dinner brings pasta and barbecued ribs. Indoor and outdoor tables have ocean views.

HĀNA Hotel Hāna-Maui Dining Room   🚹🏃♫🍽⭐ $$$$
Hāna Hwy, 96713 **Tel** *(808) 248-8211*

Here you can enjoy exquisite Pacific Rim cuisine created with organic fruits and vegetables from a nearby farm and the freshest fish available. The beautiful tropical setting overlooks the hotel's gardens. Performances by local dancers and musicians take place in the dining room once a week. The experience is a little pricey, but worth it.

KĀ'ANAPALI CJ's Deli & Diner   📋🏃 $$
2580 Keka'a Dr, 96761 **Tel** *(808) 667-0968*

Located in the Fairway Shops within the Kā'anapali Resort, CJ's is good value – nothing on the menu is more than $15. The extensive choices range from breakfast items to sandwiches, and plate lunches to pot roast. Highlights of this friendly neighborhood eatery include Internet access, a good children's menu, and homemade pastries.

KĀ'ANAPALI Leilani's on the Beach   🚹🏃🚽♫🅿 $$$
Whalers Village, 96761 **Tel** *(808) 661-4495*

This is a beachfront, island-style fish restaurant and steakhouse. The upstairs dining room has panoramic ocean views, while the downstairs cocktail *lānai* (veranda) has umbrella-shaded tables just steps from the beach. Leilani's is a great spot for drinks and *pūpū* (appetizers), watching people on the beach, or viewing Maui's fabulous sunsets.

KĀʻANAPALI Hula Grill

$$$$

Whalers Village, 96761 **Tel** *(808) 667-6636*

This lovely reproduction of a *kamaʻaina* architecture beach house will transport you back to the gentility of 1930s Hawaiʻi. Its beachfront Barefoot Bar has palm-thatched umbrellas over tables that actually sit directly on the sand. Menu favorites include *ono* (wahoo) and *ahi* (tuna) steak, lemon-ginger roasted chicken, and banana barbecue ribs.

KAʻANAPALI Sonʻz

$$$$

Hyatt Regency Hotel, 96761 **Tel** *(808) 667-1234*

Arguably the most romantic restaurant in all Hawaiʻi, this gorgeous alfresco room in the Hyatt Regency Maui Resort *(see p185)* now has food as sublime as the surroundings. The chefs prepare creative Hawaiʻi regional cuisine using mostly local produce. Enjoy the ambience as you watch the swans glide lazily on a lagoon surrounded by lush foliage.

KAHANA Royʻs Kahana Bar & Grill

$$$$

Kahana Gateway Center, 96761 **Tel** *(808) 669-6999*

Serving up the trademark East-meets-West fusion cuisine of chef Roy Yamaguchi, this restaurant is always buzzing, so book ahead. The Hawaiian fusion cuisine Yamaguchi is famous for is prepared in an open kitchen. There is an award-winning wine list and the menu has nightly specials. Crowded and noisy it can be, but this makes it fun.

KAHULUI Maui Coffee Roasters

$

444 Hāna Hwy, 96732 **Tel** *(808) 877-2877*

If you believe, as the staff t-shirts here say, "Corporate Coffee Sucks," this is your kind of place. It has been around for a long time, with good reason – it serves fantastic coffee at great proces. The light menu of salads and sandwiches is as good as the coffee, as is the service and atmosphere. You can eat in or get a cappucino to go.

KAHULUI Stillwellʻs Bakery

$

1740 Kaʻahumanu Ave, 96732 **Tel** *243-2243*

One of the best bake shops on Maui, pastry chef Roy Stillwellʻs clean, well-lit place serves up perfect lunches as well as amazing bread, rolls, cakes, pies, cookies, and pastries. The homemade soups, hearty sandwiches, and salads are all wonderful. Do not leave without something either chocolatey or creamy.

KAHULUI Kohoʻs Grill & Bar

$$

Queen Kaʻahumanu Center, 96732 **Tel** *(808) 877-5588*

Shopping center restaurants come and go yet Koho just keeps on going. The food, atmosphere, and service are consistently good and the place is as family-friendly as they come. There is something to suit every taste for breakfast, lunch, and dinner. Choices include above average plate lunches, salads, burgers, fish, and desserts.

KAHULUI Bistro Casanova

$$$

33 Lono Ave, 96732 **Tel** *(808) 873-3650*

This casual bistro is of the few restaurants open for dinner in Kahului. Local ingredients such as beef and fish, are used to create a variety of Mediterranean dishes including pastas and tapas. A great spot if youʻre looking for good food on the way to the airport, or after a show at the Maui Arts & Cultural Center.

KAPALUA The Plantation House Restaurant

$$$

2000 Plantation Course Dr, 96761 **Tel** *(808) 669-6299*

Perched above the blue Pacific and the Kapalua Resort area, this lovely restaurant is refered to by chef Alex Stanislaw as "the last house on the right." Open for breakfast, lunch, and dinner, it is evening when the menu shines brightest. Island food with Mediterranean influences dominates and there is an excellent wine list, too.

KAPALUA Sansei Seafood Restaurant & Sushi Bar

$$$

600 Office Rd, 96761 **Tel** *(808) 669-6286*

This first, wildly successful Sansei celebrated its 10th anniversary in 2006. After a decade of rave reviews locally, statewide, nationally, and internationally, the award-winning Asian rock shrimp cake, mango and crab salad handroll, and Japanese calamari salad are among the signature dishes that continue to delight diners nightly.

KAPALUA The Banyan Tree

$$$$

Ritz-Carlton Kapalua, 1 Ritz-Carlton Dr, 96761 **Tel** *(808) 669-6200*

The Ritz-Carlton Kapaluaʻs signature restaurant was redone as part of the hotelʻs $160-million renovation. The lounge offers panoramic views, and diners can enjoy Asian-inspired world cuisine from tasting menus that change daily. Fresh fish and local produce (especially Kapalua pineapple) are highlighted. Closed for lunch and Mon, Sun.

KAPALUA Pineapple Grill

$$$$

200 Kapalua Dr, 96761 **Tel** *(808) 669-9600*

Overlooking the lush greens of the Kapalua Golf Club, the newest incarnation of this restaruant is tropically decorated and offers Pacific cuisine that blends local ingredients and Asian style. A truly global wine list offers selections by the glass that are affordable and pair well with the food. It is open for breakfast, lunch, and dinner.

KĪHEI Stella Blues Café

$$$

1279 South Kīhei Rd, 96753 **Tel** *(808) 874-3779*

Located in Azeka Mauka Shopping Center, this is a bustling breakfast, lunch, and dinner spot, with a menu that has something for everyone. They label their fare New American comfort food, with dishes such as meatloaf, pot roast, stir fries, pizzas, salads, and sandwiches. Economical and good for family dining, it also serves wine and beer.

LAHAINA Aloha Mixed Plate
1285 Front St, 96761 **Tel** *(808) 661-3322*

Mixed plate is a term Hawai'i's plantation workers of yesteryear used to describe the result of sharing their various ethnic foods. This restaurant bases its menu on that tradition, with award-winning results. Try the coconut prawns or the soy sauce chicken. The open-air oceanfront location is a wonderful respite in hot Lahaina town.

LAHAINA Penne Pasta Café
180 Dickenson St, 96761 **Tel** *(808) 661-6633*

A block off Front Street in Dickenson Square, Penne Pasta Café serves up good, filling Italian food in Maui's famous tourist town. There are pastas, pizzas, salads, sandwiches, and nightly seafood specials. All are affordable as nothing on the menu is over $13.95. Most choices are large enough to share and the desserts are sublime.

LAHAINA Cheeseburger in Paradise
811 Front St, 96761 **Tel** *(808) 661-4855*

Located on the second story of a building right over the water, this open-air restaurant certainly lives up to its name, offering unparalleled views of the ocean and nearby islands, as well as of the action on lively Front Street. Giant juicy burgers are the main reason for coming here. Open daily until late.

LAHAINA Kimo's
845 Front St, 96761 **Tel** *(808) 661-4811*

Right on the waterfront in historic Lahaina town, Kimo's has a panoramic view of the ocean, neighboring islands, and glorious sunsets. Fresh Hawaiian fish, seafood, and prime rib are the mainstays. Dinners come with Kimo's caesar salad, bread, and rice. Popular with visitors and residents alike, this place is always busy, so make reservations.

LAHAINA Lulu's Lahaina Surf Club & Grill
Lahaina Cannery Mall, 1221 Honoapi'ilani Hwy, 96761 **Tel** *(808) 661-0808*

The party atmosphere makes this a fun late-night spot for casual dining and drinks. There are endless surf-videos and sports playing on the big flatscreen televisions, and the pool tables are free. Pizza, sandwiches, burgers, and four kinds of fries top the menu.

LAHAINA Mala An Ocean Tavern
1307 Front St, 96761 **Tel** *(808) 667-9394*

The idea here is to order a selection of gorgeous food in small portions. It comes this way so that it can be shared. Clams in black bean sauce, whole wok-fried *moi* (a type of fish), and an incredible fruit and ice-cream dessert named Carmel Miranda are just some of the satisfying offerings. The oceanfront setting affords wonderful sunset views.

LAHAINA Gerard's Restaurant
174 Lahainaluna Rd, 96761 **Tel** *(808) 661-8939*

Located a block off busy Front Street on the first floor of The Plantation Inn (*see p186*), Gerard's serves French food in a charming country setting. Chef Gerard Reversade remains true to his classical culinary roots, while incorporating island ingredients into his original recipes. It is open for dinner only.

LAHAINA I'o Restaurant
505 Front St, 96761 **Tel** *(808) 661-8422*

The second restaurant from the Pacific'O team focuses on contemporary Pacific cuisine with elements of European style. The extraordinary interior is as eye-popping as executive chef James McDonald's plates. In addition to this space, there is patio dining so close to the blue Pacific that you may get your feet wet.

LAHAINA Lahaina Grill
127 Lahainaluna Rd, 96761 **Tel** *(808) 667-5117*

A few steps off Front Street in the Lahaina Inn (*see p186*), this is a casual yet elegant modern restaurant offering exquisitely prepared and presented food. Signature dishes include tequila shrimp with firecracker rice and Kona-coffee-roasted rack of lamb. On the pricey side, but with reason, it is open for dinner from 6pm.

LAHAINA Longhi's
888 Front St, 96761 **Tel** *(808) 667-2288*

Longhi's is famous. In business at the same location for 30 years, it is still an "in" spot. The food is Italian, well prepared, and pricey. Most tables are next to a window, so you can enjoy the hustle and bustle of Maui's busiest town along with your food. There is a good wine list and an espresso bar. The valet parking is a plus.

LAHAINA Pacific'O
505 Front St, 96761 **Tel** *(808) 667-4341*

Creative contemporary Pacific cuisine with some delicious Asian twists is served in a setting fit for a king. The incredible oceanfront location was, in fact, a royal Hawaiian playground in ancient times. Signature dishes here include shrimp wontons and fresh fish tempura-style – both A Taste of Lahaina award winners.

LAHAINA Feast at Lele
505 Front St, 96761 **Tel** *(808) 667-5353*

A divine oceanfront location complements this unique concept in dining and entertainment. A musical tour through four Pacific Island nations accompanies a sit-down dinner of modern interpretations of their cuisines. The menu was designed by multi-award-winning chef James McDonald of adjacent Pacific'O and I'o restaurants.

Key to Price Guide *see p196* **Key to Symbols** *see back cover flap*

LAHAINA Old Lahaina Lu'au ♿ 🧒 🍽 ♫ 🍸 [P] ★ [$][$][$][$][$]

1251 Front St, 96761 ***Tel*** *(808) 667-1998*

Maui's best *lu'au (see pp216–17)*, this nightly show and dinner takes place on the beach, under the palm trees and the starry skies. Traditional Hawaiian music and dance are presented. Authentic foods including *kālua* pig, *poi* (taro paste), and *lomi-lomi* salmon are served buffet style.

MĀ'ALAEA The Waterfront Restaurant ♿ 🧒 🍽 🍸 [P] [$][$][$][$]

50 Hauoli St, 96793 ***Tel*** *(808) 244-9028*

Family owned and run, this restaurant sits right on the bay in Ma'alaea. It is known for its fresh fish – which the chef inspects before it is even off the boat – served nine different ways. Onion bread and beer cheese, along with a salad, begin each dinner. A local landmark, it is also known for its experienced staff and excellent wine list.

MAKAWAO Komoda's Store and Bakery 💳 🧒 [$]

3674 Baldwin Ave, 96768 ***Tel*** *(808) 572-7261*

For almost a century, the same family has been running Komoda's Store and Bakery in the heart of Makawao and making the goodies for it. It is always the favorite local spot for early morning specialties, especially the cream puffs and doughnuts on sticks. Arrive early as the daily supply of these outrageously tasty delights does not last long.

MAKAWAO Casanova Italian Restaurant and Deli ♿ 🧒 ♫ 🍸 [P] [$][$][$]

1188 Makawao Ave, 96768 ***Tel*** *(808) 572-0220*

Enjoy coffee, drinks, breakfast omelets, home-baked pastries, and homemade deli specialties on the porch here as you watch people parade through Makawao town. At night, a full menu of Italian specialties is served in the restaurant. Both the pizzas, from the centerpiece wood-burning oven, and the pastas come recommended.

NĀPILI The Gazebo 💳 🧒 🍽 [P] [$]

5315 Lower Honoapi'ilani Rd, 96761 ***Tel*** *(808) 669-5621*

The Gazebo is an indoor-outdoor restaurant right on the ocean that is a favorite breakfast place with the local residents and the tourists who find it. Macadamia nut pancakes are the most popular, but the pineapple and banana ones are equally delicious. There may be a wait for a table, but if so the superb view is compensation.

NĀPILI Sea House Restaurant ♿ 🧒 🍽 ♫ 🍸 [P] ★ [$][$][$]

5900 Honoapi'ilani Rd, 96761 ***Tel*** *(808) 669-1500*

You have to wind your way along the paths through Napili Kai Beach Resort *(see p187)* to get to the oceanfront Sea House Restaurant. From here, the view of the ocean and nearby islands is truly breathtaking. It is a great place for sunset watching. There is Hawaiian entertainment nightly and once a week a *hula* show is performed by children.

PĀ'IA Charley's Restaurant and Saloon ♿ 🧒 ♫ 🍸 [P] [$][$]

142 Hāna Hwy, 96779 ***Tel*** *(808) 579-9453*

Named for the owner's pet dog, a Great Dane, Charley's serves meals of suitably large proportions. The service can be slow, but that gives you time to enjoy the *huevos rancheros* (Mexican eggs) at breakfast, fresh fish sandwiches at lunch, and pasta or pizzas later on. A long bar in the back has pool tables and occasional live music.

PĀ'IA Moana Bakery & Cafe ♿ 🧒 ♫ 🍸 [P] [$][$][$]

71 Baldwin Ave, 96779 ***Tel*** *(808) 579-9999*

Delicious pastries are baked daily on the premises. Breakfast, lunch, and dinner choices are all fresh and well prepared. Diners can sit either in booths or at window-side tables. The live evening entertainment at this casual café ranges from the blues to flamenco, and from jazz to Hawaiian slack key.

PĀ'IA Mama's Fish House ♿ 🧒 🍸 [P] [$][$][$][$][$]

799 Poho Place, 96779 ***Tel*** *(808) 579-8488*

This restaurant is not only famous because it has been at its oceanfront location for more than 25 years. The fresh fish dishes it serves are excellent and extremely expensive. Even so, it is usually crowded so be sure to call ahead to reserve a table, preferably a window one. Valet parking is available.

WAILEA Gannon's ♿ 🧒 🍽 🍸 [P] [$][$][$]

100 Wailea Golf Club Dr, 96753 ***Tel*** *(808) 875-8080*

Gannon's is an elegant and spacious restaurant offering award-winning cuisine and deluxe service. Located on a hill along Wailea Golf Club's gold course *(see p227)*, the dining rooms have panoramic ocean views of the islands of Molokini and Kaho'olawe. The restaurant offers a casual fine-dining experience at breakfast, lunch, and dinner.

WAILEA Mala Wailea ♿ 🧒 🍽 🍸 [P] [$][$][$]

Marriott Wailea Beach Hotel, 3700 Wailea Alanui, 96753 ***Tel*** *(808) 875-9394*

Mala Wailea is another restaurant created by noted Maui chef Mark Ellman, one of the founders of the Hawai'i Regional Cuisine movement. His innovative dishes incorporate fresh island seafood and organic produce. Mala Wailea serves breakfast and dinner, with brunch on the weekends. Open daily.

WAILEA Tommy Bahama ♿ 🧒 🍽 🍸 [P] [$][$][$]

3750 Wailea Alanui, 96753 ***Tel*** *(808) 875-9983*

This chain of shops bills itself as the "purveyor of island lifestyles." Several, like this one, also have restaurants. The fare – fresh fish, salads, burgers, and lots of appetizers, all prepared island-style – is consistently excellent. The fun, tropical drinks are great, too. Portions are generally large, which at these prices they should be.

WAILEA Joe's Bar & Grill ⎸⬚⬚⬚⬚⬚⎹ $$$$
131 Wailea Iki Place, 96753 **Tel** *(808) 875-7767*

Joe's wife is the acclaimed Hawai'i regional cuisine chef Bev Gannon, so the food here is simply delicious. It is not just trendy, but hearty, as in the meatloaf with garlic mashed potatoes. Bev is not the only famous one in the family; Joe had his time in the limelight, as evidenced by the show-biz memorabilia that decorates the restaurant.

WAILEA Spago ⎸⬚⬚⬚⬚⬚⎹ $$$$
3900 Wailea Alanui, 96753 **Tel** *(808) 879-2999*

The menu at celebrity chef Wolfgang Puck's Spago offers Puck's classics and locally inspired dishes that fuse Hawaiian and Californian cuisines, such as Hāna hearts of palm salad and Hawaiian-style ceviche of *opakapaka* (pink snapper). Of course, it is elegant, as befits its location in the Four Seasons Resort Maui *(see p187)*.

WAILUKU A.K.'s Cafe ⎸⬚⬚⬚⎹ $$
1237 Lower Main St, 96793 **Tel** *(808) 244-8774*

Great tasting, local-style food that is good for you and affordable: this is what chef Elaine Rothermel set out to provide when she opened her pleasant small restaurant. She has succeeded. The Thai chicken, baked chicken, and turkey meatloaf are not to be missed. It is closed on Mondays and Sundays.

WAILUKU A Saigon Cafe ⎸⬚⬚⬚⬚⎹ $$
1792 Main St, 96793 **Tel** *(808) 243-9560*

Not easy to find because it is tucked away under a bridge without a sign, this is one of the most popular restaurants in central Maui. The eclectic menu features Vietnamese cuisine, with something for every appetite, including a good selection of vegetarian dishes. You may well find owner Jennifer Nguyen greeting diners when you arrive.

WAILUKU Asian Star ⎸⬚⎹ $$
1764 Wili Pa Loop, 96793 **Tel** *(808) 244-1833*

Tucked away in Wailuku's Millyard commercial area, this place is definitely worth seeking out. The efficient service makes it a popular lunch choice with folks who work nearby. Flavors are intense – try the curry lemongrass with chicken. The crispy tangerine beef is a specialty, salads are fresh, and noodle dishes are sure to please.

WAILUKU Tokyo Tei ⎸⬚⬚⬚⬚⎹ $$
1063 Lower Main St #C101, 96793 **Tel** *(808) 242-9630*

In business for more than 50 years, Tokyo Tei does local-style Japanese food exceedingly well and, somehow, cheaply. Every single dish on the menu is outstanding – the teriyaki fish, salmon, pork, and tempuras are particularly good. The sashimi is the freshest and most affordable you will find. It is not a fancy eatery, but comfortable.

HAWAI'I ISLAND

HILO Bears' Coffee ⎸⬚⬚⬚⬚⬚⎹ $
106 Keawe St, 96721 **Tel** *(808) 935-0708*

Hilo's hippest little place is where locals gather to gossip, read the paper, and enjoy coffee, tasty breakfasts of Belgian waffles, or quick lunches such as a Greek salad or a burrito. Open daily, the coffee shop has outdoor sidewalk bistro tables that are in an ideal spot for watching the people of Hilo go by.

HILO Café 100 ⎸⬚⬚⬚⬚⬚⎹ $
969 Kīlauea Ave, 96721 **Tel** *(808) 935-8683*

Named for an all-Japanese fighting battalion that became famous during World War II, Café 100 has been serving Hilo folk at outdoor picnic-style tables for more than 50 years. The huge menu features items like beef teriyaki, beef curry, *laulau* (leaf-wrapped meat or fish bundles), *kālua* pig, and soda-fountain treats. It is closed on Sundays.

HILO Ken's House of Pancakes ⎸⬚⬚⎹ $
1730 Kamehameha Ave, 96721 **Tel** *(808) 935-8711*

This 24-hour 1950s-style diner is best known for its incredible all-day breakfasts – exceptional omelets, potent coffee, and warm, friendly service. A favorite with local residents, Ken's House of Pancakes also offers a separate children's menu. A good selection of vegetarian dishes is available.

HILO Café Pesto ⎸⬚⬚⬚⎹ $$
308 Kamehameha Ave, 96721 **Tel** *(808) 969-6640*

Occupying a 1910 building that has survived more than one tsunami, this casual café is in a lovely setting near Hilo Bay. Hawai'i regional cuisine is featured here, including island fish prepared in a variety of ways, fresh organic salads, innovative pastas, and creative pizzas. This restaurant has a reputation for quality food and good service.

HILO Nihon Restaurant & Cultural Center ⎸⬚⬚⬚⬚⬚⎹ $$
123 Lihiwai St, 96721 **Tel** *(808) 969-1133*

Japanese in design, Nihon gives you culture with your sushi. This upstairs restaurant offers a beautiful view of Hilo Bay and Lili'uokalani Gardens. It is decorated with Japanese art and guests are greeted by traditional Japanese music. The food is authentic, delicious, and good value. It is closed on Sundays.

Key to Price Guide *see p196* **Key to Symbols** *see back cover flap*

HILO Restaurant Miwa
$$
1261 Kīlauea Ave, 96721 **Tel** (808) 961-4454

This neighborhood Japanese restaurant in the Hilo Shopping Center is stark and clean, with light-wood tables and a sushi bar. Combination dinners provide an opportunity to sample several menu items at a reasonble price. Miwa's is also known for its *haupia* (coconut) pie. This place is so good that reservations are recommended.

HILO Royal Siam Thai Restaurant
70 Mamo St, 96721 **Tel** (808) 961-6100

Fresh herbs and vegetables from the owner's garden enhance the Thai curries, noodles, soups, and other specialties on offer here, including Buddha Rama (a mix of spinach, chicken, and peanut sauce). This place is small, simply decorated, and inexpensive, and the food is consistently good. Closed for lunch on Sundays.

HILO Ponds Hilo
135 Kalanianaole Ave, 96721 **Tel** (808) 934-7633

Visitors to Hilo will find a delightful restaurant on Reed's Pond. The menu is American, with classics including prime rib, lobster, and escargot. Diners can enjoy the view of the pond as they chat with the chef, who visits each table personally.

HILO Seaside Restaurant
1790 Kalanianole, 96721 **Tel** (808) 935-8825

The Nakagawa family has run this Hilo institution for more than 70 years. Dining here is an experience as the restaurant sits in the middle of fish ponds; the trout, mullet, and *aholehole* fish are caught right before you arrive. Reservations are recommended as its long-standing reputation as one of the island's best eateries draws crowds.

KAILUA-KONA Big Island Grill
75-5702 Kuakini Hwy, 96745 **Tel** (808) 326-1153

Serving big portions at reasonable prices, the Big Island Grill is always packed. Worth the wait (reservations are not taken), the menu includes island favorites such as *loco moco* (egg-topped hamburger with rice and gravy) for breakfast, chicken katsu for lunch, and beef teriyaki for dinner. The drive-up window is great for those in a hurry.

KAILUA-KONA Basil's Pizzeria & Ristorante
75-5707 Ali'i Dr, 96740 **Tel** (808) 326-7836

Right across from Hulihee Palace, this oceanview restaurant is all Italian, as evidenced by the tantalizing aroma of garlic in the air. Pizza, pasta, *parmigiana*, *cacciatore*, and an assortment of other fine Italian foods are tasty and reasonably priced. There are two large dining rooms, providing seating for 100.

KAILUA-KONA Sombat's Fresh Thai Cuisine
88 Kanoelehua Ave, 96720 **Tel** (808) 969-9336

"Fresh" is the key word here; Sombat grows a lot of the ingredients used in her flavorful dishes. Choose your heat level – mild, medium hot, or Thai hot – and enjoy traditional Thai offerings such as Green Papaya Salad, Summer Rolls, and curries. This place is small and popular, so take-out is a good option.

KAILUA-KONA Huggo's
75-5828 Kahakai Rd, 96740 **Tel** (808) 329-1493

A Kona tradition, this family-run oceanside restaurant has been a favorite with locals for more than 35 years. Its spectacular setting affords diners a fabulous view of Kona Bay, making it a great place to watch sunsets, while enjoying live entertainment, cocktails, and *pūpū* (appetizers).

KAILUA-KONA Kona Inn Restaurant
75-5744 Ali'i Dr, 96740 **Tel** (808) 329-4455

This is a sound choice for open-air dining in the heart of Kailua. The restaurant is set in a historic property built by the Inter-island Steam Navigation Company in 1928 and has retained a Hawaiian theme. A nice view of Kona Bay adds to the old-fashioned charm. Island fish, seafood, prime rib, and steak feature on the menu.

KAILUA-KONA Jameson's by the Sea
77-6452 Ali'i Dr, 96740 **Tel** (808) 329-3195

Ocean views and outdoor dining on the water's edge make this a popular fine-dining restaurant. Specialties from the American-Continental menu include *filet mignon*, rack of lamb, poached *opakapaka* (pink snapper), baked stuffed shrimp, and chiffon pies. White linen tablecloths, crystal, and candlelight enhance the romantic atmosphere.

KAILUA-KONA Pahu i'a
100 Kaupulehu Dr, 96740 **Tel** (808) 325-5000

The signature restaurant at the Four Seasons Resort Hualalai (see p189), this beachfront spot is just steps away from the gently lapping waves of the Pacific. Terraced indoor and outdoor seating makes the most of the magnificent views. The cuisines of the Pacific are featured. Evening attire is suggested and reservations are recommended.

KEAUHOU Edward's at Kanaloa
78-261 Manukai St, 96739 **Tel** (808) 324-1434

Meals are served on a delightful patio, with the Pacific as the backdrop. This restaurant is a great spot for an intimate and romantic sunset dinner. It offers classic and innovative menu selections and an excellent wine list. Edward's can be hard to find within the Outrigger Kanaloa at Kona (see p189), so get directions when you call for reservations.

KOHALA COAST Canoe House 🏧 🚶 🎞 🍴 🅿 $$$
68-1400 Mauna Lani Dr, 96743 **Tel** *(808) 885-6622*

Set in the grounds of the Mauna Lani Bay Hotel *(see p189)*, the Canoe House combines a magnificent open-air setting with impressive Pacific Rim cuisine. A traditional *koa* canoe hangs from the ceiling. This is an expensive place, but the breathtaking location and marvelous sunset views make it worthwhile.

KOHALA COAST Roy's Waikoloa Bar & Grill 🏧 🚶 🎞 🍴 🅿 $$$$
250 Waikoloa Beach Dr, 96738 **Tel** *(808) 886-4321*

Although you would not think a venue of this caliber would be found in a strip mall, this is another one of celebrity chef Roy Yamaguchi's top-notch restaurants. His signatures are evident: an exhibition kitchen, trendy Hawaiian fusion cuisine, good service, and the roar of the crowd. Roy's is always packed, so it is best to make reservations.

VOLCANO Volcano Golf and Country Club 🏧 🚶 🍴 🅿 $$
99-1261 Pi'i Mauna Dr, 96785 **Tel** *(808) 967-8228*

This restaurant is located in the golf-course clubhouse at the Volcano Golf and Country Club *(see p227)*. It serves burgers and sandwiches, along with local-style dishes such as *saimin* (noodles in broth), chili and rice, and teriyaki chicken. The service is friendly and the atmosphere casual, with the dining room overlooking the fairway.

VOLCANO Kilauea Lodge & Restaurant 🏧 🚶 🍴 🅿 $$$
Highway 11, 96785 **Tel** *(808) 967-7366*

Cozy mountain decor, with a huge and historic fireplace, sets the scene for hearty European cooking. *Hasenpfeffer* (rabbit stew) is a house specialty; other favorites include freshly caught fish, duck, and venison. Dinners come with soup, freshly baked bread, and salad, and there's a good wine list. Brunch on Sundays.

WAIMEA Merriman's 🏧 🚶 🍴 🅿 $$$
65-1227 Opelo Rd, 96743 **Tel** *(808) 885-6822*

Probably the best, and certainly the busiest, restaurant in Waimea, Merriman's is owned by one of the original Hawai'i regional cuisine chefs, Peter Merriman, who also operates Hula Grill Restaurant *(see p203)* on Maui. The menu features island-reared beef, fresh seafood (sometimes caught by Merriman himself), and other local produce.

KAUA'I

ANAHOLA Duane's Ono Char-Burgers 🍽 🎞 🅿 $
4-4350 Kūhiō Highway (Hwy 56), 96703 **Tel** *(808) 822-9181*

If you blink you will miss this Kaua'i burger institution, so keep your eyes peeled on the drive north from the airport. It is a roadside stand with a few concrete tables outside, but the burgers are big, juicy, and delicious. The fries are great too. Deservedly popular, it can attract a line at lunchtime.

HANAMAULU Hanamaulu Restaurant, Teahouse & Sushi Bar 🏧 🎞 🍴 🅿 $$$
3-4291 Kūhiō Hwy, 96715 **Tel** *(808) 245-2511*

Off the beaten track, this eatery is still a local landmark. Although it is a typical Japanese teahouse, both Japanese and Chinese food, as well as plate lunches, are served. Diners can sit at the sushi bar, or at low tables on tatami floors in the teahouse (call ahead). Good Asian food has been served here for more than 75 years. Families enjoy this place.

KAPA'A Kountry Kitchen 🍽 🚶 🍴 🅿 $
1485 Kūhiō Hwy, 96746 **Tel** *(808) 822-3511*

As the name implies, this family style restaurant serves up hearty and tasty American fare: pancakes and waffles at breakfast; fried chicken and hamburgers at lunch; ice cream and apple crisp for dessert. Friendly and prompt service, flowered wallpaper, and antiques, all help to create the cozy, country atmosphere.

KAPA'A Papaya's Natural Foods 🏧 🎞 🅿 $
4-831 Kūhiō Hwy, 96746 **Tel** *(808) 823-0190*

This is the biggest health food store on Kaua'i and the food it serves is in keeping with the organic ingredients it sells. Tofu, hummus, tempeh, and all the usual health food fare is on the menu, along with baked goods, coffee, drinks, and smoothies. Order at the counter, then enjoy your food at the outdoor tables. It is closed on Sundays.

KAPA'A Eggbert's Family Specialty Restaurant 🏧 🚶 🎞 🅿 $$
4-484 Kūhiō Hwy, 96746 **Tel** *(808) 822-3787*

Eggbert's has been a local favorite for over 25 years. In an open, airy corner of the Coconut Market Place *(see p214)*, it serves breakfast until 3pm, as well as lunch and dinner. There are more than 150 styles of omelet to choose from – and then there are the Eggs Benedict and the banana pancakes. Senior and *keiki* (children's) portions are available.

KAPA'A Coconuts Island-Style Bar & Grill 🏧 🚶 🍴 🅿 $$$
4-919 Kūhiō Hwy, 96746 **Tel** *(808) 823-8777*

Busy from the time it opens at 4pm, this place is packed with people who come for the affordable and delicious food. Choices range from burgers and salads to lobster ravioli and grilled teriyaki-dipped fresh salmon. Wines by the glass, beers on tap, a great *pūpū* (appetizers) menu, and a cheerful, upbeat atmosphere all draw the crowds.

KĪLAUEA The Kīlauea Bakery & Pau Hana Pizza   🚻 P   Ⓢ

2484 Keneke St, 96746 **Tel** *(808) 828-2020*

This small and unassuming place is located in the Kong Lung complex on Kaua'i's North Shore. There are surely no better baked goods or pizzas anywhere on the island. Get there early for the best selection of breakfast goodies. Enjoy your delicious treat inside, or outside under the shade of an umbrella. Stock up for a picnic while here, too.

KOKE'E Koke'e Lodge   ♿ 🚻 🍽 P   Ⓢ

3600 Kokee Rd, 96796 **Tel** *(808) 335-6061*

Set within Koke'e State Park *(see pp170–71)*, about 4,000 ft (1,220 m) above sea level, this welcoming place is open daily from 7am–6pm and serves breakfast, lunch, and desserts. The hearty Portuguese bean soup, a house specialty, is a delicious way to warm up. The luscious *lilikoi* (passionfruit), guava chiffon, and coconut pies are home-made.

LĪHU'E Hamura Saimin & Halo Halo Shave Ice   🗒   Ⓢ

2956 Kress St, 96766 **Tel** *(808) 245-3271*

Though not particularly attractive to look at, this place is famous for having the best *saimin* (noodles and broth) around. Crowded even late at night, it is affordable as the most expensive item on the menu costs $5. Fresh *lilikoi* (passionfruit) pie is the specialty dessert. Go through the side entrance for shave ice, another local treat.

LĪHU'E Tip Top Café & Motel   ♿ 🚻 P   Ⓢ

3173 Akahi St, 96766 **Tel** *(808) 245-2333*

This spotlessly clean, large dining room has 1950s-style booths and orchids on every table. Breakfasts and lunches are hearty. The macadamia pancakes are legendary at breakfast, while the oxtail soup is the highlight at lunch. This café-bakery has been in business since 1916 and is still a local favorite. It is closed on Mondays.

LĪHU'E Café Portofino   ♿ 🚻 🚻 🎵 🍽 P   ⓈⓈⓈ

3481 Ho'olaulea Way, 96766 **Tel** *(808) 245-2121*

Café Portofino serves Italian fare created with authentic ingredients imported from Italy. Breads, ice cream, and desserts are made on the premises. Located in the Kaua'i Marriott, the restaurant has a romantic atmosphere, with candelit tables, and soft music performed by a harpist or classical guitarist. Open for dinner only.

LĪHU'E Duke's Canoe Club Barefoot Bar & Restaurant   ♿ 🚻 🚻 🎵 🍽 P 🌟   ⓈⓈⓈ

3610 Rice St, 96766 **Tel** *(808) 246-9599*

Named for legendary Hawaiian surfer and Olympic champion Duke Kahanamoku, this place is decorated with his memorabilia, including three of his surfboards. Oceanfront at the Kaua'i Marriott Resort *(see p191)*, it is one of the busiest spots in town. The sunset views are incredible, the menu is affordable, and the music is live.

LĪHU'E JJ's Broiler   ♿ 🚻 🚻 🍽 P   ⓈⓈⓈ

3416 Rice St, 96766 **Tel** *(808) 246-4422*

JJ's at Anchor Cove Shopping Center has a simple winning feature: open-air dining with a great ocean view. Burgers, sandwiches, and vegetarian dishes are served at lunch; seafood, steak, and pasta at dinner. Slavonic steak (tenderloin in butter, wine, and garlic) is the signature dish. Portions are large and there are daily specials at reasonable prices.

LĪHU'E Gaylord's at Kilohana   ♿ 🚻 🚻 🍽 P   ⓈⓈⓈⓈ

3-2087 Kaumuali'i Hwy, 96766 **Tel** *(808) 245-9593*

Located at Kilohana, Kaua'i's legendary plantation estate, Gaylord's offers gracious open-air dining matched by unhurried service and a menu ranging from pasta to prime rib. Sunday brunch is served here and there is an extensive wine cellar. Today the historic estate includes a complex of shops and galleries.

PO'IPŪ Casa Blanca at Kiahuna   ♿ 🚻 🚻 🎵 🍽 P   ⓈⓈ

2290 Po'ipū Rd, 96756 **Tel** *(808) 742-2929*

This small, open-air restaurant is located at the Kiahuna Swim and Tennis Club. The best food on offer here has Mediterranean and African influences: such as Basque *piperrada* (pepper omelet) at breakfast, Algerian chicken skewers, and North African lamb with fennel and harissa. Tapas and children's menus are available.

PO'IPŪ The Beach House   ♿ 🚻 🚻 🍽 P   ⓈⓈⓈ

5022 Lawai Rd, 96756 **Tel** *(808) 742-1424*

With a spectacular oceanfront setting, The Beach House is one of the best spots on Kaua'i for sunset drinks, appetizers, and dinner. The excellent menu offers the chef's creative twists on island favorites, made with fresh local ingredients. The outstanding food, good service, and fantastic location make this one of the island's top restaurants.

PO'IPŪ Casa Di Amici   ♿ 🚻 🚻 🎵 🍽 P   ⓈⓈⓈ

2301 Nalo Rd, 96756 **Tel** *(808) 742-1555*

Italian-Mediterranean fare and alfresco dining make this a hidden delight. Tucked away in a residential neighborhood in Po'ipū, Casa Di Amici serves risottos, pastas, and specials, all prepared by the owner-chef. Diners come for the relaxing atmosphere, tasty food, and fairly reasonable prices. It is open for dinner only.

PO'IPŪ Roy's Po'ipū Bar & Grill   ♿ 🚻 🚻 🍽 P   ⓈⓈⓈⓈ

2360 Kiahuna Plantation Dr, 96756 **Tel** *(808) 742-5000*

Chef Roy Yamaguchi has become internationally known and operates restaurants across the US. Most are crowded and noisy and have exhibition kitchens so that diners can watch their food being prepared. The food is typically creative, delicious, and worth the price. This one, in the Po'ipū Shopping Village *(see p214)*, is no exception.

SHOPPING IN HAWAI‘I

Pineapples, macadamia nuts, Kona coffee, alohawear, T-shirts, tropical flowers – these are the things that top visitors' shopping lists, and they are easy to find. Traditional Hawaiian crafts, such as *kapa* cloth, pandanus baskets, and Ni‘ihau shell *lei*, are harder to find and usually more costly – but beautiful, and

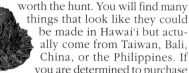

Coconut frond hat

worth the hunt. You will find many things that look like they could be made in Hawai‘i but actually come from Taiwan, Bali, China, or the Philippines. If you are determined to purchase "the real thing," check carefully. The addresses and telephone numbers of all the shops mentioned in the text are given on page 213.

A woman weaving traditional *lei* garlands, a popular Hawaiian souvenir

SHIPPING

For a charge, most stores and galleries will ship goods worldwide. Alternatively, you can use the **United States Postal Service** to send purchases home. Courier companies such as **DHL**, **FedEx**, and **UPS** are another option and can be contacted by phone or email. They provide insurance, delivery confirmation, and tracking, and offer a range of delivery times and costs. Some restrictions may apply to the type of item that can be sent and the destination of the package. You will be asked to fill out a form giving a short description of the goods and stating their monetary value. Keep receipts of the transaction in case any items should get lost in transit.

WHERE TO SHOP

Supermarkets, grocery shops, Longs Drugs stores, and discount shops, such as ABC Stores and K-Mart, have the best prices for things like macadamia nuts, jam, and coffee. These are the best places for cheap souvenirs, too, while museum shops are often good for Hawaiian crafts.

Anyone who likes secondhand shops should enjoy scouring shops and home sales for collectibles ("Hawaiiana"), from aloha shirts to vintage postcards, at bargain prices. The islands are big on secondhand shops and private garage sales. Check the Friday edition of the newspapers for weekend garage sales. The papers also list crafts fairs and market days.

WHEN TO SHOP

You can shop 24 hours a day, seven days a week if you wish – some supermarkets and convenience stores never close.

Malls and large stores are normally open from 10am to 9pm, Monday to Saturday, and often on Sunday (but the hours are usually shorter). Small stores open from about 9am to 5 or 6pm, Monday to Saturday, and are closed on Sundays.

HOW TO PAY

Travelers' checks in US dollars and credit cards are accepted more or less everywhere in Hawai‘i (*see p240*). However, it is a good idea to carry at least some cash for purchases at roadside stands and small, family-run stores.

Remember that sales tax of 4.17 percent is added to every purchase made in Hawai‘i, and that this tax will be added to the total bill by the cashier.

FRUIT AND FLOWERS

Many visitors take the fresh flavors and aromas of Hawai‘i home with them. You can take coconuts, pineapples, and papayas (but no other fruit) through customs, as long as they are passed by the **US Department of Agriculture (USDA)** inspection.

It is best to buy such fruit prepackaged at airport shops or other reputable stores that specialize in "take home" fruits. There are many of these stores in Hawai‘i, such as the **Maui Tropical Plantation & Country Store** near Wailuku. Someone at your hotel should know the best place on any particular island. These same places sell sterile cuttings and

Roadside stand selling tropical Hawaiian fruit on Maui's windward coast

seeds of tropical plants that have been passed by USDA. You can have your purchases delivered to the airport from which you are leaving or sent directly to your home address.

You can export all fresh flowers, subject to agricultural inspection, apart from jade vines, gardenias, and *mauna-loa*. Hawai'i Island is the best place to buy anthuriums, while you should buy protea and exotics in Maui. You can export *lei*, but most last only a very short time; check with the florist or *lei*-maker, because some *lei* are very attractive when dried. Alternatively, you could consider buying a nonperishable *lei* made of nuts, feathers, seeds, or shells, for example *(see p29)*. The best places to buy flower *lei* are the small shops in Honolulu's China-town, but the stands at Honolulu International Airport have a good selection, too.

Macadamia nuts, in easy-to-pack cans

If you are unsure whether or not you'll be able to take a particular item home with you, check first by tele-phoning the USDA.

FOOD AND DRINK

Although mangoes, guava, and *liliko'i* (passion fruit) are not permitted out of the islands, chutneys, jams, jellies, and other products made with these fruits are great buys.

World-famous Kona coffee comes from Hawai'i Island, but coffee is now grown on Maui and Kaua'i too. All coffees are available in whole-bean or ground, flavored, instant, and decaffeinated varieties.

Macadamia nuts also come in many forms, from dry-roasted and salted to honey-flavored or chocolate-covered. Adventurous gastronomes may like to try taro chips and "crack seed" – preserved and sea-soned nuts, fruits, seeds, and sweets. All these products are sold at supermarkets, grocery stores, convenience stores, and specialty shops throughout the islands. **Shirokiya** (Honolulu), a Japan-based department store, also sells a great variety of unusual prepared food.

Hawai'i has two wineries. The **Tedeschi Winery** on Maui makes a couple of good red table wines, one sparkling wine, and, its most famous product, Maui Blanc – a light pineapple wine. The **Volcano Winery** on Hawai'i Island is producing some interesting wines from various tropical fruits while waiting for its grapevines to mature.

ART

Like Gauguin, many artists have followed their muse to the Pacific. Unlike Gauguin, the majority are not very good. There are literally dozens of "galleries," mostly in tourist shopping areas. Some specialize in sales of very expensive work that has no investment value – in spite of what the resident "consultants" tell you. If you need advice, someone at your hotel should be able to direct you to a reliable source; museums can often be of help, too.

There is some wonderful art to be found in Hawai'i. And much of it – in the form of lithographs, posters, and even cards – is affordable. Dietrich Varez of Volcano (on Hawai'i Island), for example, lovingly creates earth-brown linoleum block prints depicting local legends. They are glorious, easy to find, and cheap, at about $20 apiece. You will find his work in the **Volcano Art Center** gallery on Hawai'i Island is **Studio 7** in Hōlualoa.

The **Viewpoints Gallery** in Makawao (Maui) is a collective representing some fine local artists.

One of the many art galleries on Front Street in Lahaina, Maui

You can also rely on good quality at the **Village Gallery** and **Lahaina Arts Society** in Lahaina, the **Avalene Gallery** in Makawao, and **Nohea Gallery** in Honolulu.

COLLECTIBLES

Just about anything Hawaiian from the 1940s to the 1970s is now considered collectible: postcards, Matson steamship menus, even kitsch ceramic *hula* girls, and especially old aloha shirts known as "silkies."

You'll find such things in the little shops on Wailuku's Market Street and in "antique" shops such as **Bailey's Antiques** and **Aloha Antiques & Collectibles** in Honolulu, and **The Only Show in Town** in Kahuku (O'ahu); **Mauna Kea Galleries** in Kamuela and **Seconds to Go** in Honoka'a (Hawai'i Island); and the **Pā'ia Trading Company** on Maui; You may find it more fun to go hunting for collectibles in secondhand stores and garage sales.

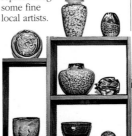

Display of blown-glass vases and other objects in a Maui gallery

Man weaving a coconut-leaf hat on a Hawai'i Island street

CRAFTS

Hawai'i teems with artisans. Hand-crafted bowls of mango, monkeypod, or *koa* wood make beautiful presents and mementos. You can also buy *koa* hair ornaments, chopsticks, and key chains. Wooden objects can be found in craft shops in most big towns.

Hawai'i also has many expert weavers. Coconut leaf is often used, but *hala* (pandanus) is better quality. Mats, bags, and hats are all popular buys. Ceramic bowls, vases, and plates are also popular. **The Island's Best** in Honolulu is a good bet for these.

It is virtually impossible to find any vintage Hawaiian quilts to buy (most are treasured family heirlooms), but new quilts, quilt kits and other crafts can be found at the **Maui Crafts Guild** in Pā'ia or the **Gallery of Great Things** on Hawai'i Island. Hawaiian kapa (bark cloth) is hard to find and most *kapa* goods for sale are imported from Samoa or Tonga.

Combing the crafts fairs is a fun and rewarding way to see what is available. Museum shops are also good sources, as are the many specialty shops, including **Sand & Sea** on Maui and **Ola's Hanalei** on Kaua'i.

JEWELRY

Costume jewelry is made from everything you can think of – ceramic, paper, plastic, metals, and more – and can be found at crafts fairs.

Fine jewelry made of pearls, coral, jade, silver, and gold is sold in department stores and in the dozens of specialty shops, such as **Precision Goldsmiths** in Wailuku and Kaua'i's **Jim Saylor Jewelers**. "Heritage jewelry," Victorian gold jewelry with names and designs inscribed in black enamel, is popular. It is also expensive, so be sure to buy from a reliable dealer.

The most precious pieces of Hawaiian jewelry available are Ni'ihau shell *lei*. The shops on Kaua'i are the best places to buy them, but be sure to do some advance research. A simple choker may cost as little as $25, while museum-quality, multi-strand, waist-length *lei* typically cost thousands of dollars.

BOOKS AND MUSIC

The big bookstores, such as **Barnes & Noble** (O'ahu), **Waldenbooks** (everywhere), and **Borders** (O'ahu, Maui, Kaua'i, and Hawai'i Island), have the best choice of books about Hawai'i. Borders also carries an excellent selection of Hawaiian music. **Native Books Na Mea Hawaii**, in Honolulu, has a wide range of Hawaiian-language books.

Wooden bowl from the Maui Crafts Guild

In most music stores, including the locally based **Request**, both traditional and contemporary Hawaiian music is available.

CLOTHES AND FABRIC

The days of tourists strolling down the street dressed in matching polyester *mu'umu'u* and aloha shirts seem to have gone. Even the state's biggest producer of alohawear, **Hilo Hattie**, now sells attractive cotton or cotton-blend island fashions in its many fashion centers. **Jagger's** (Pā'ia, Maui), **Sig Zane Designs** (Hilo, Hawai'i Island), and **Reyn's** and **Macy's** (both are statewide department stores) stock some stunning Hawaiian-style clothing in the latest fashions, colors and subtle prints.

Mamo Howell is big in the world of Hawaiian couture, but you might want to think about whether you will be able (or want) to wear your expensive *mu'umu'u* back home.

Sarongs are popular beachwear among local women and men. They are sold everywhere and cost $10–35, depending on the fabric and design. Most places offer tips on how to wear what is basically a couple of yards of material finished on all four sides.

Hawai'i is a great place to stock up on swimsuits, and it can surely claim to be the T-shirt capital of the world. T-shirts are sold everywhere, emblazoned with every imaginable design and logo. In particular, **Crazy Shirts**, which has a number of stores statewide, is considered by many to stock the highest quality shirts with the best designs.

Sarongs displayed outside a shop on O'ahu's North Shore

DIRECTORY

SHIPPING

DHL
Tel (800) 225-5345.
www.dhl.com

FedEx
Tel (800) 463-3339.
http://fedex.com

United States Postal Service
Tel (800) 275-8777.
www.usps.gov

UPS
Tel (800) 742-5877.
www.ups.com

FRUIT & FLOWERS

Dole Plantation
64-1550 Kamehameha Hwy, Wahiawā, O‘ahu.
Tel (808) 621-8408.
www.dole-plantation.com

Maui Tropical Plantation & Country Store
1670 Honoapi‘ilani Hwy, Wailuku, Maui.
Tel (808) 244-7643.
www.mauitropical
plantation.com

Take Home Maui
121 Dickenson St, Lahaina, Maui.
Tel (808) 661-8067.
www.takehomemaui.com

US Department of Agriculture (USDA)
Honolulu International Airport, Honolulu, O‘ahu.
Tel (808) 837-8092.

FOOD AND DRINK

Shirokiya
Ala Moana Center, Honolulu, O‘ahu.
Map 3 A4.
Tel (808) 973-9111.
www.shirokiya.com

Tedeschi Winery
‘Ulupalakua, Maui.
Tel (808) 878-6058.
www.mauiwine.com

Volcano Winery
35 Pi‘imauna Drive, Volcano, Hawai‘i Island.
Tel (808) 967-7772.
www.volcanowinery.com

ART

Avalene Gallery
1156 Makawao Ave, Makawao, Maui.
Tel (808) 572-8500.
www.avalenegallery.com

Lahaina Arts Society
Old Lahaina Courthouse, Lahaina, Maui.
Tel (808) 661-0111.

Nohea Gallery
Ward Warehouse, 1050 Ala Moana Blvd, Honolulu, O‘ahu. **Map** 2 D5.
Tel (808) 596-0074.
www.noheagallery.com

Studio 7
Māmalahoa Hwy, Hōlualoa, Hawai‘i Island.
Tel (808) 324-1335.

Viewpoints Gallery
3620 Baldwin Ave, Makawao, Maui.
Tel (808) 572-5979.
www.viewpoints
maui.com

Village Gallery
120 Dickenson St, Lahaina, Maui.
Tel (808) 661-4402.
www.villagegallery
maui.com

Volcano Art Center
Hawai‘i Volcanoes National Park, Hawai‘i Island.
Tel (808) 967-7565.
www.volcanoartcenter.org

COLLECTIBLES

Aloha Mahalo Antiques & Collectibles
926 Maunakea St, Honolulu, O‘ahu. **Map** 1 A2.
Tel (808) 536-1828.

Bailey's Antiques
517 Kapahulu Ave, Honolulu, O‘ahu.
Tel (808) 734-7628.
www.alohashirts.com

Mauna Kea Galleries
2005 S King St, Honolulu, O‘ahu.
Tel (808) 941-4901.
www.maunakea
galleries.com

The Only Show in Town
56-901 Kamehameha Hwy, Kahuku, O‘ahu.
Tel (808) 293-1295.

Pā‘ia Trading Company
106 Hāna Hwy, Pā‘ia, Maui. *Tel (808) 579-9472.*

Seconds to Go
Mamani St and Rickard Place, Honoka‘a, Hawai‘i Island. *Tel (808) 775-9212.*

CRAFTS

Gallery of Great Things
Parker Square, Waimea, Hawai‘i Island.
Tel (808) 885-7706.

Maui Crafts Guild
69 Hāna Hwy, Pā‘ia, Maui.
Tel (808) 579-9697.
www.mauicrafts
guild.com

Ola's Hanalei
5016 Kūhiō Hwy, Hanalei, Kaua‘i.
Tel (808) 826-6937.
www.olashanalei.com

Sand & Sea
83A Hāna Hwy, Pāia, Maui. *Tel (808) 579-9377.*

The Island's Best
Ala Moana Center, Honolulu, O‘ahu.
Tel (808) 949-5345.

JEWELRY

Jessica's Gems
Whalers Village, Kā‘anapali, Maui. *Tel (808) 661-4223.*

Jim Saylor Jewelers
1318 Kūhiō Hwy, Kapa‘a, Kaua‘i. *Tel (808) 822-3591.*

Precision Goldsmiths
16 N Market St, Wailuku, Maui. *Tel (808) 986-8282.*
www.precision
goldsmiths.com

BOOKS AND MUSIC

Barnes & Noble
Kahala Mall, 4211 Wai‘alae Ave, Honolulu, O‘ahu.
Tel (808) 737-3323.

Borders
Ward Centre, 1200 Ala Moana Blvd, Honolulu, O‘ahu. **Map** 2 E5. *Call for the nearest branch.*
Tel (808) 591-8995.

Native Books Na Mea Hawaii
Ward Warehouse, 1050 Alamoana Blvd, Honolulu O‘ahu. **Map** 2 D5. *Tel (808) 596-8885.* www.
nativebookshawaii.com

Request
10 N Market St, Wailuku, Maui.
Tel (808) 244-9315.

Waldenbooks
Kahala Mall, 4211 Wai‘alae Ave, Honolulu, O‘ahu.
Tel (808) 737-9550. Call for the nearest branch.
www.waldenbooks.com

CLOTHES AND FABRIC

Crazy Shirts
Ala Moana Center, Honolulu, O‘ahu. **Map** 3 A4.
Tel (808) 973-4000. Call for the nearest branch.
www.crazyshirts.com

Hilo Hattie
700 N Nimitz Hwy, Honolulu, O‘ahu.
Tel (808) 535-6500.
www.hilohattie.com

Jagger's
100 Hana Hwy, Pā‘ia, Maui. *Tel (808) 579-9221.*

Macy's
Ala Moana Center, Honolulu, O‘ahu.
Tel (808) 941-2345. Call for the nearest branch.

Mamo Howell
Ward Warehouse, 1050 Ala Moana Blvd, Honolulu, O‘ahu. **Map** 2 D5.
Tel (808) 591-2002.
www.mamohowell.com

Reyn's
Ala Moana Center, Honolulu, O‘ahu. **Map** 3 A4.
Tel (808) 949-5929. Call for the nearest branch.
www.reyns.com

Sig Zane Designs
122 Kamehameha Ave, Hilo, Hawai‘i Island.
Tel (808) 935-7077.
www.sigzane.com

Malls and Shopping Centers

There are literally hundreds of shopping options in Hawai'i, including huge malls and shopping centers that stay open late. While shopping centers do not dominate the landscape as they do in parts of the United States, they are still a common feature of Hawai'i's main towns. Most malls have one large department store, together with smaller shops and boutiques, as well as restaurants, movie theaters, and a beauty salon or day spa. Some even have stages for performances and present a full calendar of entertainment, including *hula* shows, concerts, and amateur talent contests.

HONOLULU AND WAIKĪKĪ

Honolulu and Waikīkī's many shopping centers offer an outstanding selection of goods and services. The largest and most well-known is the **Ala Moana Center**, with department stores such as Macy's, Sears, Nordstrom's, and hundreds of other outlets. The **Royal Hawaiian Shopping Center** is home to designer boutiques like Cartier and Hermès. The **International Marketplace** is an open-air bazaar offering jewelry, apparel, and souvenirs. Other popular shopping spots include the waterfront complex **Aloha Tower Marketplace**, **Kahala Mall**, **King's Village**, and **Koko Marina Center**.

The well-known Hilo Hattie logo

O'AHU

Bargain hunters can follow their instincts at **Waikele Premium Outlets**, with 50 discount outlets including Banana Republic, Guess, and Tommy Hilfiger. The **Windward Mall** has more than 80 gift, clothing, and food outlets. **Pearl Highlands Center** has stores such as Payless Shoe Source, Old Navy, and Sam's Club, along with Ultrazone Hawai'i, where shoppers can try an interactive game of laser tag. At **Pearlridge**, a monorail connects two shopping centers.

MOLOKA'I AND LĀNA'I

Both Moloka'i and Lāna'i each has one large town whose main street has most of its shops. On Moloka'i, shoppers can find everything from fishing gear to clothing and food on Ala Malama Street in Kaunakakai. Check out **Friendly Market Center**. Shopping on Lāna'i is centered around Dole Park, Lāna'i City. Visit **Pine Isle Market** and **Richard's Shopping Center**, an old-fashioned general store.

MAUI

Maui's largest department store, Macy's, is in the island's biggest mall, **Queen Ka'ahumanu Center**. Others, such as **Whalers Village** and **The Shops at Wailea**, offer upscale shopping on the oceanfront. **Pi'ilani Shopping Village** in Kīhei has the state's largest Safeway and Hilo Hattie for souvenirs. **Lahaina Cannery Mall**, housed in a refurbished pineapple cannery, sells everything from aloha wear to fine art. **Maui Marketplace** offers Borders Books & Music, The Sports Authority, and Old Navy. Other shopping spots include **Kukui Mall** and **Nāpili Plaza**, a neighborhood-style center with a military museum.

Entrance to the Aloha Tower Marketplace, Honolulu

HAWAI'I ISLAND

The main shopping districts on Hawai'i Island are in the towns of Kailua-Kona, Waimea, and Hilo. In Kailua-Kona there are several small shopping centers, including **Coconut Grove Market Place** and **Kona Coast Shopping Center**. Just outside Kailua-Kona, the **Keauhou Shopping Center** is home to one-off shops selling hand-blown glass, ceramics, mermaid ornaments, and *hula* dolls. **Waimea Center** has a supermarket, a bakery, and apparel and gift stores. The upscale **Kings' Shops** in Waikoloa are comprised of art galleries, boutiques, and designer stores. In Hilo, **Prince Kūhiō Plaza**, the island's largest mall, includes mainland brand stores, such as Sears and Macy's, and smaller outlets that carry apparel, crafts, and surf gear. WalMart, Borders Books & Music, Hilo Hattie, and a food court are found in the **Waiakea Center**.

KAUA'I

The **Po'ipū Shopping Village** features an open-air garden setting and an array of services, eateries, and specialty stores selling jewelry, art, apparel, and accessories.

In Kapa'a, the open-air **Coconut Market Place** is a good spot for searching out resort wear, collectibles, and local arts and crafts. In addition to the shops and galleries at **Kaua'i Village**, look out for a heritage center and the Kaua'i Children's Discovery Museum.

Kukui Grove Center is Kaua'i's largest shopping center. Included here such well-known stores such as Macy's, Sears, K-Mart, Borders Books & Music, a variety of smaller shops, and a four-screen cinema. The plantation-themed **Princeville Shopping Center** has more than 35 shops and restaurants, along with a supermarket, a bank, a hardware store, a post office, and a clinic. Other popular shopping centers include **Ching Young Village Shopping Center** and **Rice Shopping Center**.

DIRECTORY

HONOLULU AND WAIKĪKĪ

Ala Moana Center
1450 Ala Moana Blvd,
Honolulu, O'ahu.
Map 2 F4.
Tel *(808) 955-9517.*
www.alamoana.com

Aloha Tower Marketplace
1 Aloha Tower Dr,
Honolulu, O'ahu.
Map 1 A3.
Tel *(808) 528-5700.*
www.alohatower.com

International Marketplace
2330 Kalākaua Ave,
Waikīkī, O'ahu.
Map 4 E5.
Tel *(808) 971-2080.*
www.international
marketplacewaikiki.com

Kahala Mall
4211 Wai'alae Ave,
Honolulu, O'ahu.
Map 4 F5.
Tel *(808) 732-7736.*
www.kahalamall
center.com

King's Village
131 Ka'iulani Ave,
Waikīkī, O'ahu.
Map 4 E4.
Tel *(808) 944-6855.*
www.kings-village.com

Koko Marina Center
7192 Kalaniana'ole Hwy,
Honolulu, O'ahu.
Map 4 F5.
Tel *(808) 395-4737.*
www.kokomarina
center.com

Royal Hawaiian Shopping Center
2201 Kalākaua Ave,
Waikīkī, O'ahu. **Map** 4 D4.
Tel *(808) 922-0588.*
www.royalhawaiian
center.com

O'AHU

Pearl Highlands Center
1000 Kamehameha Hwy,
Pearl City, O'ahu.
Tel *(808) 456-1000.*
www.pearlhighlands
center.com

Pearlridge Mall
98-1005 Moanalua Rd,
Aiea, Hawai'i Island.
Tel *(808) 488-0981.*
www.pearlridge
online.com

Waikele Premium Outlets
97-790 Lumiaina St,
Waipahu, O'ahu.
Tel *(808) 676-5656.*
www.premiumoutlets.
com/waikele

Windward Mall
46-056 Kamehameha
Hwy, Kane'ohe, O'ahu.
Tel *(808) 235-1143.*
www.windwardmall.com

MOLOKA'I AND LĀNA'I

Friendly Market Center
90 Ala Malama St,
Kaunakakai, Moloka'i.
Tel *(808) 553-5595.*

Pine Isle Market
356 Eighth St,
Lāna'i City, Lāna'i.
Tel *(808) 565-6488.*

Richard's Shopping Center
434 Eighth St,
Lāna'i City, Lāna'i.
Tel *(808) 565-6047.*

MAUI

Kukui Mall
1819 South Kīhei Rd,
Kīhei, Maui.
Tel *(808) 877-7073.*

Lahaina Cannery Mall
1221 Honoapi'ilani
Hwy, Lahaina, Maui.
Tel *(808) 661-5304.*
www.lahainacannery
mall.com

Maui Marketplace
270 Dairy Rd,
Kahului, Maui.
Tel *(808) 873-0400.*

Nāpili Plaza
509 Nāpilihau St,
Nāpili, Maui.
Tel *(808) 872-4318.*

Pi'ilani Shopping Village
297 Pi'ikea Ave,
Kīhei, Maui.
Tel *(808) 874-8900.*

Queen Ka'ahumanu Center
275 Ka'ahumanu Ave,
Kahului, Maui.
Tel *(808) 877-4325.*
www.queenkaahumanu
center.com

The Shops at Wailea
3750 Wailea Alanui,
Wailea, Maui.
Tel *(808) 891-6770.*
www.shopsatwailea.com

Whalers Village
2435 Kā'anapali Pkwy,
Kā'anapali, Maui.
Tel *(808) 661-4567.*
www.whalersvillage.com

HAWAI'I ISLAND

Coconut Grove Market Place
75-5818 Ali'i Dr, Kailua-
Kona, Hawai'i Island.

Keauhou Shopping Center
78-6831 Ali'i Dr,
Kailua-Kona, Hawai'i.
Tel *(808) 322-3000.*
www.keauhou-
resort.com

Kings' Shops
250 Waikoloa Beach Dr,
Waikoloa Beach Resort,
Hawai'i Island. **Tel** *(808)
866-8811.* www.
waikoloabeachresort.com

Kona Coast Shopping Center
74-5588 Palani Rd,
Kailua-Kona,
Hawai'i Island.
Tel *(808) 326-2262*
www.konashopping.com

Prince Kūhiō Plaza
111 E Puainako St,
Hilo, Hawai'i Island.
Tel *(808) 959-3555.*
www.princekuhio
plaza.com

Waiakea Center
324 Maka'ala St,
Hilo, Hawai'i Island.
Tel *(808) 961-9115.*

Waimea Center
65-1158 Mamalahoa Hwy,
Waimea, Hawai'i Island.
Tel *(808) 885-7727.*

KAUA'I

Coconut Market Place
4-484 Kūhiō Hwy,
Kapa'a, Kaua'i.
Tel *(808) 822-3641.*
www.coconutmarket
place.com

Ching Young Village Shopping Center
5-5190 Kūhiō Hwy,
Hanalei, Kaua'i.
Tel *(808) 826-7222.*
www.chingyoung
village.com

Kaua'i Village
4-831 Kūhiō Hwy,
Kapa'a, Kaua'i.
Tel *(808) 822-3900.*
www.kauaivillage.com

Kukui Grove Center
3-2600 Kaumuali'i Hwy,
Līhu'e, Kaua'i. **Tel** *(505)
245-7784.* www.
kukuigrovecenter.com

Po'ipū Shopping Village
2360 Kiahuna Plantation
Dr, Po'ipū, Kaua'i.
Tel *(808) 742-2831.*

Princeville Shopping Center
5-4280 Kūhiō Hwy,
Princeville, Kaua'i.
Tel *(880) 826-9497.*

Rice Shopping Center
4303 Rice St,Līhu'e, Kaua'i.
Tel *(800) 246-0311.*

ENTERTAINMENT IN HAWAI'I

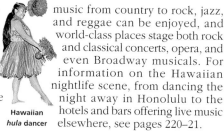

Music, song, and dance are as important to Hawaiians as the food that they eat and the air they breathe. From the musicians strumming in virtually every hotel lounge to the Merrie Monarch Festival (known as the "Olympics of *hula*"), Hawai'i is alive with the sounds of music. Besides Hawaiian rhythms, all kinds of

Hawaiian hula dancer

music from country to rock, jazz, and reggae can be enjoyed, and world-class places stage both rock and classical concerts, opera, and even Broadway musicals. For information on the Hawaiian nightlife scene, from dancing the night away in Honolulu to the hotels and bars offering live music elsewhere, see pages 220–21.

Hawaiian tourist magazines, a good source of entertainment information

PRACTICAL INFORMATION

The Friday edition of *The Honolulu Advertiser* has the most complete entertainment listings; the neighboring islands' newspapers also have entertainment sections once a week. Local radio stations and posters plastered all over town are other sources, along with free local newspapers such as *Honolulu Weekly*. Your hotel should have up-to-date listings.

TICKET OUTLETS

It is best to buy tickets in advance for major events such as the Broadway shows that are occasionally put on in Honolulu. You can charge tickets to a major credit card for many events by telephoning **Ticket Master**.

If you're buying tickets in person, there is sure to be a convenient ticket outlet near your hotel for almost any event; check with the hotel's guest services department. Music stores sell most concert tickets, for example.

Local people are not known for making plans a long way in advance, so there are usually tickets to be had at the door for smaller events.

If you want to attend the really big shows – the Merrie Monarch Festival in April or February's NFL Pro Bowl, for example – you should plan your holiday around them. Tickets for these must be purchased months in advance. You should also note that hotel rooms are at a premium during particularly big events.

HAWAIIAN MUSIC, HULA, AND LŪ'AU

A great deal of the Hawaiian entertainment that is most popular with visitors – from the sounds of traditional chants and slack-key guitar (*kī hō'alu*) to traditional foods and *hula* costumes – has been "adjusted" for Western tastes. However, as a result of the cultural renaissance that has occurred in the state over the last decade, traditional Hawaiian entertainment is now accessible to anyone who wishes to experience it. Virtually every hotel offers Hawaiian music of some description on a regular, if not daily, basis, and many put on *hula* shows, too. Such performances are usually free.

The **Waikīkī Shell** in Kapi'olani Park is a magnificent outdoor spot that hosts many concerts of Hawaiian music and *hula* throughout the year.

"The Shell" was once home to the famous Kodak Hula Show, which was started by Kodak in 1939. Although the show no longer exists the Waikīkī Shell has not lost its fame and continues to be one of O'ahu's top entertainment venues.

Small shows staged at island shopping centers are often the most authentic. They usually feature students of Hawaiian music and dance from *hālau hula* (*hula* schools) and are almost always free.

For a unique treat, enjoy the remarkable talent of the two Brothers Cazimero, whose extraordinary voices and skill on the guitar and bass combine to produce one of Honolulu's best shows. Check the listings in the newspapers or tourist magazines for details of shows.

Most of the major hotels offer *lū'au* – the traditional feasts of the islands. Prices

The impressive sight of a traditional Hawaiian feast or *lū'au* in Lahaina, Maui

Colorful pageant at the Polynesian Cultural Center on O'ahu *(see p92)*

are approximately $50–100 for adults and half that for kids. On O'ahu, try the **Paradise Cove Lū'au** in 'Ewa, about 25 miles (40 km) from Waikīkī; tickets include the bus from town. The best place to go on Maui is, without doubt, **Old Lahaina Lū'au**, in a lovely setting overlooking the ocean.

The only waterfront *lū'au* in Kailua-Kona (Hawai'i Island) is held at **King Kamehameha's Kona Beach Hotel**, while the one at secluded **Kona Village Resort** is well known as the most authentic on the islands. On Kaua'i, be sure to make reservations in advance for the **Tahiti Nui Lū'au** in Hanalei, which takes place every Wednesday night and is perhaps Hawai'i's most "local-style" – that is, most boisterous – *lū'au*.

You can also enjoy a more authentic and inexpensive experience by checking the local newspaper for fundraisers and other *lū'au* put on by civic groups. If you get really lucky and are invited to a big Hawaiian family party, accept the invitation. You will have the experience of a lifetime.

POLYNESIAN SHOWS

These shows are Hawai'i's real extravaganzas, and usually include a *lū'au*-style meal as well as exhibitions of music and dance from Pacific islands like Tahiti, Samoa, Tonga, and Fiji. All the islands have them. While they may vary in scale, Polynesian shows are broadly similar in content – never failing to deliver women wearing grass skirts.

The **Polynesian Cultural Center** in Lā'ie (O'ahu) stages several shows daily, including "*Mana!,*" an evening show featuring a cast of over 100, and the newest and most Hawaiian show, the *Ali'i Lū'au*. An alternative on O'ahu is **Creation: A Polynesian Odyssey**, staged at the Sheraton Princess Ka'iulani Hotel in Waikīkī.

The Hyatt Regency Maui offers **Drums of the Pacific**, and the *lū'au* at the **Royal Lahaina Resort** features a Polynesian show. Finally, you can also try the show at the **Hilton Waikoloa Village Resort** on Hawai'i Island.

EVENING SHOWS

In Honolulu, mimicry features in the lively Las Vegas-style show put on by the **Society of Seven**, a group of veterans who have been appearing at Outrigger Waikīkī on the Beach for more than 30 years. **Cirque Polynesia** blends Hawaiian culture with dazzling acrobatics, including thrilling high-wire routines.

On Maui, evening shows are inspired by Hawaiian myths, legends, and lore. The **Feast at Lele** is an exquisite evening dinner show on the beach that showcases the cultures of the South Pacific. Magic is the focus at **Warren & Annabelle's**, where guests are entertained by the piano-playing ghost of the wife of a 19th-century whaler, as well as mystified by a modern magician in an interactive show. Cocktails and appetizers are available for an extra charge.

Kahuā Ranch on Hawai'i Island draws from another part of Hawai'i's heritage, the *paniolo* (cowboy) experience. After enjoying a hearty chuck-wagon barbecue, you can dance to live music and participate in ranch games such as roping and horseshoes.

On Kaua'i, you can enjoy an enchanted evening of musical theater, entertainment, and dining featuring a full production of the Broadway musical **South Pacific** at the Kaua'i Beach Hotel.

Concerts by big international names from Tony Bennett to Sting and legendary rock bands like the Eagles appear at major O'ahu venues such as the spectacularly restored **Hawai'i Theatre**, the **Neal Blaisdell Concert Hall**, and **Aloha Stadium**. Maui's top spot is the impressive $32-million **Maui Arts & Cultural Center**, with an outdoor amphitheater and several different auditoriums for concerts, plays, and art-house films.

The biggest stars of all are of course up in Hawai'i's night sky. Almost all the heavenly bodies in the southern hemisphere are visible from Hawai'i. Operators of star-gazing tours include **Mauna Kea Stargazing Tour** and **Haleakalā National Park**. Some hotels and charter boats also offer excursions for viewing the night sky.

The thrilling Cirque Polynesia show, a multi-million dollar spectacular

Hula at the Maui Ukulele Festival, Maui Arts & Cultural Center

THEATER

For anything other than small community theater, Honolulu is the place to be. At least a couple of Broadway musicals show up each year, usually at the **Neal Blaisdell Concert Hall**. Past shows include *Les Miserables, Cats,* and *Phantom of the Opera.* The **Mānoa Valley Theatre** presents local productions of the cream of Broadway and off-Broadway. Hawai'i's oldest company, the **Diamond Head Theatre**, offers a mixed bag of performances each season, as does the **Kumu Kahua Theatre** – some of whose shows are written locally.

On weekends, at any time of year, it should be possible to see a performance by at least one of Maui's four community theater groups – the Maui Academy of Performing Arts, Maui Community Theatre, the Baldwin Theater Guild, and Studio Hāmākua Poko. Most often the place is one of the two theaters inside the **Maui Arts & Cultural Center** in Kahului, although the Maui OnStage Theater uses the lovingly restored **'Īao Theater** in historic Wailuku.

Hawai'i Island has several community theater groups, too: Akebono Theater, Aloha Community Players, and Hilo Community Players. The lovely **Kahilu Theatre** in upcountry Waimea is a wonderful spot.

On the Garden Isle, the Kaua'i Community Players offer an almost continuous program of performances throughout the year. There is a beautiful performing arts center on the campus of **Kaua'i Community College**.

OPERA, CLASSICAL MUSIC, AND DANCE

The state's resident opera company, **Hawai'i Opera Theatre**, stages three or four operas from January to April each year. These are held in Honolulu's **Neal Blaisdell Concert Hall**, where Broadway productions such as *Phantom of the Opera*, *Les Miserables*, *Miss Saigon*, and *Chicago* have also been staged. You should also look out for performances by the **Hawai'i Youth Symphony Association**, made up of student musicians from all the islands.

Every year at least one of the mainland's most reputable ballet companies travels across the Pacific to perform in Hawai'i, usually at the Neal Blaisdell Concert Hall. The **Ballet Hawai'i** – the islands' oldest ballet troupe – presents the *Nutcracker Suite* every winter for the holiday crowds, plus another ballet in summer. The **Iona Contemporary Dance Theatre** perform unique works that combine dance with theater.

The **Maui Arts & Cultural Center**, which is also known

as the "MACC," is Maui's premier venue for performing and visual arts. The complex includes two theaters, an outdoor amphitheater, and a gallery. Performances include classical music, rock, pop, and many other styles by an array of nationally and internationally famous artists.

The Classical Music Festival takes place every June at various Maui venues, with a series of classical concerts performed over two weekends.

FILMS AND FILM FESTIVALS

A large and, for the most part, free film festival, the **Hawai'i International Film Festival**, takes place each November. Scores of films are shown at various theaters on O'ahu (some of which charge admission) in the first week, and on the neighboring islands the second week; even tiny communities are included.

New films normally open in Honolulu at the same time as on the mainland. In addition to the many spots that specialize in big Hollywood movies, the University of Hawai'i, community colleges, and other venues present art-house, foreign, and classic films on a regular basis. Check the Friday edition of *The Honolulu Advertiser* for the latest listings. You can go to the movies on the neighboring islands, too, but the choice there is a great deal more limited. It was not that long ago that Maui got its first multiplex cinema. The **Maui Arts & Cultural Center** presents seasons of foreign and art-house films.

On the island of Hawai'i, the Big Island Film Festival, devoted to independent narrative film, presents screenings, workshops, and celebrity appearances. On the neighboring islands, there are special showings of non-blockbuster films, often presented by community colleges, civic organizations, and various nonprofit groups.

Maui
Arts & Cultural Center
M A K A N A   A L O H A
Sign for the top cultural place on Maui

DIRECTORY

TICKET OUTLETS

Ticket Master
Tel (808) 521-2101.
www.ticketmaster.com

MAJOR VENUES

Aloha Stadium
99-500 Salt Lake Blvd,
'Aiea, O'ahu. *Tel (808)
486-9300.* www.aloh
astadiumhawaii.gov

Hawai'i Theatre
1130 Bethel St, Honolulu,
O'ahu. **Map** 1 A2.
Tel (808) 528-0506.
www.hawaiitheatre.com

Maui Arts &
Cultural Center
1 Cameron Way, Kahului,
Maui. *Tel (808) 242-
7469.* www.mauiarts.org

Neal Blaisdell
Concert Hall
777 Ward Ave, Honolulu,
O'ahu. **Map** 2 D3.
Tel (808) 591-2211.
www.blaisdellcenter.com

Waikīkī Shell
2805 Monsarrat Ave,
Kapi'olani Park, Honolulu,
O'ahu. *Tel (808) 591-2211.*
www.blaisdellcenter.com

HAWAIIAN MUSIC,
HULA, AND LŪ'AU

King Kamehameha's
Kona Beach Hotel
75-5660 Palani Road,
Kailua-Kona, Hawai'i
Island. *Tel (808) 329-2911.*
www.konabeachhotel.com

Kona Village Resort
Queen Ka'ahumanu Hwy,
Ka'ūpūlehu-Kona,
Hawai'i Island.
Tel (808) 325-5555.
www.konavillage.com

Old Lahaina Lū'au
1251 Front St,
Lahaina, Maui.
Tel (808) 667-1998.
www.oldlahainaluau.com

Paradise Cove Lū'au
92-1089 Ali'inui Drive,
Kapolei, O'ahu. *Tel (808)
842-5911.* www.
paradisecovehawaii.com

Tahiti Nui Lū'au
5-5134 Kūhiō Highway,
Hanalei, Kaua'i.
Tel (808) 826-6277.

POLYNESIAN
SHOWS

Creation: A Poly-
nesian Odyssey
Sheraton Princess Ka'iulani
Hotel, 120 Ka'iulani Ave,
Waikīkī, O'ahu. **Map** 4 E4.
Tel (808) 922-5811.

Drums of the
Pacific
Hyatt Regency Maui,
200 Nohea Kai Dr,
Kā'anapali, Maui.
Tel (808) 667-4420.
www.maui.hyatt.com

Hilton Waikoloa
Village Resort
425 Waikoloa Beach Dr,
Kohala Coast, Hawai'i
Island. *Tel (808) 886-1234.*
www.hiltonwaikoloa
village.com

Polynesian
Cultural Center
55-370 Kamehameha
Hwy, Lā'ie, Oahu.
Tel (808) 293-3333.
www.polynesia.com

Royal Lahaina
Resort
2780 Keka'a Dr,
Kā'anapali, Maui. *Tel
(808) 661-3611.* www.
royallahainaluau.com

EVENING SHOWS

Cirque Polynesia
Hyatt Regency Maui, 200
Nohea Kai Dr, Lahaina,
Maui. *Tel (808) 667-4540.*
www.cirquepolynesia.com

Feast at Lele
505 Front St,
Lahaina, Maui.
Tel (808) 667-5353.
www.feastatlele.com

Kahuā Ranch
Waikoloa, Hawai'i Island.
Tel (808) 987-2108.
www.kahuaranch.com

Haleakalā
National Park
PO Box 369,
Makawao, Maui.
Tel (808) 572-4400.
www.nps.gov/hale

Mauna Kea
Stargazing Tour
737 Kanoelehua Ave,
Hilo, Hawai'i Island.
Tel (808) 969-9507.
www.jackshawaii.com

Society of Seven
Outrigger Waikīkī on the
Beach, 2335 Kalākaua
Ave, Waikīkī, O'ahu.
Tel (808) 922-6408.
www.outrigger.com

South Pacific
Hilton Kaua'i Beach
Resort, 4331 Kaua'i
Beach Dr, Līhu'e, Kaua'i.
Tel (808) 245-1955.

Warren &
Annabelle's
900 Front St, Lahaina,
Maui. *Tel (808) 667-6244.*
www.warrenand
annabelles.com

THEATER

Diamond Head
Theatre
520 Makapu'u Ave,
Honolulu, O'ahu.
Tel (808) 733-0274.
www.diamondhead
theatre.com

'Iao Theater
68 N Market St, Wailuku,
Maui. *Tel (808) 244-8680.*
www.mauionstage.com

Kahilu Theatre
67-1185 Māmalahoa Hwy,
Waimea, Hawai'i Island.
Tel (808) 885-6868.
www.kahilutheatre.org

Kaua'i Community
College Performing
Arts Center
3-1901 Kaumuali'i Hwy,
Līhu'e, Kaua'i. *Tel (808)
245-8270.* www.kauai.
hawaii.edu/pac

Kumu Kahua
Theatre
46 Merchant St,
Honolulu, O'ahu. **Map** 1
A3. *Tel (808) 536-4441.*
www.kumukahua.org

Mānoa Valley
Theatre
2833 E Mānoa Rd,
Honolulu, O'ahu. *Tel (808)
988-6131.* www.
manoavalleytheatre.com

OPERA,
CLASSICAL MUSIC,
AND DANCE

Ballet Hawai'i
650 Iwiler Rd, Honolulu,
O'ahu. *Tel (808) 521-8600.*
www.ballethawaii.org

Hawai'i Opera
Theatre
848 S Beretania St, Hono-
lulu, O'ahu. **Map** 2 E4.
Tel (808) 596-7858.
www.hawaiiopera.org

Hawai'i Youth
Symphony
Association
Suite 201, 1110 University
Ave, Honolulu, O'ahu.
Map 4 D1. *Tel (808) 941-
9706.* www.hiyouth
symphony.org

Iona Contemporary
Dance Theatre
130 Ulupa St,
Kailua, O'ahu.
Tel (808) 262-0110.
www.iona360.com

FILMS AND FILM
FESTIVALS

Big Island
Film Festival
68-1851 Lina Poepoe St,
Waikoloa, Hawai'i Island.
Tel (808) 883-0394.
www.bigislandfilm
festival.com

Hawai'i
International
Film Festival
680 Iwilei Rd, Suite 100,
Honolulu, O'ahu.
Map 1 A3.
Tel (800) 528-3456.
www.hiff.org

Maui Film Festival
16 Baldwin Ave, Pa'ia,
Maui. *Tel (808) 572-
3456.* www.mauifilm
festival.com

Nightlife

Traditionally, Hawai'i is an early-to-bed, early-to-rise place. Night owls may, however, find enough to keep them occupied, especially in Honolulu and Waikīkī on O'ahu. There is a fair bit of nightlife on Maui as well, but do not expect to find much on the other islands. Having said that, many bars and hotel lounges provide live entertainment. On any night of the week you can find almost any kind of music – rock, pop, blues, jazz, country, reggae, and, of course, Hawaiian – either performed live or spun by a DJ. Check listings in each island's local newspapers for an up-to-date guide to what is on while you are there.

Partying goes on well into the night at the fashionable Ocean Club, Honolulu

HONOLULU AND WAIKĪKĪ

Honolulu has a flourishing club scene. **Pearl Ultra Lounge** is a swanky nightclub with unusual theme parties. Dance outdoors at pier-side **Gordon Biersch**, dress up for a night at **Rumours**, or enjoy the casual atmosphere at **Scruples Beach Club**. For lively parties, head to the **Pipeline Café**, a comedy club, dance hall, and concert venue.

Waikīkī's clubs stay open late – the **Jazz Minds Art & Café**, for example, closes at 2am. **Zanzabar** features themed nights, the latest dance music, and cutting-edge DJs. **Level 4** has all the glitz of Las Vegas. For chilled-out live jazz, try **Lewer's Lounge**.

Some hotels also host hip dance clubs, such as **Twist and Shout** in the Hanohano Room at the Waikīkī Hotel (see p179), where you can dine and dance with a view. Restaurants also double up as nightclubs later in the evening: **Indigo** (see p196) serves dinner until 9:30pm; then the club is open every night until 1am. **Chai's Island Bistro** (see p198) becomes a club on Saturdays from 10pm to 2am.

MOLOKA'I AND LĀNA'I

Not much nightlife is to be found on either of these quiet islands. What there is takes place in the hotels. **Hotel Moloka'i** (see p183) hosts live entertainment in its oceanfront dining room and once a week everyone and anyone brings their ukuleles and joins in a local-style jam session. It is a casual, fun, and unique island experience.

On Lāna'i, you will also find a relaxed scene. Check out entertainment at the **Four Seasons Lodge at Kō'ele** or the **Hale Aheahe Lounge**.

MAUI

Most of Maui's nightspots are in Lahaina and Kīhei, where there are lots of bars and lounges offering live entertainment. **Mulligan's On the Blue** in Wailea offers a Hawaiian dinner show a few nights a week, live jazz or rock on other nights, and traditional Celtic music on weekends.

In Lahaina, the **Hard Rock Café** presents a live reggae band weekly, while **Paradice Bluz** features a lively schedule of local bands and dancing to DJ-spun grooves.

The popular nightspots from the last century have been replaced by modern clubs such as **Timba** in Lahaina and **Ambrosia** in Kīhei, where DJs spin discs for the late-night set, with state-of-the-art video, sound, and lighting technology.

HAWAI'I ISLAND

The Big Island's nightlife centres on Kailua-Kona and Hilo. However, there are great bars with DJs and dancing, and some with live bands, around the island. Again, you will find musical variety: country and western, reggae, rock, hip hop, and Hawaiian.

There is a host of bars and restaurants that feature live music and dancing at night. Among these are **Bongo Ben's**, **Lulu's**, **Huggo's on the Rocks**, and **Blue Dragon**.

Just about every hotel has a lounge offering live Hawaiian music; choose from the chic **Honu Bar** at the Mauna Lani Bay Hotel (see p189), the open-air **Reef Lounge** at Hāpuna Beach Prince Hotel (see p189), and **Hawaii Calls** at the Waikoloa Beach Marriott (see p189).

KAUA'I

Kaua'i is not known for its nighttime scene, but live entertainment and dancing can be found in restaurants, bars, and clubs, as well as in the resort hotels. **Hanalei Gourmet** serves dinner and then has live entertainment after dark, usually modern Hawaiian or R&B. The hip **Sushi Blues** in Hanalei has a weekly schedule of performances that include jazz, blues, and swing music. In Kapa'a, live entertainment accompanies pool and darts at the **Lizard Lounge and Deli**. There is also a sports bar, with DJs and dancing, at **Rob's Good Times Grill** in Līhu'e's Rice Shopping Center. **The Landing Pad** at Princeville Airport has live entertainment on weekends and a DJ dance night on Thursdays.

Hawaiian dancer at a dinner show

DIRECTORY

HONOLULU AND WAIKĪKĪ

Chai's Island Bistro
1 Aloha Tower Dr,
Honolulu, O'ahu.
Map 1 A3.
Tel (808) 585-0011.
www.chaisisland
bistro.com

Gordon Biersch
Aloha Tower Marketplace,
1 Aloha Tower Dr,
Honolulu, O'ahu.
Map 1 A3.
Tel (808) 599-4877.
www.gordonbiersch.com

Indigo
1121 Nu'uanu Ave,
Honolulu, O'ahu.
Map 1 A2.
Tel (808) 521-2900.
www.indigo-hawaii.com

Jazz Minds Art & Café
1661 Kapi'olani Blvd,
Honolulu, O'ahu.
Map 3 A3.
Tel (808) 945-0800.

Level 4
2233 Kalākaua Ave,
Honolulu, O'ahu. **Map** 4
E4. *Tel (808) 926-4441.*
www.14waikiki.com

Lewer's Lounge
Halekulani Hotel,
2199 Kālia Rd,
Waikīkī, O'ahu.
Map 4 D5.
Tel (808) 923-2311.
www.halekulani.com

Pearl Ultra Lounge
1450 Ala Moana Blvd,
Honolulu, O'ahu. **Map**
2 F4. *Tel (808) 944-8000.*
www.pearlhawaii.com

Pipeline Café
805 Pohukaina St,
Honolulu, O'ahu.
Map 1 B4.
Tel (808) 589-1999.
www.pipelinecafe.com

Scruples Beach Club
2310 Kūhiō Ave,
Honolulu, O'ahu.
Map 4 E4.
Tel (808) 923-9530.

Twist and Shout
Sheraton Waikīkī Hotel,
2255 Kalākaua Ave,
Waikīkī, O'ahu. **Map** 4
D5. www.sheraton
waikiki.com

Zanzabar
2255 Kūhiō Ave,
Honolulu, O'ahu.
Map 4 D4.
Tel (808) 924-3939.

MOLOKA'I AND LĀNA'I

Four Seasons Lodge at Kō'ele
Keōmuku Hwy,
Lāna'i City, Lāna'i.
Tel (808) 565-7300.
www.lodgeatkoele.com

Hale Aheahe Lounge
Four Seasons Resort
at Mānele Bay,
1 Mānele Bay Rd,
Mānele, Lāna'i.
Tel (808) 565-2000.
www.fourseasons
manelebay.com

Hotel Moloka'i
Kamehameha V Hwy,
Kaunakakai,
Moloka'i.
Tel (808) 553-5347.
www.hotelmolokai.com

MAUI

Ambrosia Martini Lounge
1913 S Kihei Rd,
Kihei, Maui.
Tel (808) 891-1011.
www.ambrosiamaui.com

Hard Rock Café
900 Front St,
Lahaina, Maui.
Tel (808) 667-7400.
www.hardrock.com

Mulligan's on the Blue
Wailea Blue Golf Course,
100 Kaukahi St,
Wailea, Maui.
Tel (808) 874-1131.
www.mulligansonthe
blue.com

Paradice Bluz
744 Front St,
Lahaina, Maui.
Tel (808) 667-5299.
www.paradicebluz.com

Timba
505 Front St,
Lahaina, Maui.
Tel (808) 661-9873.
www.timamaui.com

HAWAI'I ISLAND

Blue Dragon Musiquarium
61-3616 Kawaihae Rd,
Kamuela, Hawai'i. *Tel
(808) 882-7771.* www.
bluedragonhawaii.com

Bongo Ben's
75-5819 Ali'i Dr,
Kailua-Kona, Hawai'i.
Tel (808) 329-7366.
www.dirtyjakes.com

Hawaii Calls Lounge
Waikoloa Beach Marriott,
69–275 Waikoloa Beach
Dr, Waikoloa, Hawai'i.
Tel (808) 886-6789.
www.marriott.com

Honu Bar
Mauna Lani Bay Hotel,
68-1400 Mauna Lani Dr,
Kohala Coast, Hawai'i.
Tel (808) 881-7911.
www.maunalani.com

Huggo's on the Rocks
75-5828 Kahakai Rd,
Kailua-Kona, Hawai'i.
Tel (808) 329-1493.
www.huggos.com

Lulu's
75–5819 Ali'i Dr,
Kailua-Kona, Hawai'i.
Tel (808) 331-2633.
www.lulushawaii.com

Reef Lounge
Hāpuna Beach Prince
Hotel, 67-100 Kaunaoa
Dr, Kohala Coast, Hawai'i.
Tel (808) 880-1111.
www.princeresorts
hawaii.com

KAUA'I

Hanalei Gourmet
5-5161 Kūhiō Hwy,
Hanalei, Kaua'i. *Tel (808)
826-2524.* www.
hanaleigourmet.com

The Landing Pad
Princeville Airport,
5-3541 Kūhiō Hwy,
Princeville, Kaua'i.
Tel (808) 826-9561.

Lizard Lounge and Deli
Waipouli Town Center,
4771 Kūhiō Hwy,
Kapa'a, Kaua'i.
Tel (808) 821-2205.

Rob's Good Times Grill
Rice Shopping Center,
4303 Rice St,
Līhu'e, Kaua'i.
Tel (808) 246-0311.

Sushi Blues
Ching Young Village
(upstairs),
5-5190 Kūhiō Hwy,
Hanalei, Kaua'i.
Tel (808) 826-9701.
www.sushiandblues.com

OUTDOOR ACTIVITIES

With its hot climate, Hawai'i is a great place for outdoor activities, many of which are focused on the ocean. All over the islands you will find people surfing, swimming, paddling, windsurfing, or fishing at all hours of the day. The abundance of coral and exotic marine life is a big attraction for divers and snorkelers, too. Whale watching is a popular activity

Hawai'i's colorful yellow tang fish

in the spring and numerous boat tours allow visitors to get up close and personal with these awesome marine mammals. On land, there are many attractive, well-maintained hiking trails, as well as paths for horseback riding, which provide a great way to enjoy the islands' fine scenery. For more information on Hawai'i's world-leading golf courses see pages 226–7.

Snorkeler enjoying a close encounter with a trumpet fish

SNORKELING, SCUBA DIVING, AND SNUBA

Snorkeling and scuba diving are at the top of the list of Hawai'i's most popular outdoor activities. Early morning is the best time to observe the fish. Some snorkel sites are dangerous during high wave action, so check the conditions first. Darting butterfly fish, rainbow parrotfish, bright yellow tangs, and sea turtles are all common sights. For equipment rental at good prices, **Snorkel Bob's** has outlets on O'ahu, Maui, Kaua'i, and Hawai'i Island.

The leeward sides of the islands have the best dive sites, most of which are only accessible only by boat. Some good dive operators are: **Aaron's Dive Shop** (O'ahu), **Bubbles Below** (Kaua'i), **Extended Horizons** (Maui), **Fair Wind Cruises** (Hawai'i Island), See pages 32–33 for more information about snorkeling and dive sites.

Another way to enjoy Hawai'i's magnificent undersea environment is

snuba, a cross between scuba diving and snorkeling. This shallow water diving system allows you to go many places that snorkelers cannot reach. The approximate depth of a snuba dive is 20 ft (6 m). Snuba is not difficult to learn, there is no certification required, and few restrictions apply. Anyone over the age of eight can snub. Many snorkel cruises offer snuba for an additional charge.

SWIMMING

The waters off Hawai'i are cool and inviting. Maui and O'ahu have the best beaches, particularly Maui's Kā'anapali Coast and the southern and windward shores of O'ahu, where the surf is usually gentle. World-famous Waikīkī Beach is one of the best

swimming spots, but locals generally prefer nearby Sans Souci. On O'ahu's windward side both Kailua Beach and Lanikai Beach are mellow and uncrowded with lovely, clear water. Hawai'i Island's Mauna Kea Beach is also good.

If you enjoy serious wave action, look out for Hawai'i's "rough-water" swimming contests, such as the demanding summer North Shore Roughwater Swim Series on O'ahu. The ocean is dangerous. Safety tips for anyone entering the water are given on page 238.

SURFING, BODY-SURFING, AND WINDSURFING

Athletes from around the globe flock to Hawai'i to test their mettle at some of the world's best surf breaks. With 7 miles (11 km) of excellent surf spots between Hale'iwa and Sunset Beach, O'ahu's North Shore is the surfing capital of the world, and site of the annual Triple Crown contest *(see p31)*. But there is a cornucopia of world-class surf breaks around the rest of the O'ahu coast, and also on the coasts of Maui and Kaua'i. Waikīkī's gentle rollers are ideal for beginners. Beach boys offer surfing lessons, just like in the old days, and boards can also be rented here. Chun's Reef on O'ahu's North Shore

Surfer taking a break between rides on the Hawaiian surf

Novices being given a windsurfing lesson at Kailua Beach Park on O'ahu

is a good place for beginners. **Surf-n-Sea** rents boards here and also offers lessons.

The Lahaina Breakwall, east of Lahaina, is another popular spot for beginners. You can rent surfboards from **Honolua Surfco**, **Local Motion**, and other Maui surf shops. The **Nancy Emerson School of Surfing** offers lessons; **Windsurf Kaua'i** rents boards and offers lessons on Kaua'i. Call the **Surf News Network** for general information.

You can surf all year, but the waves reach their peak from November through April, when the north shore of any island can be dangerous for experienced surfers – let alone beginners. The power of the ocean in Hawai'i is beyond description and many visitors get into trouble after paddling out into big surf. The best advice is "Never surf alone."

Body-surfing, in which riders wearing flippers lie flat on a bodyboard or boogie board (see p30), is also popular. At O'ahu's Makapu'u and Sandy Beach, waves crash onto a shallow sandy shorebreak, and body-surfers shoot through the tube barely ahead of the lip of the wave. Point Panic in Honolulu is also a favorite spot. All three of these places are dangerous, but for spectators they are fantastic.

Beginners can get their fins wet at O'ahu's Bellows Beach and Waikīkī Beach, Maui's Wailea Beach, and Kaua'i's Shipwreck Beach. To rent bodyboards, try **Aloha Beach Service** in Waikīkī, **Local Motion** in Lahaina, and **Progressive Expressions** on Kaua'i.

Windsurfing has a big following. The sport's hub is Maui's North Shore, Ho'okipa Beach being the top spot for acrobatics. On O'ahu, Kailua Bay suits all ability levels, and Diamond Head's constant winds and breaking waves make it a windsurfer's delight. Windsurfers replace surfers at Sunset Beach when the wind blows strongly.

Lessons and equipment are available from: **Naish Hawai'i** (O'ahu), which is owned and run by world-champion windsurfer Robbie Naish; **Secondwind** or **Hi-Tech Surf Sports**, both on Maui; and **Windsurf Kaua'i** in Hanalei, on Kaua'i.

KAYAKING, CANOEING, AND SAILING

Kayaking is all the rage in Hawai'i. Favorite spots include O'ahu's Kailua Bay and Kaua'i's Wailua River. The kayak is also one of the preferred ways to visit Kaua'i's great Nā Pali Coast. Kayaks can be rented from **Go Bananas** or **Twogood Kayaks Hawai'i** (O'ahu), **South Pacific Kayaks** (Maui), and **Outfitters Kaua'i** (Kaua'i).

Traditional Hawaiian canoe paddling in outrigger canoes is popular, too. The October Nā Moloka'i Hoe race (see p35) is the most important contest of its kind in the world. Regattas are held on weekends in several places, but the sport is run by tightly knit clubs, making it hard to participate. However,

Waikīkī beach boys will take you out to ride the waves in an outrigger near the Moana Hotel (see p64).

Hawai'i is a major stopping-place for boats crossing the Pacific, and the state has a strong seafaring tradition of its own. Two of the world's biggest regattas, the Kenwood Cup and the Trans Pacific Race, take place in Hawai'i.

Kāne'ohe Bay on O'ahu is the best place for small boat sailing, though Waikīkī is also suitable. The **Hawai'i Yacht Club** and **Waikīkī Yacht Club** take on experienced deckhands for Honolulu's weekly Champagne Race (so named because the winners are given champagne). Races are held on Friday afternoons.

FISHING

Hawai'i is famous for its deep-sea fishing – above all on the Kona Coast, where record catches are often made of Pacific blue marlin, yellow-fin tuna, and other gamefish. This area is the best for trips, but charters can be arranged on all the islands. **Sea Verse** operates in Honolulu while **Blue Hawai'i Sportfishing** is based in Kailua-Kona, Hawai'i Island. On Maui, you can arrange fishing trips with **Hinatea Charters** and **Aerial Sportfishing Charters**. *Hawai'i Fishing News* is a good source of infomation.

Hawai'i's long shoreline offers lots of surf casting for smaller fish, such as snapper and giant *ulua* (jack). Take care if you fish; conditions in the best surf-casting places can be hazardous.

Women kayak training on the gentle waters of Waikīkī's Ala Wai Canal

Cyclist on a scenic bike ride through Waikīkī's Ala Moana Park, away from the multitudes at the beach

CYCLING AND MOUNTAIN BIKING

Narrow shoulders and variable road quality make Hawai'i a poor place for bike riding. Mountain biking trails are limited too, but those that do exist are of good quality. Trails above Pūpūkea on O'ahu's North Shore are very popular, with ocean views and challenging riding.

South of Kula on Maui, in the Polipoli Springs Recreation Area, several miles of trails snake through ravines and forests of eucalyptus and giant ferns. An easier but extremely popular adventure is the sunrise descent down Haleakalā, a 38-mile (61-km) stretch starting in Haleakalā National Park (see pp128–9) that contains 21 switchbacks and superb views.

For quality mountain bike rentals, try **Raging Isle Sports** in Hale'iwa, O'ahu, or **Haleakalā Bike Co**, **West Maui Cycle and Sports**, or **South Maui Bicycles** on Maui.

HIKING

An extensive network of state and national parks crisscrossed by trails makes Hawai'i great hiking territory. The terrain ranges from barren volcanic desert to lush fern rainforest with waterfalls and cool swimming holes.

There are trails to suit everyone in terms of both accessibility and difficulty. Two of the finest are Kaua'i's Kalalau Trail along the stunning, rugged Nā Pali Coast (see pp168–9) and the Kaupō Trail, which descends from Haleakalā's volcanic moonscape to the lush rainforest of the Kīpahulu Valley (see p126).

Clubs and environmental groups, including the **Sierra Club**, **Nature Conservancy**, and the **Hawai'i Nature Center**, organize hikes on a number of islands. Some of the state, national, and county parks have campsites for longer stays (see p177).

Changing weather conditions can be a serious hazard when hiking; flash floods in narrow ravines are common, and hikers disappear with alarming regularity. It is dangerous to hike alone. Before you set off, leave word of your plans and your expected time of return with a friend or someone at the hotel. Pack water, a flashlight, warm clothes, and a blanket in case you become stranded.

Hiker enjoying the wild scenery of Haleakalā National Park, Maui

WHALE WATCHING

Every winter humpback whales migrate from the North Pacific to the warm waters around the Hawaiian islands to mate and bear their young. Although it is certainly possible to see whales from the shoreline, you will get a better look by getting out onto the water.

Almost every charter boat offers whale-watching cruises in the peak viewing season of January through April. Whale-watch cruises usually last two hours and many have a marine biologist or knowledgeable narrator on board. Try operators such as **Wild Side Specialty Tours** on O'ahu or **Paragon Charters** on Maui.

Tours may be on anything from large boats to kayaks. Boats may have a hydrophone, an underwater microphone, which allows you to listen to the haunting whale song. Humpback whales are protected by U.S. laws that prohibit approaching whales any closer than 300 ft (90 m).

A humpback whale, in Hawaiian waters from January to April

OTHER ACTIVITIES

Hawai'i's mild climate lends itself to all warm weather activity. In-line skating and jogging are common pastimes, particularly on O'ahu. There are busy public tennis courts on the four major islands.

Two good horseback riding trails are along the Moloka'i cliffs and in Maui's Kīpahulu Valley. Horses or rides can be organized through **CJM Country Stables**, **Moloka'i Mule Ride**, and **Paniolo Riding Adventures**.

More daring activities include caving, zipping through the tree tops, or freefalling from an airplane. Contact **Skyline Eco-Adventures** or **ATV Tours** for more information.

DIRECTORY

SNORKELING, SCUBA DIVING, AND SNUBA

Aaron's Dive Shop
307 Hahani Street, Kailua, O'ahu. *Tel (808) 262-2333.* www.hawaii-scuba.com

Bubbles Below
PO Box 157, Eleele, Kaua'i. *Tel (808) 332-7333.* www.bubblesbelow kauai.com

Extended Horizons
94 Kupuohi St, Suite A-1, Lahaina, Maui. *Tel (808) 667-0611.* www.extended horizons.com

Fair Wind Cruises
78-7130 Kaleiopapa St, Kailua-Kona, Hawai'i Island. *Tel (808) 345-0268.* www.fair-wind.com

Snorkel Bob's
700 Kapahulu Avenue, Honolulu, O'ahu. *Tel (808) 735-7944.* www.snorkelbob.com

75-5831 Kahakai Road, Kailua, Hawai'i Island. *Tel (808) 329-0770.*

3350 Lower Honoapi'ilani Road, Lahaina, Maui. *Tel (808) 667-9999.*

3236 Po'ipū Road, Kōloa, Kaua'i. *Tel (808) 742-2206.*

SURFING, BODY-SURFING, AND WINDSURFING

Aloha Beach Service
2365 Kalakaua Avenue, Waikīkī, O'ahu. *Tel (808) 922-3111.*

Hi-Tech Surf Sports
425 Kōloa Street, Kahului, Maui. *Tel (808) 877-2111.* www.surfmaui.com

Honolua Surfco
845 Front St, Lahaina, Maui. *Tel (808) 661-8848.* www.honoluasurf.com

Local Motion
1295 Front St, Lahaina, Maui. *Tel (808) 661-7873.* www.localmotion hawaii.com

Naish Hawai'i
155A Hāmākua Drive, Suite A, Kailua, O'ahu. *Tel (808) 262-6068.* www.naish.com

Nancy Emerson's School of Surfing
505 Front St, Suite 224B, Lahaina, Maui. *Tel (808) 244-7873.* www.mauisurfclinics.com

Progressive Expressions
5428 Kolōa Road, Kōloa, Kaua'i. *Tel (808) 742-6041.* www.progressive expressions.com

Secondwind
111 Hāna Hwy, Kahului, Maui. *Tel (808) 877-7467.* www.secondwind maui.com

Surf News Network
Daily updates on water conditions, weather, etc. *Tel (808) 593-2170.* www.surfnewsnetwork.com

Surf-n-Sea
62-595 Kamehameha Hwy, Hale'iwa, O'ahu. *Tel (808) 637-9887.* www.surfnsea.com

Windsurf Kaua'i
PO Box 323, Hanalei, Kaua'i. *Tel (808) 828-6838.*

KAYAKING, CANOEING, AND SAILING

Go Bananas
799 Kapahulu Avenue, Honolulu, O'ahu. *Tel (808) 737-9514.* www.gobananaskayaks.com

Hawai'i Yacht Club
1739-C Ala Moana Blvd, Suite C, Honolulu, O'ahu. *Tel (808) 944-9666.* www.hawaiiyachtclub.org

Outfitters Kaua'i
2827A Po'ipū Rd, Kōloa, Kaua'i. *Tel (808) 742-9667.* www.outfitterskauai.com

Paragon Charters
5229 Lwr Kula Rd, Kula, Maui. *Tel (808) 244-2087.* www.sailmaui.com

South Pacific Kayaks
95 Halekauai St, Kīhei, Maui. *Tel (808) 875-4848.* www.southpacific kayaks.com

Twogood Kayaks Hawai'i
345 Hahani Street, Kailua, O'ahu. *Tel (808) 262-5656.* www.twogood kayaks.com

Waikīkī Yacht Club
1599 Ala Moana Blvd, Honolulu, O'ahu. *Tel (808) 955-4405.* www.waikikiyachtclub.com

FISHING

Aerial Sportfishing Charters
Slip #9, Lahaina, Maui. *Tel (808) 667-9089.* www.aerialsportfishing charters.com

Blue Hawai'i Sportfishing
Kailua-Kona, Hawai'i Island. *Tel (808) 895-2970.* www.konamarlin fishing.com

Hawai'i Fishing News
6650 Hawai'i Kai Drive, Suite 201, Honolulu, O'ahu. *Tel (808) 395-4499.* www.hawaiifishing news.com

Hinatea Charters
Slip 27, Lahaina Harbor, Lahaina, Maui. *Tel (808) 667-7548.*

Sea Verse
Kewalo Basin, Slip C, Honolulu, O'ahu. *Tel (808) 591-8840.*

CYCLING AND MOUNTAIN BIKING

Haleakalā Bike Co
810 Ha'ikū Rd, Suite 120, Ha'ikū, Maui. *Tel (808) 575-9575.* www.bikemaui.com

Raging Isle Sports
66-250 Kamehameha Hwy, Building B, Hale'iwa, O'ahu. *Tel (808) 637-7707.*

South Maui Bicycles
1993 S. Kīhei Road, #5, Kīhei, Maui. *Tel (808) 874-0068.*

West Maui Cycles
1087 Limahana Pl, Maui. *Tel (808) 661-9005.* www.westmauicycles.com

HIKING

Hawai'i Nature Center
2131 Makiki Heights Dr, Honolulu, O'ahu. *Tel (808) 955-0100.* www.hawaiinaturecenter.org

Nature Conservancy
923 Nu'uanu Avenue, Honolulu, O'ahu. *Tel (808) 537-4508.* www.nature.org

Sierra Club
111 Bishop St, Honolulu, O'ahu. *Tel (808) 538-6616.* www.sierraclubhawaii.org

WHALE WATCHING

Paragon Charters
5229 Lwr Kula Rd, Kula, Maui. *Tel (808) 244-2087.* www.sailmaui.com

Wild Side Specialty Tours
Wai'anae Boat Harbor, A-11, Wai'anae, O'ahu. *Tel (808) 306-7273.* www.sailhawaii.com

OTHER ACTIVITIES

ATV Tours
PO Box 800, Kalaheo, Kaua'i. *Tel (808) 742-2734.* www.kauaiatv.com

CJM Country Stables
1831 Poipu Rd, Kōloa, Kaua'i. *Tel (808) 742-6096.* www.cjmstables.com

Moloka'i Mule Ride
Kualapu'u, Moloka'i. *Tel (808) 567-6088.* www.muleride.com

Paniolo Riding Adventures
Kawaihae, Hawai'i Island. *Tel (808) 889-5354.* www.paniolo adventures.com

Skyline Eco-Adventures
P.O. Box 880518, Pukalani, Maui. *Tel (808) 878-8400.* www.skylinehawaii.com

Golf

With year-round warm, sunny weather and more than 80 challenging courses on six different islands, Hawai'i is a golfer's paradise. The courses, carved from brilliant green valleys and dramatic lava fields, are as varied as the islands. Lush fairways are bordered by tropical rainforests and sandy beaches. Distractingly scenic panoramas reveal sparkling blue sea, neighboring islands, and even breaching whales. There are championship courses across the state, created by some of the biggest names in golf – Arnold Palmer, Jack Nicklaus, and Robert Trent Jones, Sr and Jr. *Golf Magazine* lists eight in its Top 25 US Golf Resorts; no other state boasts more than two.

The challenging and scenic Turtle Bay Resort Golf Club, O'ahu

GENERAL INFORMATION

Most of Hawai'i's golf courses are open to the public. Municipal courses usually have low green fees. Resort courses are more expensive, but are generally open to all players, not only to resort guests. Private courses are for members only, but some set aside a day for non-members to play. Military courses are open to military personnel and their dependents.

Winner celebrates at the Mercedes Championships

Most courses have driving ranges and fully-stocked pro shops that provide equipment rental, instruction, and clinics.

Green fees usually include the use of a cart and range from less than $30 on a municipal course to in excess of $200 for a round on a plush resort course. However, many Hawai'i courses do offer discounted rates – twilight fees, junior discounts, and multiple-round discounts for those who want to play a second round on the same day or use the same course more than once in a week.

Golf packages are available at many hotels and resorts. These typically combine accommodations and golf rounds or discounted green fees with extras such as meals, instruction, video analysis, and golf logo items.

MAJOR TOURNAMENTS

In January, The MasterCard Championship, at Hawai'i Island's Four Seasons Resort Hualālai *(see p189)*, opens the Champion's tour season. Top golfers gather again for the Mercedes Championships on Kapalua Resort's Plantation Course, Maui. This exclusive tournament features the likes of Tiger Woods, Ernie Els, and Vijay Singh. January also sees the Sony Open *(see p37)*, held at the Wai'alae Country Club on O'ahu. In February, The Wendy's Champions Skins Game at Maui's Wailea Golf Club is one of the greatest weekends of the golfing calendar.

For more than 13 years, the Po'ipū Bay Golf Course on Kaua'i has played host to the PGA Grand Slam of Golf in November. In the same month, the top lady golfers come to Turtle Bay Resort's Palmer Course on O'ahu for the SBS Open.

O'AHU

Ala Wai Golf Course is one of the busiest municipal courses in the world. Arnold Palmer's **Hawai'i Prince Golf Club** offers three challenging nine-hole layouts. Considered the toughest course in the US, **Ko'olau Golf Club** features extreme elevation changes and winding ravines. **Turtle Bay Resort Golf Club** has the George Fazio Course and the Arnold Palmer Course, where the back nine meander through a tropical forest and a wetlands bird sanctuary. The course at **Ko Olina Golf Club** has no parallel fairways.

MOLOKA'I AND LĀNA'I

Moloka'i offers the **Ironwood Hills Golf Club**, a municipal course along scenic hillsides. On little Lāna'i, **The Experience at Kō'ele** (upcountry) and **The Challenge at Mānele** (seaside) are top-ranked championship resort courses. In contrast, the public **Cavendish Golf Course** has nine holes and no fees (but do leave a donation in the box).

The Experience at Kō'ele, Lāna'i; one of Hawai'i's many superb courses

Putting at hole seven on the Blue Course at Wailea Golf Club, Maui

MAUI

Maui's fabulous weather and awe-inspiring beauty provide the backdrop for some of the world's most breathtaking golf experiences. The three courses at the **Kapalua Resort** are gorgeous, with long fairways and tall evergreens running down to the sea. Opened in 1993, **Mākena Golf Course** offers some of the most spectacular views of any golf course in Hawai'i. Designed by Robert Trent Jones, Jr., it winds its way up the slopes of Haleakalā *(see pp128–9)*, reaching an elevation of 800 ft (240 m) above sea level. At **Wailea Golf Club**, there are three courses – the Gold, the Emerald, and the Blue.

HAWAI'I ISLAND

Hawai'i Island boasts 20 world-class golf courses, many carved from black lava and overlooking beautiful seascapes. The first resort course built on the island is one of two in the state designed by legendary golf course architect Robert Trent Jones, Sr. **Mauna Kea Golf Course** has dramatic changes in elevation and incredible views of the snowcapped volcanic mountain from which it takes its name, as well as spectacular holes along the rugged coastline. **Volcano Golf and Country Club** is situated at a lofty 4,000 ft (1,220 m), along the rim of the active Kīlauea volcano *(see pp152–3)*. One of the

world's most unusual golf courses, it provides visiting players with a memorable experience. The par-72 course has 18 holes and you may have to look out for wild turkeys and nene geese.

KAUA'I

Kaua'i's golf courses feature waterfalls, fern forests, and flowers on lush layouts sculpted from rainforests, canyons, and sea cliffs. At **Po'ipū Bay Golf Course**, the carts have satellite navigation systems that indicate the distance to the hole and pin placement. **Princeville Golf Club** has two courses, one with three nine-hole layouts in one.

Bunkers on Mauna Kea Golf Course, Hawai'i Island

DIRECTORY

O'AHU

Ala Wai Golf Course
404 Kapahulu Ave,
Honolulu. **Map** 4 F3.
Tel (808) 296-2000.

Hawai'i Prince Golf Club
91-1200 Fort Weaver Rd,
'Ewa Beach.
Tel (808) 944-4567.
www.princeresorts
hawaii.com

Ko'olau Golf Club
45-550 Kionaole Rd,
Kāne'ohe.
Tel (808) 247-7088.
www.koolaugolfclub.com

Ko Olina Golf Club
92-1220 Alii Nui Dr,
Kapolei.
Tel (808) 676-5300.
www.koolinagolf.com

Turtle Bay Resort Golf Club
57-091 Kamehameha
Hwy, Kahuku.
Tel (808) 293-8574.
www.turtlebayhotel.com

MOLOKA'I AND LĀNA'I

Cavendish Golf Course
Keomoku Rd,
Lāna'i City, Lāna'i.

The Challenge at Mānele
1233 Fraser Ave, Mānele,
Lāna'i. *Tel (808) 565-2222.*
www.fourseasons.com/
manelebay/golf

The Experience at Kō'ele
Lāna'i Ave, Lāna'i City,
Lāna'i. *Tel (808) 565-4653.*
www.fourseasons.com/
manelebay/golf

Ironwood Hills Golf Club
Kalae Hwy, Kualapu'u,
Moloka'i.
Tel (808) 567-6000.

MAUI

Kapalua Golf Club
Kapalua Resort,
300 Kapalua Dr.
Tel (808) 669-8044.
www.kapaluamaui.com

Mākena Golf Course
Mākena Resort,
5415 Mākena Alanui Dr.
Tel (808) 891-4000.
www.makenagolf.com

Wailea Golf Club
100 Wailea Golf Club Dr,
Wailea Resort.
Tel (808) 875-7540.
www.waileagolf.com

HAWAI'I ISLAND

Mauna Kea Golf Course
62–100 Mauna Kea Beach
Dr, Kohala Coast. *Tel*
(808) 822-5400. **www**.
princeresortshawaii.com

Volcano Golf and Country Club
Pi'i Mauna Road, Volcano.
Tel (808) 967-7331.

KAUA'I

Po'ipū Bay Golf Course
2250 Ainako St, Kōloa.
Tel (808) 742-8711.
www.poipubaygolf.com

Princeville Golf Club
Princeville.
Tel (808) 826-1105.
www.princeville.com

WEDDINGS IN HAWAI'I

Beautiful and sensual, Hawai'i is the ultimate destination for lovers. Everything you could want for the perfect romantic escape is here – balmy weather year round, magnificent sunsets, star-studded night skies, brilliant rainbows, fragrant blossoms, and magical settings. In this tropical paradise there is no end to the variety of ways in which you can get married. Exchange your vows barefoot on a sparkling white sand beach or by a secluded waterfall. Have a traditional wedding in a tropical garden or a picturesque chapel. Sail into the sunset for a ceremony at sea, or fill a formal ballroom with family and friends. You can even declare your love under the waves or while falling through the air.

Conch shell, blown to signal start of ceremony

A garlanded couple exchanging rings in a traditional Hawaiian-style wedding

WEDDING DETAILS

The range of professional wedding services on offer in Hawai'i is as extensive as the choice of venues and ceremony types. Whether you want a wedding that is intimate, elegant, or unusual, wedding planners are available to assist in every way and can make recommendations to fit your personal taste and budget.

The **Hawai'i Visitors and Convention Bureau** and the individual visitors' bureaux on each island have websites with sections on weddings and honeymoons. These include directories of services provided by their members.

Many hotels offer wedding packages that include everything from a champagne toast to a private in-room dinner prepared by a top chef, and from a fragrant flower *lei* greeting to a Hawaiian blessing.

If you decide to handle the details yourself, check the *Yellow Pages* phone book for the island in question. Local professional associations provide useful lists of coordinators, officiants, photographers, videographers, musicians, and entertainers. They also list bridal gown boutiques, tuxedo rentals, hair, makeup, and nail stylists, caterers, florists, and more.

A HAWAIIAN WEDDING

A Hawaiian blessing is just one aspect of genuine island-style nuptials. Other special features include the blowing of the conch shell to signal the start of the ceremony, soft island music, the officiant performing the ceremony in the Hawaiian language (as well as in English), and fresh flower *lei*, worn and exchanged by the bride and groom.

It is also possible to opt for a Western ceremony and the limitless stunning locations available mean you can make your vows in a memorable setting.

GAY AND LESBIAN WEDDINGS

The State of Hawai'i does not legally recognize gay marriages and will not issue a license to same-sex couples. However, there are many gay-friendly wedding planners listed on the Internet who offer commitment ceremonies. Try www.hawaiigayweddings.com and www.mauialoha gayweddings.com

BEACH WEDDINGS

Hawai'i offers countless golden beaches that make perfect wedding settings. If you get married at **Kapi'olani Park** *(see pp72–3)* on O'ahu, your wedding photos could show the world-renowned Waikīkī Beach and Diamond Head in the background. **Hāpuna Bay** *(see p140)*, near Kawaihae on Hawai'i Island, has a gorgeous long stretch of white sand and sparkling turquoise water.

On Kaua'i, one of the most spectacular settings is **Hanalei Bay** *(see p166)*, where steep cliffs shrouded in emerald-green vegetation contrast against the dazzling white sand and deep-blue sea.

A bride and groom hand in hand on the beach at the Maui Prince Hotel, Mākena *(see p186)*

Gazebo surrounded by flowers and lush greenery, an ideal garden wedding setting

Maui has mile upon mile of beautiful beaches, but it may be difficult to find one that you can have all to yourselves. The bay at **Kapalua** *(see p115)*, on the west side of the island, makes a picture-perfect wedding setting. The beach here is a white sand crescent that fronts the lovely bay, with the nearby islands of Moloka'i and Lāna'i floating on the horizon.

Hawai'i's state and county beaches allow beach wedding ceremonies without a charge, but you must obtain a permit.

GARDEN WEDDINGS

Foster Botanical Gardens, a serene oasis in Honolulu's Chinatown *(see p59)*, is a popular wedding venue. It is well stocked with beautiful plants from tropical regions around the globe. Another popular choice is **Hawai'i Tropical Botanical Garden** *(see p147)*, a short distance north of Hilo on Hawai'i Island. These gardens overlook Onomea Bay: the Twin Rocks that stand as sentinels in the bay are said to embody two legendary lovers. The **Kepaniwai Heritage Gardens** *(see p119)* on Maui are colorful and fragrant and have pavilions representing each ethnic group that has settled on the island, from the Japanese and the Chinese to the Portuguese.

Gardens that are administered by state and county parks do not charge a fee for wedding ceremonies, however it is necessary to apply for a permit in advance.

CHURCHES AND CHAPELS

Each island has a picturesque historic church built in the 1800s, when Christian missionaries first arrived. Today these churches are chosen as locations for many Hawaiian weddings. Honolulu's grand **Kawaiaha'o Church** *(see pp54–5)* once served Hawaiian royalty. On Maui, the intimate **Keawala'i Church** *(see p120)* in Mākena, built in 1832, is set on the edge of a peaceful bay and surrounded by palms gently swaying in the breeze. The oldest church on the islands, **Moku'aikaua Church** *(see p134)* on Hawai'i Island, is built of lava stone and its steeple is the highest structure in Kailua-Kona. The inter-denominational **Kōloa Church** in the Po'ipū area of Kaua'i *(see p173)* also has a beautiful steeple, as well as ornate columns, high ceilings, and seating for over 200 guests.

Old-style steepled church, Hawai'i Island

Almost every hotel in Hawai'i offers wedding packages and several have lovely chapels on their own grounds.

In Honolulu and Waikīkī, there are chapels at the **Hilton Hawaiian Village Beach Resort** *(see p181)*, the **Sheraton Moana Surfrider** *(see p180)*, and the **Renaissance Ilikai Waikīkī Hotel** *(see p181)*.

Located on a magnificent stretch of O'ahu's south shore, the lovely **Kahala O Ke Kai Chapel** is part of the gorgeous Kahala Hotel *(see p181)*. At Turtle Bay Resort *(see p182)*, on the north shore of O'ahu, the **Wedding Pavilion**, located on the tip of scenic Kuilima Point, is a dramatic glass-walled sanctuary. Here wedding parties can arrive at and depart the ceremony in the utmost style, riding in Turtle Bay Resort's own horse-drawn carriage.

On Maui, the **Wailea Seaside Chapel**, part of the Grand Wailea Resort *(see p187)*, is impressive and picturesque. Its exterior resembles a New England church and inside there are chandeliers hanging majestically from the high vaulted ceiling and glorious stained-glass windows.

On Hawai'i Island, the Sheraton Keauhou Bay Resort *(see p189)* offers a romantic white seaside wedding chapel, **Bayside Chapel**, which is secluded from the rest of the property.

The striking interior of Wailea Seaside Chapel at the Grand Wailea Resort

Tying the knot underwater, in a scuba marriage ceremony

UNUSUAL WEDDINGS – LAND, AIR, AND SEA

There are many out-of-the-ordinary wedding ceremony options to be enjoyed in Hawai'i. For instance, couples can get married on the summit of one of Hawai'i's breathtaking dormant volcanoes – **Diamond Head** *(see p73)* on O'ahu, **Haleakalā** *(see pp128–9)* on Maui, or **Mauna Kea** *(see p146)* on Hawai'i Island. Permits are needed, but the location itself is free of charge.

Alternatively, you can let a helicopter whisk you away to your special beach or hidden waterfall. On Maui, Hawai'i Island, and Kaua'i **Blue Hawaiian Helicopters** can organize this.

Another heavenly option is saying your vows while skydiving. On O'ahu, you can arrange to do this with **Skydive Hawai'i** or the **Pacific Skydiving Center**.

There are a variety of possibilities for a romantic wedding at sea. You might choose to say your vows sailing into the sunset on the **Alala Catamaran** – or on a yacht provided by **Kamanu Charters** or **Shangri-La Private Sailing Charters**.

Kaua'i's legendary Fern Grotto *(see p162),* a natural amphitheater full of luxuriant greenery, is perfect for a secluded wedding. For the journey there, **Smith's Motor Boat Service** will provide a private boat, on which

musicians can serenade you with the romantic Hawaiian Wedding Song as you cruise up the Wailua River.

In an underwater scuba ceremony, dolphins, turtles and colorful reef fish will be your witnesses as you write the words "I do" and exchange rings. **Eve Eschner Hogan** on Maui, or **Beach Weddings Hawai'i** on Hawai'i Island can arrange to make this happen for you. On O'ahu, Mau'i, and Hawai'i Island, another underwater option is to charter a private submarine cruise for your ceremony with **Atlantis Submarines**.

Musician at an Hawaiian-style wedding

LEGALITIES

Both the bride and groom must be present when the license is issued and each must provide valid picture identification (a driver's license or passport). Your birthplace, and the names of your parents will be noted on the license application. If relevant, final divorce decree information is also needed, as is written permission from a parent or legal guardian for those under 18 years of age. No waiting period, blood tests, or vaccinations are required. The license is good for 30 days and the $60 fee must be paid in cash.

The central marriage license office is located in O'ahu at the **Hawai'i State Department**

of Health. An appointment to obtain the license should be scheduled directly with a license agent. For agent contact information, call the local branch of the Hawai'i State Department of Health. After the wedding, the officiant sends the license for filing as the official marriage certificate. A certified copy is mailed to the couple around 120 days later. The license agent can speed up this process by forwarding a $10 fee.

VOW RENEWALS

Many married couples want to do it all over again and arrange a vow renewal ceremony. These can be as creative and personal as you want them to be and there is the same endless variety of locations and ceremonies available as there is for first-timers. Since the ceremony is purely symbolic, not legal, a minister or judge is not required to perform it, nor is it necessary to obtain any form of marriage license. Outrigger Waikīkī on the Beach *(see p180)* and Outrigger Reef on the Beach *(see p179)* invite guests who are newlyweds or celebrating an anniversary to renew their vows at a complimentary ceremony on Waikīkī Beach. This nondenominational Hawaiian celebration is conducted by a practicing *kahu* (priest) and includes a traditional chant, *hula* *(see pp26–7),* song, and flower *lei* garlands.

Hawaiian dancers at a vow renewal ceremony on Waikīkī Beach

DIRECTORY

INFORMATION

Big Island Visitors Bureau
250 Keawe St, Hilo, HI 96743.
Tel (808) 961-5797.
www.bigisland.org

Hawai'i Visitors and Convention Bureau
Suite 801, 2270 Kalākaua Ave, Honolulu, HI 96815.
Tel (808) 923-1811.
www.gohawaii.com

Kaua'i Visitors Bureau
4334 Rice St, Līhu'e, HI 96766.
Tel (808) 245-3971.
www.kauaidiscovery.com

Kaua'i Wedding Professionals Association
www.kauaiwedpro.com

Maui Visitors Bureau (also Lāna'i and Moloka'i)
1727 Wili Pa Loop, Wailuku, Maui 96793.
Tel (808) 244-3530.
www.visitmaui.com

Maui Wedding Association
www.mauiwedding association.com

O'ahu Visitors Bureau
733 Bishop St, Suite1520, Honolulu, O'ahu.
Tel (808) 524-0722.
www.visit-oahu.com

BEACH WEDDINGS

Hanalei Bay
Permits: Kaua'i County Beach Parks, 4444 Rice St, Līhu'e, Kaua'i, HI 96766.
Tel (808) 241-6660.

Hāpuna Bay
Permits: Hawai'i Island State Parks, P.O. Box 936, Hilo, Hawai'i Island, HI 96721.
Tel (808) 974-6200.

Kapi'olani Park
Permits: 3902 Paki Ave, P.O. Box 3059, Honolulu, Oahu, HI 96815.
Tel (808) 545 4344.

GARDEN WEDDINGS

Foster Botanical Gardens
Permits: Honolulu Dept of Parks and Recreation, 50 N Vineyard Blvd, Honolulu, HI 96817.
Tel (808) 522-7066.
www.honolulu.gov/parks

Hawai'i Tropical Botanical Garden
Pepe'ekeo Scenic Dr, Hawai'i Island.
Tel (808) 964-5233.
www.htbg.com

Kepaniwai Heritage Gardens
'Iao Valley Rd, Maui.
Tel (808) 270-7230.

CHURCHES AND CHAPELS

Bayside Chapel
Sheraton Keauhou Bay Resort, 78-128 Ehukai St, Kailua-Kona, Hawai'i Island.
Tel (808) 930-4900. www.sheratonkeauhou.com

Hilton Hawaiian Village Beach Resort
2005 Kālia Rd, Honolulu, O'ahu. *Tel (808) 949-4321.*
www.hilton.com

Ilikai Waikīkī Hotel
1777 Ala Moana Blvd, Honolulu, O'ahu.
Tel (808) 949-3811.
www.ilikaihotel.com

Kahala O Ke Kai Chapel
5000 Kahala Ave, Honolulu, O'ahu.
Tel (808) 739-8888.
www.kahalaresort.com

Kawaiaha'o Church
957 Punchbowl St, Honolulu, O'ahu.
Tel (808) 522-1333.

Keawala'i Congregational Church
190 Mākena Rd, Mākena, Maui.
Tel (808) 879-5557.

Kōloa Church
3269 Po'ipū Rd, Kōloa, Kaua'i.
Tel (808) 742-9956.

Moku'aikaua Church
75-5713 Ali'i Dr, Kailua-Kona, Hawai'i Island.
Tel (808) 329-0655.

Moana Surfrider
2365 Kalākaua Ave, Waikīkī, O'ahu. *Tel (808) 923-3111.* www.moana-surfrider.com

Wailea Seaside Chapel
Grand Wailea Resort, 3850 Wailea Alanui, Wailea, Maui. *Tel (808) 875-1234.*
www.grandwailea.com

Wedding Pavilion
Turtle Bay Resort, 57-091 Kamehameha Hwy, Kahuku, O'ahu.
Tel (808) 293-8811.
www.turtlebayresort.com

UNUSUAL WEDDINGS

Alala Catamaran
Ocean Sports, 69-275 Waikoloa Beach Dr, Waikoloa, Hawai'i Island.
Tel (808) 886-6666.
www.hawaiiocean sports.com

Atlantis Submarines
Maui: Suite 175, 658 Front St, Lahaina.
Tel (808) 667-2224.
Hawai'i Island: 75-5669 Ali'i Dr, Kailua-Kona.
Tel (808) 329-6626.
O'ahu: 1600 Kapi'olani Blvd, Honolulu. *Tel (808) 973-9811.* www.atlantis adventures.com

Beach Weddings Hawai'i
Kailua-Kona, Hawai'i Island. *Tel (808) 328-9239.* www.beach weddingshawaii.com

Blue Hawaiian Helicopters
Maui: *Tel (808) 871-8844.*
Hilo, Hawai'i Island:
Tel (808) 961-5600.
Waikoloa, Hawai'i Island:
Tel (808) 886-1768.
Līhu'e, Kaua'i:
Tel (808) 245-5800.
www.bluehawaiian.com

Diamond Head
Diamond Head Rd, Honolulu, O'ahu.
Tel (808) 587-0300.

Eve Eschner Hogan
P.O. Box 943, Pu'unene, Maui. *Tel (808) 573-7700.*
www.hearthpath.com

Haleakalā
Haleakalā National Park, Haleakalā Crater Rd, Maui.
Tel (808) 572-4440.

Kamanu Charters
P.O. Box 2021, Kailua-Kona, Hawai'i Island.
Tel (808) 329-2021.
www.kamanu.com

Mauna Kea
Hwy 200, Hawai'i Island.
Tel (808) 933-0734.

Pacific Skydiving Center
68-760 Farrington Hwy, Dillingham Airfield, O'ahu.
Tel (808) 637-7472.
www.pacific-sky diving.com

Shangri-La Private Sailing Charters
Suite 109B, 5095 Napilihau St, Lahaina, Maui.
Tel (808) 665-0077.
www.sailingmaui.com

Skydive Hawai'i
68-760 Farrington Hwy, Dillingham Airfield, O'ahu. *Tel (808) 637-9700.* www.hawaii skydiving.com

Smith's Motor Boat Service
Wailua Marina State Park, Wailua, Kaua'i.
Tel (808) 821-6892.
www.smithskauai.com

LEGALITIES

Hawai'i State Department of Health
1250 Punchbowl St, Honolulu, O'ahu.
Tel (808) 586-4545.
Maui: *Tel (808) 984-8201.*
Lāna'i: *Tel (808) 565-6411.*
Moloka'i: *Tel (808) 553-3663.* Kaua'i: *Tel (808) 241-3498.* Hawai'i Island: *Tel (808) 974-6008.*
www.hawaii.gov/health

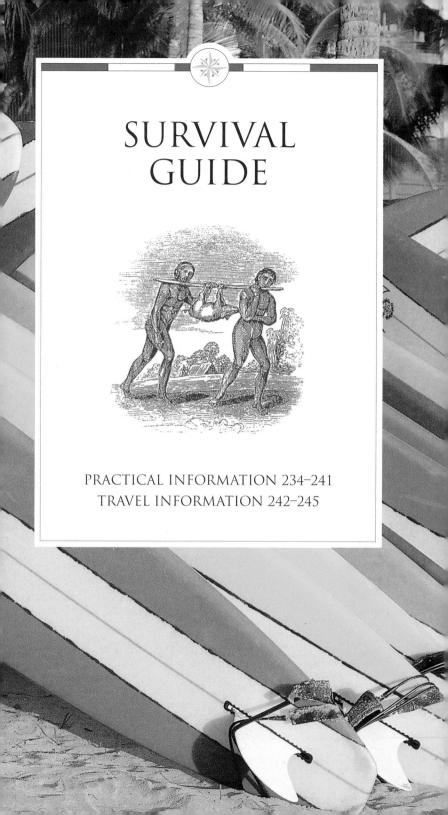

SURVIVAL
GUIDE

PRACTICAL INFORMATION

Tourism is Hawai'i's most important industry. From the bright lights of Waikīkī and Honolulu to the remote waterfalls of Maui's Hāna district, the islands offer something for everyone – whatever the budget. There is no escaping the fact that paradise can be expensive: the cost of living in the state is thought to be about 40 percent higher than that in the rest of the US. For those planning a money-is-no-object

Hawai'i Visitors and Convention Bureau sign

vacation, all kinds of luxuries await. But visitors on a more modest budget can have an equally memorable trip. Hawai'i is a great destination all year round, but you will enjoy better prices if you choose to visit in the off season – between September and December. At any time of year, however, many of the islands' biggest attractions are free, and many others, including national parks and larger museums, charge only low admission prices.

Aloha Week, always a colorful time for visiting Hawai'i

WHEN TO GO

Hawai'i's fabulous weather makes it a year-round destination. The difference in the numbers of visitors coming to the islands in the "high season" and the "off season" is not as great as it used to be.

However, the most popular time to visit begins with the Christmas holidays and lasts through April. It is a good idea to make advance reservations for these periods as flights, hotels, and car rentals get booked up early. Prices are at their highest at this time of year, too.

Although summer vacation time from June through August is busy, especially with families traveling, more deals are available then than in the winter months. September to mid-December is generally considered the off season and bookings are easier to come. Another plus is

that activities, attractions, restaurants, and hotels are not as crowded in the fall.

Some visitors plan their stay in Hawai'i around special events and holidays, such as the Honolulu Marathon *(see p36)*, the Ironman Triathlon *(see p35)*, and Aloha Week *(see p35)*.

For more information about visiting Hawai'i and its year-round events schedule, contact either a branch of the **Hawai'i Visitors and Convention Bureau** (HVCB), or one of the individual island tourist offices.

CUSTOMS AND AGRICULTURAL INSPECTIONS

Bottle of local wine

Foreign visitors staying at least 72 hours have the following duty-free allowance: 1 liter of wine or alcohol; 200 cigarettes or 100 cigars (as long as they are not Cuban), or 4.4 lbs (2 kg) of smoking tobacco; and $100 worth of gifts. You

are not permitted to bring foodstuffs or plants from any foreign country into Hawai'i.

Regardless of its destination, all luggage is subject to an agricultural inspection on departure from the state. Only certain produce and flowers may be taken out of the islands, so be sure to ask about this when making a purchase. No such restrictions are imposed on the export of processed foods.

VISAS AND PASSPORTS

The conditions for entering Hawai'i are the same as for visiting other parts of the US. Citizens of the UK, most European nations, New Zealand, and Australia need a passport that is valid for at least six months after their trip, an onward or return ticket, and a completed Electronic System for Travel Authorization (ESTA) form, available online. From September 2010 there will be a charge for the ESTA form. Canadian citizens are only required to show their passport to enter the US. Citizens of all other countries need a valid passport and a tourist visa, which can be obtained from a US consulate or embassy.

No inoculations are required unless you come from, or have stopped in, an area suffering from an epidemic, particularly cholera or yellow fever.

Hawai'i has two main languages: English and Hawaiian *(see p256)*. You may see signs written in Hawaiian but will rarely hear it spoken. Many people in the tourist industry also speak Japanese.

◁ **Multicolored surfboards for rent on Waikīkī Beach**

VISITOR INFORMATION

Visitor information desks at all island airports provide maps and guides, and major hotels usually have a knowledgeable and helpful guest services desk. Each island also has a tourist information center – either a branch of the Hawai'i Visitors and Convention Bureau (HVCB), or another visitor association. If you need information before leaving home, contact a HVCB representative abroad or a tourist office in Hawai'i.

Old-fashioned Surrey horses and carriage on Waipi'o Valley Wagon Tour (see p142)

OPENING HOURS

Most businesses are open on weekdays from 9am to 5pm (for banking hours see p240). Shopping malls and many stores are open from 10am to 9pm Monday to Saturday; other stores close earlier, between 5pm and 7pm. Sunday shopping is more limited, but some supermarkets, convenience stores, and gas stations are open 24 hours a day, seven days a week.

Although the opening hours of attractions vary, most admit visitors daily. Some close on major public holidays such as Christmas and Thanksgiving.

ALCOHOL AND SMOKING LAWS

The minimum legal age for drinking in Hawai'i is 21. It is illegal to drink in a state or national park, or to carry an open container of alcohol in your vehicle. Grocery stores, supermarkets, and convenience stores sell beer, wine, and spirits, all of which can be bought seven days a week.

Smoking is prohibited in public spaces, such as shops, theaters, nightclubs, restaurants, bars, and elevators. In hotels, it is allowed only in guest rooms designated as smoking accommodation.

SPECIAL VACATIONS AND GUIDED TOURS

If you want to explore the natural beauty of Hawai'i, but prefer to leave the organizing to someone else, there are a number of companies specializing in such vacations. These include **Gorp Travel**, the **Sierra Club**, and the **Nature Conservancy of Hawai'i**.

In addition, many other companies offer guided tours of attractions on individual islands. The largest and most reliable of these firms are **Roberts Hawai'i** and **Pleasant Island Holidays**. They offer packages that include inter-island flights, accommodations, bus tours, and car rental.

In any case, your hotel's guest services desk should be knowledgeable about guided tours of specific attractions and be able to give you advice on how to book them.

ELECTRICITY

The electricity supply in Hawai'i is at the standard US 110–120 volts. If you will need to operate 220-volt appliances while on the islands, remember to pack both a voltage converter and a plug adapter with two flat, parallel prongs.

Most hotel rooms have coffee- or tea-making facilities and sockets for shavers; some also provide hair dryers.

Standard American plug

DIRECTORY

HAWAI'I VISITORS AND CONVENTION BUREAU OFFICES

Australia
The Walshe Group Ltd, Level 6, 117 York St, Sydney, NSW 2000. *Tel (612) 9286-8936.* www.hawaiitourism.com.au

Germany
The Mangum Group, Sonnenstr. 9, 80331 München. *Tel (89) 23 66 21 97.* www.hawaii-tourism.de

New Zealand
The Walshe Group Ltd, Level 7, Citibank Building, 23 Customs St East, Auckland. *Tel (649) 977-2234.* www.hawaiitourism.com.nz

United Kingdom
Hills Balfour Ltd, Colechurch House, 1 London Bridge Walk, London SE1 2SX. *Tel (020) 7367 0900.* www.hawaii-tourism.co.uk

ISLAND TOURIST OFFICES

O'hau
733 Bishop St, Suite 1520, Honolulu, O'hau. *Tel (808) 524-0722.*

Maui
1727 Wili Pa Loop, Wailuku, Maui. *Tel (808) 244-3530.* www.visitmaui.com

Hawai'i Island
250 Keawe St, Hilo, Hawai'i Island. *Tel (808) 961-5797.* www.bigisland.org

Kaua'i
4334 Rice St, Līhu'e, Kaua'i. *Tel (808) 245-3971.* www.kauaidiscovery.com

SPECIAL VACATIONS AND GUIDED TOURS

Gorp Travel
www.gorptravel.com

Nature Conservancy of Hawai'i
Tel (808) 537-4508. www.nature.org

Pleasant Island Holidays
Tel (808) 922-1515. www.pleasantislandholidays.com

Roberts Hawai'i
Tel (808) 954-8600. www.robertshawaii.com

Sierra Club
Tel (415) 977-5522. www.sierraclub.org/outings/national

A typically friendly Hawaiian waiter in traditional dress

ETIQUETTE, TIPS, AND TAXES

Hawai'i is a friendly, casual place where hugs and kisses on the cheek are common greetings. It may appear that islanders are never in a hurry, so prepare yourself for Hawai'i's leisurely pace.

Clothing is casual, too: pack sandals, sneakers, shorts, and casual evening wear. If you visit in winter, or plan to scale mountains, you should take long pants and a sweater or jacket, plus sturdy shoes.

It is customary to tip good service. The standard restaurant tip is 15 percent of the check; you should tip taxi drivers 10–15 percent of the fare; baggage handlers at least $1 per piece of luggage; and valet parking attendants $2.

Hawai'i has a 4.17 percent sales tax on all goods and services and an additional hotel tax of 9.25 percent, making a total of 13.42 percent tax on accommodation.

In Hawai'i it is good manners to respect the rights of property owners and not trespass on their land.

SINGLE TRAVELERS

Small hotels, bed and breakfasts, and campsites are the best bet for single travelers. **Singles in Paradise** organizes Hawai'i vacations. Guided tours are also a good way to meet people. Islanders will often "adopt" a single traveler, so you may end up a guest at a big family party.

SENIOR CITIZENS

Senior citizens (in most cases, this means those age 62 and over) can claim discounts at many attractions, including national parks, and at some hotels, restaurants, and shops, upon presentation of their photo ID. Always ask about discounts and check local publications such as the *Honolulu Advertiser* or *The Maui News* or contact the Department of Parks and Recreation *(see p151)* for special events.

American Association of Retired Persons (AARP) members get discounts for rooms, cars, and tours. The nonprofit **Exploritas** offers educational trips for senior citizens that include accommodations, meals, lectures, guided tours, and activities.

CHILDREN

Hawai'i is great for families. Most hotels allow children to share a room with their parents at no extra charge, and many also have family suites. Larger hotels often have kids' programs and babysitters. Restaurants are child-friendly and even if there is no special menu, they will often provide youngsters with

a hamburger, or even a peanut butter and jelly sandwich.

Most tour operators will specify if there are any restrictions concerning children for their activity. In cars, children must occupy a child safety seat or wear a seat belt.

VISITORS WITH DISABILITIES

Hawai'i welcomes visitors with disabilities. Most hotels and restaurants, and many attractions have wheelchair ramps, reserved parking, and specially equipped toilets.

The **Disability and Communication Access Board** website provides information on access to beaches, parks, shopping centers, attractions, and rental vehicles. You can also find information about support services here, including parking permits, telecommunications services, and service dogs. The **Statewide Independent Living Council of Hawai'i** also provides information and assistance for disabled travelers.

Parking for people with disabilities

GAY AND LESBIAN TRAVELERS

Hawai'i shares its *aloha* with all and welcomes gays and lesbians as it does everyone else. There are many gay-friendly accommodations, restaurants, bars, and beaches on all the islands. On O'ahu, the hub of gay and lesbian activity is in Waikīkī. **Hula's Bar and Lei Stand** is one of the best known gathering places. Contact the **PFLAG** for more information on gay venues.

A kids' program at the Kā'anapali Beach Hotel *(see p184)*

HAWAI'I TIME

Hawai'i has a time zone all of its own – known as Hawai'i Standard Time (HST). The West Coast of the US mainland is two hours ahead of Hawai'i, and the time difference increases by one hour each time you move east into a new time zone. Unlike the rest of the US, Hawai'i does not put its clocks forward for summer daylight saving, so some of the time differences listed below increase by one hour when the respective countries switch to summer time. In the Northern Hemisphere this is generally from March or April to October.

City and Country	Hours + HST	City and Country	Hours + HST
Athens (Greece)	+12	Moscow (Russia)	+13
Auckland (New Zealand)	+22	New York (US)	+5
Beijing (China)	+18	Paris (France)	+11
Berlin (Germany)	+11	Perth (Australia)	+18
Chicago (US)	+4	Rome (Italy)	+11
Dublin (Ireland)	+10	Sydney (Australia)	+20
Hong Kong (China)	+18	Tokyo (Japan)	+19
London (UK)	+10	Toronto (Canada)	+5
Los Angeles (US)	+2	Vancouver (Canada)	+2
Madrid (Spain)	+11	Washington, D.C. (US)	+5

CONVERSION CHART

US Standard to Metric
1 inch = 2.54 centimeters
1 foot = 30 centimeters
1 mile = 1.6 kilometers
1 ounce = 28 grams
1 pound = 454 grams
1 US quart = 0.947 liter
1 US gallon = 3.8 liters

Metric to US Standard
1 centimeter = 0.4 inch
1 meter = 3 feet 3 inches
1 kilometer = 0.6 mile
1 gram = 0.04 ounce
1 kilogram = 2.2 pounds
1 liter = 1.06 US quarts

RECOMMENDED READING

If you want to read up on the islands, there are many titles to choose from. *Shoal of Time* by Gavan Daws (University of Hawai'i Press) is an entertaining history of the islands, though you may prefer James Michener's epic, *Hawaii* (Random House) – a historical novel that is considered by many to be essential reading.
Paradise News (Penguin), a novel by David Lodge, also makes a good vacation read. Or try Jack London's *Stories of Hawaii* (Mutual). *Hawaii: A Natural History* by Sherwin Carlquist (Doubleday) is all you will need on the flora and fauna, while *Hawaiian Mythology* by Martha Beckwith (University of Hawai'i Press) contains all the most important legends.

RELIGIOUS SERVICES

Thanks to Hawai'i's rich cultural mix, a wide range of religious services – from Catholic to Buddhist – can be found in Honolulu, and the choice is only slightly more limited on the other islands. Ask at your hotel or at the local visitor information center about services, or check in the Friday or Saturday editions of the local paper for details.
 If you visit native Hawaiian religious sites, be sure to treat them with the utmost respect. It is best not to leave your own offerings, and you should not move or remove anything under any circumstances.

RESPECT FOR THE LAND

The land, or *'āina* ("that which feeds"), is the most important element of the local culture. Traditional Hawaiians believe that humans are merely stewards of the land, put here to protect and nurture it, not to exploit it. They believe that every natural object, from a whale to a grain

DIRECTORY

SINGLE TRAVELERS

Singles in Paradise
Tel (808) 662-1212.
www.singlesinparadise.com

SENIOR CITIZENS

AARP
Tel (888) 687-2277.
www.aarp.org

Exploritas
Tel (800) 454-5768.
www.exploritas.com

VISITORS WITH DISABILITIES

Disability and Communication Access Board
919 Ala Moana Blvd, Room 101, Honolulu, O'ahu. *Tel (808) 586-8121.* www.state.hi.us/health/dcab

Statewide Independent Living Council of Hawai'i
841 Bishop St, Suite 201, Honolulu, O'ahu. *Tel (808) 585-7452.* www.hisilc.org

GAY AND LESBIAN TRAVELERS

PFLAG
92-954 Makakilo Dr, Honolulu, O'ahu. *Tel (808) 672-9050.* www.pflag.org

Hula's Bar and Lei Stand
134 Kapahulu Ave, 2nd Floor, Waikīkī, O'ahu. *Tel (808) 923-0669.* www.hulas.com

of sand, has life and a soul. You should therefore treat everything with great respect.
 Do not remove anything from its home; if you pick up a shell to look at it, for example, remember to put it back where you found it. Littering is both offensive and illegal.

Sidewalk sign warning against the effects of careless dumping on local marine life

Health and Personal Security

Lifeguard sign,
Kūhiō Beach

Despite being in the tropics, Hawai'i carries remarkably few health risks (it boasts the highest life expectancy in the US). No immunizations are necessary, there are no land snakes to worry about, and only a few nasty creepy-crawlies. You should be aware of certain potential dangers if you go hiking or camping, but generally it is the sun and the ocean that pose the biggest threats to your health. Hawai'i does not have a serious crime problem, but you should take the normal precautions and use your common sense.

OCEAN SAFETY

The Pacific Ocean is as powerful as it is beautiful. Whether or not you are an experienced swimmer, pay careful attention to the conditions of the sea. If you have not surfed before, do not try it without proper instruction.

Always ask the lifeguard on duty about the state of the ocean, and heed the posted warnings. If you aren't used to identifying dangerous currents, avoid unguarded beaches. Note that some beaches can be perfectly safe in summer but very dangerous in winter.

When you're in the water, swim facing away from the beach. So-called rogue waves arrive as if from nowhere and can sweep you out to sea. Should you get carried out by a rip current, try to swim with it until it dissipates – usually 50–100 yds (45–90 m) from shore. Never swim alone,

watch out for surfers, and keep a very close eye on children. Always check for rocks, coral, and other potential dangers below the surface. You are advised to wear protective foot gear such as reef slippers whenever possible.

Should you happen to cut yourself on coral, clean the cut thoroughly with antiseptic. If you step on a sea urchin, the spine is likely to break off, leaving a tip embedded in your skin.

Signs warning of currents, dangerous shore break, and big surf

This will dissolve in several days, but applying vinegar may speed up the process.

Jellyfish are fairly common in Hawai'i. You're most likely to see them washed up on the shore. Their stings vary from mild to severe, the worst being that of the Portuguese

man-of-war. If you are stung by a jellyfish, the best remedy is to apply a paste of vinegar and meat tenderizer.

Encounters with sharks are very rare; should you see one, simply swim back to shore as quickly and quietly as you can.

SUN, HEAT, AND OTHER NATURAL HAZARDS

Whether you're fair or dark-skinned, it is vital to protect yourself against the harsh Hawaiian sun. Be sure to wear a hat and sunglasses, and use plenty of sun block. You should consider wearing a T-shirt if you plan to snorkel for more than just a short time.

Introduce yourself to the sun gently after you first arrive, and at any stage try to stay out of the sun between 11am and 2pm, when the rays are at their strongest; even on overcast days, the ultraviolet rays penetrate the clouds. Heat can be a danger too. Drink plenty of fluids and avoid being out in high temperatures for long periods without breaks to let your body cool down.

Mosquitoes do not carry malaria, but they can still be a real nuisance. Black widow spiders and scorpions are a potential danger to be aware of if you are planning to hike or camp in the wilds.

PERSONAL SAFETY

Although not completely free of crime, Hawai'i is still a remarkably safe place. Violent crime is rare.

Use common sense. Do not hitchhike; avoid hiking alone, and being in dark or remote areas at night. If in doubt, ask your hotel whether or not a particular area is safe.

Carry minimal cash when you go out, and do not take your passport unless you need to change travelers' checks. Leave your best jewelry at home, and other valuables in a safe – either in your room or at the hotel front desk.

THE FOLLOWING ARE PROHIBITED:
Alcoholic Beverages   Animals
Ball Playing   Camping
Flying Disc   Littering

Lifeguard on duty at Kūhiō Beach Park, Waikīkī

Fire engines in the station, ready for an emergency call

The main possibility of theft is from a rented vehicle. Never leave any valuables in the car; thieves are skilled at dealing with door and trunk locks.

LOST PROPERTY

Even though you have only a slim chance of retrieving stolen property, you should report all stolen items to the police. Keep a copy of the police report for when you make your insurance claim.

Most credit cards have toll-free numbers for reporting a loss, as do companies issuing travelers' checks *(see p241)*. If you need a replacement passport, contact your embassy or consulate.

TRAVEL INSURANCE

Travel insurance cover of a minimum of $1 million is highly recommended, mainly because of the high cost of medical treatment. Make sure the policy covers emergency medical care, accidental death, trip cancellation, and loss of baggage or documents.

MEDICAL TREATMENT

Even the smallest towns in Hawai'i have some kind of medical center, although the facilities on Moloka'i and Lāna'i are not as extensive as those on the main islands. As you would expect, Honolulu's medical services are the best equipped in the state.

Ask at your hotel if you need a doctor, dentist, or any other healthcare professional. All medical care is expensive: even a simple visit to a doctor can cost over $100. Hospitals take most credit cards, but doctors and dentists will usually want to be paid in cash. Visitors without insurance documents may need to pay in advance.

Anyone on prescription drugs should take along a supply and ask their doctor for a copy of the prescription in case more is needed. Pharmacies are plentiful (Long's Drugs has branches on all the islands), and you can buy some medicines in supermarkets and convenience stores.

Suntan lotions and sun block, on sale in stores all over Hawai'i

DRINKING WATER

It is generally safe to drink the tap water, although in some areas, such as upcountry Maui and parts of Hawai'i Island, the water is susceptible to pollution from acid rain.

Never drink from freshwater streams or pools. A bacterial disease, leptospirosis, can be contracted by drinking untreated water or exposing cuts or abrasions to fresh water.

EMERGENCIES

In an emergency, the police, ambulance, or fire services can be reached by dialing 911. For emergencies in the water, call the **Coast Guard, Search and Rescue**. There is also a 24-hour **Suicide and Crisis Line**.

If you need emergency cash, transfer it from your bank at home, or use American Express's **Moneygram** service.

In the event of natural disasters, such as hurricanes or tsunamis, contact the **American Red Cross** or the **Hawai'i State Civil Defense**.

DIRECTORY

MEDICAL TREATMENT

Hilo Medical Center
1190 Waiānuenue Avenue.
Tel (808) 974-4700.

Kona Community Hospital
79-1019 Haukapila St,
Kealakekua, Kona.
Tel (808) 322-9311.

Lāna'i Community Hospital
628 7th Street, Lāna'i City.
Tel (808) 565-8450.

Maui Memorial Medical Center
221 Mahalani Street, Wailuku.
Tel (808) 244-9056.

Moloka'i General Hospital
Kaunakakai. *Tel (808) 553-5331.*

Queen's Medical Center
1301 Punchbowl St, Honolulu.
Tel (808) 538-9011.

Wilcox Memorial Hospital
3420 Kūhiō Highway, Līhu'e.
Tel (808) 245-1100.

EMERGENCY NUMBERS

All Emergencies
Tel 911 to alert police, fire, and medical services.

Coast Guard, Search and Rescue
Tel (800) 522-6458.

Moneygram
Tel (800) 926-9400.

Suicide and Crisis Line
Tel (808) 832-3100.

NATURAL DISASTERS

American Red Cross
Tel (808) 734-2101.
www.hawaiiredcross.org

Hawai'i State Civil Defense
Tel (808) 733-4300.
www.scd.hawaii.gov

Banking and Communications

Keypad on a bank's cash dispenser

Money matters in Hawai'i are similar to those in the rest of the US. So, don't even think about taking any currency other than US dollars. And since credit cards and travelers' checks are the most common form of currency, it is easy to avoid carrying lots of cash around. Communications are straightforward too, and the postal services are very good given Hawai'i's isolation.

Branch of the First Hawaiian Bank

BANKING

All banks are open Monday to Friday from 8:30am to 3pm, and many stay open until 6pm on Fridays. A few offer longer weekday hours and also open on Saturdays.

The two largest banks – First Hawaiian Bank and Bank of Hawai'i – have many branches throughout the islands. Other banks with branches on all the islands include American Savings Bank, Central Pacific Bank, and Territorial Savings.

ATMS

All bank branches, and many stores, shops, markets, and gas stations, have ATM machines. You can use your credit card to withdraw cash from an ATM if you do not have a bank card. The main ATM systems are Cirrus and Plus, which accept MasterCard, VISA, and various bank cards. Look on the back of your card to see which network your bank belongs to and remember to have your PIN ready. There is a fee payable on some ATM transactions.

CHANGING MONEY

Although you may find a currency exchange desk at the airport, it is probably best to wait until you get to your destination. Larger hotels usually have a currency exchange desk. You will, however, get a better rate directly from a bank or by using an ATM machine affiliated with a major bank.

CREDIT CARDS

Anyone without a credit card may feel like a social outcast in Hawai'i. Credit cards can be used to pay for almost anything – from admission tickets to hospital bills. It is also standard practice for car rental companies and hotels to take an imprint of your card as security; rental companies may require a sizable cash deposit from visitors who do not have a credit card.

The most widely accepted cards are VISA and MasterCard. American Express, Diners Club, Discover, and JCB are also commonly taken. The credit card companies have

special toll-free emergency numbers to call if you lose your card.

Although it can be useful to use your credit card to withdraw cash from ATMs, remember that extra charges may apply beyond those charged for a bank card.

TRAVELERS' CHECKS

Travelers' checks are the safest form of currency to carry with you, since lost or stolen checks can be easily refunded. In many instances, you can use them as if they were cash: US dollar travelers' checks are accepted as payment by many businesses. Change will be given in cash.

To exchange your checks into cash directly, go to a bank. Note that travelers' checks in other currencies will be of no use at all.

TELEPHONE CALLS

Making telephone calls in Hawai'i is easy. The area code for the state is 808. You do not need to use the area code when making local calls (i.e., within one island). Inter-island calls count as long distance, and the number must be preceded by 1-808 when dialing. Calls to other US area codes must be preceded by 1.

It costs 50 cents to make a local call from a public phone. Otherwise, the charge varies according to the time of day and the distance. The cheapest rates are from 11pm to 8am Monday to Thursday, and

A public pay phone, which takes either coins or phone cards

A post office on Moloka'i

from 11pm Friday to 8am Monday. The cost of calls made from a hotel room is much higher than the normal rate. Most hotels should have a pay phone in the lobby that guests can use.

Given that you will need lots of change to make long-distance calls from a pay phone, you may want to buy a phone card (usable on touch-tone phones).

Many businesses have toll-free phone numbers, which are preceded by either 1-800 or 1-888 rather than 1-808. These are toll-free only if accessed from within the United States.

Directory assistance for the island you are on is 1-411; for the others it is 1-808-555-1212.

INTERNET ACCESS

There are many Internet cafés dotted around each island, with a particular concentration in Honolulu. Most hotels in Hawai'i offer Internet access in their guest rooms.

Some hotels also have a business center available, where guests can check email and surf the Internet.

Public libraries and independent postal services also offer Internet access; there are fees associated with using either of these services. In the case of libraries, you can get access by purchasing a temporary library card.

Most of the islands have free Wi-Fi spots; you will find a directory at www.wififree spot.com/ha.html.

POSTAL SERVICES

Post offices are usually open from 8:30am to 4:30pm, Monday to Friday, and on Saturday morning. Smaller post offices may have shorter hours. Mailboxes can be found on the streets of all major cities and towns. You can also purchase stamps and send mail from your hotel's front desk.

Sending a letter within the US costs the same, regardless of the destination. The time it takes for ordinary mail to reach the US mainland from Hawai'i depends on where you mail it. From Honolulu it should not take more than four days; from the other islands around a week. Mail to the rest of the world takes longer still.

US stamps with tropical plants

NEWSPAPERS, MAGAZINES AND INFORMATION

Hawai'i has a single statewide daily newspaper – the *Honolulu Star-Advertiser*. Hawai'i Island, Maui, and Kaua'i each has at least one daily paper, as well as weeklies. National newspapers, such as the *Wall Street Journal*, *USA Today*, and *The New York Times*, are easy to find in Honolulu and in many of the larger hotels throughout Hawai'i.

Local magazines worth looking out for include *Honolulu* and *Hawai'i*, a bimonthly general interest publication. You can pick up free visitor guides at airports,

on Waikīkī street corners, and at malls on the other islands. Many car rental companies will provide you with a free local driving guide as part of the rental transaction.

Many newspapers also have online editions; there is a list at www.world-newspapers.com/hawaii.

TELEVISION AND RADIO

All the main US television networks – ABC, CBS, PBS, NBC, and FOX – have local affiliate stations; check local listings on each island for the channel numbers. There are also a few interesting home-grown cable stations.

You can tune into dozens of local and state radio stations, but do not expect to pick up much if you are surrounded by volcanoes.

TRAVEL INFORMATION

One of the world's most popular tourist destinations, Hawai'i entertains more than six million visitors a year (which is about six times its resident population). A few steamship lines include Hawai'i on their itineraries, but most visitors arrive by air. This will usually get you as far as Honolulu, but that's only the start. (As residents and regular visitors will undoubtedly inform you, if you've seen only O'ahu, you haven't really seen Hawai'i.) Travel from one island to another is done mainly by air, although there are a handful of ferry services (plus some luxury cruises). As for exploring individual islands, the only reliable way to get around is by car; public transportation is minimal except on O'ahu.

Hawaiian Airlines plane

FLYING TO HAWAI'I

Given that so many visitors go to Hawai'i, there are a vast number of flights, mainly to Honolulu. Most people fly via the US or Canada, and there are many good connections from Los Angeles and other West Coast cities. United Airlines, American Airlines, and Air New Zealand all fly direct from Europe, but normally you'll need to change planes.

The more you shop around the better air fare you'll get. There are literally dozens of deals available, and it's worth taking the time to do some research, or to trust a reliable travel agent to do it for you.

There are various ways to cut the cost of your fare. Most importantly, the cheapest deals are generally available in off-peak months – namely May, June, September, and October. So-called discounted fares often come with advance purchase requirements and other restrictions, particularly involving cancellations. Be sure to check these carefully before you purchase the ticket to avoid unpleasant surprises at the last minute.

Most airlines also offer cheaper deals if you travel to arrive on a weekday. It's better to arrive in Hawai'i during the week anyway, since local residents often fly between islands on weekends, making airport (and hotel check-in) crowds even larger than normal. Weekend reservations may also be difficult to come by at short notice.

Logo for go! Airlines, an inter-island carrier

The Hawaiian Islands are the earth's most isolated landmass, so be prepared for a long flight; the shortest flight time is about five hours – from Los Angeles. From Europe, expect up to 18 hours traveling.

HAWAI'I'S AIRPORTS

Hawai'i's transportation hub is **Honolulu International Airport**, 10 miles (16 km) west of Waikīkī, on O'ahu. Its two terminals handle about 1,000 international, domestic, and inter-island flights daily. **Kahului Airport** is Maui's major airport, with inter-island and several mainland flights daily. A few flights from Kahului make up some of the eight daily connections to tiny **Hāna Airport** on Maui's east coast. **Kapalua-West Maui Airport**, 6 miles (10 km) north of Lahaina, has just one runway (and no telephone). The airport serves the Kā'anapali and Kapalua resort areas.

On Moloka'i, little **Moloka'i Airport** is situated 8 miles (13 km) northwest of the island's main town, Kaunakakai. It sees 20 inter-island flights per week and is open only when a flight is about to arrive or depart. There's also a tiny airstrip on the Kalaupapa Peninsula.

Only inter-island carriers use **Lāna'i Airport**, with its one-room terminal 4 miles (6.5 km) southwest of Lāna'i City.

Kona International Airport, near Kailua-Kona on Hawai'i Island, has the state's prettiest terminal; its check-in counters and snack bars are housed in small thatched huts. It handles mostly inter-island services, as does **Hilo International Airport**, 3 miles (5 km) east of downtown Hilo. **Waimea-Kohala Airport**, in the grasslands south of Waimea, services Trans Air flights only.

Līhu'e Airport, just a few miles east of Kaua'i's capital, sees the occasional United Airlines long-haul flight. Kaua'i's North Shore is served by **Princeville Airport** (no telephone), with flights to and from Maui, Moloka'i, and Lāna'i via Honolulu.

Plane taxiing on the runway at Honolulu International Airport

Departure building at Keāhole-Kona Airport on Hawai'i Island

GETTING INTO TOWN FROM THE AIRPORT

Approximate one-way taxi fares from various airports into town are: $20 from Honolulu airport to Waikīkī; $15 from Hilo airport into downtown Hilo; $25 from Keāhole-Kona to Kona; $55 from Kahului to Kā'anapali; $6 from Ho'olehua to Kaunakakai; $8 from Līhu'e airport into Līhu'e, and $18 north to Kapa'a. Buses and shuttle vans serve some airports and resorts – they are often free for resort guests.

On O'ahu, **Airport Waikīkī Express** runs a shuttle bus between Honolulu airport and Waikīkī for about $8 per head. The **SpeediShuttle** links Maui's Kahului airport with resorts. Fares are $13–32, depending on the destination.

PACKAGE TOURS

There are lots of package tours to Hawai'i for visitors to choose from. These include air and hotel costs, car rental, inter-island travel, and often some activities and meals. Try to book tours through a reliable travel agent since prices and itineraries vary enormously.

Local travel agents, inter-island airlines, Robert's Hawai'i, and Pleasant Island Holidays *(see p235)* all offer packages and sometimes discounts on

activities and meals. Both deals and itineraries change frequently, so try to check close to your departure date or make arrangements when you get to Hawai'i.

INTER-ISLAND AIR TRAVEL

No one should visit Hawai'i without exploring beyond Honolulu and the island of O'ahu. It is easy enough for you to arrange excursions to the outer islands before you leave home, but this can also be done after arrival.

Several airlines offer an inter-island service. The two largest are **Hawaiian Airlines** and **go! Airlines**. Round-trip prices between any two islands can vary greatly, from $38 to $200, as these airlines offer special fares throughout the year.

Other carriers are smaller commuter lines. **Island Air** connects Honolulu with Maui's Kahului and Kapalua-West Maui airports, Moloka'i, and Lāna'i. **Ni'ihau Helicopters** run a tour of the private island of Ni'ihau *(see p173)*. This is quite a pricey tour (it costs over $365 per person), but it touches down at a couple of beaches and is the only way to visit the island. The helicopter trip leaves two times a day from Hanapēpē on Kaua'i.

Travel magazines for individual Hawaiian islands

(see p235)

(see p173)

DIRECTORY

AIRLINES WITH FLIGHTS TO HAWAI'I

Air New Zealand
Tel (800) 262-1234.
www.airnewzealand.com

American Airlines
Tel (800) 223-5436.
www.aa.com

Japan Airlines
Tel (800) 525-3663.
www.jal.com

Qantas
Tel (800) 227-4585.
www.qantas.com

United Airlines
Tel (800) 824-6200.
www.ual.com

MAJOR AIRPORTS

Hilo International Airport
Tel (808) 961-9321.

Honolulu International Airport
Tel (808) 836-6413.

Kahului Airport
Tel (808) 872-3893.

Kona International Airport
Tel (808) 329-3423.

Lāna'i Airport
Tel (808) 565-6757.

Līhu'e Airport
Tel (808) 241-3913.

Moloka'i Airport
Tel (808) 567-6361.

AIRPORT SHUTTLES

Airport Waikīkī Express
Tel (808) 954-8652.

SpeediShuttle
Tel (808) 242-7777.

INTER-ISLAND AIRLINES

go! Airlines
Tel (888) 435-9462.
www.iflygo.com

Hawaiian Airlines
Tel (800) 367-5320.
www.hawaiianair.com

Island Air
Tel (800) 652-6541.
www.islandair.com

Ni'ihau Helicopters
Tel (877) 441-3500.
www.niihau.us

Public Transportation, Cars, and Ferries

It is undeniable that if you don't have a car your horizons will be rather limited in Hawai'i. Having your own vehicle provides both freedom of movement and the chance to be spontaneous (most locals keep a swimsuit and towel in their car because they never know when the beach will look too good to resist). Those dependent on public transportation will be able to reach few destinations beyond the confines of cities with an airport. Some of Hawai'i's most spectacular landscapes are out of bounds even to four-wheel-drive vehicles; this is when hikers can come into their own.

Birds on the highway

Waikīkī Trolley, plying the streets and sights of Honolulu

PUBLIC TRANSPORTATION

O'ahu is alone in having a good public transit system. Called **TheBus**, its buses will take you almost anywhere on the island for $2. Luggage is not allowed, so these buses are not very useful for the airport.

Other companies, the **Waikīkī Trolley** and Aloha Tower Trolley among them, serve Honolulu and Waikīkī, with a hop-on, hop-off service to major sights.

On Maui, the county government and Roberts Tours cooperate to offer the **Maui Bus Service**, which runs nine routes providing service between various Central, South, West, North Shore, and Upcountry areas. It operates seven days a week, including holidays. The Kahului and Wailuku Loops are free; all other routes are $1 per boarding (exact fare required). The Upcountry and Haiku routes also make

Route map for O'ahu buses

a stop at Kahului Airport. Further information and a schedule are available on the Maui Bus Service website.

The **Kaua'i Bus** operates on a fixed route Monday through Saturday. The standard fare is $1.50.

On Hawai'i Island, the **HeleOn Bus** runs in both Hilo and Kailua-Kona, as well as islandwide. There is also a shuttle that stops along Ali'i Drive at all major hotels and shopping centers. Called the **Ali'i Shuttle**, its fare is $2 each way.

TAXIS

Taxis can be found at airports and outside major hotels, but the only place where it is relatively easy to hail a cab is Honolulu. Elsewhere, call a taxi by phone. There are no taxis in Hāna or Kalaupapa. **Lāna'i City Service** is a limited taxi service.

CAR RENTAL

You must be 21 (25 in some cases) and have a valid driver's license and credit card to rent a vehicle in Hawai'i. Most companies rent cars, vans, and four-wheel-drive vehicles. The large rental companies – such as **Alamo**, **Avis**, **Hertz**, and **National** – all have desks at the main airports. The **Lāna'i City Service** also has a range of vehicles for rent.

It is best to book a car before you leave home, if only to get the car you want. Rates start at about $35 per day, but there are discounts for weekly rental, and you can get good deals if you book via some airlines.

You must pay $3 tax per day, and you can also add $10–18 per day by taking out Loss Damage Waiver (LDW). This protects you from Hawai'i's "no fault" policy, which means that in the event of an accident, you are responsible for damage done to the rental car, regardless of fault. Your own insurance policy or credit card may cover rental cars, so check. Most rental contracts forbid even four-wheel-drive vehicles from using unpaved roads.

Cars should be returned with a full tank; fill it beforehand to avoid the high gas prices charged by the rental agencies.

MOTORCYCLING AND BIKING

Mopeds and motorcycles can be rented on all the four main islands. It is not mandatory to wear a helmet, but it is a good idea to do so.

You can rent bicycles easily too. People seem to use them mainly for getting about town rather than for touring.

Car rental pick-up area at the airport

RULES OF THE ROAD AND SAFETY

Seat belts are mandatory in Hawai'i, and children under three must sit in approved car seats. Pedestrians always have right of way, and you can turn right after a full stop at a red light unless otherwise stated.

Distances between gas stations can be long, so it's a good idea to keep the tank at least half full. Always check the weather, as many roads wash out during or after heavy rains.

Local people are seldom in a hurry, so allow plenty of time for any journey. Also, residents never use their horns, so on narrow roads check your mirrors regularly and pull over to let cars pass. If you break down, call the rental company.

When you ask for directions, people will often give you landmarks to follow. On O'ahu you'll hear "Go diamondhead" (southeast) or "Go ewa" (northwest), and on all the islands you'll hear the words *mauka* ("toward the mountain") and *makai* ("toward the sea"). Many signs are in Hawaiian, so if you are getting help ask to be shown the way on a map.

PARKING

It's fairly easy to find free parking in Hawai'i, except in metropolitan Honolulu. Be sure to heed all signs. If there's no free parking, use a parking garage instead; you can often get your parking ticket validated by a restaurant, shopping center, or attraction and so park at little or no charge. Valet parking is provided at all major hotels and many restaurants.

Expeditions inter-island ferry crossing Lāna'i's Mānele Bay

FERRIES

Hawai'i has just one ferry route, which crosses the 'Au'au Channel to link the island of Maui with Lāna'i. The ferry company **Expeditions** runs several daily ferries on this crossing, and in the winter the service doubles as a whale-watching cruise. The ferries depart from Lahaina Harbor and dock at Mānele Bay on Lāna'i about an hour later. The fare is approximately 50 percent less than the equivalent air fare. However, be warned that the crossing can sometimes become quite rough.

CRUISES

In the old days there would have been *hula* dancers and *lei* greeters in colorful lines along Honolulu's piers to welcome the cruise ships filled with tourists. Times have changed, and most people arrive by plane. However, several luxury lines stop in Hawai'i as part of a broader itinerary. They include **Princess Cruises**, **Cunard**, **Royal Caribbean International**, and **Norwegian Cruise Lines**.

Floodlit cruise ship dominating the Honolulu oceanfront

General Index

Acknowledgments

Dorling Kindersley would like to thank the following people whose contributions and assistance have made the preparation of this book possible.

Contributors
Gerald Carr is Professor of Botany at the University of Hawai'i, Manoa and a resident of O'ahu. Bonnie Friedman runs a public relations firm on Maui, contributes regularly to Hawaiian publications, and volunteers in a Hawaiian language immersion school. Rita Goldman is a freelance writer and editor who has lived on Maui since 1978. Clemence Mclaren is a Honolulu-based writer and teacher. Melissa Miller, a native of Honolulu, is a poet, storyteller, grant writer, and nonprofit consultant. Alex Salkever is a Hawai'i-based journalist specializing in sports. Stephen Self is Professor of Geology at the University of Hawai'i, Manoa and a resident of O'ahu. Greg Ward, an established travel writer who has written extensively on the Hawaiian islands, is also the author of *Hawaii: The Rough Guide*. Paul Wood, freelance writer, editor, writing teacher, and long-term resident of Maui, is the author of *Four Wheels Five Corners: Facts of Life in Upcountry Maui.*

Design and Editorial
Emma Anacootee, Stephen Bere, Hilary Bird, Louise Bolton, Julie Bond, Arwen Burnett, Barbara Carr, Chris Barstow, Sherry Collins, Karen Constanti, Nicola Erdpresser, Jane Ewart, Fay Franklin, Emily Green, Emily Hatchwell, Des-Helmsley, Kim Kemp, Maite Lantaron, Nicola Malone, Linda Mather Olds, Georgina Matthews, Alison McGill, Simon Melia, Robert Mitchell, Kate Molan, Mary Ormandy, Sangita Patel, Mani Ramaswamy, Lee Redmond, Amir Reuveni, Ellen Root, Collette Sadler, Sands Publishing Solutions, Mary Sutherland, Rachel Symons, Conrad Van Dyk, Karen Villabona, Greta Walker, and Stewart Wild.

Special Assistance
Alana Waikiki, Sheryl Toda and Tracey Matsushima at Bishop Museum, Four Seasons Resort Maui at Wailea, Elizabeth Anderson at Haleakalā National Park, Richard Rasp at Hawai'i Volcanoes National Park, Julie Blissett at HVCB (UK), Sharon Brown at Kalaupapa National Historical Park, www.luciesfarm.com, Geraldine Bell at Pu'uhonua O Hōnaunau National Historical Park, Stouffer Renaissance Wailea Beach Resort, Bill Haig and Linda Matsunaga at TheBus, the State Parks Administrator at Waimea Canyon and Koke'e State Park, and RM Towill Corporation for artwork reference.

Additional Special Photography
Philip Dowell, DK Studio/Steve Gorton, Frank Greenaway, John Heseltine, Nigel Hicks, Dave King, Neil Mersh, Andrew McKinney, James McConnachie, David Murray and Jules Selmes, Ian O'Leary, Roger Philips, Clive Streeter, Greg Ward, Andrew Whittuck, and Jerry Young.

Photograhy Permissions
Dorling Kindersley would like to thank the following for their kind permission to photograph at their establishments and for their assistance with photography: Sharon Clark at the Hawai'i Film Office, George Applegate HVCB Big Island, Connie Wright at the HVCB Moloka'i, Department of Interior and the National Park Service 106–7, 116–117 and 128–129 and all other churches, museums, restaurants, hotels, shops, galleries, and other sights too numerous to thank individually.

Picture Credits
t = top; tl = top left; tlc = top left center; tc = top center; trc = top right center; tr = top right; cla = center left above; ca = center above; cra = center right above; cl = center left; c = center; cr = center right; clb = center left below; cb = center below; crb = center right below; bl = bottom left; b = bottom; bc = bottom center; bcl = bottom center left; br = bottom right; d = detail
Works of art have been reproduced with permission of the following copyright holders:
Stage design for L'Enfant et les Sortileges 1981, courtesy Tradhart, (c) David Hockney 1981: 71b.
The publisher would like to thank the following individuals, companies, and picture libraries for their kind permission to reproduce their photographs:
Akg, London: 25t, 45t; Museum of Mankind, London 24c; ALAMY IMAGES: Caroline Commins 126br; Hank deLespinasse 194cla; Douglas Peebles Photography/ Douglas Peebles 127cra; Douglas Peebles Photography/ Thomas Dove 155ca; David Fleetham 22bc, 32cl; Robert Fried 230c, 236tl; Dennis Hallinan 90-91; D. Hurst 195c; Andy Jackson 121br, 127cr, 229tl; Jacques Jangoux 11br; Andre Jenny 229cr, 240cl, 241tl; Jon Arnold Images/Walter Bibikow 11cl; David L. Moore 134tl; nagelestock.com 10cla; Photo Resource Hawaii/Ann Cecil 11tr; Photo Resource Hawaii/David Franzen 141tr; Photo Resource Hawaii/David Olsen 15bc; Photo Resource Hawaii/David Schrichte 32br, 33tl, 234cl; Photo Resource Hawaii/ Dylan Dawson 15c; Photo Resource Hawaii/Franco Salmoiraghi 142tl; Photo Resource Hawaii/G. Brad Lewis 144-145, 228cl; Photo Resource Hawaii/Jim Cazel 16c, 16bl, 120br; Photo Resource Hawaii/Mark Wilson 17c; Photo Resource Hawaii/Tor Johnson 16t, 226cl; Photo Resource Hawaii/Wayne Levin 17tr; Travis Rowan 33br; Stephen Frink Collection/James D. Watt 23bl; Stephen Frink Collection/Masa Ushioda 224cr; ALEXANDER AND BALDWIN SUGAR MUSEUM, Maui: 123bl; Allsport UK Ltd.: Vandystadt/sylvain Cazenane 31c; ARCHIVE PHOTOS: 28tr, 44b, 45b; ASTON HOTELS & RESORTS: 176bl.

Courtesy of BAMBOO RIDGE PRESS: Cover illustration From *Wild Meat And The Bully Burgers* With Kind Permission of The Artist Cora Yee 25b; BIOFOTOS: Heather Angel 21ca; BISHOP MUSEUM, Honolulu: 42c, 43t, 44c, 68br, 68cr, 69t, 152b; Charles Furneaux 135cr; Engraved By JG Woods 1878 30tr; BRIDGEMAN ART LIBRARY, London: Museum of Mankind, London 28c, 29t; National Library Of Australia, *Canberra Captain Cook C1820* by John Webber Engraved By Josef Selb C1820 41b; Scottish National Portrait Gallery *Robert Louis Stevenson (1850–94)* 1892 by Count Girolamo Pieri Nerli 25c(D); PAUL J BUKLAREWICZ: 26cl; GERALD CARR: 20br, 21tc/bc; JEAN LOUP CHARMET: *From Voyage Autours du Monde* by Louis Choris 1822 8–9; 26tr, 40t; CIRQUE HAWAII: 217br; BRUCE COLEMAN COLLECTION: Jeff Foot Productions 115b; CORBIS UK LTD: Bettman Archive 44t, /acme 149t, /upi 63t, 65b; Mark A. Johnson 116-117; David Muench 126tl; Amos Nachoum 23cla; Douglas Peebles 56br, 118cr, 154tr, 195tl,

227tl, 230br; Randy Faris: 228tc; Roger Ressmeyer 155br; Reuters/Lucy Pemoni 17bl; Tony Roberts 226br, 227cr; Jim Sugar 14; Karl Weatherly 10crb; Stuart Westmorland 143br. CULVER PICTURES, Inc, New York: 41c, 43c, 43b, 44c, 68tl; CURRENT EVENTS, Kailua-kona: 135cl; RON DAHLQUIST: 20c, 31tl, 33cr, 21br, 37t, 82cb, 83tr, 100cb, 110ca, 121cl, 123tr, 127cl, 129br.

ET ARCHIVE, London; National Maritime Museum *Death of Cook* by J Cleavely 41t; EXPEDITIONS INTER-ISLAND FERRIES: 245t.

FOUR SEASONS RESORT HUALALAI: 177bl; PETER FRENCH: 19b, 20tr, 21tr, 36b, 102t, 135cla, 168b, 170cb.

GETTY IMAGES: The Image Bank/Bruce Forster 10tc; CHERYL GILBERT: 135br; GO!: 242cr; GRAND WAILEA RESORT HOTEL & SPA: 229br; RONALD GRANT ARCHIVE: Paramount Pictures *Blue Hawaii* (1961) 165; GRAPEVINE PRODUCTIONS; 193tl.

ROBERT HARDING PICTURE LIBRARY: Nakamura 174–5; HAWAI'I VOLCANOES NATIONAL PARK: 155cl; Dave Boyle 154cl; Norrie Judd 154br; HAWAIIAN AIRLINES: 242t; HAWAIIAN HISTORICAL SOCIETY: 14b, *From Voyage Autours du Monde* by Louis Choris 1822 38; HAWAIIAN LEGACY ARCHIVE: 24tl; EVE ESCHNER HOGAN: 230tl; HONOLULU ACADEMY OF ARTS: Gift of Mrs. C. Montague Cooke, Jr, Charles M. Cooke III And Mrs. Heatin Wrenn in Memory of Dr. C. Montague Cooke, Jr 1951 *Nahienaena* Robert Dampier 111t.

IMAGE BANK, London: 50; IMAGE QUEST MARINE: James D. Watt 22bl, 32tr; Masa Ushioda 22crb, 23clb; INTERNATIONAL COFFEE ORGANISATION, London: 135clb.

KAPALUA RESORT ON MAUI: 226cb; © KAUA'I MUSEUM: 169t; KŌKE'E NATURAL HISTORY MUSEUM: David Boynton 170ca. KONA COFFEE CULTURAL FESTIVAL: 134cr.

LAHAINA TOWN ACTION COMMITTEE: 110b; LEONARDO MEDIA BV: 176cra; 236bl; ANTHONY LIMERICK: 110tr, 112t, 153t/b, 193b, 239t, 240tl/tr, 241t, 243t, 244b.

MAUI ARTS & CULTURAL CENTER: 218h; MAUI OCEAN CENTER: Darren Jew 119br; WWW.MAUI-WEDDING-PHOTOGRAPHY: Shasta Rose 228br.

NASA, Houston: 12c; NATURE PHOTOGRAPHERS: Brinsley Burbidge 20cb/bl, 167c; James Hancock 169cr; Paul Sterry 169cl; PETER NEWARK'S AMERICAN PICTURES: engraved by N Currier 1852 42t; NHPA: Stephen Kraseman 21cb.

MAUI CRAFTS GUILD: Randy Miller 212c.

OCEAN CLUB HONOLULU: 220cla; OSF/PHOTOLIBRARY: Botanica/Bob Stefko 23crb; David Fleetham 22tl; Pacific Stock/Dave Fleetham 22clb, 22-23, 33cl; Pacific Stock/Jim Watt 23cra.

PACIFIC STOCK: 40c; Bob Abraham 27b, 34c, 242b; Rita Ariyoshi 212b; Joe Carini 34b; Dana Edmunds 36t; Bill Schlidge 168t; Greg Vaughan 28bl, 29cb, 35b; DOUGLAS PEEBLES: 5tl, 18c, 52ca, 82ca, 84, 95b, 123tl, 142b, 143tr, 156, 171c, 224b; PHOTOLIBRARY: David Cornwell 33tl; PHOTO RESOURCE HAWAII: David Bjorn 30–1; David Boynton 26bl, 167t; Randy Jay Braun 27c; John Callahan 1, 34t, 37b, 210c; Monte Costa 45ca; Edmunds Dana 90-91, Tami Dawson 82t, 173b; David Franzen 57b; Nikiolas Konstantinou 136br; Jon Ogata 171t; Franco Salmoiraghi 83b, 131b, 157b, 140br, 192br; Joe Solem 35t; Jamie Wellner; Lani Breheme Yamasaki 12c; Photo Tropic: David S Boynton 169b; PHOTOSHOT/NHPA: Pete Atkinson 23tr; Kevin Schafer 23bc; PICTURES COLOUR LIBRARY: 27t; PLANET EARTH PICTURES: Pete Atkinson 89t; John Lythgoe 21bl; PRIVATE COLLECTION: 9 Inset, 24tr, 39b, 42brb, 47 Inset, 81 Inset, 175 Inset, 233 Inset. SCOTT ROWLAND: 18b.

SCIENCE PHOTO LIBRARY: Royal Observatory, Edinburgh 130; Soames Summerhays 152tr; MIKE SEVERNS PHOTOGRAPHY INC.: Mike Severns 22tr; THE STOCKMARKET: 26–27; SURFER PUBLICATIONS: Jeff Divine 31b; Tom Servais 30bl/bc/br, 31tr; KEVIN AND CAT SWEENEY: 135bla, 184c.

TEDESCHI VINEYARDS: 104tl, 234b; TELEGRAPH COLOUR LIBRARY: S Benbow 222b; Colorific/Jean Paul Nacivet 13t. BRETT UPRICHARD: 29ca. Greg Ward: 18t, 101t, 168c. NIK WHEELER 216br; WORLD PICTURES: 80–81, 85b.

Front Endpaper: all special photography except Douglas Peebles: Tl/tlc; Science Photo Library: Royal Observatory, Edinburgh b.

JACKET: Front – AWL IMAGES: Travel Pix Collection. Back–ALAMY IMAGES: Craig Ellenwood cla; Rick Strange clb; DORLING KINDERSLEY: Rob Reichenfeld bl, tl. Spine – AWL IMAGES: Travel Pix Collection. Maps ERA-Maptech Ltd, Dublin, Ireland.

All other images @ Dorling Kindersley. For further information see: www.dkimages.com

Glossary of Hawaiian Terms

Hawaiian began as an oral language. It was first put into written form by the missionaries who arrived in the 1820s. The teaching and speaking of Hawaiian was banned from the early 1900s, and by the time the native cultural renaissance began in 1978 the beautiful, melodious language was almost totally lost. Immersion programs are producing new generations of Hawaiian speakers. Fluent speakers are still few, and native speakers are even more rare. Still, you will hear Hawaiian words liberally sprinkled in conversation and in the islands' glorious music, and see it written on some signs.

Summary of Pronunciation

The Hawaiian language has just 12 letters: the five vowels plus h, k, l, m, n, p, and w.

unstressed vowels:

a	as in "above"
e	as in "bet"
i	as y in "city"
o	as in "sole"
u	as in "full"

stressed vowels:

ā	as in "far"
ē	as in "pay"
ī	as in "see"
ō	as in "sole"
ū	as in "moon"

consonants:

h	as in "hat"
k	as in "kick"
l	as in "law"
m	as in "mow"
n	as in "now"
p	as in "pin"
w	as in "win" or "vine"

The 'okina (glottal stop) is found at the beginning of some words beginning with vowels or between vowels. It is pronounced like the sound between the syllables in the English "uh-oh."

ali'i	ahlee-ee
liliko'i	leeleekoh-ee
'ohana	oh-hahnah

The kahakō (macron) is a mark found only above vowels, indicating vowels should be stressed.

kāne	kah-nay
kōkua	koh-koo-ah
pūpū	poo-poo

Everyday Words

'āina	aye-nah	land
aloha	ah-loh-ha	hello; goodbye; love
hale	ha-leh	house
haole	how-leh	foreigner; Caucasian
hula	who-la	Hawaiian dance
kāhiko	kaa-hee-koh	old; traditional
kama'āina	kah-mah-aye-nah	familiar; resident
kāne	kah-nay	man
kapa	kah-pah	bark cloth
keiki	kay-kee	child
kōkua	koh-koo-ah	help
kumu	kooh-mooh	teacher
lānai	luh-nigh	porch; balcony
lei	layh	garland
lua	looah	bathroom; toilet
mahalo	muh-ha-low	thank you
mu'umu'u	moo-oo-moo-oo	long billowing dress
'ohana	oh-hahnah	family
'ono	oh-noh	delicious
pau	pow	done
puka	poo-kah	hole
wahine	w(v)ah-he-nay	woman
wikiwiki	w(v)eekee-w(v)eekee	quickly

Geographical and Nature Terms

'a'ā	ah-aah	rough, jagged lava
kai	kaee	ocean
koholā	koh-hoh-laah	humpback whale
kona	koh-nah	leeward side
ko'olau	koh-oh-lowh	windward side
kukui	kuh-kooh-eeh	candlenut tree
makai	muh-kaee	toward the sea
mauka	mau-kuh	toward the mountains
mauna	mau-nah	mountain
nēnē	nay-nay	Hawaiian goose
pāhoehoe	pah-hoy-hoy	smooth lava
pali	pah-lee	cliff
pu'u	poo-oo	hill
wai	w(v)hy	fresh water

Historical Terms

ahupua'a	ah-hoo-poo-ah-ah	a division of land, from mountains to sea
ali'i	ahlee-ee	chief; royalty
heiau	hey-yow	ancient temple
kahuna	kah-hoo-nah	priest; expert
kapu	kah-poo	forbidden; taboo
kupuna	koo-poo-nah	elders; ancestors
luakini	looh-ah-kee-nee	human sacrifice temple
maka'āinana	mah-kah-aye-nanah	commoner
mana	mah-nah	supernatural power
mele	meh-leh	song
mo'o	moh-oh	lizard
oli	oh-leeh	chant
pili	pih-leeh	grass for thatching
pu'uhonua	pooh-ooh-hoh-nuah	place of refuge

Food Words

'ahi	ah-hee	yellowfin tuna
aku	ah-koo	skipjack; bonito
a'u	ah-oo	swordfish; marlin
haupia	how-peeah	traditional coconut pudding
imu	ee-moo	underground oven
kalo	kah-loh	taro
kālua	kah-looah	food baked slowly in underground oven
kiawe	key-ah-veh	wood used for grilling
laulau	lau-lau	steamed filled ti-leaf packages
liliko'i	lee-lee-koh-ee	passion fruit
limu	lee-moo	seaweed
lomi-lomi salmon	low-me low-me	raw salmon pieces with onion and tomato
lū'au	loo-ow	Hawaiian feast
mahimahi	muh-hee-muh-hee	dorado; dolphin fish
ono	oh-no	wahoo
opah	oh-pah	moonfish
'ōpakapaka	oh-pah-kah-pah-kah	blue snapper
poi	poy	pounded taro root
pūpū	poo-poo	appetizer
uku	oo-koo	gray snapper
ulua	oo-looah	jackfish; pompano

Pidgin

Hawai'i's unofficial conglomerate language is commonly heard on playgrounds, in shopping malls, and backyards throughout Hawai'i. Here are some words and phrases you may hear:

brah	brother, pal
broke da mout'	great food
buggah	pal or pest
fo' real	really
fo' what	why
grinds	food; also to grind
howzit?	how are you?; how is everything?
kay den	okay then
laydahs	later; goodbye
li' dat	like that
li' dis	like this
no can	cannot
no mo' nahting	nothing
shoots!	yeah!
stink eye	dirty look
talk story	chat; gossip

Honolulu Bus Routes

3-11-53-54

9-40-40A-42-43-52-62

1-7

1-10

3-11-53-54

Kalihi

MO'OKAULA STREET

N SCHOOL STREET

LILIHA STREET

10-13

13

10-19-20

7-10

7-10

9-40-40A-42-43-52-62

DILLINGHAM BOULEVARD

11-53-54

2-3-13

55-56-57-57A-65

6-15

Punch Bo

Iwilei

NIMITZ HIGHWAY

19-20

1-11-19-20-40-40A-42-43-52-53-54-62

19-20-40-40A-42-43

1-1L-2-3-9-11-13-53-54-62

6-55-56-57-57A-65

4-6

1-1L-2-3-9-11-13-40-40A-42-43-52-53-54-62

Downtown Honolulu

Sand Island

SAND ISLAND STATE PARK

1-1L-2-3-4-9-11-13-19-20-40-40A-42-43-52-53-54-62

19-20-42

1-1L-2-13

HONOLULU CHANNEL

Kalaeola

42

1-1L-2-13

17-18-43

19-20-42-55-56-57-57A

3-9-40-40A-42-52-53-62

KAKA'AKO WATERFRONT PARK

65

Ala Moana

ALA MOANA BOULEVARD

5-6-23-24-55-56

ALA MOANA RECREATION

KEY

—	Freeway
6	Bus route and number
—	City Express route A
—	City Express route B
—	Country Express route C
—	Country Express route E
✈	Airport
⛴	Ferry port
◼	Main sightseeing areas

MĀMALA BAY

0 kilometers 1

0 miles 1

SIGHTS

1 King Kamehameha Statue
2 Kawaiaha'o Church
3 Mission Houses Museum
4 'Iolani Palace
5 State Capitol
6 St. Andrew's Cathedral

7 Fort Street Mall
8 Aloha Tower Marketplace
9 Hawai'i Theatre
10 Hawai'i State Art Museum
11 Chinatown

1 Bishop Museum
2 O'ahu Cemetery
3 Royal Mausoleum
4 Queen Emma Summer Palace
5 National Memorial Cemetery of the Pacific

6 Honolulu Academy
7 The Contemporary
8 Lyon Arboretum
9 Kapi'olani Park
10 Pearl Harbour